The Feeling of the Form

signale
modern german letters, cultures, and thought

Series Editor: Paul Fleming, Cornell University
Peter Uwe Hohendahl, Founding Editor

Signale: Modern German Letters, Cultures, and Thought publishes new English-language books in literary studies, criticism, cultural studies, and intellectual history pertaining to the German-speaking world, as well as translations of important German-language works. Signale construes "modern" in the broadest terms: the series covers topics ranging from the early modern period to the present. Signale books are published under a joint imprint of Cornell University Press and Cornell University Library. Please see http://signale.cornell.edu/.

The Feeling of the Form

*Empathy and Aesthetics from
Büchner to Rilke*

Joseph R. Metz

A Signale Book

Cornell University Press and Cornell University Library
Ithaca and London

Cornell University Press and Cornell University Library gratefully acknowledge the College of Arts & Sciences, Cornell University, for support of the Signale series.

Copyright © 2025 by Joseph R. Metz

All rights reserved. Except for brief quotations in a review, this book, or parts thereof, must not be reproduced in any form without permission in writing from the publisher. For information, address Cornell University Press, Sage House, 512 East State Street, Ithaca, New York 14850.

First published 2025 by Cornell University Press
and Cornell University Library

Librarians: A CIP catalog record for this book is available from the Library of Congress.

ISBN 9781501783586 (hardcover)
ISBN 9781501783593 (paperback)
ISBN 9781501783609 (pdf)
ISBN 9781501783616 (epub)

For Claudi, Ben, and Alexander

Contents

Acknowledgments	ix
Note on Translations, Page References, and General Sources	xiii
Introduction: The Feeling of the Form	1
1. The Materialist Unconscious: Necromantic Empathy in Robert Vischer and Georg Büchner	52
2. Adalbert Stifter: Resistances of Form and Feeling	125
3. Bad Metaphors: Catachresis and Coercion in Rainer Maria Rilke	217
Coda: The Afterlives of *Einfühlung*	286
Works Cited	297
Index	315

Acknowledgments

The contributions of many kind and generous people helped make this book possible. I am grateful to the editors at Cornell University Press, the editorial board of the Signale series, the production staff at Westchester Publishing Services, and the anonymous reviewers of the manuscript; insightful comments from all these individuals helped make *The Feeling of the Form* a stronger book. In particular, I would like to thank Paul Fleming, Kristen Gregg, Mahinder Kingra, Mary Kate Murphy, and Kizer Walker at CUP; Abigail Michaud and the copyeditors at Westchester Publishing; and Rachel Lyon for creating the index. At the University of Utah, this book was supported by the University Research Committee (URC), which awarded me valuable leave time to work on the study. The contents of the book are solely my responsibility and do not necessarily represent the official views of the URC, the Vice President for Research Office, or the University of Utah. Margaret Toscano, then chair of the Department of World Languages and Cultures, along with the URC and university administration, provided crucial support in rescheduling the leave when circumstances made this necessary.

Conferences of the American Comparative Literature Association and the International Rilke Society offered me the opportunity to workshop ideas that would later become important to the book, as did the Awe and Attention Symposium at the University of Utah. Audience comments by Biddy Martin on a presentation I gave many decades ago helped me think about the question of flows in Stifter; the results of this line of thought influenced part of the trajectory of my reading of *Der Hochwald* in this book's second chapter. Some of the ideas in that section of the chapter, as well as some parts of my discussion of Rilke's essay "Über den Dichter" in chapter 3, were also originally developed in substantially different form in my previous writings.

Ongoing conversations about philosophy, virtual reality, technology, and nature with my friend and colleague Alf Seegert at the University of Utah helped inspire some of the concerns of the book; Alf additionally read and provided valuable feedback on an early draft of chapter 1. Karin Baumgartner, Scott Black, Vince Cheng, Katharina Gerstenberger, and Matt Potolsky, also friends and colleagues at the University of Utah, commented on early versions of the first chapter, reviewed the prospectus, suggested authors relevant to the study, or helped me think through crucial aspects of the revision process. Classroom dialogue with students in my courses "Empathy, Medicine, and the Human Condition," "The Sublime," "Aesthetics-Empathy-Form," and "German Realism" helped energize my continuing engagement with the book's sphere of ideas. Outside the University of Utah, Haun Saussy offered helpful comments, and Tobias Wilke provided a difficult-to-obtain document.

Numerous friends, family members, and mentors sustained me throughout the years before, during, and after the writing of the book. My parents, Archie and Dora Metz, who did not live to see the completion of this book, were my first and continuous sources of love and support; in many ways, they inspired me to enter academia to begin with. My friends Roy Bjellquist, Doug Cogan, Thérèse De Raedt, Rainer Orth, Ralf Saborrosch, Margaret Toscano, and others continue to weave me into a tapestry of love and meaning. Teachers from college, graduate school, and beyond have shaped my thinking. I will not attempt to put into words the debt I owe Lama Thupten Dorje Gyaltsen Rinpoche. And it would also be impossible to express the depth of my love and gratitude for my wife Claudia and my children Ben and Alexander. Many others who cannot be listed by name also played a role in the emergence of this book; I acknowledge them here. In the broadest sense, I acknowledge and thank the totality without which neither this book nor anything else would be possible.

NOTE ON TRANSLATIONS, PAGE REFERENCES, AND GENERAL SOURCES

I have used published translations of German sources when available, as indicated in the list of works cited. Exceptions are the poems "Der Hund" ("The Dog") by Rilke and "Auf eine Lampe" ("To a Lamp") by Mörike, where the published translations serve as occasional supplements to my own versions. For some main sources, especially Vischer's *Ueber das optische Formgefühl* (*On the Optical Sense of Form*) and Stifter's *Turmalin* (*Tourmaline*), I have sometimes modified the published translation or provided my own rendering of particular passages; these instances are noted in the body or with an explanatory note. When quoting both a published translation and the German original in the same passage, I provide first the page number of the translation, then a shortened version of the German title followed by the original page number (e.g., 106, *Formgefühl* 23). All translations from German sources for which no translator is noted in the works cited are my own. When providing broad etymologies of common terms, I paraphrase relevant sections of entries from Etymonline.com. The instances are not cited separately; rather my general use of this reference source is acknowledged here.

Introduction

The Feeling of the Form

> The subjective pattern of our perceptive feelings and the objective pattern of the form perceived are one and the same phenomenon differently thought of.
>
> —Vernon Lee and Clementina Anstruther-Thomson, *Beauty and Ugliness*

At the beginning of Steven Kotler's 2019 cyberpunk novel *Last Tango in Cyberspace*, protagonist Lion Zorn, an "empathy tracker" on the trail of a mysterious designer drug that induces in its human users radical emotional identification with animals, steps off his plane into a "shimmering world"—an airport where "everything scrolls, winks, and blinks, but softly, like Sunset Strip on mute" (Kotler 1). As Kotler writes, Zorn "can feel it, all this kinesis, like a twitch in his brain stem. It's old code, an ancient alert system. Any shiver in the outer peripheral registers as another living creature, another consciousness, potentially an opportunity, possibly a threat. This airport shivers too, even at this late hour" (1).

The short passage crystallizes fifty years of theory and research about empathy. Indeed, it encapsulates much of the concept's first half century (1873–1925), when both the English word *empathy* and the German term *Einfühlung*, first translated as "empathy" by the Cornell psychologist Edward Titchener in 1909, were neologisms with strikingly different connotations than they have today.[1] Coined by the German aesthetic theorist Robert Vischer (1847–1933) in his 1873 dissertation *Ueber das optische Formgefühl: Ein Beitrag zur Aesthetik* (*On the Optical Sense of Form: A Contribution to Aesthetics*),[2] *Einfühlung*—literally "feeling one's way into" or "feeling *oneself* into"—originally meant *not* the capacity to feel or imagine what another human being is feeling but rather the projection of human feelings and "life" into *form*, especially inanimate form: nonliving nature, abstract lines and shapes, and works of art. Now almost forgotten, this earliest meaning of empathy was, by the beginning of the twentieth century, a dominant, if not the dominant, concept in German and European aesthetic theory, as well as a link to the roots of modern Western philosophical aesthetics not in the notion of beauty but in the ancient Greek *aísthesis*, "sense perception." It is on this Greek root that Alexander Baumgarten drew when he introduced the concept of aesthetics into Enlightenment philosophical discourse. Aesthetics, as first described in Baumgarten's 1735 *Meditationes philosophicae de nonullis ad poema pertinentibus* (*Philosophical Meditations on Some Requirements of the Poem*), meant, as Kai Hammermeister summarizes, a "theory of sensibility as a gnoseological faculty, that is, a faculty that produces a certain type of knowledge" (4)—for Baumgarten, knowledge gained

---

1. See Titchener 21. Lanzoni notes that Cambridge philosopher James Ward may have independently proposed "empathy" as *Einfühlung*'s translation, likewise in 1909 ("Introduction" 9). The term itself is formed in analogy to the older, Greek-derived English word "sympathy": *empátheia* = "en" or "em" ("in") + "páthos" ("feeling").

2. Hereafter *Über das optische Formgefühl*, *Optisches Formgefühl*, or *Formgefühl*.

through the senses (including the perception of sensible form) rather than through reason. In his more famous *Aesthetica* (1750 and 1758), Baumgarten expanded the concept: Aesthetics was now "a science of sensual cognition, as well as a theory of art. The general aim for Baumgarten [was] to establish the latter by means of the former" (Hammermeister 7). The aim of the earliest empathy theorists, especially Robert Vischer, was not dissimilar.

When *Einfühlung* entered English as "empathy" thirty-six years after Vischer's introduction of the concept, empathy theorists were only just beginning to ascribe greater importance to what would eventually become the term's primary, present-day meaning of interpersonal or intersubjective fellow-feeling. But the presence of the human (and thus, at least potentially, of the interpersonal) was always fundamental, even in the earliest empathy theory, and the borders between the original, aesthetic understanding of *Einfühlung* and our current interpersonal conception of empathy were from the beginning uncannily porous. As Vischer himself states, "Natural love for my species is the only thing that makes it possible for me to project myself mentally [into objects]" (103). And without the existence and projective capacity of the human sensorium and mind—as well as, as we shall see, the form of the human body as the "measure" of aesthetic perception—no identification with (or even *of*) the "other" would be possible. Indeed, it is this ambiguous, at times dialectical, always fraught relationship between self and otherness that will haunt the theory and artistic representation of both (aesthetic) *Einfühlung* and (intersubjective) empathy from the beginning, and that will come to occupy a central place in this book.

Kotler's futuristic novel is itself about empathy. Its hero Zorn is, as noted, an "empathy tracker," a diviner of future global trends, pursuing an animal rights cult called, improbably but satisfyingly, "the Rilkeans" (after Rainer Maria Rilke, subject of the last part of this book, renowned for his ostensibly empathic *Dinggedichte*, "thing poems," about animals and objects). Indeed, in a particularly satisfying turn, the Rilkeans' identifying bodily marker is a barcode tattoo on the back of their necks; the bars, one might imagine, evoke the staves of the cage behind which a powerful but imprisoned panther, the object of the speaker's empathy, famously paces in the earliest and perhaps most well known of Rilke's *Dinggedichte*.³ *Tango*'s fourth chapter even includes a lengthy overview of the history of the word "empathy" that, while not entirely accurate in some of its details, does convey a sense of the term's spectrum of meaning and original grounding in German aesthetics. It is in its opening paragraphs, however, where the novel's grasp of, or influence by, the theoretical history of *Einfühlung* is most revealing.

Returning to these passages, we find an assembly of phenomena and experiences that conspicuously stages key concerns of early *Einfühlungstheorie* (theory of aesthetic empathy). Upon arriving in New Jersey, Zorn experiences the airport as an aesthetic phenomenon. Reflecting both Baumgarten's original understanding of aesthetics as an extra- or para-rational knowing through the senses and the current popular use of the word as a synonym for the "look of things," the terminal's "parade of razor-thin screens, angled atrium glass, and staccato mirror work" (1) interfaces with Zorn's feeling and judgment. The building presents as *kinetic form*: "Everything scrolls, winks, and blinks, . . . like Sunset Strip on mute." The sense of perceived motion ("[Zorn] can feel it, all this kinesis") is crucial. Indeed, highlighting the importance of motion to early *Einfühlungstheorie*, the first substantial unit of *Empathy: A History*, Susan Lanzoni's comprehensive study of the development of the concept of empathy from its nineteenth-century German roots to the present, carries the title "Empathy as the Art of Movement" (vii); the unit frames *Einfühlung*'s relation to broader aesthetic theory and practice in terms of kinesis. Significantly, Zorn feels the *airport*'s kinesis "like a twitch in his brain stem," evoking in Kotler's fictional twenty-first-century future what had come to dominate the first empathy theorists' actual nineteenth-century present: the rise of neurophysiology and the development of an understanding of human aesthetic response as based in nerve functioning (an understanding without which *Einfühlung* would not have developed, as it did, into

---

3. See Rilke, "Der Panther." The name of Kotler's protagonist, Lion Zorn, also metonymically evokes this panther, as well as the other animals with whom the empathy drug's users identify. *Zorn* is of course also German for anger or rage.

the core of the once-prestigious laboratory discipline of psychological or physiological aesthetics).

Perhaps most importantly, Kotler's passage presents an image of the *form* of the airport—its angled glass and winking screens—as *alive*, at least in Zorn's perception: "Any shiver in the outer peripheral registers as another living creature, another consciousness, potentially an opportunity, possibly a threat. This airport shivers too, even at this late hour." The notion is pivotal to foundational empathy theory. As Vischer puts it in *Über das optische Formgefühl*, "I project my own life into the lifeless form" (104). In *Einfühlung*, or empathy in Vischer's original, aesthetic sense, inanimate form "registers as another living creature," but only because I have projected myself or "my life" into it—a variation of the widespread "thought-figure" (*Denkfigur*) of projection that Jutta Müller-Tamm identifies as operating across a broad range of sensory physiology, cultural theory, aesthetics, and literature from the eighteenth to the twentieth centuries.[4] Indeed, one of the fundamental problems of empathy already begins with the German word *Einfühlung* itself, whose active *-ung* ending and directional prefix *ein-* open up an unsettling ambiguity. The term simultaneously suggests projecting or "feeling one's way into" something that is already there—experiencing its existent contours "from the inside," as it were—*and* inscribing, installing, or placing oneself precisely at the site of this "other" (or Other's) interiority: *dis*-placing it, in other words.

The observation by British aestheticians and empathy theorists Vernon Lee and Clementina Anstruther-Thomson that opens this introduction points beyond this paradox, but also deepens it: "The subjective pattern of our perceptive feelings and the objective pattern of the form perceived are one and the same phenomenon differently thought of" (*Beauty and Ugliness* 227).[5] Here, we find a

---

4. See her comprehensive study *Abstraktion als Einfühlung: Zur Denkfigur der Projektion in Psychophysiologie, Kulturtheorie, Ästhetik und Literatur der frühen Moderne.*

5. *Beauty and Ugliness* notes which sections were written by Lee, which by Anstruther-Thomson, and which by both; I follow this citation convention in my parenthetical references to the book. However, since the later works on empathy by Lee I discuss in chapter 2 were single-authored and further elaborate Lee's

radical blurring or conflation of subject and object, inner and outer, self and other—a bringing into focus, so to speak, of the terms and relations that form the core of *Einfühlung*, but also a potential undermining of this same core. Can there be *Einfühlung*, that is, when it is functionally impossible, or at least difficult, to distinguish between or determine the borders of self and other? Or is this very difficulty the operative definition of empathy itself?

Finally, like early empathy theory, Kotler's passage offers a picture of the world, and of Zorn's responses to it, as a fluid display of shimmering, shivering motion and emotion: "a shimmering world," "everything scrolls, winks, and blinks," "he can feel it, all this kinesis," "this airport shivers, too." The *feeling of the form*—Zorn's empathic reception, or projection, of the airport's materiality (or, the aesthetic experience of the phenomenological unit "Zorn-airport")—registers as a flickering oscillation of affect, "potentially an opportunity, possibly a threat." Perhaps coincidentally, but intriguingly, Kotler places this scene of the shifting, unstable, and potential-laden interaction between feeling and form at the suggestively named *Liberty* International Airport (1), recalling philosopher Brian Massumi's understanding of affect as an unfixed—that is, *free*-flowing—intensity of feeling, as opposed to the more restrictively defined or "owned" emotions.[6] In "An Inventory of Shimmers," their introduction to *The Affect Theory Reader* (and a piece whose title itself evokes the "shimmering" feel of Kotler's airport), Gregory J. Seigworth and Melissa Gregg fortuitously build an additional bridge between affect—for them, the "body's ... immersion in and among the world's obstinacies and rhythms" (1)—and the paradoxes of *Einfühlung* when they write that "with affect, a body is as much outside itself as in itself ... until ultimately such firm distinctions cease to matter" (3).

The implications of all these concerns shall come to occupy us in this book. Indeed, one of the aims of the present study is to tease

---

views, in part through engagement with German *Einfühlungstheorie*, I as a rule use the name "Lee" and the designator "Lee's empathy theory" throughout this study when discussing the overall theory's tenor and principles, including those that appear in *Beauty and Ugliness*.

6. See Massumi, "The Autonomy of Affect."

out and recover some of the hidden or unexplored layers, including the uncannier layers, of the earlier, aesthetically focused understanding of empathy—to explore what is at stake in the conceptualization of *Einfühlung* as a process occurring at the intersection of feeling and form. But I also aim to complicate *Einfühlung* by exploring *its* intersection with questions, and feelings, of intersubjective empathy: questions and feelings that, in the literary and theoretical texts I investigate, often unfold in markedly aesthetic contexts and ways (including conspicuous displays of form, self-reflexive stagings of artistic concerns, and moments of Baumgarten-like "knowing through the senses").

This book is about the feeling of the form; it therefore looks at multiple aspects of feeling and form in correspondingly diverse ways. With regard to *form*, for example, the study addresses the role of empathy-inspiring forms ("objects" in the "external" world) as theorized by Vischer's early *Einfühlungstheorie*; it likewise considers formal features of literary texts (narrative voice, rhythm and punctuation, and tropic forms such as catachresis), the implications of the logic of broadly conceived generic forms (such as theatrical performance, or, more precisely, performance's representation in the different generic form of prose fiction), and certain philosophical considerations of the problem of form as such (that is, the problem of how form comes to be perceived *as* form). Regarding *feeling*, I explore the broad atmosphere of "the uncanny" (*das Unheimliche*), feeling-laden instances of psychopathology and of the pleasure in melodrama and tragedy, experiences of bodily intensity or affect in Massumi's sense (that is, beyond specific emotions), and the implicit feelings of coercion and semiotic incommensurability aroused by strained or "bad" metaphor, among other examples. Most importantly, however, the book explores the *linkages* of feeling and form—the concepts' intersection points—especially as they traverse the different but also revealingly interrelated concepts of aesthetic *Einfühlung* and intersubjective empathy. For example, when read closely, how do the rhetoric and image-inventory of the inaugural statements of *Einfühlungstheorie* think the relation of feeling to form, including the mobilization of human feeling by (or toward) form and the ways that the forms of material objects and of human bodies can become figures or "forms" of each other? How might the broad "logical form" of theater (that is, performance or aesthetic simulation), as it shapes one of the novellas this study analyzes, relate to feeling, and what implications might questions of the formal or aesthetic performance of feeling have for the larger problem of empathy and knowing "other minds"? How, in another of this study's analyses, might our "feeling into" formal features of literary style (rhythm, syntax, and punctuation) arouse experiences of bodily intensity and empathic identification that challenge the seeming ideological investments of a text's plot? And how might the simultaneous (and possibly contesting) feelings of coercion and rhetorical "failure" evoked by the "inadequate" form of catachresis introduce empathic and semiotic paradoxes that have ethical stakes for our relations with an Other? In each of these cases, feeling and form are thought not separately but together; in many of them, questions of *Einfühlung* (the relation of our feelings to inanimate or aesthetic form), though different from questions of interpersonal empathy, open onto questions with ethical implications for interpersonal empathy itself. For if human self-projection or feeling into form constitutes a standard definition of *Einfühlung* as construed by much of the scholarship summarizing this now less well known branch of aesthetic theory, close attention to the words of Vischer's treatise and of the literary texts in its broad intellectual and sensual orbit reveals a more complex picture, and more complex stakes: a picture in which an entire range of multidirectional exchanges among feelings and forms, subjects and objects, selves and others generates a shifting field of border relations that together constitute an expanded understanding of aesthetic *Einfühlung*, intersubjective empathy, and the connections between them.

The Feeling of the Form is, first and foremost, a book of close readings—sometimes of entire texts, sometimes of smaller, but especially relevant, parts of texts—that travel backward and forward in time from the hub of Vischer's *Über das optische Formgefühl*. These include readings of Vischer himself, of his uncanny mid-nineteenth-century precursor, the German dramatist and neuroanatomist Georg Büchner (1813–1837), of Büchner's seemingly opposite but oddly related near contemporary, the Austrian novelist Adalbert Stifter (1805–1868), and of the twentieth-century poet Rainer Maria Rilke (1875–1926), erstwhile student of Vischer's intellectual heir, the psychologist and renowned empathy theorist Theodor Lipps (1851–1914). The readings place Vischer in dialogue with Büchner, Rilke with Lipps, and, for reasons I will elaborate below, Stifter with Vernon Lee (1856–1935), an "honorary German" due to her intensive engagement with the German *Einfühlungstheorie* of Karl Groos and, later, Lipps. The analyses trace how empathy, often in both senses of the term, is performed in and as specific texts; they likewise offer provisional answers to larger questions raised by the texts' explicit or implicit, theoretical or concrete linkages between feeling and form.[7]

In another sense, however, the book is a "para-history" of *Einfühlung*: not a conventional history or history of influence but an excavation of *Einfühlung*'s hidden forerunners, resonances, implications, and descendants, a walk through its parenthetical dimensions, or a holographic unfolding of its implicate order. As David Bohm writes, "In a television broadcast, the visual image is translated into a time order, which is 'carried' by the radio wave. Points that are near each other in the visual image are not necessarily 'near' in the order of the radio signal. Thus, the radio wave carries the visual image in an implicate order. The function of the receiver is then to explicate this order, i.e., to 'unfold' it in the form of a new visual image" (188). The meaning-field of *Einfühlung* represents an implicate order existing before, during, and after the appearance of the actual term *Einfühlung*; the texts explored in this study are explicate manifestations of this order "unfolded" by the "receiver" of close reading, even when they are not overtly connected to the discrete historical emergence of the term or concept *Einfühlung*.

Taken together, the study's two faces—close readings and para-history—allow us to explore various stakes of *Einfühlung* that have not been treated, or treated from these perspectives with this study's authors, before; they likewise allow us to make surprising discoveries, driven by the unique interpretive and formal demands

---

7. I am grateful to an anonymous reviewer of the manuscript for the formulation "how empathy is performed in and as texts."

of specific texts, about the relations among *Einfühlung* and intersubjective empathy, feeling and form. They expose, first, the anxieties lurking beneath the largely positive-sounding surface of the 1873 birth of *Einfühlungstheorie*—anxieties about uncanny resurrection, pathological identification, and a figuratively "demonic" possession by (or of) the Other—and show how these worries were already anticipated and made explicit by *Einfühlung*'s mid-nineteenth-century incubation period, here crystallized in Büchner. Specifically, they expose the links of the rise of *Einfühlung* to concerns of the German 1830s and 1840s that will act as *Einfühlung*'s midwife: the transition from vitalism and *Naturphilosophie*, with their sense of the whole of nature as profoundly "alive," to materialist science, with its associated "death of nature," as Carolyn Merchant calls it in her book of that title. In *The Forces of Form in German Modernism*, Malika Maskarinec observes that aesthetic empathy helps address the modern problem of "alienation from a world of things" (60): In her view, *Einfühlung* "compensates for the seeming disregard of natural objects by investing them with feelings those objects would otherwise lack, and so it counteracts a merely cognitive or intellectual relationship to things" (66–67). As I will argue, however, the "compensation" provided by Vischer's *Einfühlungstheorie* is a profoundly ambiguous one, and in one way no help at all: From the milieu of the death of nature, Vischer's *Einfühlung* arises as a "ghost story" or post-Romantic revenant, uncannily reanimating the lost "life" of the natural world and permeated by a classic constellation of unconscious fears and desires (including the desire to reanimate and the fear of reanimating).[8] Yet just as the first half of the nineteenth century sets up and makes visible a series of anxieties, shared in different but related ways by both aesthetic and interpersonal empathy, that will haunt the later formulation of *Einfühlungstheorie*, the decades around 1840 simultaneously open avenues of curiosity, exploration, and even potential escape—alternative paths within

---

8. For a different, more positive view of the late nineteenth-century German "overcoming" of materialism that does not specifically focus on *Einfühlung*, see Monika Fick's account of the turn-of-the-century reception of Vischer's predecessor Gustav Fechner in her *Sinnenwelt und Weltseele* below.

Einfühlung's implicate order. Like Büchner's, Stifter's texts also invite retroactive interpretation through the lens of *Einfühlungstheorie*: in Stifter's case, the lens of Lee's post-Vischerian, body-oriented empathy theory, with its focus on movement and breath. Reading Stifter's style (rhythm, syntax, and punctuation) in the light of Lee helps us understand his implicit, unrecognized coding of the textual "body" of narrative as *gendered* body, as well as the potential role of this "form body" as an unexpected site of resistance to the otherwise patriarchal investments of the very story it articulates. As I show, the stakes of this imagined dialogue between Stifter and Lee can be unfolded even more fully by placing *their* "conversation" into dialogue with later, affect-focused theorists (Massumi, Julia Kristeva) with whom they resonate. An additional Stifter text anticipates impending questions of "other minds," artificial intelligence, and virtual reality that will become important for subsequent thinkers (Alan Turing) and for the blurry border between aesthetic and interpersonal empathy. And at the end of the book, in my discussion of Rilke and Lipps, we will see how certain problems announced between the lines at the beginning of *Einfühlungstheorie*—problems of the role of metaphor and of the limits of the exchange of "selves" and "others" that metaphor implies—may themselves paradoxically become part of a "solution" to ethical questions of empathy, particularly when empathy and metaphor are viewed through the twenty-first-century philosophical lens of object-oriented ontology. In each of these cases, we find what Walter Benjamin might call a "dialectical image": present and past thought become legible in terms of each other, each revealing aspects of the other that might otherwise have remained invisible.[9] This is perhaps most evident in the case of Büchner and Vischer, where reading the two authors together simultaneously troubles Büchner's presumed representation of pathology—and Vischer's of empathic "health." In Stifter's and Rilke's cases, too, the conversing voices of multiple time periods illuminate each other: Viewed through the lens of later thought, the ostensibly "regressive" Stifter appears as a (perhaps unconscious) pioneer of that very thought, and Rilke's poetic practice, reframed from an object-oriented

---

9. See Benjamin, *The Arcades Project* 463.

perspective, bears witness both to the gaps in his teacher Lipps's theoretical understanding of *Einfühlung* as metaphor and to the ethical potential of those gaps.

The "para-historical" questions may therefore be summarized thus: What anxieties and problems, already implicit in the decades leading up to Vischer's dissertation, does the aesthetic, philosophical, and rhetorical formulation of the concept of *Einfühlung* open up? How does *Einfühlung* arrive in the course of a series of historical developments to meet, but also further ambiguously articulate, distinct challenges, fears, needs, and desires (materialism, the death of nature, reanimation)? What other, sometimes less anxious or more open potentials of *Einfühlung* are proleptically embedded in the same mid-century incubation period that gave rise to Vischer's pronouncements—possibilities perhaps invisible to Vischer, but latent in literary writers before him (Stifter) and explicit in empathy theorists (and other thinkers) after him (Lee, Massumi)? And, in the heyday and aftermath of *Einfühlungstheorie*, how might some of the same coordinates and concerns that troubled the birth of *Einfühlung* (the uncanniness of metaphors of self-other exchange, for example) offer homeopathic "healing" for problems of aesthetic and intersubjective empathy? To frame the pursuit of these questions, let us turn first to a brief history of *Einfühlung*, then to relevant problems of feeling and form, an overview of chapters and conceptual goals, and finally to some differences between this book and existing German studies work on empathy and *Einfühlung*.

Einfühlung: A Brief History

Empathy, whether aesthetic or intersubjective, deals with the relation of selves to others; it therefore perhaps always carries ethical stakes. As Fritz Breithaupt points out, interpersonal empathy, in addition to its widely touted benefits, also allows for a striking number of "dark sides": potential loss of self, "side taking" (or the rigid division of the world into friends and enemies), the "vampiristic" appropriation or erasure of others' experiences, and the sadistic desire for another to feel pain *so that* one can feel empathy, among other possibilities (*Dark Sides* 1–17). Even when seen as largely prosocial, the definition and scope of the most common present-day understanding of empathy—loosely, an intersubjective capacity to feel "along with" or from the perspective of another human being, to feel or imagine what another human being is feeling—is itself far from clear. Indeed, it has become something of a scholarly ritual to introduce discussions of empathy with the disclaimer that it is nearly impossible to pin down the term, especially in contradistinction to the older concept of "sympathy," and to point out that philosophers, psychologists, and medical professionals deploy the word in sometimes subtly, sometimes widely differing ways. Meghan Marie Hammond, for example, explains that since the mid-twentieth century, "sympathy" has come to mean "feeling for," while empathy suggests "feeling with"; however, she also reminds us that earlier uses of *sympathy* covered much of the same definitional ground as later conceptions of interpersonal empathy (6). And Remy Debes notes that "ever since . . . Titchener . . . introduced the term 'empathy' into English . . . , 'empathy' has either been used synonymously with 'sympathy,' or, even if distinguished from sympathy by one author, nevertheless defined in ways that other authors happily reverse, ignore, contradict, reject, dilute, delimit, and in general, redefine" (286–87). Among the many current meanings of empathy, Lanzoni finds "emotional resonance or contagion, motor mimicry, a complex cognitive and imaginative capacity, perspective taking, kinesthetic modeling, a firing of mirror neurons, [and] concern for others" (*Empathy* 3).[10] Derek Matravers, attentive to the term's evolution from the aesthetic concept of *Einfühlung*, laments that "empathy is an unholy amalgam of . . . different claims involving imagining another's perspective, mirroring the properties of others (whether things or people), projecting our mental states into others (whether

---

10. Mirror neurons are "premotor neurons that fire both when an action is executed and when it is observed being performed by someone else. . . . Action observation causes in the observer the automatic activation of the same neural mechanism triggered by action execution" (Gallese, "Mirror Neurons" 520). Coplan and Goldie provide a thorough overview of recent understandings of empathy from multiple perspectives (philosophical, psychological, historical, ethical, medical, and neuroscientific) in their introduction (ix–xlvii).

things or people), and taking on the emotions of others" (12); he ultimately concludes that empathy today means "using our imagination as a tool . . . to adopt a different perspective in order to grasp how things appear (or feel) from there" (1–2). This definition, while broad enough to gesture toward the experiences of (sentient) nonhuman others, clearly finds its most comfortable terrain in imagining the mental, emotional, and affective lives of other people. Things are not made simpler by the fact that German, under the influence of English, eventually retranslated *Einfühlung*, its word for human self-projection into objects, *back* into German as *Empathie*, or feeling with another *living* creature (Lanzoni, *Empathy* 10–13; Curtis and Koch, Vorwort 7)—a move that reflects the transnational shift toward today's prevailing interpersonal (or at least interanimal) understanding of empathy and away from the older, object-focused horizon of *Einfühlung*.

Vischer's initial 1873 definition of *Einfühlung*, or aesthetic empathy, seems more straightforward: The human body "unconsciously projects its own bodily form—and with this also the soul—into the form of the object" (92). Yet we already enter a zone of ambiguity when we ask just what Vischer might mean here by "soul" (*Seele*) (*Formgefühl* vii). Although this *Seele* is presumably not the divine spark posited by theistic religions but rather, as in Freud's use of the term, human feelings, mind, and psychic life, the question of *actual* souls—and the ambiguous implications of the "divine" (or demonic) human (in)ability to confer them on "dead" objects—will become, as we shall see in the next chapter, a central source of Vischer's anxieties. And Vischer's "projection" (*Versetzen*) (*Formgefühl* vii) of human bodily form is both less ethereal and weirder than the rendering by his English translators Harry Francis Mallgrave and Eleftherios Ikonomou might suggest: The German word also carries the active, even physical, sense of "displacing," "transferring," "transplanting," "transporting," and "relocating." Paul Guyer summarizes Vischer's dense explication of *Einfühlung* as "the union of [human] subjective response with the perception of 'objective form' . . . based on the projection of our own bodily form or attitude into the perceived form of objects, a projection that, because of the union of our own body and soul, carries with it the projection of our own emotional as well as physical characteristics into the perception of the object" (392). Müller-Tamm's synopsis is simpler: In *Einfühlung*, by "recalling the dimensions and movements of the human form and their associated feelings, impersonal natural and abstract forms appear as the carriers of human affect" (231). Lanzoni puts the matter perhaps most succinctly when she characterizes the early understanding of *Einfühlung* as "bodily engagement with form" (*Empathy* 9). This engagement—what Guyer describes as the "union" of human feelings with "objective" forms, predicated on a corresponding union of our own "bodies and souls"—was, for Vischer, profoundly *physiological*: "My principal concern . . . became to explain mental stimulation in every case precisely through and together with bodily stimulation" (92). It was also, as we will see, considerably stranger and more complex than a one-sided model of projection allows.

Vischer's dissertation "radically altered the aesthetic discussion of an era" (Mallgrave and Ikonomou 22). As Debes notes, interest in *Einfühlung* spread with "startling speed" throughout Germany, much of Europe, and the United States (287). Müller-Tamm calls *Einfühlungstheorie* the dominant aesthetic doctrine of the last third of the nineteenth century (214), and Oxford aesthetician E. F. Carritt could write at the dawn of World War I that "in various forms [*Einfühlung*] may be said to be the most commonly accepted [aesthetic theory] of our time" (qtd. in Lanzoni, *Empathy* 42).[11] By the end of the nineteenth century, empirical study of the somatic mechanisms of *Einfühlung* formed the core of the young but highly popular discipline of psychological or physiological aesthetics: the attempt to explain human responses to the sensuous phenomena of form as the effects of physiological and neurological processes, and the corresponding efforts to experimentally test, measure, and record these responses. As Robert Michael Brain explains, psychological aesthetics encompassed "physiological and laboratory approaches that examined how line, color, sound, or perception of movement produced a corresponding movement in the beholder's eye muscles, breathing, vascular system, or bodily musculature, stimulating either fellow feeling or revulsion" (*Pulse* xv). Psychological aesthetics evolved in

---

11. Lanzoni quotes Carritt's *The Theory of Beauty* (Methuen, 1914), 273.

tandem with the late nineteenth-century rise of German scientific psychology as a whole—Wilhelm Wundt established the first psychological laboratory in Leipzig in 1879, just six years after the publication of Vischer's *Über das optische Formgefühl*—and mirrored the "cultural prominence" of the growing field of experimental physiology, which "in its late nineteenth-century heyday... featured the most high-profile, numerous, and highly funded network of laboratories of any scientific discipline [and] often provided the model for the disciplinary expansion of physics, chemistry, and other laboratory sciences" (Brain, *Pulse* xv).

If Vischer's concept of *Einfühlung*, which he developed nearly in its entirety while still a philosophy student in Tübingen, was thus spectacularly influential, it did not arise in a vacuum. Vischer's own father and mentor Friedrich Theodor Vischer, himself a professor at Tübingen and, by some accounts, the most famous German aesthetician of his day, had proposed similar ideas in his two six-volume works *Ästhetik; oder, Wissenschaft des Schönen* (*Aesthetics; or the Science of the Beautiful*, 1846–1857) and *Kritische Gänge* (*Critical Pathways*, 1861–1873). Mallgrave and Ikonomou note the parallel development of Vischer's theories with analogous notions independently put forward by his contemporary, the then-leading philosopher Hermann Lotze (20); Vittorio Gallese contends that Vischer *fils* was deeply influenced by Lotze's earlier work on human self-projection into animals and objects ("Being Like Me" 112). And Vischer himself attributed his discovery of *Einfühlung*—indeed, its definition as the "projection of our own bodily form, and with this also the soul, into the form of the object"—to inspiration from the psychologist Karl Albert Scherner's 1861 book *Das Leben des Traums* (*The Life of the Dream*), which, famously, went on to influence Freud's more well-known dream theory.[12]

Just as importantly, as Müller-Tamm argues, the stage for the appearance and significance of *Einfühlung* was set by the unique

---

12. See Mallgrave and Ikonomou 18–20; Guyer 390; Curtis, "Einführung" 19–25; Vischer 92; Matravers 7; and Lanzoni, *Empathy* 32. The grammar and punctuation of the Vischer quotation has been modified slightly for syntactical reasons; cf. Vischer 92.

fusion of philosophy, science, and aesthetics in the nineteenth-century German-speaking world.[13] It was this fusion that would stake out a territory for *Einfühlung* different from the one occupied by sympathy, many of whose ethical and philosophical implications, explored earlier in the anglophone realm by David Hume, Adam Smith, and Edmund Burke, were precursors to the modern, intersubjective understanding of empathy.[14] And if Johann Gottfried Herder's late-1770s treatises on sculpture, nature, and the human "soul" were perhaps the first to prefigure both the philosophical-aesthetic assumptions and the vocabulary of Vischer's *Einfühlungstheorie*, the broader conceptual conditions for the rise of *Einfühlung* itself were provided above all by Kant, whose *Kritik der reinen Vernunft* (*Critique of Pure Reason*, 1781) and its resultant "Copernican Revolution in philosophy" understood human perception not as the unmediated "seeing" of an external world but rather as the human cocreation, or even creation, *of* that world according to the cognitive conditions set by a priori categories of understanding: the world *as* the sculpture, as it were, of the human mind.[15]

---

13. Müller-Tamm makes this argument in detail in *Abstraktion als Einfühlung*. In the following paragraphs on *Einfühlung*'s nineteenth-century prehistory, I am greatly indebted to her presentation, especially her account of Kant's influence on the rise of German sensory physiology.

14. See Hammond 6. Keen (*Empathy* 42–44) and Greiner (paragraph three) maintain that Hume's and Smith's treatment of sympathy not only anticipated later conceptions of intersubjective empathy but also recognized bodily phenomena (motor mimicry, relations between abstract forms and human emotions) that would later become central to aesthetic *Einfühlungstheorie* as well. Burke's thought prefigures both intersubjective empathy and physiological aesthetics (*Philosophical Enquiry* 47–48, 124); Braungart notes Burke's influence on German aesthetics and science, including on figures (Herder, Fechner) who would play important roles in the development of *Einfühlung* (58–61). The (mainly) separate paths of interpersonal and aesthetic empathy converge overtly in Theodor Lipps, who expanded *Einfühlungstheorie* to include other human beings (Hammond 72–73). Lipps would translate Hume's 1739–1740 *Treatise of Human Nature* into German in 1904–1906; on its possible influence on his thought, see Voss 32 and Guyer 397.

15. On Herder's striking prefiguration of and influence on the history, terminology, and concerns of *Einfühlungstheorie* (including his use of the verb *sich einfühlen*), see Curtis, "Einführung" 17–18 and especially Braungart's discussion of Herder's "Plastik" and "Vom Erkennen und Empfinden der menschlichen Seele" (55–107, 195). As Braungart writes, "Practically every central argument and idea

Kant's privileging of a "productive" subjectivity, with its blurring of the borders between inner and outer realities, found ready reception and elaboration—indeed, in important ways helped give birth to—the pervasive universalism of German Romanticism, with its recurrent motifs of pantheistic feeling, human oneness with nature, and pathetic fallacy. It is therefore unsurprising to find another of the first proleptic formulations of Vischer-like *Einfühlung* in the early Romantic Novalis (here, from his story "Die Lehrlinge zu Sais" ["The Novices of Sais"], written in 1798–1799 and published in 1802): "No one will grasp nature who does not have an organ for it, who does not . . . merge with all natural entities, who does not, in intimate multifarious kinship with all bodies, through the medium of sensation *feel himself into them* [*sich in sie hineinfühlt*], as it were" (31, my emphasis).[16] But for the full-fledged concept of *Einfühlung* to emerge, Kantian philosophy and Romantic aesthetics would have to meet science. This meeting had already begun to occur in the Czech physiologist Jan Evangelista Purkinje's 1819 research into the eye's "productive activity" in creating entoptic phenomena, or visual phenomena whose origin is internal to the eye itself (Müller-Tamm 34), and in Goethe's 1810 *Farbenlehre* (*Theory of Colors*), which many scholars identify as a decisive influence on the development of German physiology.[17] As Jonathan Crary writes, the *Farbenlehre* represents "the inseparability of two models usually presented as distinct and irreconcilable: a physiological observer who will be described in increasing detail by the empirical sciences in the nineteenth century, *and* an observer posited by various 'romanticisms' and early modernisms as the active, autonomous producer of his or her own visual experience" (69). But, as Müller-Tamm points out, the marriage of aesthetics and science truly came to fruition with the rise of neuroanatomy and its offspring, the increasingly important German fields of neurophysiology and sensory physiology, in the decades from 1820 to 1840 (30–45, 140, and passim)—a formative period for both the

---

in the discussion of *Einfühlung* was already present in Herder, at least in rudimentary form" (62).
    16. Curtis also notes the passage ("Einführung" 18).
    17. See for example Müller-Tamm 29–45 and 71–80.

neuroanatomist Büchner and for Stifter, erstwhile seeker of an academic career in physics (Coen 65). Indeed, the development of *Einfühlung*, its understanding of aesthetics, and the neurophysiological sphere with which it was interwoven unfolded in a decidedly Kantian fashion (Müller-Tamm 147–48).

Kant's Copernican Revolution may have inspired not only the enthusiastic elaboration of projective subjectivity as Romantic universalism and—responding to the notion of a projected world in a more anxious vein—the development of "holistic" *Naturphilosophie* as an attempt to overcome the Kantian gap between *Erscheinung* (appearance) and *Ding-an-sich* (thing-in-itself) (Heidelberger 2). Ironically, it may also have fostered the growth of the very empirical-scientific approaches that would eventually secure the decline of holistic and universalist thinking (and particularly of *Naturphilosophie*) itself. As Müller-Tamm writes, the Enlightenment's "emphatic discovery of the nervous system" and the subsequent physiological experiments of Germany's late and post-Romantic age transferred Kantian theories of perception, knowledge, and projective subjectivity "into the realm of empirical science" and its ascendant "neurological understanding of the human being" (11). This was the period of the "subjectivizing" of vision, driven in part by Goethe and Purkinje and famously analyzed by Crary in his seminal *Techniques of the Observer* (1990): the period of the shift, that is, from conceiving of vision as governed by "stable and fixed" Newtonian laws of optics, exemplified by the camera obscura (Crary 14–16), to viewing sight as rooted in the "corporeal subjectivity of the observer" (69)—the "unstable" human body, with its complex array of physiological, neurological, and sensory systems, now seen as operating separately from each other to "actively produce" optical (and other) experience (69–71). A critical moment in this shift was the pathbreaking work of the German physiologist Johannes Müller (1801–1858), whose experimental confirmation and 1826 formulation of the law of specific nerve energies, or the ability of distinct categories of sensory nerves (visual, auditory, and so on) to produce *different* sensations (light, sound) from the *same* stimulus, somatically "verified" the Kantian split between appearance and thing-in-itself and strikingly translated the a priori rules of the *Critique of Pure Reason* into physiological terms (Crary 81–93; Müller-Tamm 32–44).[18] As Müller-Tamm writes, nineteenth-century commentators already called this fusion of Kant and the body "physiological idealism" (11).

Importantly, proto- and early sensory physiologists and "physiological Idealists" studied aesthetic phenomena in both senses of the term *aesthetics*: Baumgarten's knowledge-producing objects of sensible perception, and phenomena (color, line, abstract patterns) that might serve as formative components of works of art.[19] Thus, sensory physiology "reache[d] into the aesthetic domain," "integrating aesthetics into the physiological theory of perception" (Müller-Tamm 11, 44). In addition to Müller, among the most instrumental figures in this nineteenth-century German dialectic of aesthetics, philosophy, and science were Schopenhauer, whose intense concern with aesthetic questions and formidable influence on the arts were paralleled, as Crary notes, by his singular determination to explain aesthetics physiologically (74–77); Gustav Fechner, founder of "psychophysics," or the quantitative study of the relations between nerve stimuli and their resultant perceptions; Müller's more famous pupil Hermann von Helmholtz, whose groundbreaking experiments on vision and acoustics laid the foundations for the development of psychology as a discipline; and Müller and Helmholtz's student Wilhelm Wundt, "the father of experimental psychology," who, as I have noted, established the first psychological laboratory in 1879 in Leipzig. It was out of this milieu that Vischer's concept of *Einfühlung* emerged and soon became the focus of psychological-aesthetic research in Germany's new, Wundt-inspired laboratories. As Müller-Tamm explains, aesthetics remained central to German experimental science throughout the nineteenth century (29); reciprocally, *Über das optische Formgefühl* cites Wundt's experiments in optics as support for its aesthetic claims (96–97) and shows the marks—and conflicts—of Müller's, Fechner's, and Helmholtz's scientific

---

18. Müller's successors Wundt and Helmholtz both considered Müller's law an empirical, physiological proof of Kant's notion of a priori understanding (Müller-Tamm 78–79n24). The law has since been modified in the light of subsequent brain research.

19. Cf. Müller-Tamm 33–36.

thought.²⁰ When Nietzsche thus writes in his 1887 *Genealogy of Morals* that the "physiology of aesthetics" is "practically untouched and unexplored so far" (547–48), the exploration he seeks is in fact going on all around him.²¹

The fin-de-siècle work of philosopher and psychologist Theodor Lipps, Vischer's intellectual successor and the most prominent theorist of *Einfühlung* in Germany and beyond, marked perhaps aesthetic empathy's apotheosis, but also its incipient decline. Though still concerned with Vischer's projection of human feelings into objects, Lipps was the first to explore in detail the aesthetic and psychic mechanisms of empathic projection into other human beings. He thus forms a bridge backward to earlier British thinking about sympathy and forward to the twentieth century's predominantly intersubjective understanding of empathy. In turn-of-the-century Munich, where he arrived to teach at the Ludwig-Maximilian University the year after Vischer left a temporary position there for a professorship in Göttingen (Guyer 396), Lipps would go on to become the young Rilke's professor for aesthetics, influence Freud's work, and develop a conception of *Einfühlung* that many see as a precursor to the discovery of mirror neurons and the resultant "embodied simulation" theories of empathy of the 1980s and 1990s.²²

---

20. Müller-Tamm additionally understands Lichtenberg, Albrecht von Haller, and (the French and pre-Kantian) Condillac as precursors to "physiological idealism" and projective *Einfühlung* (108–12). Mallgrave and Ikonomou note the aesthetician Johann Friedrich Herbart's posthumous influence on experimental science in the second half of the nineteenth century, including on Fechner and Wundt (10–16); Vischer will state in *Formgefühl* that his treatise was written in refutation of Herbart's claim that form can exist without (emotional) content, which must be "empathically" supplied by the observer (89).

21. Nietzsche's statement occurs in the context of his critique of Schopenhauer's aesthetics; it is thus possible that it is only Schopenhauer's treatment of the physiology of aesthetics that leaves Nietzsche dissatisfied. Müller-Tamm presents compelling evidence from Nietzsche's posthumous papers that the philosopher was familiar with sensory physiology and had read much Helmholtz in the 1870s (170–90); this makes his claim that the physiology of aesthetics was "practically untouched" difficult to understand.

22. On Lipps as a bridge from aesthetic to interpersonal empathy, see Hammond 72–74; on his theoretical foreshadowing of mirror neurons, see Gallese, "Mirror Neurons" 523–26. As opposed to standard simulation theories of empathy, which posit that we understand others by "imagining" ourselves in their position

But writing in 1906, Lipps famously (or infamously) defined *Einfühlung* as "objectified self-enjoyment" ("Einfühlung und ästhetischer Genuss" ["Empathy and Aesthetic Pleasure"] 100), a formulation that would seem to lend weight to the criticism leveled by his early phenomenologist colleagues that aesthetic empathy, even when understood to encompass interpersonal dimensions, paid insufficient attention to the Otherness of the other, the other's actual experience—or in fact assimilated the Other to the Self.[23]

Lipps, and the entire theoretical hegemony of *Einfühlung*, would soon experience challenges from other quarters as well. Just two years after Lipps's essay on objectified self-enjoyment, the art historian Wilhelm Worringer—himself, like Rilke, one of Lipps's former students—would publish his just-finished dissertation *Abstraktion und Einfühlung: Ein Beitrag zur Stilpsychologie* (*Abstraction and Empathy: A Contribution to the Psychology of Style*); the book, which proposed a contrasting, ostensibly empathy-opposing pole of crystalline geometrical form or "abstraction" to counter *Einfühlung*'s dominance of aesthetic theory, would, like Vischer's *Formgefühl*, revolutionize a generation's understanding of art. *Abstraktion*

(Matravers 27), Gallese sees empathic identification as "embodied," "prerational," "mandatory," and "nonintrospectionist"—a process rooted not in the imagination but in mirror neurons and their corresponding "intercorporeity" ("Mirror Neurons" 523–24). His thinking thus offers neurophysiological explanations for the "instantaneous" empathic resonance between our own and others' bodily and emotional states that Lipps identified in his research; cf. Hammond 73–74. On Lipps's influence on Freud, see Gallese, "Mirror Neurons" 525 and Agosta 66–82. As Agosta notes, despite having adopted Vischer and Lipps's vocabulary, Freud used the word *Einfühlung* in the context of interpersonal relations, not in the sense of projective aesthetic empathy; his English translators frequently render Freud's *Einfühlung* as "sympathetic understanding" (66–67). On the similarities and differences between Freud's psychoanalytic theory of projection and the self-projection of *Einfühlungstheorie*, see Müller-Tamm 193–209 and 214–48. Due to Freud's distance from the distinct terminological usage and concerns of *Einfühlungstheorie*, I (like the majority of work on German empathy theory) do not treat him as belonging to this tradition.

23. Through his participation in the Munich Circle of early phenomenologists, Lipps influenced the growth of phenomenological thought; he came under fire from Circle member Max Scheler and Husserl's student Edith Stein, one of the first to focus primarily on interpersonal empathy, for his application of *Einfühlung* to the problem of other minds (Debes 294–95, 313–17). For a critique of Lippsian *Einfühlung* as the erasure of the Other's difference, see Voss 40–45.

und Einfühlung, for example, is frequently credited with "explaining" the contemporaneously arising movement of German Expressionism.[24] Critics have since pointed out that Worringer's arguments rely on a conspicuous (though productive) misreading of Lipps, questioned whether abstraction differs all that fundamentally from the projective mechanisms of *Einfühlung*, and debated whether Worringer's book in fact had a significant effect on the decline of aesthetic empathy at all (Waite; Müller-Tamm; Koss). Müller-Tamm, for example, as the title of her study *Abstraktion als Einfühlung* (*Abstraction as Empathy*) suggests, sees abstraction and empathy not as contraries but as structurally related processes, both subsumed within the larger concept or "thought-figure" of projection (250). Mallgrave and Ikonomou (20–21), Maskarinec (13), and others note that abstract geometrical forms had been staple objects of aesthetic empathy since the beginning, a point borne out by Vischer, Lipps, and numerous psychological-aesthetic experiments. And Brain contends that the turn away from *Einfühlungstheorie* after World War I had more to do with growing criticism that the affective and bodily focus of *Einfühlung* had somehow contributed to the war itself than with the influence of any book (*Pulse* xx–xxiii, 226–28). Whatever the case, by the end of the Weimar years, *Einfühlung* in Vischer's and Lipps's sense had faded as Germany's foremost aesthetic theory, "killed," perhaps, by some combination of Worringer's ideas, Brecht's new theater of anti-empathic alienation, the revision of cultural values provoked by the war, and, ironically, the very laboratories that had first made *Einfühlung* the center of their psychological-aesthetic experiments, then failed to find enough uniformity in human responses to aesthetic phenomena to justify further interest in the research.[25]

Of course, the decline of *Einfühlungstheorie* did not simply leave *Einfühlung* without a legacy. In many ways, as I consider briefly at the conclusion of this book, aesthetic empathy was absorbed into

---

24. For a critique of these views, see Jennings.
25. On the contribution of Brecht's Epic theatre to the decline of *Einfühlung*, see Curtis and Koch, Vorwort 7; on psychological-aesthetic laboratory experiments as causes for the fading of the *Einfühlungstheorie* that inspired them, see Koss 117–20.

new media, psychological phenomena, and political practices. And the history I have sketched above is only a cursory overview: I will return to or add relevant details in the subsequent chapters. What is clear, however, is how the meaning of the word *empathy* has changed and how *Einfühlung*, the neologism that gave rise to another neologism and that originally meant—simplified—the projection of human feelings into objects, emerged from a strikingly "German" intersection: the heritage of Kantian philosophy, the continuing centrality of aesthetics to nineteenth-century German thought, including natural-scientific thought, and the rise, throughout the nineteenth century, of German neuroanatomy, neurophysiology, and experimental psychology. In the remainder of this introduction, I lay out a road map for how the present book will unfold this constellation.

Problems of Feeling and Form

A book about feeling and form will be concerned with problems of both. Indeed, the concept of *aísthesis*, or knowing through the senses, itself depends at least in part on questions of form—whether forms thought to be found "out there" (visual, tactile, audible) or, in Kantian fashion, forms "formed" by the synthesizing activity of our minds. Taking this latter point first, we might say that the problem of form covers a spectrum ranging from the physio-philosophical question of how form is perceived *at all*, through the question of our numerous engagements with (presumably) physical or tangible forms, such as the various "objects" *Einfühlung* is concerned with and believes it "feels itself into" (artworks, details of nature, abstract shapes), to issues of specific or generic forms, including artistic and literary genres and the particular structural elements and formal features of individual texts. In his *History of Six Ideas*, Władysław Tatarkiewicz lists five main understandings of form, including "an arrangement of parts," "what is directly given to the senses," "the boundary or contours of an object," "the conceptual essence of an object," and "the contribution of the mind to the perceived object" (220–21). Angela Leighton notes that there are "more than twenty dictionary definitions" of form, among them "shape, design, outline, frame, ideal, figure, image, style, genre, order," and "body" (2). As Caroline Levine emphasizes:

> Over many centuries, *form* has gestured to . . . conflicting, sometimes even paradoxical meanings. Form can mean immaterial idea, as in Plato, or material shape. . . . It can indicate essence, but it can also mean superficial trappings, such as conventions—*mere forms*. Form can be generalizing and abstract, or highly particular (as in the form of *this* thing is what makes it what it is, and if it were reorganized it would not be the same thing). Form can be cast as historical, emerging out of particular cultural and political circumstances, or it can be understood as ahistorical. (2)

Regarding literary form in particular, Levine writes that "critics habitually use . . . form in two competing ways: first, as an overarching textual unity (such as the marriage plot or epic), but also as the many, smaller and more varied techniques that go into structuring and shaping a text (such as metaphor, the couplet, peripeteia, the cliffhanger, monologue)" (40). As Leighton puts it, mobilizing both semantics and materiality, the form of a text is "the shape of the text on the page, the shape of its sound in the air, and the matter of which it speaks" (16). Seeking commonalities amid this profusion of thought about form, Levine proposes a capacious definition that encompasses "all shapes and configurations, all ordering principles, all patterns of repetition and difference" (3).

At the philosophical beginning (and one of the deepest levels) of the form problem as it relates to empathy, both aesthetic and intersubjective, is the problem of form as posed by Kant. This is simultaneously a self-other problem. As Andrew Bowie summarizes the *Critique of Pure Reason*, "Kant is insistent . . . that we can only know the world as it *appears* to us via the constitutive a priori 'categories' of subjectivity which synthesise intuitions into cognisable forms. The world as an object of truth is therefore actively constituted by the structures of the consciousness we have of it, which means that we cannot know how the world is 'in itself.' Instead of cognition following the object, the object comes to depend upon the subject's constitution of it *as* an object by giving it a repeatable identity in a predicative judgement" (17). In Kant's words, "Our representation of things, as they are given to us, does not conform to these things as they are in themselves, but ... these objects, as appearances, conform to our mode of representation" (*Critique of Pure Reason* 24). Thus, as Mallgrave and Ikonomou write, form for Kant is "that which allows the manifold of appearances to be ordered in certain relations" (5).

Müller-Tamm contends that most major nineteenth-century contributors to the prehistory of *Einfühlung*, with their diverse variations on "physiological idealism," or the construction of the "outside" world by the activity of the nerves, brain, and sense organs, were in a crucial sense in dialogue with Kant, alternately accused by their opponents of being too Kantian or not Kantian enough (147–48). Lipps, at the height of *Einfühlungstheorie*, does not escape this dialogue: "Form is always a 'Being-Formed-By-Me,' or is my activity" ("Einfühlung und ästhetischer Genuss" 106)—the "me" here being the synthesizing powers of the human mind. Karl Groos, writing in the wake of Vischer, famously argued not only for the influence of internal bodily sensations on our interaction with form ("Ästhetisches Miterleben" ["Aesthetic Involvement"] 161–68) but also for the necessity of "inner imitation" (*innere Nachahmung*)—the mental abstraction of "appearance" (*Schein*) from sense data, or the "imitation" of the contours of an external object by the movements of consciousness—for the perception of form to take place at all (*Einleitung in die Aesthetik* [*Introduction to Aesthetics*] 84–106). Lee and Anstruther-Thomson, more corporeally radical than Groos, initially proposed that dynamic bodily motion itself was required for seemingly external forms to appear: "It is we, the beholders, who ... *make form exist* in ourselves by alteration in our respiratory and equilibratory processes, and by initiated movements of various parts of the body" (*Beauty and Ugliness* 236). As Jesse Prinz points out, Lee's theory, which she saw as affirming both the Kantian tradition of recognizing "apparently objective existences" as "function[s] of our mind" and the later psychophysiological understanding of these functions as themselves "processes of what we rather arbitrarily distinguish from [mind] as *body*" (*Beauty and Ugliness* 236), likewise anticipates the still later approach to form represented by present-day research in embodied cognition or "enactivism" (Prinz 322–31):

As enactivist philosopher Alva Noë argues, sensorimotor skills are themselves "conceptual skills," translating sensory stimulation into "experience with world-presenting content" (183).

These approaches, with their blurry and differently proportioned combinations of "subjective" and "objective," "internal" and "external," "mental" and "bodily" elements, arguably raise more questions about form than they answer. Not only do they tie the problem of form to the question of "where the self begins and where it ends," as Müller-Tamm puts it with regard to the broader issue of projection in general (146): A close reading of these thinkers, such as I undertake with Vischer in the next chapter, also reveals considerably more ambiguity regarding the origin, locus, and trajectory—what I will call the "vector"—of *Einfühlung* (and, with it, form) than a unidirectional model of projection allows. As Groos writes in a representative, paronomastic, and polysemic formulation that captures the simultaneity of different empathic trajectories, inner imitation "brings both a form and a content to consciousness, for it *forms what is external—internally*," "*builds the outside—into the inside*," and "*imagines the external*" (*bildet das Aeußere—ein*) (*Einleitung* 100, my emphasis).

Form is part of what David Chalmers calls the "hard problem of consciousness," or why the processing of sensory information by the body is accompanied by subjective or phenomenal experience (here, the experience of form).[26] Perhaps most profoundly, it is part of the even larger question of how and at what scale the "substance" of the universe, whether "mind" or "matter" (all imprecise terms here), becomes conscious at all—and of whether the concepts of mind and matter, the commonly felt distribution of the experiential field into subject and object, *and* the *Einfühlung* said to account for a certain relationship between consciousness and form are themselves phantoms of an erroneously dualistic logic. Even if we limit ourselves to the more narrowly focused question of the relationship

---

26. See Chalmers 203: "Why is it that when electromagnetic waveforms impinge on a retina and are discriminated and categorized by a visual system, this discrimination and categorization is experienced as a sensation of vivid red?" (We might replace "red" with "spatial extension," "rectangularity," and so on.) For one possible answer to Chalmers's question, see Dennett.

of *Einfühlung* to form, we encounter numerous ambiguities and implicit dangers. When Lipps, for example, writes that the objects with which we empathize contain a "piece of me" ("Einfühlung und ästhetischer Genuss" 108), it is not always easy to tell whether this is because "I" have already claimed "possession" of these objects ("sofern sie 'meine' Gegenstände sind" [insofar as they are *my* objects], 108) or because the objects have "devoured" and now "possess" something of the empathizer's "self." Particularly in Vischer, at the origin of *Einfühlungstheorie*, the question of the vector of empathy is especially pronounced: Subject and object, self and other form an eternally turning, mutually conditioning circle, a process that ultimately undermines the ontological status of both. But additional uncanny effects also pervade the further manifestations of *Einfühlung* and form throughout the book.

We will not solve the form problem here; more important perhaps is how one works with it. In her *Forms: Whole, Rhythm, Hierarchy, Network*, Levine interweaves the study of form with the analysis of political power, or, more precisely, shows how the latter is always interwoven with and operating through the former. Forms, she writes, "make order"; thus "forms are the stuff of politics" (3). Expanding the definition of form to include not only literary texts but also "management hierarchies" (22), types of cultural theory, and diverse "social arrangements" such as the disciplinary routines of schools (2), Levine employs close formalist analysis to "rethink the historical workings of political power and the relations between politics and aesthetics" (xiii). As she argues, building on the theory of "affordances," or the "potential uses or actions latent in materials and designs," each form "lays claim to a limited range of potentialities"; we should therefore ask not what forms "do" but rather "what potentialities lie latent—though not always obvious—in aesthetic and social arrangements" (6–7). This politically attentive formalism, she contends, "offers a promising way forward" in contesting "unjust arrangements of power" (xiii).

The Feeling of the Form is less overtly political than Levine's study; it focuses not on a broad Foucauldian range of social formations (with their implications for the exercise of power) or on the strict intersections between aesthetics and politics (such as might have interested Benjamin or the Frankfurt School) but on a corpus of literary and theoretical texts. However, the book is political insofar as it presupposes or asks ethical questions about self-other relations; and since form indeed can rarely be fully separated from its political "affordances" (the political uses that a form implicitly allows), my "formalist" consideration of particular forms will also open onto political dimensions. Thus my examination of the formal device of catachresis in the book's last chapter is simultaneously an exploration of the ways "bad metaphor" and its complicating of *Einfühlung* might paradoxically help us relate more ethically to "the Other." In my chapter on Stifter's *Hochwald* in particular, Levine's notion of "colliding forms" (18–19)—the fact that "aesthetic and political forms may be nested inside one another, and that each is capable of disturbing the other's organizing power" (16–17)—may be especially helpful in understanding the fraught and mutually destabilizing relationship between, on the one hand, the "caughtness" of Stifter's female protagonists in the demands of patriarchal societal and familial structures and, on the other, the possible "escape" offered by the intense affective energies of the body, as articulated by the form of Stifter's prose: its syntactical rhythms and punctuation. And this form itself—syntax, rhythm, and punctuation—might be seen as providing the "affordance" for connecting Lee's theory of feeling and *Einfühlung*, with its emphasis on the rhythms of body and breath, to Stifter's narrative.

When we think about the connections between form and feeling, the complexities increase. As noted earlier, form in this study will not be thought separately from feeling, especially when *Einfühlung* and intersubjective empathy are at stake (I will return momentarily to the necessary distinctions between, but also the productive interface of, the two types of empathy for our analysis). Indeed, one way to think about aesthetics in this book is as the coming together of feeling and form, here in the context of empathy. As the title of Vischer's own treatise makes clear, aesthetic empathy *is* "the feeling of the form"—*das Formgefühl*. Although Mallgrave and Ikonomou render Vischer's "Formgefühl" as "sense of form," the broader translation "feeling of the form" is perhaps more revealing. The gerund vividly captures feeling's simultaneous status as noun and verb, statal and active; it likewise leaves open whether feeling is something done *to* "form" (form as feeling's object) or is something form *has* or *does*—a capacity, intrinsic quality, or accompanying mood. Form's suspension between object and subject is itself a version of the vector problem that haunts *Einfühlung*. Writing three-quarters of a century after Vischer, philosopher Susanne K. Langer could still contend that "feeling does inhere somehow in every imaginal form," at least for "people of artistic discernment" (54). And this is of course what psychological aesthetics set out to test: the relation of sensible form to "sensed" form, to perceived feeling or sensation.

What is the feeling that is associated with form, projected into form, inheres in form, or is evoked by form (or all of the above)? At least since Wundt divided human affect into "sensation" (*Empfindung*), "feeling" (*Gefühl*), and "emotion" (*Gemütsbewegung*) (Mallgrave and Ikonomou 15), the term *feeling* has presented particular challenges. Vischer's *Über das optische Formgefühl* itself contains, in addition to *Einfühlung*, an entire catalogue of neologisms for microsubtleties of affective response: "Anfühlung," "Nachfühlung," and "Zufühlung," for example (*Formgefühl* 24–25), rendered valiantly by Mallgrave and Ikonomou as "attentive feeling," "responsive feeling," and "immediate feeling" (106–7). In his seminal study *The Particulars of Rapture: An Aesthetics of the Affects*, Charles Altieri chooses "affect" as the umbrella term for "the entire range of states that are bounded on one side by pure sensation and on the other by thoughts"—in other words, the "immediate modes of sensual responsiveness to the world characterized by an accompanying imaginative dimension"—and offers the following taxonomy: "Feelings are elemental affective states characterized by an imaginative engagement in the immediate processes of sensation. Moods are modes of feeling where the sense of subjectivity becomes diffuse and sensation merges into something close to atmosphere, something that seems to pervade an entire scene or situation. Emotions are affects involving the construction of attitudes that typically establish a particular cause and so situate the agent within a narrative and generate some kind of action or identification. Finally, passions are emotions within which we project significant stakes for the identity that they make possible" (2).

The Feeling of the Form uses the term "feeling" more loosely than does Altieri—that is, at times interchangeably with "emotion" and "affect," or to include "immediate processes of sensation," as in my discussion of syntax, punctuation, and breath in Stifter—except where differentiation is necessary for my argument. The term *affect*, however, deserves special consideration, as it is not just a synonym for "feeling" broadly defined but is also used, as I have noted, by Massumi and others to indicate an undifferentiated flow of felt "intensity" as opposed to "fixed," "named," and personally "owned" emotions.[27] This understanding, inherited from Spinoza by way of Deleuze, has been adopted by influential branches of affect theory and will be important for parts of this book. As Massumi writes, summarizing Deleuze and Guattari, "*L'affect* (Spinoza's *affectus*) is an ability to affect and be affected. It is a prepersonal intensity corresponding to the passage from one experiential state of the body to another and implying an augmentation or diminution in that body's capacity to act" (notes xvi).[28] Some affect theory, then, "designates feelings as personal, emotions as social, and affects per se as the biological substrate of emotion" (Leitch et al., "Sianne Ngai" 2639).[29] In the chapters to follow, I indicate when I am using "affect" in Massumi's sense. For Ernst van Alphen and Tomáš Jirsa in *How to Do Things with Affects: Affective Triggers in Aesthetic Forms and Cultural Practices*, affect is a bridge between feeling and form, an intermediary process or "stage" of intensity "triggered" by forms of various types ("structure," "aesthetics," "social and political ... practices") and in turn triggering feelings, broadly understood— "emotions," "moods," "sensations," "bodily responses" (4–5). As we see in the *Einfühlungstheorie* of Groos and Lee, however, the

---

27. In psychology and psychoanalysis, "affect" is sometimes used more controversially as a technical term to describe a patient's outward presentation of feeling as judged from the ostensibly "objective" perspective of the analyst (i.e., as distinct from the patient's "subjective" experience of their own emotions); see Leitch et al., "Sianne Ngai" 2639.

28. See also Deleuze, *Difference and Repetition* 222–61 and Spinoza, *Ethics* 154.

29. On variations in the understanding of key concepts in different strands of affect theory, see Leitch et al., "Sianne Ngai," 3rd ed., 2638–40; on these different strands themselves and the expansion of the concept of affect beyond affect theory proper, see Alphen and Jirsa 1–3.

trajectory of the process may also be reversed: Bodily responses, that is, can "trigger" the perception of form.

One of the most exciting contemporary attempts to think form and feeling (as well as formalist criticism and affect theory) together may be found in the work of film theorist Eugenie Brinkema (*The Forms of the Affects*, 2014; *Life-Destroying Diagrams*, 2022). She is skeptical of what she understands as the practice—widespread, in her estimation, in much affect theory—of treating affect "in the singular," as always the same type of "diffuse unmediated sensation," "pure state of potentiality," or "vague shuddering intensity" (*Forms of the Affects* xiii–xvi). This reduction, along with the concomitant association of affect with the "expression" of the artist or the "I-experience" of the spectator (*Forms* 31–32, 36), not only produces theoretical readings that are, she maintains, "the same every time" but also leaves us unable to contend with the "definite particular[s]" in which "ethics, politics, aesthetics—indeed, lives—must be enacted" (xv). Rather than being a formless flow, she argues, affect "manifests in, as, and with textual form" (25), "tak[ing] shape in the details of specific . . . forms and temporal structures" (37). She therefore calls for "slow, deep" close analysis of textual elements "often ignored or reduced to paraphrase," as well as of "more ephemeral problematics such as duration, rhythm, absences, elisions, ruptures, gaps, and points of contradiction (ideological, aesthetic, structural, and formal)" (37).

My own concerns and methods overlap with Brinkema's in several ways, especially in their emphasis on close analysis, the interwovenness of feeling and form, and the "ruptures, gaps, and points of contradiction" in texts. And, fascinatingly, the Spinoza epigraph with which Brinkema opens (and that guides) *The Forms of the Affects*—"I shall consider human actions and desires in exactly the same manner, as though I were concerned with lines, planes, and solids" (vii)—implicitly allows us to link her formalism to the interests of psychological aesthetics and much early empathy theory, especially that of Vischer and Lipps, with their own fascination with "lines, planes, and solids." As Maskarinec notes, Lipps regarded "points, lines, and planes" as "exemplary objects" for *Einfühlung* (13): "The paradigmatic object of empathic experience is neither another person nor a figural (or narrative) representation of a person but a simple spatial form" (59). Brinkema's epigraph thus both illuminates the points of contact between affect theory and *Einfühlungstheorie* (which does not appear in her book) and, as it were, closes the circle connecting one of the newest approaches to theorizing the relationship between feeling and form to some of the oldest. Unlike Brinkema's scrupulous unfolding of the entire signifying field opened by the affects that "saturate" and manifest in a text's diverse array of forms (178), however, the present study at times takes a step back in abstraction, speculating on the *stakes* of feeling's entwinement with form or on what "feeling oneself into" certain forms might mean for the conscious or unconscious projects of empathy theorists, literary authors, and readers. I do, however, in my chapter on Stifter's narratives, attend to affect's "saturation" of form, either *ex negativo* (in the story *Turmalin*) or in excess (in *Der Hochwald*). If in that chapter I also draw perhaps more heavily on Massumi's understanding of affect as a diffuse experience of bodily intensity or "unmediated sensation" than Brinkema might endorse, I hope to temper her imagined criticism by placing my reading of intensity in *Der Hochwald* in the context of the text's political tensions: the context, that is, of how characters' bodies (and the "body" of narration that creates them) become sites of the "colliding forms" (Levine) of patriarchal politics and Massumian affect.

The chapters to follow look at some of the broader implications of the intersections of feeling and form for *Einfühlung* and intersubjective empathy; more precisely, they oscillate dialectically between close analysis of specific formal, rhetorical, and figural features of texts and these broader implications. In chapter 1, for example, I explore how Vischer's inaugural *Einfühlungstheorie* itself understood the relation between feeling and form, how it positioned form (of the human body and of objects) as the necessary condition for aesthetic empathy, but also how it introduced conspicuous anxieties—a *feeling* of the uncanny—regarding the ambiguous origin, trajectory, and locus of empathy and its objects, the potentially pathological affects involved in empathic exchange, and the possibly "diabolical" stakes of the empathic project overall. In reading

Büchner as a proleptic companion to Vischer, I consider, among other even more crucial elements to be discussed below, the earlier author's famed formal techniques of free indirect discourse and radical, attributionless citation—themselves at times "uncanny" ways one thing can become another. In chapter 2, I analyze, as noted, the relations between form (syntax, rhythm, and punctation) and feeling (Massumian affect and intensity) in Stifter's *Hochwald* and their resonances with Vernon Lee's somatic *Einfühlungstheorie*. I also, in a different part of the chapter, trace the function of the "logical form" of theater as thematized in Stifter's later novella *Turmalin*: how theater's form as the performance of feeling intersects with the larger formal structure of Stifter's narrative, the presence of a key character whose role in the fiction is to *represent the representation* of feeling as *pure formalism*, and the ramifications of these textual elements for empathy and self-other relations. In chapter 3, I not only investigate how the feelings of rhetorical "coercion," frustration, and semiotic inadequacy evoked by the tropic form of catachresis or "bad metaphor" in Rilke lead to seemingly contradictory ethical paths with respect to empathy—I also closely analyze other formal elements of Rilke's poetry and essays (sonic slippage, punctuation, the moves of rhetorical argumentation) to investigate how the poet's aesthetic and ethical investments intersect with, draw on, and problematize the *Einfühlungstheorie* of his teacher Theodor Lipps.

No single, overarching theory of the relations among feeling, form, and empathy structures the book; rather, each chapter presents a series of specific readings that pursue individual but broadly related questions about the intersections of these elements. Nevertheless, a certain narrative arc and constellation of issues, concerns, methods, and aims animates the study. Let us turn now to these and to a more precise overview of the chapters.

Conceptual Goals and Chapter Overview

As noted earlier, the primary aim of *The Feeling of the Form* is to offer readings that travel backward and forward in time from the

1873 hub of Vischer's *Über das optische Formgefühl*, unfolding the "implicate order" or pre-and para-history of *Einfühlung*. The emphasis is on readings: the study hopes, through attentive analysis, to open illuminating perspectives not just on the interactions of feeling, form, and empathy but also on the rhetorical workings of texts. Broadly speaking, each chapter pairs a literary author with a principal empathy theorist, though any of the theorists may make an appearance in any chapter. The intensity of the treatment of the theorist varies with the needs and goals of the chapter, and each chapter ventures beyond the scope of concerns of its "main" theorist. In chapter 1, Vischer himself is the primary focus of analysis, with Büchner serving as a necessary key to crucial aspects of Vischer's theory; in chapters 2 and 3, Stifter and Rilke take center stage, with the theoretical writings of Lee and Lipps acting as important pathways into thinking what is at stake in the literary texts. In each case, however, it is the real or imagined dialogue between literature and *Einfühlungstheorie* that allows the full dimensions of the chapter's specific configuration of feeling, form, *Einfühlung*, and intersubjective empathy to come into view.

In similarly dialogic fashion, the chapters' readings frequently draw on or "converse" with later, twentieth- and twenty-first-century movements and thinkers—Freud, Turing, virtual reality and artificial intelligence, Kristeva, Massumi, object-oriented ontology—with which or whom the earlier writers resonate, thus allowing deeper understanding of the writers' stakes. The study's method itself is a colloquy of approaches—close rhetorical and formal analysis, "depth" and "surface" reading, aspects of cultural history and psychoanalysis, affect theory and object-oriented philosophy—whose juxtaposition, interaction, and points of contact and difference tell us more about the texts we are exploring than any monolithic approach would alone.[30] In the course of this exploration, we will see that Vischer's *Einfühlung* arises in the late nineteenth century as a complex response to paradigm shifts and crises in the preceding, mid-century decades of the German-speaking world. As a polyvalent phenomenon, it simultaneously reflects or channels—in a way,

---

30. On surface reading, see Best and Marcus.

represents the culmination of—the anxieties of the earlier period, attempts to repair them through a complicated series of scientific, philosophical, and aesthetic maneuvers, *and* uncannily recapitulates or extends the earlier anxieties in different form. Both the content and the very emergence of Vischer's *Einfühlung*, that is, are uncanny. But the same mid-century period that laid the groundwork for the emergence of an anxious and uncanny *Einfühlung* also initiated a bifurcated path. It opened other questions, potentials, and promises for aesthetic empathy—implicit (if problematically conflicted) in Stifter, resonant with Lee, or later articulated by Rilke in his dialogue with Lipps—that offer possible, at least partially positive, alternatives to the constellation of dangers and fears about self-other relations present in Vischer. Thus, the book's questions about *Einfühlung*, feeling, and form are also in some sense ethical questions.

Chapter 1, "The Materialist Unconscious: Necromantic Empathy in Robert Vischer and Georg Büchner," reads *Über das optische Formgefühl* in consort with the narrative fragment *Lenz*, Büchner's groundbreaking 1839 depiction of the mental illness and correspondingly distinctive sensory perceptions of the Sturm und Drang playwright Jakob Michael Reinhold Lenz—a man who, as Büchner vividly reimagines in his depiction of key events from the playwright's life, tried and failed to raise the body of a lifeless child from the dead. The chapter is concerned less with actively analyzing form per se (although it does include discussion of *Lenz*'s formal elements) than with understanding how Vischer *theorized* the relations between form and feeling in his inaugural formulation of *Einfühlung*—and with how *Lenz* proleptically exposes both the reasons for and the implications of this formulation. As I show, Vischer's treatise contains, beneath or distributed across the surface of its rhetorical celebration of the new aesthetic concept of *Einfühlung*, uncanny anxieties aroused by this concept itself: anxieties about perilous self-other relations (including diabolical "possession" of and *by* the Other), the nearness of empathy to pathology, and especially the meaning of the simultaneously divine and demonic human reanimation of a world of "dead" form. The historical grounds for these anxieties were coming ever more clearly into focus in Büchner's post-Romantic 1830s, with their profound scientific transformations (including transformations of the science that underlay Büchner's anatomical research and Vischer's neurologically based aesthetics): the development of German neurophysiology in the context of the destabilizing transition from vitalism and *Naturphilosophie*, with their belief in a holistic, organic, "living" universe, to scientific materialism, with its view of nature as a site of purely physical and chemical reactions—dead matter. It is this liminal time that frames Büchner's work. And if Vischer's *Einfühlung* arises in response to materialism's perceived deadening of the world, it is also, like *Lenz* (and as *Lenz* foretells), itself the tale of an uncanny resurrection. As both a site of resistance to, or at least ambivalence about, post-vitalist modernity *and* a product of that modernity itself (materialist neurophysiology), its attempt to reanimate dead form can only "succeed" by becoming the very modern ghost story it fears.[31] Other varieties of empathy—the fictionalized Lenz's "feeling into" the beings and objects he encounters, Büchner's empathy for Lenz himself and subsequent "resurrection" of the suffering playwright as a fictionalized, "formal" avatar—do not escape these and other anxieties. Ultimately, Vischer's and Büchner's ambivalence about the resurrective powers of empathy, both aesthetic and interpersonal, channels the corresponding anxieties of what I call a "materialist unconscious": what scientific materialism longs for and fears.

Chapters 2 and 3 turn to in-depth analysis of the relations among form, feeling, and empathy, both aesthetic and interpersonal, in the form and content of literary texts. Chapter 2, "Adalbert Stifter: Resistances of Form and Feeling," closely reads *Der Hochwald* (*The Mountain Forest*, 1844) and *Turmalin* (*Tourmaline*, 1853), two novellas by Stifter, Büchner's Austrian near contemporary and fellow barometer of mid-century materialist anxieties. The chapter traces the ways the same period that laid the foundations for Vischer's uncanny formulation of *Einfühlung* also prefigured other pathways and possibilities for aesthetic empathy than those foregrounded (or

---

31. On the ways manifestations of a historical period can turn against the conditions that gave rise to them, see Janet Ward and especially Pijarski, to whose work I am indebted for inspiring me to think about Vischer's *Einfühlung* as a site of resistance to modernity.

implicit) in Vischer's theory: pathways that point to later developments in *Einfühlungstheorie*, affect and gender theory, and the understanding of other minds more generally. The first part of the chapter, a new reading of *Turmalin*, considers multiple levels of the thematization of the logical form of theater—broadly, the simulative performance of the *form of feeling*—as an aesthetic and ethical problem across *Turmalin*'s diegetic and formal dimensions. Theatrical art and theories of acting form central concerns in the novella, but perhaps the text's most revealing figure (both character and trope) is an *inadvertent* actor—a girl who *formally performs* expressions of feeling without being able to feel their content herself. Yet these simulations, like those of the professional actor whose stage performances and actions outside the theater catalyze key developments in the story, have a real-world effect on those who spectate her "acting." Like the girl, the novella's experimental form "misses" affect and transparently reliable or accessible empathic anchors. Fragmentary narration and the elision of key events and emotional high points—the textual presence, that is, of feeling only in "virtual" form—forces us to infer the affective content of crucial story elements. As I show, Stifter's experimental novella is also an "empathy experiment" that opens onto "modern" questions of other minds, virtual reality, and artificial intelligence that will be important for thinkers like Turing: It asks whether there is a difference between "real" feeling and its formal simulation and what it means to "feel oneself into" another if that other is only known as pure formalism, a virtual effect.

The second half of the chapter juxtaposes Stifter's *Hochwald* with turn-of-the-(twentieth)-century writings by Vernon Lee, whose bodily theory of aesthetic empathy builds on and substantially expands the German *Einfühlungstheorie* of Karl Groos and whose intensely corporeal understanding of *Einfühlung* parallels and retroactively illuminates *Der Hochwald*'s aesthetic strategies. Pairing Stifter and Lee, two writers at first glance distant from the geographical and temporal centers of German empathy theory, reveals that Stifter not only foreshadows but also, like Lee, moves strikingly beyond the types of *Einfühlung* later to be envisioned by Vischer. Read together with Lee, Stifter's *Hochwald* indexes the feeling of its form not primarily in objects but as pulses, beats, breath, movement, and full bodily response; its unique deployment of idiosyncratic punctuation, repetition, spaces, and rhythms forms an inventory of "intensities" that anticipates affect theory. These intensities at the formal level are mirrored by the novella's content, which stages the simultaneous constraint and escape of "intense" (*innig*) flows of Massumian affect, particularly at the site of the body of the central character Clarissa. Placing this understanding of *Der Hochwald* in further dialogue with influential Enlightenment-era theories of the beautiful and sublime and with Kristeva's notion of a "semiotic chora" of bodily stases and flows underlying language, we find Stifter's text to be "about" the relation of empathy and *Einfühlung* to the gendered voice and gaze. Correspondingly, the analysis asks whether there is an unrecognized "parallel Stifter" operating alongside the traditionally patriarchal figure this author is often taken to be: a Stifter whose aesthetic of the small and *innig* (intense, but also intimate, heartfelt) empathically produces a textual form that the gender norms of the nineteenth century might characterize as *feminine*—the body of the text as female body. But especially where they seem to resist the patriarchal ideologies of their day, Stifter's textual experiments, like Vischer's theories, are also problematically complicit with what they resist.

Chapter 3, "Bad Metaphors: Catachresis and Coercion in Rainer Maria Rilke," moves beyond the foreshadowing and birth of *Einfühlung* to the concept's zenith and aftermath. Rilke is the German-language poet perhaps most closely associated with a striking and idiosyncratic blend of intersubjective and aesthetic empathy—empathy with animals and objects, as expressed in his famous *Dinggedichte*. His work is contemporaneous with that of Theodor Lipps, Europe's most influential representative of *Einfühlungstheorie* and Rilke's professor for aesthetics at the University of Munich. The impact of Rodin and Cézanne on Rilke's art has long been noted; however, the possible role of Rilke's teacher Lipps, the first to theorize *Einfühlung* together with intersubjective empathy, has been almost entirely overlooked. As I show in the chapter, empathy in Rilke functions—appropriately for a poet—like a metaphor, and specifically like *bad metaphor* or catachresis. Here, I mean "bad metaphor" in both the stylistic and the ethical sense, as a specific sort of hinge between form and feeling: a tropic form whose relationship between vehicle and tenor is "coerced," and that itself coercively forms or "forces" the reader's feeling and vision. Strikingly, Lipps's version of *Einfühlungstheorie* is itself conspicuously rooted in the coercive operations of metaphor: the problematic practice of transforming the qualities—the feelings and forms—of the other into a set of metaphors for the self. Writing at the peak of Lipps's own substantial publication output on *Einfühlung*, Rilke develops a poetics of empathy as bad metaphor that parallels and at times adopts Lipps's practice. At the same time, however, Rilke's bad metaphors—"bad" now in the sense of "insufficient"—complicate, reverse, and disrupt Lipps's project. Rilke's very catachreses save his texts from the presumption of direct or even adequate correlation with their "objects" or "others"—an aporia in *Einfühlung* that paradoxically both ratifies and undermines the concept's long-standing reliance on an understanding, derived from Kant and "physiological idealism," of the world as mind- and body-projected. By closely reading, in broad conversation with Lipps, the interaction of feeling and form in a number of Rilke's lesser-known but especially revealing poems and essays, the chapter tells the story of empathy's relation to bad metaphor: from the young Rilke's empathic obsession with the legal and linguistic injustices of a 1901 court case in which bad metaphor literally becomes deadly; to the role of empathy-forcing catachresis in a language of "disastrous saying" and unsayability in Rilke's poetry; to the perils of Lipps-inflected metaphor in Rilke's instrumentalizing identification with non-Western others; to metaphor's transformation of Rilke into a Vischerian "dead object" of, paradoxically, Rilke's *own* empathy; and finally to Rilke's anticipation of something like present-day object-oriented ontology, with its recognition of the inevitability of bad metaphor in any encounter with another. Reading Rilke alongside object-oriented ontology's problematization of Kant allows us to return to several of the dilemmas with which the book, and early *Einfühlungstheorie*, began—the world as self-projection, human bodies and feelings and external objects and forms as metaphors of each other, the uncanniness of self-other exchange—and possibly offer an alternative to them. In that alternative, all metaphor is a species of catachresis, and catachresis ironically becomes the "best" metaphor: a defense, that is, against the self's possession of (or by) the Other, and perhaps also the basis for an ethics based on aesthetics. A brief coda about the "afterlives" of *Einfühlung* after its supposed death in the Weimar Republic closes the book.

The study's ethical trajectory, then, moves from fears about the implications of *Einfühlung*'s animation of dead form and reciprocally "colonial" model of self-other relations, through the philosophical and political curiosity articulated by alternative approaches to thinking "otherness" (Stifter's novellas), to the potential, though still ambiguous, protection of the space of the other through bad metaphor—ambiguous because bad metaphor is simultaneously (negatively) coercive and (positively) "inadequate." Along the way, we will periodically ask whether some of the ethical and philosophical conundrums of empathy, both intersubjective and aesthetic, arise at least in part from empathy's problematically dualistic assumptions. Certain apparent changes in *Einfühlungstheorie* itself—the movement from Vischer's efforts to explain "mental stimulation ... precisely through and together with bodily stimulation," especially neurophysiological stimulation (92), to Lee's concern with the full spectrum of bodily motion, breath, and circulation in the empathic "creation" of objects, to Lipps's emphasis on the more purely "mental" aspects of mind as the root of empathic projection—represent, apart from the sorts of differences, developments, and debates that occur in any field, perhaps less a trajectory than a palimpsest or kaleidoscope, with more or less divergent areas or dimensions coming serially into focus. That is, to return to the image of the implicate order, Vischer, Lee, and Lipps do not so much "advance" empathy theory as *unfold* it, "explicating" the broader *Einfühlungstheorie(n)* already implicit in Vischer himself and in the three theorists' literary precursors. Rilke then continues this unfolding.

Before leaving this overview of chapters and goals, let us return briefly to the question of *Einfühlung* versus—or perhaps better, *with*—intersubjective empathy. On the one hand, as this introduction has recounted, the two terms are patently definitionally distinct: *Einfühlung* is human self-projection into inanimate form, and empathy, at least in current usage, is a capacity possessed by one human being vis-à-vis another. Central parts of the study depend on this difference, and the following chapters therefore clearly indicate wherever possible when they are speaking of interpersonal and when of aesthetic empathy or *Einfühlung*. And, since *The Feeling of the Form* begins with a reading of Vischer and draws on at least two other essential *Einfühlungstheoretiker* (theorists of aesthetic empathy), aesthetic empathy or *Einfühlung* in particular plays a conspicuous role in the book's arguments. On the other hand, as my overview of the chapters suggests, the two concepts are also, if not inextricably, then at least profoundly and problematically—perhaps even "uncannily"—interwoven. Vischer theorizes the dynamics of feeling oneself into objects, but also maintains that it is only "natural love" for the human species (103)—as Guyer explains it, the intersubjectively empathic "drive ... for union with other human beings" (394)—that makes this *Einfühlung* possible. Büchner empathizes interpersonally with the historical Lenz, whose fictionalized avatar empathizes *aesthetically* with the inanimate forms and objects he encounters in Büchner's tale. The narrator's, and our, "narrative empathy" (a virtual version of intersubjective empathy) with *Der Hochwald*'s protagonist Clarissa is complexified by what Lee's theory of aesthetic empathy or *Einfühlung* makes visible about Clarissa's body—and the text's. Lipps himself blurs the border between *Einfühlung* and intersubjective empathy through his practice of turning human others into metaphor-supplying "objects," and Rilke finds in bad metaphor a limit to interpersonal and aesthetic empathy alike. The histories and concepts of *Einfühlung* and interpersonal empathy might perhaps be productively thought of as resembling a network of railway tracks: describing at times different paths, at times intersecting, converging, traveling together, and diverging again, presenting both crucial distinctions and crucial connections. In keeping with these observations, *The Feeling of the Form* not only maintains separation between intersubjective empathy and *Einfühlung*: It also pursues salient aspects of their interconnection and interplay, differentiating or thinking the concepts together as directed by the workings of the texts under consideration and the pathways opened by analysis. In any case, both concepts are necessary for an understanding of Büchner, Stifter, and Rilke. With these thoughts in mind, let us turn in conclusion to some of the ways *The Feeling of the Form* differs from related work on *Einfühlung* and intersubjective empathy both in general and in German studies in particular.

The Feeling of the Form, German Studies, and Empathy

Interpersonal empathy, whether represented by theories of reader response, narrative empathy (readers' "intersubjective" empathy with fictional characters), or the depiction of empathy between literary characters themselves, dominates much of the work in literary-critical empathy studies in the United States. Particularly in the wake of Suzanne Keen's seminal *Empathy and the Novel* (2007), questions of the possible relationships among literature, empathy, and altruism have especially come to the fore—questions, that is, about whether engaging empathically with literary texts can increase readers' prosocial behavior or help transform them into morally improved persons. Keen herself remains cautious. As she writes, fiction can provide a "no-strings-attached opportunity" for readers to experience empathy free from real-world barriers; however, the evidence that such experiences translate into extratextual action is "not robust" (*Empathy and the Novel* 167–68). Readers, she concludes, "may enjoy empathy freely without paying society back in altruism" (168). To pursue these still-open questions, literary studies has partnered with various forms of psychology, moral philosophy, and cognitive neuroscience (Keen, "Empathy Studies" 126). Psychologists David Comer Kidd and Emanuele Castano, for example, attracted considerable attention when they published experimental evidence seemingly confirming that "reading literary fiction" does indeed improve "theory of mind" (here, the ability to recognize and understand others' mental and emotional states); their 2013 study in the journal *Science* has itself since been contested (Panero et al.).

My own aims differ considerably from these trends. Although, as I have pointed out, *Einfühlung* in *The Feeling of the Form* is frequently thought together with questions of intersubjective empathy raised by the specific texts under consideration, the focus is not on the interpersonal alone. What is at stake is the two concepts' interplay, with aesthetic empathy or *Einfühlung* often leading the dance, as it were. Put otherwise, even when questions of intersubjective empathy come to play a significant role in the analyses to follow, these questions cannot be separated from other fundamental questions of *aesthetic* empathy—the feeling of the form—out of which they arise, on which they depend, and whose implications they articulate. Likewise, although this study is concerned with ethics and therefore, in a broadly understood sense, with "reader response," it does not investigate how individual readers or populations respond to the texts it addresses or whether these texts measurably contribute to moral improvement. The ethical questions it raises are, like its interpersonal questions, a function of its aesthetic and formal questions.

These aesthetic and formal questions are not pursued from the side of a historical survey of scientific-theoretical, psychological-aesthetic, or laboratory-experimental investigations into the relations of physiology to form, such as Robert Michael Brain undertakes with regard to the pan-European (but especially French) arts in his *The Pulse of Modernism: Physiological Aesthetics in Fin-de-Siècle Europe* (2015). Instead, a central contribution of this study is its readings, both close and surface, particularly of literary texts (which here serve as the primary "canon" of *Einfühlung*'s pre- and para-history), but also of *Einfühlungstheorie* itself. My reading of Vischer's *Über das optische Formgefühl*, for example, represents to my knowledge one of the only close analyses of this inaugural treatise of *Einfühlungstheorie*—a reading, that is, dedicated not only to understanding and summarizing the treatise's theoretical "content points" (the currently dominant mode of approaching Vischer's text) but also, and even more importantly, to tracing the rhetorical operations and figural implications of his language itself, the "unconscious" of his imagery and the anxieties it opens onto.[32] Similarly, by attending closely to formal features of Stifter's novellas, the study provides new interpretations of these narratives that, in the context of *Einfühlung* and intersubjective empathy, challenge traditional understandings of Stifter's relation to gender or link his stories in sur-

---

32. The other properly "close" analysis of Vischer's treatise of which I am aware is Tobias Wilke's 2014 article "Einfühlung als Metapher"; see chapter 1.

prising ways to contemporary concerns of virtual reality and artificial intelligence. And the chapter on Rilke presents original analyses of several of his lesser-known texts that, while they have not received the critical attention of his more famous writings (indeed, in some cases have received virtually no critical attention), are particularly revealing with regard to the intersections of empathy, aesthetics, and ethics. In this regard, *The Feeling of the Form* has less in common with most American literary empathy criticism than with Meghan Marie Hammond's 2014 study *Empathy and the Psychology of Literary Modernism*, which also draws extensively on Vischer, Lipps, and Lee (among others) in the service of robust readings of literary texts. Hammond's book, however, exclusively treats English and American rather than German literature and, as its title indicates, restricts itself to the modernist period. It is also more classically "historicist" than the present study. Unlike the dominant methods of Hammond's work (and more unusually for literary empathy studies overall), my readings—particularly of Stifter's *Hochwald* and Rilke's poetry—are significantly inflected by textual formalism: they examine blocks of syntax, the acoustic resonances of words, and at times even individual punctuation marks for their interface with questions of *Einfühlung*, affect, and intersubjective empathy.

Given *Einfühlung*'s German origins and decades-long prominence in German aesthetic theory, surprisingly few books address the concept's points of contact with German literature. In English, Maskarinec's *The Forces of Form in German Modernism* (2018) reads German literary and visual texts of the (again) modernist age in part through the lens of *Einfühlungstheorie*. However, as Maskarinec points out, the authors she discusses "largely distance themselves from Vischer's language of projection" (9), and her study itself is more concerned with the relation of forces such as "gravity, weight, equilibrium, and fall" (11) to form than with *Einfühlung* per se.

In German, some of the most prominent work in literary empathy studies has been done by Fritz Breithaupt. His 2009 *Kulturen der Empathie* (*Cultures of Empathy*) focuses, as its title suggests, not on *Einfühlung* but on intersubjective empathy (*Empathie*) and on what a narrative-based understanding of empathy might tell us about the structure of fellow-feeling in the "real world." The German literary texts he discusses stem primarily from periods predating those I treat in *The Feeling of the Form*.[33] As Breithaupt argues, "Human empathy is substantially shaped by narrative thinking and arises on the basis of narrative paradigms and constraints" (*Kulturen* 114). Specifically, interpersonal empathy arises as a feeling of "affiliation" (*Zugehörigkeit*) generated by "taking sides in a three-person scene" (116), or a situation in which "an observer witnesses the nonharmonious interaction of at least two individuals and mentally sides with one of the two parties without necessarily intervening in the action" (152–53). The feeling of affiliation is catalyzed by the "emotional and rational strategies" the observer undertakes to "narratively legitimize" her choice of sides (116). Breithaupt links narrative and the aesthetic to cognitive neuroscience: We understand others by involving them in "mental narratives" (10), and mirror neurons themselves function like narratives in miniature, prompting us to predict others' behavior as we might do when reading a plot (186) and arousing our heightened feelings of having a separate "self" when this predictability is thwarted (53). *Kulturen* insists that sides must be taken for empathy to arise or for narrative to "be" narrative (168–71)—a position perhaps troubled by Stifter's ambiguous tales, which do not typically present the sorts of "absolutized" "good" and "bad" characters Breithaupt sees as ideal coordinate points for the production of empathy (192).

Breithaupt's later *The Dark Sides of Empathy* (2019, originally *Die dunklen Seiten der Empathie*, 2017) is more directly related to the concerns of this study. *The Dark Sides* probes "the terrible things we do because of our ability to empathize with others" (1), including "exploitation, vampirism, . . . sadism," and "self-loss" (1, 17); it thus resonates with my exploration of empathy's relation to the uncanny, the pathological, and other perils to self and others, as well as with questions of our enjoyment of others' suffering in tragedies (162–70) such as *Der Hochwald*. Despite a dedicated discussion of *Einfühlung* (77–81), *The Dark Sides*, even more so than *Kulturen*, focuses on broadly sociological formations and nonliterary examples of the problematic functioning of interpersonal empathy in extratextual

---

33. The exception is Fontane's *Effi Briest*, written between Vischer and Rilke.

situations (Stockholm Syndrome, humanitarian aid, helicopter parenting, stalking). However, building on the arguments of *Kulturen*, *The Dark Sides* links interpersonal empathy to aesthetics through the model of generic forms such as narrative and drama: "We can empathize because we can aestheticize—clarify—the situation of the other ... [by turning them into] a character in a play we watch and experience" (12). If this claim trusts perhaps too strongly in a "clarity" that aesthetic forms may in fact not provide, other aspects of Breithaupt's connection of interpersonal empathy to aesthetics have important implications for both ethics and affect: "Empathy increases our aesthetic perception ... by widening the scope of that which we experience; ... by providing us with more than one perspective of a situation, thereby multiplying our experience of the situation; and ... by intensifying that experience" (223).

Two additional studies in German have particular relevance for *The Feeling of the Form*, especially its discussion of Vischer.[34] The first, Monika Fick's *Sinnenwelt und Weltseele: Der psychophysische Monismus in der Literatur der Jahrhundertwende* (*Sense-World and World Soul: Psychophysical Monism in Turn-of-the-Century Literature*, 1993), explores the role of monism—here, the holistic conception of the unity of mind and body, psychological and physical, and, by extension, self and world—in German literature around the turn of the twentieth century. While it only briefly mentions *Einfühlungstheorie*, Fick's book extensively analyzes the thought and

---

34. A third study, Braungart's *Leibhafter Sinn* (*Incarnate Sense*, 1995), might also be mentioned here. It seeks to trace an alternative, nonlinguistic "discourse of modernity" in which meaning arises in and through the sensuously experiencing body (1–2). Although the majority of Braungart's literary analyses focus on the modernist period, his book provides a compelling prehistory of *Einfühlung* (including aspects of Kantian idealism, sensory physiology, and psychology) grounded in a detailed reading of Herder's aesthetics. A fourth study, *Einfühlung: Theorie und Kulturgeschichte einer ästhetischen Denkfigur 1770–1930* (*Empathy: Theory and Cultural History of an Aesthetic Thought-Figure 1770–1930*) by Thomas Petraschka, appeared as the final manuscript of *The Feeling of the Form* was being prepared for publication; I am therefore unable to treat it in depth here. As its title suggests, like Müller-Tamm's work on projection, Petraschka's book presents a broad historical overview of the development of *Einfühlung* as a "thought-figure"; it also contains explication of key ideas in early *Einfühlungstheorie* and concise excurses on Vischer, Rilke, and Lee.

influence of Gustav Fechner, a late proponent of *Naturphilosophie*-inflected ideas and, as I noted earlier, one of *Einfühlung*'s important precursors (his *Elemente der Psychophysik* [*Elements of Psychophysics*] appeared in 1860). As Fick argues, the roots of the German modernist version of monism may be found in Fechner's psychophysics, with its avowal of the inseparability of mental and physical processes and corresponding "ensoulment of the physical" (12–18, 39–52). Fechner's work, which received a widespread popular reception at the turn of the century, thus helped fuel the growing reaction against nineteenth-century scientific materialism, with its reduction of mind to a secondary function of matter (43–56). Fick sees Fechner-inspired monism as having achieved broad acceptance by the turn of the century, that is, of having established, at least in the neoromantic and early modernist literary spheres, an understanding of the material world as indeed "ensouled" (*beseelt*) (51–52)—an effective alternative to the previous century's physicalism. In my study, I am more concerned with the anxieties of the twentieth century's liminal predecessors. If Vischer's *Einfühlung* might be seen as contributing to the rise of the tendencies Fick notes—a bridge, as it were, between Fechner and twentieth-century monism—then its proposed "projection of life into lifeless form" (Vischer 104, modified) or ensoulment of the physical is not the sort of (relatively) unproblematically successful phenomenon Fick seems to take fin-de-siècle monism to be. Rather, Vischer's *Einfühlung* exhibits the ambivalences and anxieties of a nascent or intermediate stage—a moment when challenges to materialism were not at all guaranteed to "succeed." More importantly, it is *uncanny*: not only because it repeats (before neoromanticism) some of Romanticism's characteristically uncanny content or because it is a "return" of Romantic universalism "made strange" by the pressures of intervening epistemic shifts (although it is all of this) but also because it harbors its own anxieties, prefigured by Büchner, about whether it *can* succeed—and about the dangers and guilt that might be awakened *should* it. I will return to these issues in the next chapter.

Müller-Tamm's *Abstraktion als Einfühlung: Zur Denkfigur der Projektion in Psychophysiologie, Kulturtheorie, Ästhetik und Literatur der frühen Moderne* (*Abstraction as Empathy: On the Thought-*

Figure of Projection in the Psychophysiology, Cultural Theory, Aesthetics, and Literature of Early Modernism, 2005), whose account of the career of physiological idealism strongly influenced my overview of the scientific path to *Einfühlungstheorie* earlier in this introduction, is indispensable for placing the development of *Einfühlung* in its historical context. The book provides a comprehensive overview of the factors leading from the Enlightenment to the appearance of *Einfühlungstheorie* and of the theory's place in late nineteenth- and early twentieth-century thought. Despite *Einfühlung*'s prominent position in the book's title, however, aesthetic empathy is only one part of the larger narrative that forms the study's true subject: the history and manifestations of the "thought-figure of projection" in European modernity. As Müller-Tamm argues, starting with post-Kantian physiological idealism or the "sensory-physiological subjectivizing of perception and experience" in the first half of the nineteenth century (11), the figure and processes of projection have dominated the conceptualization of human interaction with the world across a diverse array of phenomena in philosophy, the sciences, and aesthetics up to the modernist period (9); these include Müller's law of specific nerve energies (32), Freudian psychoanalysis (196ff.), and Expressionism (19, 66). Perhaps most strikingly, following Crary (and, ultimately, Nietzsche), Müller-Tamm reads physiological perception and projection, and thus also *Einfühlung*, in terms of a broadly understood, linguistic-turn-inflected theory of arbitrary signification.[35] As she writes, in the wake of Müller's law of specific nerve energies, nineteenth-century "sensory physiology ... defined the process of perception as a semiotic process—the world of perception has no similarity with real things, but is the result of a multi-part process of translation" (184). At the center of *Einfühlungstheorie*, then, was not "trust in an ... unquestionable 'meaning' [*Sinnhaftigkeit*] of the body" (218) but rather a "'medialization' or metaphorization of perception," a "fictionalizing of reality" (12).

Müller-Tamm's approach has the virtue of comprehensiveness and clarity; however, it also suffers from certain drawbacks. The paradigm of projection as a single, overarching figure uniting disparate texts,

---

35. Cf. Crary 71, 90–91, as well as Nietzsche, "On Truth and Lying."

phenomena, and movements works best at a certain distance. In offering a broad cultural history and wide-ranging canon of texts from the eighteenth century to the 1920s, *Abstraktion* must at times sacrifice close reading and the nuances of textual specificity, particularly in the case of theoretical works like Vischer's. As close attention to these nuances—individual words, images, connotations, and rhetorical moves—shows, however, even in supposed exemplars of projection theory like Vischer, the operations of projection are themselves far from simple. Rather than the unidirectionality implied by the model of human self-projection "*into*," projection often simultaneously arrives from the other, "object" side as well, or dissolves into numerous microvectors, seemingly moving in opposite directions at once.

As I have noted, *The Feeling of the Form* does not attempt to present a comprehensive historical overview: It focuses on individual readings of texts and on rhetorically specific intersections of *Einfühlung* and interpersonal empathy. It also tells a different story than Müller-Tamm's account of the broader thought-figure of projection: a story about the stakes of *Einfühlung*'s uncanny animation of nature in a materialist world, the different paths opened by the crossings of *Einfühlung* with the body and metaphor, and the ethical implications of some of these crossings. The juxtapositions uncovered or invited by the study's para-history and implicate order point to the ways these crossings themselves open onto surprisingly contemporary concerns—affect theory, artificial intelligence, virtual reality, object-oriented ontology—not previously pursued in German studies work on empathy. This, as I have noted, allows diverse phenomena across time and space to illuminate each other, each becoming more or differently legible in the light of the others. Finally, the study tells a story guided by the unique and heterogeneous details of texts: Rather than seeking a common, overarching, or unifying paradigm, it seeks to proliferate difference.

Sendoff

In her introduction to *The Varieties of Empathy in Science, Art, and History*, an issue of *Science in Context*, Susan Lanzoni asks, "Does empathy tell us about others, or in the end, just ourselves? Do we project ourselves into the other and in so doing, obscure the reality of the other's experience, or does empathy allow us to grasp an authentic sense of the other's experience? As a term of relation, does empathy tend to privilege the self or the other? And, finally, is there a stress on difference or similarity across the empathic divide?" (288). Such questions are essential to an exploration of the "interstices between bodies and things, ... selves and others" (287): interstices, that is, that span both aesthetic and interpersonal empathy. Just as importantly, however, we might ask whether the concept and rhetoric of empathy, both intersubjective and aesthetic, obscure the equally significant question of on what basis we might, in an ultimate rather than provisional sense, determine the reality, existence, or borders of "self" and "other" at all.

These sorts of questions hover in the background of this study, in some ways refracting its ethical concerns. Perhaps more directly, the study asks how in the realm of empathy, the aesthetic continues to haunt the interpersonal like a ghost—a fact that seems to pull the ethical along with it, or us into the realm of the ethical. From a certain perspective, that is, the problem of aesthetic empathy turns out to be the "aesthetic problem of empathy": *Einfühlung* begins its life as an aesthetic concept but remains, even after its double translation—first into "empathy," then into an intersubjective mode of feeling with another—an aesthetic problem. With these thoughts in mind, let us go back to the beginning.

1

THE MATERIALIST UNCONSCIOUS

Necromantic Empathy in Robert Vischer and Georg Büchner

The history of *Einfühlung* begins with a diabolical resurrection. About a third of the way through "Feeling and Emotion" ("Gefühl und Gemüth"), the central, longest, and perhaps most important chapter of Robert Vischer's *Über das optische Formgefühl*, we encounter the following passage:

> With organic nature, empathy [*Einfühlung*] functions symbolically to animate a plant and to anthropomorphize an animal; only toward other human beings does it act as a doubling of self. . . . We are also reminded here of stories of the spontaneous resurrection [*unwillkürliche Wiederbelebung*] of a corpse and the many legends that tell of skeletons engaged in nocturnal dances and the dead walking abroad. In medieval legends the devil takes possession of a corpse and causes it to behave as if alive— for instance, the tale of a Parisian nobleman whom the devil seduced by animating the corpse of a beautiful girl recently hanged [*den der Teufel in der schönen Leiche eines gehenkten Mädchens verführt*].
> (106, *Formgefühl* 23)

What is striking here is the text's abrupt leap from organic nature, plants, and animals—phenomena traditionally associated with personification and pathetic fallacy, and thus unsurprising candidates for Vischer's understanding of *Einfühlung*—to reanimated corpses, dancing skeletons, demonic possessions, and the devil. Like a revivified corpse itself, Vischer's odd supplement seems a weird "body" within the treatise's main argument. Despite its strangely insistent nature ("we *are also* reminded here of"), the passage's sudden turn to the macabre appears at first glance to follow only tenuously from what has come before and to present a particularly eccentric—and sinister—list of what *Einfühlung* supposedly reminds us of. Yet on closer examination, what seems an afterthought turns out to be, tellingly, the point: Vischer's treatise as a whole is conspicuously concerned with death, and especially with the figuration of *Einfühlung* as the resurrection or reanimation of the not-quite-living and outright dead. Indeed, uncanny anxieties haunt the text. Not only does the chain of associations evoked by *Einfühlung* lead inexorably to death: The resulting resurrection of the dead *by Einfühlung* is also allegorized as frighteningly demonic ("The devil takes possession of a corpse and causes it to behave as if alive"). Even empathy "toward other human beings" ends with a "doubling of self," an image as likely to evoke foreboding and the death-heralding doppelgänger of Gothic Romanticism as it is to inspire the comforts of fellow-feeling. Thus, not only did Vischer's inaugural formulation of *Einfühlungstheorie* supply early empathy theorists with an extensive inventory of ideas, terms, and models for thinking about the processes through which the human body "objectifies itself in spatial forms" and unconsciously "projects its own . . . form—and with this also the soul—into the form of the object" (Vischer 92): It left the unfolding history of *Einfühlung* with something more uncanny, spooky, and unsettling as well. To borrow Breithaupt's differently used term, right from the beginning, *Einfühlung* unfolds in the shadow of its own "dark sides." Indeed, confronted with *Einfühlung*'s founding document, we must ask ourselves what forces, implications, and anxieties are at stake in the image that literally and figuratively climaxes (and therefore in a certain sense governs) the strange register of things Vischer insists aesthetic empathy reminds us of: the image of *Einfühlung*'s "reanimation of a corpse"—of a "beautiful girl recently hanged," no less—as the devil's seduction.

Almost forty years before *Über das optische Formgefühl*, Georg Büchner staged German literature's perhaps most famous scene of *failed* resurrection. The titular mentally ill protagonist of the narrative fragment *Lenz*, begun in 1835 and published posthumously in 1839—a man much given, at least in Büchner's retelling, to "objectifying his body in spatial forms" and "projecting its own form, and with this also the soul, into the form of the object"—attempts and spectacularly fails to raise a recently perished girl from the dead:

> Lenz shuddered when he touched the cold limbs and saw the [girl's] half-open glassy eyes. The child seemed so forsaken and he himself so alone and isolated; . . . he fell to his knees, he prayed with the full misery of despair that God send him a sign and bring the child back to life. . . . Then he got up and took the child's hand and said loudly and firmly: Arise and walk! But the walls echoed back his voice so dispassionately they seemed to mock him, and the corpse remained cold. He fell to the ground, half out of his mind. . . . A song of hell triumphant was in his breast. (53)

Here, it is Lenz's failure to resurrect the girl—his failure, as it were, to "seduce" her to live—that transforms *him* into the devil: "It seemed to him as if he alone existed, as if the world lay only in his imagination, as if there were nothing but himself, eternally damned, Satan himself; alone, tormented by his imaginings" (71–73). This solipsistic vision would seem to eliminate the possibility of empathy or *Einfühlung*: There is no "other" to project oneself into. Yet the vision also recalls, in diabolical form, certain structural frameworks for the *emergence* of *Einfühlung* (Kant's a priori categories of understanding, Müller's "physiologically Idealist" conception of the nervous system's relation to the world), as if—to press a dualist into the ambiguously monist service of *Einfühlung*—Descartes were his own demon.

What do these two scenes, separated by more than a quarter century, have to do with each other? In this chapter, I read *Über das optische Formgefühl* together with *Lenz* to show how Vischer's treatise contains, beneath or distributed across the surface of its inaugural formulation of *Einfühlungstheorie*, a series of uncanny anxieties aroused by the concept of *Einfühlung* itself: anxieties about perilous self-other relations (including "possession" of and by the Other), the nearness of empathy to pathology, and especially the meaning of the simultaneously divine and "demonic" human reanimation of a world of dead form. As I discussed in this book's introduction, Vischer's theory emerged from a nexus of intersecting philosophical and scientific transformations, among them the Kantian legacy of anthropocentric projection, the rise of empirical physiology and neuroscience, and the gradual transition from the vitalist impulses of German *Naturphilosophie*, with its belief in the universe as a holistic, living organism, to the scientific-materialist view of nature as a fragmented site of purely physical and chemical reactions. The latter transformation is particularly important for framing both Vischer and Büchner: Materialist and vitalist tendencies mixed and wrestled during the pivotal years of Büchner's neuroanatomical and literary career, and this agonistic mid-nineteenth-century milieu likewise formed the intellectual foundation for the development of Vischer's neurophysiologically conceived theory of aesthetic empathy. Indeed, as I argue, Vischer's *Einfühlungstheorie* is not just the univalent result or culmination of decades of rising materialist neuroscience. In its focus on the (re-) animation of dead form, it is simultaneously an equivocal attempt to revivify the "dead," post-Romantic, materialist world, staged from within that world itself—an internally ambivalent, counter-Weberian "re-enchantment," as it were.[1] *Einfühlung*, which would soon become the central concept or working thesis of the laboratory discipline of psychological aesthetics, was therefore both a product and catalyst of a particular sort of modernity—a neurophysiological-materialist modernity—*and*, strikingly, a reaction against or resistance to this

---

1. On disenchantment, see Weber's "Science as a Vocation." On late nineteenth-century counter-materialist attempts to "re-enchant the world," see Bayertz on monism in the German Darwin-popularizer Ernst Haeckel, who wrote shortly before and after Robert Vischer (97–103, here 99). Bayertz's essay does not treat *Einfühlungstheorie*; on one occasion, he uses the word *Einfühlung* in a general sense to describe viewers' "overcoming of the separation between subject and object" through absorption in the representational world of artworks (102). On modernist attempts at re-enchantment, see Janet Ward 92.

modernity: a seemingly new tool with the "magical" power to resurrect the old (including, perhaps, aspects of the Romantic worldview itself). Yet, unlike the more serene turn-of-the-century monistic strivings analyzed by Monika Fick, the magic of *Einfühlung* cannot be separated from its accompanying anxieties about dead nature, the killing and reanimating of life, and possessing or being possessed by the Other: the entire demonic register of necromancy. Put otherwise, from its outset, Vischer's *Einfühlung* is *uncanny*. Like *Lenz* (and as *Lenz* foretells), aesthetic empathy is a post-Romantic revenant or "ghost story"—not only because it stages the repetition of some of Romanticism's characteristically uncanny content or because it is a return of Romantic universalism "made strange" by the pressures of intervening materialism but also because it harbors its own anxieties, prefigured by Büchner, about what dangers and guilt might ensue should the resurrective, aesthetic-empathic project succeed.[2]

In the readings to follow, I explore the uncanny links among *Einfühlung*, death, and reanimation in *Über das optische Formgefühl* to understand what this constellation reveals about the mechanisms of aesthetic empathy, the internal tensions *Einfühlung* embodies, and the problems it carries moving forward. By closely analyzing the rhetorical and figural implications of Vischer's language, I trace the "unconscious" of his imagery and the fears and desires it opens onto—fears and desires anticipated or proleptically allegorized by *Lenz*. Although present-day critics largely pay little attention to potential connections between Vischer and Büchner, the pioneering early twentieth-century phenomenological psychiatrist Wilhelm Mayer-Gross, as Yvonne Wübben points out in *Büchners "Lenz": Geschichte eines Falls* (*Büchner's "Lenz": History of a Case*), not only described Büchner's depiction of Lenz's mental illness in terms derived from psychological aesthetics and Vischerian empathy theory but also linked the empathic performance of Büchner's narrative itself to the text's *aesthetic form*. As Wübben writes, quoting and summarizing Mayer-Gross, "Especially [*Lenz*'s] 'breathless succession of sentences and words' is em-

---

2. It is unclear whether Vischer himself knew Büchner's text. Vischer's father Friedrich Theodor Vischer is reported to have described Büchner's writings as "bottom-literature [*Afterpoesie*] in the truest sense" (Meyer).

pathic [*einfühlsam*] because it shows the breakdown of the human being"; "[the text's] objectivity corresponds to the content of what it represents and to its aesthetic form" (266).³ Mayer-Gross's assessment thus points to the intersection of Vischer and Büchner's shared articulation of *Einfühlung* (and of their similarly shared articulation—explicit in Büchner, implicit in Vischer—of pathology) with two of this book's other interwoven concerns (and *their* interwovenness): the relation of feeling to form, and the relation of aesthetic to interpersonal empathy. Büchner empathizes intersubjectively with the historical Lenz, whose fictionalized, "resurrected" avatar likewise empathizes intersubjectively with the beings—and *aesthetically* with the inanimate forms and objects—he encounters in Büchner's tale. These affective processes are, as Mayer-Gross noted, staged rhetorically by the novella's form. This chapter explores all these varieties of empathy. In doing so, it moves backward and forward in time to witness Vischer and Büchner's (imagined) spooky interaction at a (temporal) distance. *Lenz*, with its conspicuous foregrounding of the problematic of resurrection and its emergence from central decades of the vitalist-materialist conflict and the post-Romantic "death of nature," sheds revealing proleptic light on Vischer's formulation of *Einfühlung*, which reciprocally illuminates Büchner's narrative. The juxtaposition of the two texts tells us more about the history, hidden life, and legacy of *Einfühlung* than either would alone. Seen in this light, Vischer's *Einfühlung*, with its figural inventory of projection, necromantic reanimation, and demonic resurrection, reveals itself to be an uncanny function of what I call the *materialist unconscious*—what scientific materialism represses, yearns for, or fears. To start exploring these concerns, let us begin where Vischer begins: with his inaugural understanding of *Einfühlung*, his analysis of the relations of feeling to form, his positioning of the "parallel forms" of the human body and "external" objects as the necessary conditions for aesthetic empathy, and his rhetoric of self-other exchange, or the ways the forms of human and other bodies can become metaphors, figures, or "forms" of each other. These concerns do not fit easily into a simple model of unidirectional

---

3. See also Mayer-Gross (here publishing as Wilhelm Mayer) on Büchner's "empathic capacity" (*Einfühlungsfähigkeit*) (890).

projection but instead evoke unsettlingly uncanny feelings about the "blurry" origin, trajectory, and locus of *Einfühlung* and its objects.

Robert Vischer, Reanimator

In its original edition, Vischer's *Über das optische Formgefühl* unfolds over some fifty-five dense, ambiguous, even frequently self-contradictory pages. More typically paraphrased than analyzed (at least since the decline of *Einfühlugstheorie* in the early twentieth century), its thesis has been summarized by commentators in sometimes minutely, sometimes meaningfully differing ways. *Einfühlung* is, or should be, "the aesthetic activity of transferring one's own feeling into the forms and shapes of objects" (Lanzoni, *Empathy* 2), "immediately experienc[ing] aesthetic objects ... in terms of emotions that we ourselves have in fact projected onto them" (Guyer 389), "the projection of human feeling onto the natural world" (Breithaupt, *Dark Sides* 77), and the "imputation of one's personal life to an inanimate object" (Barasch 104); more expansively, it is the "wholesale animation of the inanimate world" (Barasch 104), "the role that subjective feeling plays in conditioning the perception of form" (Mallgrave and Ikonomou 17), and, perhaps most unsettlingly, the "working out of one's relations with the objective world by means of objectifying oneself" (David Morgan 321). These summaries, as correct as they are in their generalities (and as telling as they are in their shifts in emphasis), still do not capture the entire strangeness of Vischer's text. For that, we require detail.

Without leaving the summaries, however, we can already discern at least two crucial coordinates: first, the overwhelming concern with inanimate objects, and second, *Einfühlung*'s uncanniness. By "uncanny," I mean here both Freud's psychoanalytic understanding of the term—the return of familiar but alienated psychic content made strange by repression[4]—and the entire inventory of phenom-

---

4. "[The] uncanny is ... nothing new or alien, but something which is familiar and old-established in the mind and which has become alienated from it ... through the process of repression" (Freud, "Uncanny" 944).

ena identified by Freud's contemporary Ernst Jentsch and discussed by Freud from a psychoanalytic perspective in his famous essay "Das Unheimliche" ("The Uncanny"): "animism" (945), "the omnipotence of thoughts" and other forms of magical thinking (949), "doubts whether an apparently animate being is really alive; or conversely, whether a lifeless object might not be in fact animate" (935), "an inanimate object [that] becomes too much like an animate one" (939), "apparent death and the re-animation of the dead" (948), and the appearance of the uncanny "double" of the self (940–41, 949n8). All these themes resonate with the strange mixture of projection, (re)animation, life-death conflation, and self-alienation (or self-devivification) we find in the critics' summaries of *Einfühlung*: "imputing one's personal life to inanimate objects," "animating the inanimate world," "objectifying oneself." Yet a more classically psychoanalytic understanding of the uncanny—the altered, unsettling return of the familiar, in this case not the repressed content of an individual psyche but the remainders of the traumatic movement of history, of the death of nature—is also at stake in the uncanniness of *Einfühlung*. To understand this more fully, we must go beyond the summaries and trace the details of how Vischer's theory enlists the body, senses, and mind in the "feeling of the form"—and how these processes shade into *art*.

"There is a way of seeing without any special effort," Vischer writes in the opening sentence of his dissertation's first chapter, "a way of mere looking that relies on physical activity only insofar as certain groups of nerves are tensed" (93). Vischer contrasts this "mere" or "passive" looking (*blosses Hinsehen*) (*Formgefühl* 1), a bodily process he figures as a sort of neural photography—"the simple reproduction or photographic impression of the object on our retina" (93)—with the "active," "conscious" seeing of what he calls "Schauen," or what Mallgrave and Ikonomou render as "scanning": the dynamic process of visually caressing and bringing an object to life through wandering muscular movements of the eyes (94).

Scanning forms the psychophysiological model for *Einfühlung* as a whole, whose examples and explanations move from the relatively simple to the increasingly complex. *Einfühlung* begins with body-object isomorphism: Our experience of pleasure or displeasure in perceiving a form derives from the similarity (pleasure) or dissimilarity (displeasure) of the object, "first with regard to the structure of the eye and second with regard to the structure of the whole body" (Vischer 97). Correspondingly, in proto-phenomenological fashion, "walls that have become crooked with age offend our basic sense of physical stability," and "in rooms with low ceilings our whole body feels the sensation of weight and pressure" (98). As Guyer explains, "along with feeling the harmony or resemblance between an object and our own body, or more precisely with a particular condition or posture of our body, we also feel and project into the object the emotional state that goes along with that bodily condition" (392). Human affect is thus "relocated" (*versetzt*) in things: "A cliff appears to stand at attention and squarely face us; we therefore read spiritual *defiance* into it. Its projecting angle seems to lunge out as if affected by a *passion* (impatience, curiosity, anger)" (Vischer 105). Finally, "kinesthetic imagination" (*motorische Vorstellung*) (101, *Formgefühl* 15) mentally animates static forms. As Vischer writes, "The road traced by . . . responsive feeling seems to hesitate and rush impatiently along its course" (107). The mobile eye, "scanning," sets the world in motion: "I might imagine myself moving along the line of a range of hills guided by kinesthetic imagination. . . . In the same way, fleeting clouds might carry me far away. This is no longer seeing [*Sehen*] but a *watching* [*Zusehen*]: the forms appear to move, but only *we* move in the imagination. We move in and with the forms. We caress their spatial discontinuities [*Alle Raumveränderungen tasten wir mit liebenden Händen nach*]. We scale this fir tree and reach up within it, we plunge into that abyss, and so forth" (101, *Formgefühl* 15).[5] At a fundamental level, then, Vischer's *Einfühlung* is an attempt to describe the processes through which we figuratively—but also, in the union of body, senses, and mind, literally—"feel the form": "We move in and with the forms," "We caress their spatial discontinuities," "We scale this fir tree . . . [and] plunge into that abyss, and so forth." It is likewise a way of making the human form and the forms

---

5. In the Vischer quote, the first two insertions in brackets appear in Mallgrave and Ikonomou's translation; the final insertion is mine.

of "external" objects (indeed, human *emotions* and the forms of external objects) *forms of each other*. As Vischer writes, "I stimulate, on the basis of simple nerve sensations, a fixed form that symbolizes my body or an organ of it. . . . The way in which the phenomenon is constructed also becomes an analogy for my own structure" (101). Thus it is irrelevant that in the examples above, the clouds are *actually* moving. The point is not primarily the "kinesthetic imagination" as such but *Einfühlung*'s establishing of identification—a metaphoric process—between the object (whether mobile or static) and the human body, feelings, and mind.

This feeling of the form is somatic and synesthetic (the "eye" "caresses" spatial discontinuities, seeing "carries" "me" away). Its aesthetic program becomes clearer when we look closer at its foundational unit, "scanning." This active seeing, Vischer contends, comprises two aesthetic modes figured in terms of the visual arts, with their wedding of sight and touch—one "relate[d] to drawing" (*zeichnerisch*) and the other "plastic-painterly" (*plastisch-malerisch*) (94, *Formgefühl* 2). As Vischer explains, the first type of scanning "is a [visual] drawing of lines, whereby I precisely define the contours with my fingertips, so to speak"; "the second . . . is a mapping of the masses, whereby I run my hand, as it were, over the planes, convexities, and concavities of an object, the paths of light, the slopes, ridges, and hollows of the mountain" (94, translation modified). The passages' visual haptics ensures that active seeing cannot be separated from (a metaphorical rhetoric of) touch: Like the speaker of Goethe's *Fifth Roman Elegy*, the scanner "sees with an eye that feels, feels with a hand that sees."[6] Vischer's discussion of nerve sensations, cited earlier, makes *Einfühlung*'s fusion of physiology, isomorphism between perceived object and perceiving subject (even the bodily organs of that subject), and "art" even plainer: "I stimulate, on the basis of simple nerve sensations, a fixed form that *symbolizes* [*bedeutet*] my body or an organ of it. . . . The way in which the phenomenon is constructed also becomes an *analogy* [*Analogie*] for my own structure. I wrap myself within its contours

---

6. "Sehe mit fühlendem Aug', fühle mit sehender Hand" (Goethe 261); English translation by J. Worthy (modified).

as in a garment" (101, *Formgefühl* 15, my emphasis). In both instances, *Einfühlung* is inseparable from artistic or aesthetic perception, and from this mode of perception as a broader model for human sensory, physiological, and imaginative interaction with the world. Gazing becomes drawing, painting, or sculpting; nerve sensations become "symbols" and "analogies," or even a "theatrical" dressing up in the "costumes" of the forms one perceives ("I wrap myself within its contours as in a garment"). Indeed, the treatise builds to an apotheosis of the artist: its final two chapters are titled "The Artist" ("Der Künstler") and "Artistic Reshaping" ("Das künstlerische Umbilden"); together they reach the conclusion that "every work of art ... [is] a *person* harmoniously feeling himself into a kindred object, or ... humanity objectifying itself in harmonious forms" (117, my emphasis). Already the text's opening discussion had posited the active aesthetic gaze, with its mobile muscles and receptive nerves, as that which "alone makes a complete artistic presentation possible" (94)—a point underscored by Mallgrave and Ikonomou's choice of the term "scanning," with its evocation of metrics and poetics, as their translation for Vischer's "Schauen." Indeed, Vischer's description of our pleasure in scanning repetitive but methodically varied visual forms becomes a sort of corporeal prosody of the (actual and imagined) moving body: "On this principle is based the *rhythmic* impression of form, which is nothing other than the pleasant overall sensation of a harmonic series of successful self-motions" (97).

Vischer places his discussion of the connections among the eye's muscular motions, our perception of repetitive forms, and our affective responses to the interaction of the two in the context of Wundt's experimental-physiological explorations of sight (96–97). But there is a more purely poetic-aesthetic lineage here as well: The "seeing hand" of Goethe's *Fifth Roman Elegy* also scanned metrical patterns by tapping his fingers on his lover's body. What we find in *Über das optische Formgefühl*, then, is both the aestheticization of physiology and the physiologization of aesthetics. Unlike Goethe's erotics, however, the *Einfühlung* enabled by Vischer's somatic-artistic union catalyzes, like the work of the scientist Herbert West in Lovecraft's classic horror tale "Herbert West—Reanimator," an uncanny resurrection. As Vischer writes, evoking dissection and suturing, the deathliness of "mechanical relationships," and the reanimation of the dead itself, scanning "sets out to analyze the forms dialectically (by separating and reconnecting the elements) and to bring them into a mechanical relationship. Scanning alone makes a complete artistic presentation possible, for its movement, as will be shown, is accompanied by an impelling animation of the dead phenomenon, a rhythmic enlivening and revitalization of it" (94). And, as he grandiosely concludes, "Once I have accomplished the process of scanning, the impression of seeing is repeated on a higher level. What I have seemingly separated I have reassembled into an ordered and restful unity. Again I have an enclosed, complete image.... To chaotic 'Being' I called 'Become!'—and my Summons brought Light and behold, it was Good" (94).

Vischer's account of *Einfühlung* raises unsettling questions that expose the uncanny stakes of (re)animation for his aesthetics of empathy and trouble the foundational assumptions or necessary conditions—that is, the very possibility—of empathy itself. To begin with, as his descriptions of being carried away by clouds, wrapping himself in the "garment" of forms, and understanding the "construction" of perceived phenomena as "analogies for his own structure" suggest, many of his statements point just as much to a fundamental confusion about what we might call the origin, locus, and vector of experience or self as they do to a projection of the self into (ostensibly) external objects. The image of "wrapping oneself within the contours of a phenomenon as in a garment," for example, introduces a conspicuous malleability into both "phenomenon" and "self." Unless the body-world isomorphism discussed earlier were exceptionally exact, "wrapping oneself" in a "fixed form that symbolizes my body" would seem to require the *dissolving* of fixed forms, the liquescence (or at least the waxy modification) of the object, the form of the body, or the imagined "self" (or all three)—less isomorphism than morphing, or *everything* as "garment." The ambiguity pervades the treatise. As Vischer writes in his chapter "Imagination" ("Bildvorstellung"), "There are ideas of my own (bodily) form and of other forms, but there are also ideas that are both objective and subjective. We will speak only of the latter here, as only they concern aesthetics" (99, translation modified).[7] Indeed, in the chapter, Vischer seems to insist *both* that the very idea of subjectivity depends on the prior perception or postulation of an object ("The imagining of the self [only] becomes conscious when it relates itself . . . to an object or to an idea of an object," 100, translation modified) *and* that a preexisting "body-ego" (*Körper-Ich*) searches for external forms that then become its surrogates or metaphors: "I stimulate, on the basis of simple nerve sensations, a fixed form that symbolizes my body or an organ of it" (101, *Formgefühl* 15). Thus we arrive at that "strange knack," characteristic of *Einfühlung*, of "confusing our own feeling with that of nature" (Vischer 107) and "find here, again, that peculiar confusion of our own stimulation with the thing that produces the stimulus" (108). As Guyer attempts to clarify, perhaps in fact adding to the confusion, "[Our] feelings are projected on to the object in such a way that we do not distinguish between them and the more objective perception of the object, that is, they become part of the unitary experience of the object" (393). Or, as Vischer's crucial "Feeling and Emotion" chapter puts it in an even more disconcerting and enigmatic summation of *Einfühlung*, perhaps the treatise's most revealing statement of the concept: "I project my own life into the lifeless form [*Ich traue . . . der leblosen Form mein individuelles Leben zu*], just as I quite justifiably do with another living person. Only ostensibly do I keep my own identity [*Nur scheinbar behalte ich mich selbst*] although the object remains distinct [*ein Anderes bleibt*]. I seem merely to adapt and attach myself to it as one hand clasps another, and yet I am mysteriously transplanted and magically transformed into this Other [*heimlicher Weise in dieses Nichtich versetzt und verzaubert*]" (104, *Formgefühl* 20). It is a description that, with regard to the question of the origin, locus, and vector of experience,

---

7. Vischer's original reads, "Es gibt Vorstellungen einer andern und Vostellungen meiner eigenen (Leib-) Form; es gibt aber auch Vorstellungen, die sowohl objektiv als subjektiv sind. Von diesen wollen wir hier sprechen und nur um diese kann es sich in der Aesthetik handeln" (12). Mallgrave and Ikonomou puzzlingly render "es gibt aber auch Vorstellungen, die sowohl objektiv als subjektiv sind" as "again, some ideas are objective and others subjective" (99).

stretches the notion of *Einfühlung* to, and perhaps beyond, its breaking point.

Vischer's claims are telling in what they reveal about our relation to aesthetic perception and artistic production, both literal and figurative. In his trajectory from scanning to the seeming apotheosis of the artist and, in the dissertation's final chapter, an evaluative assessment of artistic technique, we find a microcosm of the trajectory of aesthetics itself from Baumgarten's original understanding of the term as a knowing through the senses to the word's currently dominant definition as a theory of beauty and ugliness in nature and art. More significantly, Vischer's account merges both definitions, so that we see the ways in which knowing through the senses is always already an "artistically" aesthetic act: that is, an act of the creation of form, and thus, broadly conceived, an act of art making. As Vischer writes, "The eye has initiated a process that travels through the entire nervous system, the entire soul, the entire person. It is the hidden end purpose of all naïve form [*Bilden*] to portray this process [*Nachleben*]" (115, *Formgefühl* 38).[8] In narrowing the distance between the making of "art" proper and the physiological and sensory processes common to all—both are for Vischer a "Bilden," with its evocation of forming, shaping, sculpting, and indeed the "image" (*Bild*) itself—Vischer's *Einfühlung* installs artistic perception and presentation (or representation, "Darstellung") (94, *Formgefühl* 3) at the center of *all* perception and phenomenal display. It thereby makes everyone an artist—of empathy. Indeed, Vischer's figuring of vision and nerve responses as prosody, analogy, and symbol, as well as his explicit comparison of the two modes of scanning to sketching and sculpting, already place art *before* life, or figure the latter as predicated on the former. They effectively position artistic techniques and genres as prior to the bodily or biological organs and actions that presumably precede and give rise to them—the artificial, that is, as prior to the "natural." As Tobias Wilke argues in one of the few close readings of Vischer's rhetoric, empathy in Vischer's treatise is less corporeal than metaphorical: *Einfühlung*, especially the figurative language Vischer

---

8. The second bracketed insertion in the Vischer quote is Mallgrave and Ikonomou's.

uses to discuss it, does not so much scientifically explain physiological processes as constitute a "poetics of description" that, at least in part, tropically constructs the theoretical knowledge seemingly obtained by the application of the concept of *Einfühlung* itself (343–44).[9] From a certain perspective, then, Vischer's aesthetic empathy is suggestively "aestheticist," even proto-decadent. Unlike these movements, however (and despite Vischer's enthusiastic tone throughout the treatise), the art(ifice) of empathy is not unproblematically celebratory but ambivalent, vexed, and uneasy—for its apparent paean to the creative power of aesthetic perception conceals a reaction formation against the fear of the loss of life. Indeed, even the vital physiological process, "initiated by the eye," that "travels through the entire nervous system, the entire soul, the entire person," is ambiguously figured as something already lost, something that paradoxically only "lives" as a series of posthumous effects ("Nachleben," *Formgefühl* 38)—an uncanny remnant or "undead" phenomenon whose *second* uncanny doubling or re-presentation ("dieses Nachleben darzustellen") is the "hidden end purpose of all … form" or "Bilden" (115, *Formgefühl* 38).

Before turning to this loss of life—or, more precisely, death and uncanny resurrection—that forms the recurrent ground of Vischer's formulations of *Einfühlung*, let us spend a moment considering what his aesthetic or artistic models are *not*. For, from one perspective, despite their permeation with deathly imagery, these models might also simultaneously be read as gestures *against* death, or against certain understandings of deathliness. Vischer's models are not, for example, *photography*, a passive process of "the simple reproduction … of the object on our retina" (93) that he equates with "mere" seeing and that is immediately surpassed by the dynamic and creative aesthetic activity—the "sketching," "painting," "sculpting," and "rhythmic" versifying—of "scanning." This is in keeping with a widespread and, at first glance, incongruous-seeming realist-period ambivalence

---

9. Wilke's concern with the rhetorical subordination of physiological processes to art in Vischer intersects with my own; unlike my reading, however, Wilke's deconstructive analysis focuses primarily on the inability of Vischer's text to access bodily "reality" outside the mediation of figurative language.

about, if not outright hostility to, its own age's invention of the "realistic" medium of photography. As I will discuss further in chapter 2, at least since Baudelaire, many realists viewed the (arguably) pure mimesis of this quintessentially technological and modern medium not as an ally—indeed, not as *art*—but as a further step in the deadening automatization of life (Pijarski 148–49). Thus, in positioning scanning and its resultant *Einfühlung* against photography, Vischer positions aesthetic empathy against—or, rather, in some way *attempts* to position it against—"death."

In a related vein, scanning, despite its primary definition as active seeing, is not sight alone. It is a synesthetic or holistic compendium of the arts: vision, rhythm, drawing, movement, and so on (we gaze, we move, we trace, we are carried away). Perhaps most importantly, it restores the traditional connection of sight to touch, Goethe's "seeing hand"—a connection that, as Crary argues, had been severed by the neurological "separation of the senses and industrial remapping of the body" in the 1800s (19). Thus, the sensory and aesthetic fusion inherent in scanning and its "offspring" *Einfühlung* might once again be understood as a strike or defense against (figurative) death: the death represented by certain consequences of modernity. Put otherwise, paradoxically, Vischer's aestheticization of physiology can be read as an act of resistance against a particular manifestation of modernity—the neurological "physiologization" of aesthetics—of which *it itself is a product*.

These paradoxes return us to the ironies, and uncanniness, of "resurrective" *Einfühlung*, where life cannot be separated from death. As I have noted, Vischer maintains that scanning "sets out to analyze the forms dialectically (by separating and reconnecting the elements) and to bring them into a mechanical relationship.... Its movement ... is accompanied by an impelling animation of the dead phenomenon, a rhythmic enlivening and revitalization of it" (94). A fundamental assumption of the passage is that the relevant forms or phenomena to be scanned are *dead*. Equally important is the passage's rhetorical proximity to the laboratory—perhaps less Wundt's here than Herbert West's or Frankenstein's. In describing the processes underlying both "all artistic intuition" (94) and our everyday visual perception as an "analytical" separation and reconnection of elements, a bringing together into a "mechanical relationship," and an "impelling animation of the dead phenomenon, an enlivening and revitalization of it," Vischer figures his universal artist, observer, and empath not only as an experimental scientist, chemist, or engineer but also as a *mad* scientist, rogue surgeon, necromancer, or galvanist who sutures together and reanimates the material—the materialist—world's inert mechanistic parts or cadaver. Indeed, when he asserts that "to chaotic 'Being' [he] called 'Become!'—and [his] Summons brought Light and behold, it was Good" (94), he assumes the role not just of Frankenstein but of God himself. That is, he attempts to align himself with the original act of creation, including the creation of "actual" life, not just its reanimated copies. But for all his reconnecting and reassembling (or perhaps precisely because of them), the resurrector remains a failed god. The result of the "revitalizing" perceptual or artistic process is once again, tellingly, *dead nature*—an object "ordered" and "brought to rest," or an image whose stasis, completeness, and totalizing (en-)closedness suggest the finality of a tomb: "What I have seemingly separated I have reassembled into an ordered and restful [*beruhigte*] unity. Again I have an enclosed, complete image [*geschlossenes Gesammtbild*]" (94, *Formgefühl* 3). More precisely, the image is uncanny, existing somewhere in the liminal space between life and death—once again the undead, the aesthetic zombie.

The underlying templates of uncanny animation and the aesthetic zombie traverse the question of the origin, locus, and vector of self in the passage I identified earlier as Vischer's quintessential formulation of *Einfühlung*, exposing disconcerting implications of how he understands aesthetic empathy to work: "Thus I project my own life into the lifeless form [*Ich traue also der leblosen Form mein individuelles Leben zu*]. . . . Only ostensibly do I keep my own identity [*Nur scheinbar behalte ich mich selbst*] although the object remains distinct [*ein Anderes bleibt*]. I seem merely to adapt and attach myself to it as one hand clasps another, and yet I am mysteriously transplanted and magically transformed into this Other [*heimlicher Weise in dieses Nichtich versetzt und verzaubert*]" (104, *Formgefühl* 20). This is a model of *Einfühlung* as projection, transfusion, and transplantation, but it is also, despite the declarations of its opening sentence ("Thus I project . . ."), a conspicuously bidirectional one, and one that effectively inscribes death as much as it bestows life. For the logic, and ambiguous rhetoric, of the passage's conflation of "living" subject with "dead" object or "form"—the reciprocal transformation, equalization, position swapping, or content exchange of the two, as it were—not only makes the dead alive but the living dead. Put in the form of a question, has the subject enlivened the object, or, in being transformed into it, taken on the object's "death"? Deathliness—of things, of art—is retroactive, working temporally backward upon life. And, compounding the strangeness, *Einfühlung* here additionally suggests the *replacement* of the self by an uncanny double ("I am mysteriously [*heimlicher Weise*] transplanted and magically transformed into this Other"), the "possession" of the self *by* that Other (that is, the making of the transformed and now occulted self into the Other's possession), or, conversely, the remainderless replacement, possession, colonization, or consumption of the Other *by the self* (or all three). As Vischer ominously writes, "We . . . have the . . . ability to impose our own physical form onto, and incorporate it into, an objective form [*unsere eigene Form einer objektiven Form zu unterschieben und einzuverleiben*], in much the same way as wild duck hunters hole up in a blind to attack their quarry unseen" (104, *Formgefühl* 20, translation modified). Even Vischer's suggestion that a "pure and complete union between the subjective and the objective imagination . . . can take place only when the latter involves another human being" (103) effectively renders that other human being a "thing"—here, a thing that we can imagine possessing subjectivity. In any direction, it is a self-other exchange perhaps less magical than demonic. As we see both in the surface meaning and in the more unsettling subterranean implications of Vischer's formulation "heimlicher Weise versetzt und verzaubert"—and as Freud will famously assert nearly a half century after Vischer—the "heimlich" exists along a spectrum that eventually converges with its seeming opposite, the "unheimlich" ("Uncanny" 931–34). I shall return to these issues as my discussion progresses.

Nervous Feelings

If there is indeed magical—or demonic—transformation at play in Vischer's portrayal of *Einfühlung*, then his treatise leaves little doubt that one of the key conjurers responsible for this sorcery is the nerve. Indeed, *Über das optische Formgefühl* repeatedly highlights the crucial role of the nervous system in *Einfühlungstheorie*'s physiologization of aesthetics or conceptualization of "aesthetic response as a bodily engagement with form" (Lanzoni, *Empathy* 9)—what Vischer describes as his "principal concern ... to explain mental stimulation in every case precisely through and together with bodily stimulation" (92). As Vischer writes, channeling Fechner and other early sensory physiologists, "Whether similar or dissimilar, the form of the object ... relates to our bodily form, as well as to its conditioned forms of motion, only with the aid of hidden or apparent kinesthetic stimuli, that is to say, through nerve or muscle sensations" (95–96). The nerve in particular is the connection between body and mind: "Our body ... all at once receives an aggregate of nerve vibrations; our mind thus has the first prescient flash of an inner conception" (93). Or, as Vischer sums it up, a "mental act" (*geistiger Akt*) is "essentially at the same time an act of the central nervous system" (*wesentlich zugleich ein Akt der Centralnerven*) (*Formgefühl* 12, my translation).[10]

As discussed in this book's introduction, physiological or psychological aesthetics, understood both as the foregrounding of the interdependent network of body, senses, and mind in shaping aesthetic phenomena and as the application of empirical and experimental research methods to the study of aesthetic experience, arose from a multifaceted nineteenth-century German scientific milieu, the interaction of whose parts allowed a particular neurological conception of *Einfühlung* to flourish. As neuroscientist Mary A. B. Brazier writes, the century's advances in neuroanatomy led to the development of the field that would come to be called neurophysiology (*History* v). In this context, it would be difficult to imagine Vischer's neurally informed notion of empathic projection without the foundations laid

---

10. Mallgrave and Ikonomou's translation softens the point: "[Mental activity] also essentially involves the central nervous system" (99).

by another German thinker in whom the scientific tendencies—and antinomies—of the age converged: the early nineteenth-century comparative anatomist and pioneering physiologist Johannes Müller. Müller's formulation of the law of specific nerve energies in 1826 blurred the locus of experience in ways that should now be familiar from *Über das optische Formgefühl* and helped guarantee what Müller-Tamm calls the "physiological victory procession of the nervous system as the organic substratum of subjectivity" (104). As Müller states the law in his renowned *Handbuch der Physiologie des Menschen* (*Elements of Physiology*, 1833–1840), "the same cause, such as electricity, can simultaneously affect all sensory organs, since they are all sensitive to it; and yet, every sensory nerve reacts to it differently; one nerve perceives it as light, another hears its sound, another one smells it; another tastes the electricity, and another one feels it as pain and shock.... Sensation is not the conduction of a quality or state of external bodies to consciousness, but the conduction of a quality or state of our nerves to consciousness, excited by an external cause" (qtd. in Pearce 115).[11]

Implicit in Müller's model is the view that what appears as the external world is in fact the mentally interpreted internal activity of the human sensorium, including the "self-seeing" of the eye's neural net or the retina's excitation pattern projected outward: "physiological Kantianism" (Müller-Tamm 108), or the translation of the legacy of Kantian idealism into physical terms.[12] Here, nerves condition experience analogously to Kant's a priori categories of understanding, and the "quality or state" they "conduct to consciousness" requires psychological interpretation and externalizing reprojection in order to be viewed as a world. Müller's *Handbuch* itself—the "locus classicus" of projection theory (Müller-Tamm 120) and, as Crary explains, the "basis for the dominant work in mid-nineteenth-century psychology and physiology" (89)—went on to become perhaps the most significant medical textbook of its era

---

11. Pearce quotes *Elements of Physiology* (n.p.), W. Baly's translation of Müller's *Handbuch*.
12. Cf. Schnädelbach 97–100; Crary 77 and 88–92; and Müller-Tamm 11–31. On controversies regarding Müller's law, see Brazier, *History* 57–58.

and to establish "one of the most influential ways in which an observer was figured in the nineteenth century" (Crary 89). The medical student Georg Büchner cites the *Handbuch*'s 1835 edition as a source in his own 1836 neuroanatomy dissertation *Mémoire sur le Système nerveux du Barbeau (Report on the Nervous System of the Barbel)* (316, 339, 369), and Müller himself would go on to endorse Büchner's research (Reddick, *Georg Büchner* 14).

Yet if Müller's, Büchner's, and Vischer's nineteenth century was a "golden age of neurophysiology" (Brazier, "Rise" 212), it was also an age of epistemic and ideological conflict at the heart of understanding the human being and the natural world—an age that formed the uneasy border zone between declining Romantic and pre-Romantic conceptions of vitalism and *Naturphilosophie* on the one hand and the rising forces of scientific materialism on the other. Although the German lands, like much of post-seventeenth-century Europe, were not spared the impact of Cartesian thought and its partition of the world into *res cogitans* and *res extensa*, "living" mind and "dead" matter, Germany in the early 1800s, with its formidable and specifically German *naturphilosophische* tradition, nonetheless represented something like a refuge island of panpsychic, organicist, and holistic thought in the overall sea of dualism. The vitalist sense of the irreducibility of life to material processes and *Naturphilosophie*'s understanding, championed by Schelling, of the entirety of nature as an organic, living, and creative whole—*Naturphilosophie* as vitalism's "last potent movement," as Brazier puts it (*History* 71)—remained significant directions in German science until at least the middle of the nineteenth century, often existing alongside, then finally succumbing to, a rival physicalist and materialist monism.[13] It was this physicalist monism that, as Fick writes, would again come to be challenged, at least in fin-

---

13. Brazier contends that *Naturphilosophie* gave way to scientific materialism in the middle of the nineteenth century (*History* 71); Roth argues that the transition to materialism did not conclude in the 1840s and that the turn from *Naturphilosophie* may not have been decisive for the rise of the "exact" sciences in Germany (9–11). Walker notes that post-Romantic philosophical idealism often continued to exist side by side with scientific materialism in the German nineteenth century ("Two Realisms" 113).

de-siècle aesthetic circles, by a resurgent "metaphysical" monism inspired by turn-of-the-century German Fechner reception (44–50)—a development in which, I argue, Vischer's *Einfühlung* played an early, less recognized, and especially ambivalent or "uncannily" anxiety-ridden part.

Perhaps not surprisingly, nerves themselves became the flash point and emblem of the vitalist-materialist conflict in German thought when the physicist Hermann von Helmholtz, Müller's former student, contested his erstwhile teacher regarding the speed and meaning of nerve impulse transmission. Müller, at this point in his career a vitalist and *Naturphilosoph*, had maintained that nerves conducted immaterial "life forces" incomprehensibly and instantaneously, or at least at speeds beyond human measurement; Helmholtz, a materialist since at least 1845 (Agutter and Wheatley 123–24), set out specifically to measure just such nerve signal velocity as a quantifiable function of physiochemical processes in the body. His success in 1850 helped move the scientific community significantly closer to the abandonment of vitalism and *Naturphilosophie* and toward the consensus triumph of the materialist worldview (Brazier, *History* 65–68). Already in the 1840s, in a series of publications frequently regarded as "materialist manifestos," another of Müller's students, Emil Heinrich Du Bois-Reymond, along with the physiologist Ernst Brücke and others, had laid the groundwork for a radical materialism by arguing that all phenomena of life could be explained as physiochemical processes; Du Bois-Reymond would go on to insist that even cultural and moral problems could be understood in terms of physiochemical reactions (Agutter and Wheatley 123–24; Brodersen 26–28). Brazier contends that Müller moved from vitalist and *naturphilosophische* views to materialism over the course of his career, likely under the influence of Du Bois-Reymond (*History* 56–59), while Udo Roth writes that Müller never fully abandoned *Naturphilosophie* despite his later rejection of Schelling (10). Whatever the case, Müller's own massively influential and professedly vitalist *Handbuch der Physiologie des Menschen* ironically ended up furthering the materialist position he at that point claimed to disavow. As Crary explains, the *Handbuch*, "one of the last influential texts to argue the case of vitalism," in fact "contained the very empirical information that was to finally extinguish vitalism as an acceptable idea" (88). Müller's book, like Helmholtz's nerve experiments, effectively (and apparently against its author's intentions) "reduced the phenomenon of life to a set of physiochemical processes that were observable and manipulable in the laboratory.... The distinction ... between the organic and the inorganic collapses under the sheer weight of Müller's inventory of the mechanical capacities of the body" (Crary 88–89).

Müller, then, occupied a liminal space in the era's paradigm conflict, and Vischer, later in the century, assimilated—and embodied—a likewise liminal current. If Vischer did not know Müller's *Handbuch* directly, he likely knew its central premises and strategies through his familiarity with the work of the "father of experimental psychology" Wilhelm Wundt, whose 1860s research on optics he cites in *Über das optische Formgefühl* (96–97) and who, like Helmholtz and Du Bois-Reymond, was one of Müller's former students. Indeed, through Wundt, the intellectual heir to some of the most important figures on both sides of the vitalist-materialist divide, Vischer inherits the combined *Naturphilosophie*, "rigorously empirical ... psychology" (Crary 142), and physiologically conceived mind-body monism of Fechner's psychophysics, the radical materialism of Helmholtz, *and* the vitalism-cum-materialism of Müller. Yet if Vischer's conceptualization of *Einfühlung* recalls elements of its Romantic prehistory—Vischer writes of *Einfühlung*'s "pantheistic urge for union ... directed toward the universe" (109)—one also finds in his treatise something quite different than the *naturphilosophische*-vitalist sense of nature as a unified, creative, living force. Channeling the materialists, as well as, perhaps, the scientific positivism of his father Friedrich Theodor Vischer (Curtis 19–20; Müller-Tamm 222), Vischer describes inorganic nature in particular as "patchwork—dead material" (*Stückwerk, todtes Material*) (106, *Formgefühl* 23): neither alive nor ensouled, but the charnel house of form. This is the form that requires, as Vischer's discussion of scanning puts it, "impelling animation" and "reassembly" on a "higher level." As Müller-Tamm concludes, following this strand of Vischer's logic to its materialist, indeed, quasi-nihilist end point, "at the center of the theory of aesthetic empathy [*Einfühlungslehre*] stood ... the meaninglessness of nature" (218).

In beginning to trace *Einfühlung*'s uncanniness, I have noted the concept's early inseparability from such unsettling phenomena as the doubling of the self, the replacement or possession of the self by the Other, and the absorption of this Other by the self. I have likewise noted *Einfühlung*'s emergence from the shifting border between life and "death" as the vitalism of Romanticism gives way to the physiochemical materialism of the realist age. What does Vischer's ambiguous position on this map mean for his theory of aesthetic empathy? Put otherwise, how does *Einfühlung* become the channel—the "nerve," as it were—along which an uncanny galvanizing signal runs between Vischer's realist present and his Romantic past?

Empathy, a Ghost Story

As has often been noted, "supernatural" elements do not disappear from discourse with the passing of Romanticism. Rather, they are explained as something else, repurposed to meet new ideological ends, or otherwise deployed, consciously or unconsciously, to answer the signifying needs of a new era.[14] A similar process is at work in Vischer's *Einfühlung*. Like the infamous Chinese ghost in Fontane's *Effi Briest*—and, like that ghost, uncanny in both its content and its function—*Einfühlung* represents the "return with a difference" of Romantic modes of apprehension or *Auffassung*: in this case not as a tool of discipline or control (as in *Briest*) but as an attempt to mitigate the depradations of a materialist age. That this attempt recapitulates Romantic "apprehension" in its other sense—anxiety—and introduces new apprehensions as well marks aesthetic empathy as a ghost story indeed.

For a treatise announcing, and to a certain extent celebrating, a new aesthetic concept, *Über das optische Formgefühl* is permeated by a strangely pronounced uneasiness about its own neologistic central term—by a conspicuous rhetoric of the uncanny and spooky surrounding and constructing the notion of *Einfühlung* itself. As Vischer writes in the pivotal "Feeling and Emotion" chapter, *Einfühlung*,

---

14. See for example Begemann, "Gespenster des Realismus."

activating once raw sensory stimuli and the "motor activity of the senses" have been mentally processed or transformed into "imagination," "now imagines itself as turning toward the *interior* of the [perceived] phenomenon" (108): "By virtue of this central projection, exchange, and return," *Einfühlung* "take[s] on a life of its own [*eigenartiges Leben*]. It looks at its second self as it sits reshaped in the object and intuitively [*ahnungsvoll*] takes it back to itself, yet without discerning it clearly or knowing why" (108, *Formgefühl* 27). Here, *Einfühlung* itself is "alive" (one might say that Vischer personifies, "feels himself into," or empathizes *with empathy*): It "looks," "takes back," "discerns," and "knows" (or, as the passage tells us, *fails* to discern and know). Yet it is also *doubled*, or doubles the self. As Vischer writes, *Einfühlung* "looks at" its "second self," which "sits" somehow "reshaped in the object"—one of the dead objects Vischer highlights throughout the treatise. Yet the object is not *entirely* dead: Along with Yeats, we may "call it death-in-life and life-in-death."[15] For the second self that *Einfühlung* "looks at" in the object is positioned by the logic of the passage as another *Einfühlung*—an *Einfühlung* that lurks in the object itself, refashioned by the object's form, looking back at us and turning *us* into objects in the field of vision or experience, as Lacan might say.[16]

This ambiguous locus and directionality of *Einfühlung* and (re)animation, along with the rhetoric of doubled selves, place us once again on uncanny ground, including the ground of the doppelgänger: the fatal twin from German *Schauerromantik* whose appearance traditionally heralds the death of the subject who observes it (Freud, "Uncanny" 940–41). As if in a radical version of Lacan's famous discussion of Holbein's *Ambassadors*, this "second *Einfühlung*" turns the entire object into an anamorphic blot: Through the empathic processes of "projection, exchange, and return," we are simultaneously "called into the picture, and represented here as caught" (Lacan 92) *and* sent back to ourselves as *something else*—two meanings of "possessed." As Vischer's original German makes clear, the "life"—or death—"of its own" that *Einfühlung*

---

15. "Byzantium," line 16.
16. Cf. Lacan, *The Four Fundamental Concepts of Psycho-Analysis* 65–119.

takes on after returning from its "exchange" with objects is an "eigenartiges Leben" (27): one that is fundamentally uncanny, peculiar, weird, or strange. Accordingly, *Einfühlung* does not simply take its "second self" "back to itself" "intuitively" (*ahnungsvoll*) but also, as the semantic spectrum of *ahnungsvoll* announces, in a way that is *ominous* or *full of foreboding*. Indeed, as perhaps the most famous occurrence of this word in German literary history insists, to be "ahnungsvoll" is to be particularly sensitive to the hidden presence of the devil. When Goethe's Gretchen "intuits" the diabolical essence of the incognito Mephistopheles, Faust exclaims to her, "Du ahnungsvoller Engel, Du!" (*Faust* 131). Finally, the entire movement of empathic exchange in the passage evokes the feeling of opaque, "automatic," even out-of-control processes—"life of its own," "intuitively," "without discerning clearly," "without knowing why"— that are "at work behind the ordinary appearance of mental activity," as Freud summarizes Jentsch's account of the uncanny ("Uncanny" 935). Thus Vischer's *Einfühlung*, in its relation with objects, brings us into disquieting proximity to the eerie, the preternatural, perhaps even to a type of madness: "The layman sees in [madness] the work of forces hitherto unsuspected in his fellowmen, but at the same time he is dimly aware of them in remote corners of his own being" ("Uncanny" 946).

This ghost story is, as I have suggested, especially present in the treatise's signature description of *Einfühlung*: "Thus I project my own life into the lifeless form.... Only ostensibly do I keep my own identity although the object remains distinct. I seem merely to adapt and attach myself to it as one hand clasps another, and yet I am mysteriously transplanted and magically transformed into this Other" (104). As I have argued, the passage is marked by a conspicuous rhetoric of animation, transformation, transplantation, and transfusion—Jentsch's anxieties about "whether ... a lifeless object might not be in fact animate" ("Uncanny" 935). Related, and just as uncanny, is the passage's by now familiar rhetoric of the replacement of the self with another (an "Other") or of the replacement of that Other with the self: The sentence "I am mysteriously transplanted and magically transformed into this Other" is, in fact, a two-way street. Thus, from the outset, Vischer's text opens the door for what will become one of the most salient critiques of empathy (including, later, intersubjective empathy): that empathy, understood as self-projection, risks colonizing, appropriating, or "possessing" the human and nonhuman Other, or what David Morgan calls the "epistemological imperialism of the human personality responsible for overcoming all otherness, all difference with its powers of animation" (322). Grant Bollmer, writing of interpersonal empathy, puts it even more emphatically: "The 'understanding' provided by empathy annihilates the metaphysical relation of self to other, as . . . it transforms . . . the Other into the same. It converts the Other into an object to be used and consumed. . . . Empathy, then, denies the existence of the Other" (71).

Significantly, and seemingly paradoxically given the context of our previous discussion, one of the key differences Vischer's *Einfühlung* seems to want to overcome is *also* the *Otherness of death itself*. As Vischer insists in the "Feeling and Emotion" chapter, "Where there is no life—precisely there do I miss it. . . . Yes, we miss red-blooded life, and precisely because we miss it, we imagine the dead form as living" (104). Indeed, *Einfühlung* seems predicated on fears about a "life deficit" in nature: that is, about a *surfeit* of dead nature *different from life*. But since it is unclear whether living subject or dead object prevails in the empath's being "mysteriously transplanted and magically transformed into [an] Other," Morgan's "imperialism of overcoming all difference" can run in the opposite direction as well: toward the incorporation or possession of the self by the Other, the "second self," or Jentsch's "doubts whether an apparently animate being"—that is, ourselves—"is really alive" ("Uncanny" 935). As Sarah Kofman, reversing the sanguinolent imagery of Vischer's discussion of "red-blooded life," writes in another context about the uncanniness of artistic representation, the double "has devoured the life of its 'model,' sucked its blood down to the last drop" ("Melancholy" 208).[17] Either way, one side (and thus, ultimately, both sides) in the exchange is erased, eliminated.

---

17. For a discussion of self-loss in the context of intersubjective rather than aesthetic empathy, see Breithaupt's reading of Nietzsche in *Dark Sides*, especially 38–55.

Not only does re- (and de-) animation of the other exist in an exchange relationship with (de)animation of the self: Without an "other," there *is* no "self" (and vice versa), since each is dependent on the other for its definition and (logical) existence.

In each of these passages, the feeling of the uncanny is a function of the mutability, liquification, reciprocal "conformation," or exchange of forms: it is, in other words, a formal effect. As Angela Leighton puts it in *On Form*, "What is formed may be transformed" (2)—in Vischer, even across the (apparent) life-death divide. *Einfühlung*, like Vischer's uncanny, is, as a "capacity" for feeling, similarly a function of form. Not only does it require forms as its condition and channel, but it is also an *operator*: a process, empty slot, or (literally) "trans-action" that, as Leighton writes of the grammatical expression "in the *form* of," "allows one thing to turn into another" (2–3, my emphasis and hyphen).

Einfühlung, as I noted at the beginning of this section, is uncanny not only in its content but also in its function and very existence—what it "does" and what it "is"—especially with regard to its larger historical context. David Morgan distinguishes between "two broad phases in the history of [aesthetic] empathy theory": a "Romantic" phase of "enthusiastic aesthetic experience" that "sought to break down the distinction between subjective feeling and objective realities," and a "psycho-perceptual" phase that "eliminated" the earlier model's "pantheistic monism" in favor of "scientific explanation of human feeling and perception" (321–22). However, Vischer's rhetoric suggests that, at least in *Über das optische Formgefühl*, the two phases were in a sense one. It is not so much that science, with its now dominant, late nineteenth-century materialist assumptions, replaces Romanticism, but that the "life" of Romanticism *returns in* materialist science as an uncanny revenant, something familiar (as in Freud's famous definition) made strange by the repressive mechanisms of lingering trauma—the trauma of materialism itself. This return—*Einfühlung*'s "rise" from the theoretical and laboratory slab, as it were, at least in part in response to materialism's perceived deadening of the world—is itself an uncanny resurrection. As both a site of resistance to, or at any rate ambivalence about, post-vitalist modernity *and* a product of that modernity itself (materialist neurophysiology), its attempt to reanimate dead form can only succeed by becoming the very modern ghost story it fears. Its attempts to mitigate the anxieties that led to its emergence recapitulate or extend these anxieties in modified form: Unlike the allegedly successful resurgence of Morgan's "pantheistic monism" at the turn of the century (Fick 43–56), the ensoulment of the physical or "projection of life into lifeless form" of Vischer's *Einfühlung*—a possible early stage in this resurgence—is not an unproblematically triumphant phenomenon. Rather, it is a *return as a zombie*, the walking dead: the return of *Naturphilosophie after the death of nature*. The psychological-aesthetic and neurophysiological conception of *Einfühlung* allows, or rather is the figure for, this uncanny resurrection or "Nec-Romanticism": Realist science is the uncanny double of Romantic vitalism. The latter has been "mysteriously," *heimlicher Weise*, "transplanted" and "magically"—or diabolically—"transformed into this Other."

Aesthetic empathy's array of exchanges between dead and living forms, subjects and objects, and selves and others, with the attendant risks of possession by or of the Other, evokes disquieting feelings of the uncanny. Indeed, the grounding of *Einfühlung*, and of aesthetic perception and production more generally, in neurophysiological and psychological processes—Crary's "defective, inconsistent" human body, "prey to illusion and ... susceptible to external procedures of manipulation and stimulation that have the essential capacity to produce experience," even "derangement," "for the subject" (92–93)—aroused fears of the potential proximity of the aesthetic to the pathological (Müller-Tamm 229–30). This possible proximity of aesthetic to pathological experience had already been a cause for debate and concern in sensory physiology since Goethe, Purkinje, and Müller. The issue was central not only to the question of the "intrinsic" pathological or nonpathological status of entoptic phenomena, which were intensely studied during the period and formed, as Müller-Tamm points out, the experimental foundation of Müller's law of specific nerve energies (78), but also and particularly to the frequently dangerous self-experimentation carried out by early sensory physiologists on their own bodies.[18] The fears were to some extent justified. As a result of their attempts to explore the processing of sensory experience through systematic self-experimentation, physiologists of the early nineteenth century suffered severe physical injuries and psychological disturbances. Müller, for example, experienced intermittent paralysis and an eventual mental collapse around the time of his formulation of the law of specific nerve energies, and Fechner so damaged his eyesight by staring into the sun to study retinal afterimages that he isolated himself in a dark room for three years, exhibiting psychotic symptoms and barely eating (Müller-Tamm 74–94). *Einfühlung*, inextricable in Vischer's conception from a neurophysiologically and psychologically understood idea of the aesthetic, shares these "pathological" risks.

Unsurprisingly, Vischer attempts, at the conclusion of his discussion of the ways in which "the perception of exterior limits to a form can combine in some obscure way with the sensation of my own physical boundaries," to draw a "strict distinction between purely aesthetic and pathological" feelings, perception, and behavior (98–99). As he argues, the mental processes common to both the artist and the general perceiver posited by *Über das optische Formgefühl* should ideally work to counteract the pathologies potentially introduced into experience by the risks of neurosensory engagement with form, uncanny *Einfühlung*, and artistic activity itself: "Negative stimuli are isolated and overcome by concentrating on and accentuating the positive" (99). Unsettlingly, however, the scope of the negative expands to encompass the entirety of nature itself. As Vischer writes in his final chapter, "Artistic Reshaping," "The simple act of imputing emotional content [to inorganic and organic nature] must . . . be expanded into a reshaping [*Umbildung*] of natural forms—both the composition and its details—*that are always found wanting [der stets mangelhaft erfundenen Naturformen]*" (117, *Formgefühl* 42, my

---

18. Goethe, Purkinje, and Müller viewed entoptic phenomena as nonpathological; Müller saw them as "primary" phenomena that explained how everyday, externally directed vision works. However, the sensory physiologist Ewald Hering, writing in the 1860s, criticized the "pathological" "eyes" of self-experimenting researchers; see Müller-Tamm 74–82.

emphasis). Here, artifice again doubles and supersedes life, which is seen as intrinsically flawed, marked by lack, "always found wanting." The solution is a "transfiguration" familiar from the German poetic realist literature of Vischer's day: "We ... organize and intensify the essential and weaken the inessential in order to safeguard the whole.... Only by means of this visible, real reproduction is a truly clear purification and clarification [*Reinigung und Klärung*] of the natural model achieved" (114, *Formgefühl* 36). This Hegel-inflected trajectory concludes with the treatise's closing appeal for a "refin[ing] [of] the form's spirit" (*Läuterung des Formgeistes*) (117, *Formgefühl* 42), or, as Hegel puts it in his *Introdutory Lectures on Aesthetics*, a better birth, or *rebirth*, through *Geist*: "We may ... begin at once by asserting that artistic beauty stands *higher* than nature. For the beauty of art is the beauty that is born—born again, that is—of the mind [spirit]" (Hegel 4). In Vischer's words, "The world of sense ... is only a window on spiritual content"; "The artist undertakes to emancipate [the] Idea that is trapped in real life and to shape it flawlessly [*makellos*]" (120, *Formgefühl* 47).

Über das optische Formgefühl thus affords art both ordinal and valuative primacy: In both a literal and a figurative, colloquial sense, the treatise "begins and ends" with art. But there are at least two problems with this quasi-Hegelian rescue and resurrection of the world through the aesthetic. For art to rise, "life" must fall—or have already fallen. As philosopher J. M. Bernstein argues,

> What is ominous [in Hegelian aesthetics] ... is the idea that it is a *condition* for nature to become a pure vehicle of mindedness that it be dead (stone, wood, canvas, sounds and words), as if spirit could only assure itself of its ultimate and unsurpassable authority through the slaughter of nature.... Only if nature is really dead, so to speak, can the material basis of art that founds its sensuous character be an empty husk, a corpse, leaving only the mindedness of works as demanding attention, so that in works, finally, it is an issue of the mind knowing itself. (225)

This is already the case in Vischer's post-vitalist, materialist object-world. In a strange way, it is a world that privileges both matter and mind in uncanny relation. Vischer envisions what he calls the "patchwork" (*Stückwerk*) or "dead material" (*todtes Material*) of nature arising as "resurrected symbol[s] for everything organic" ("[die Natur] kann... nun, *als eine auferweckte*, Gleichnisse für alles Organische abgeben" [nature can now, as a *resurrected thing*, deliver tropes for everything organic], my translation and emphasis)—an image that pronounces nature dead on arrival, thoroughly subjected to our symbolizing processes, and in the position of what Freud might call the defenselessness of the corpse (106, *Formgefühl* 23; cf. Freud, *Totem und Tabu* 78). Additionally, despite its Christian echoes and purportedly "completely unpathological" character (Vischer 114), aesthetic rebirth, or at least Vischer's version of it, whether through art proper or empathic "scanning," is not as "flawless" or "makellos" (120, *Formgefühl* 47)—literally "im-maculate"—as claimed. Rather, the aesthetically or artistically "reshaping" gaze inflicts conspicuous violence on its object, as Vischer's register of bellicose commands makes clear: "The organic intentions must emerge and discharge themselves. The lax relationship of the parts must be made more stringent; the independence of this undisciplined and incomplete existence must be forced back into a bodily center; everything that is superfluous that swirls out... must be tempered or eradicated" (119). Or, in a further articulation of the violence of the aesthetic gaze, the treatise isolates "uncannily" fragmented—as it were, dismembered—body parts for special consideration: "the torso of Hercules, the charm of a fragmentary limb, an arm or a leg" (119).[19] In short, far from counteracting the pathological, the trio of aesthetic (that is, empathic) perception, artistic transfiguration, and neo-Hegelian "rebirth" might *itself* be seen as a variant of the pathological. It kills the phenomena it aims to resurrect, or—to put matters in terms of the Vischer passage with which this chapter began—it hangs the girl it is then at pains to reanimate.[20]

Rebirth, reanimation, and resurrection, whether Christian or diabolically otherwise, also play a central role in Büchner's *Lenz*, as do

---

19. On the uncanniness of dismembered body parts, see Freud, "Uncanny" 946.
20. Cassirer similarly criticizes *Einfühlungstheorie* for "killing" the primary or "living" phenomenological content—the "definite modes of appearing"—of perception and replacing it with the "dead matter of [mere] sensation" that requires reanimation through empathy; see *Philosophy of Symbolic Forms* 72–77, here 72–73.

aesthetic perception and production, (psycho)pathology and "madness," and the relation of life to art. Like Büchner's work as a whole, the neuroanatomist and dramatist's unfinished prose fragment about the Sturm und Drang playwright Jakob Michael Reinhold Lenz occupies a fault line between declining Romantic values of vitalism and *Naturphilosophie* and a rising realist regime of materialist, physicalist thought—a fault line that turns *Lenz* both into a ghost, like *Über das optische Formgefühl*, of its Romantic legacy and an uncanny herald of the problems raised by Vischer's formulation of *Einfühlung* later in the century. Let us now look more closely at this text—its relations among feelings, forms, intersubjective empathy, and proleptic *Einfühlung*—to see how this is the case.

Georg Büchner, Resurrection Man

The historical J. M. R. Lenz (1751–1792), subject of Büchner's groundbreaking narrative fragment, is widely said to have been—to use the outdated, undifferentiated, and problematic English equivalent of the German term of Lenz's day—"mad." Indeed, Büchner, choosing a word just becoming more popular in the last decade of Lenz's life, describes his subject's condition as "Wahnsinn" (madness) (*Lenz* 6–7).[21] Famously dismissed by Goethe from the literary circles of Weimar for his nonnormative behavior, Lenz died homeless and under mysterious political circumstances on a Moscow street.[22] The exact nature of his mental illness, likely a form of psychotic disorder, cannot, of course, be known: The classificatory categories of modern psychiatry did not exist in Lenz's time, nor in Büchner's. However, the vividness, detail, and precision of Büchner's literary "resurrection" of Lenz's suffering are so compelling that they have led more than one twentieth-century psychiatrist to find in the 1839 narrative a recognizable symptomatology of schizophrenia half a century before Kraepelin and Bleuler's description of the disease—and thus to diagnose Lenz posthumously on the basis of a

---

21. See the history of the word *Wahnsinn* in the *Deutsches Wörterbuch*.
22. For an account, see Sieburth, afterword 174–78.

literary text.[23] Büchner's presentation of Lenz's interactions with his friend Kaufmann and his host-caretaker Oberlin also leaves open the possibility that the playwright's anguish may have been—like that of Goethe's Werther, with whom both the historical Lenz and Büchner's "docufictional" (re)creation exist in complex dialogue—at least in part social: an effect of the familial, class, religious, aesthetic, and gender orders of Lenz's era.[24]

As intriguing as these speculations are, the salient question is perhaps not whether or how the historical Lenz was "mad," but how the *textual* one is. As we shall see, he is, at least in part, *empathically mad*—an example of intersubjective empathy and proto-Vischerian *Einfühlung* gone awry. He is, as it were, *pathologically empathic*. As the verses he recites near the end of the narrative suggest, having stared too long and too directly into the "sun" of sensory input, *sich einfühlen*, and self-other exchange, he now longs for Fechner's "dark room":

> O God, drowned in thy waves of light,
> Imprisoned by thy midday bright,
> My waking eyes are dreadful sore,
> O will the night come nevermore? (61)

Büchner's narrative reconstructs the historical Lenz's three-week convalescent stay with the Alsatian pastor Johann Friedrich Oberlin in the village of Waldersbach (then Waldbach) in 1778. In extreme psychological distress following his expulsion from Weimar

---

23. See for example Irle 73–83 and Mayer-Gross 889–90.
24. Sieburth calls *Lenz* "an early nineteenth-century example of the modern genre of docufiction," "an experiment in speculative biography, part fact, part fabrication" (afterword 167). The literary connections between *Lenz* and *Werther*, the literary and extraliterary relations between Lenz and Goethe, and Büchner's engagement with the writings and person of both Goethe and Lenz are especially intricate. Critics have long noted the historical Lenz's "imitation" of Goethe's personal life and writings (including, prominently, *Werther*), as well as the potential function of Büchner's *Lenz* both as a challenge to Goethe's negative depiction of Lenz in *Dichtung und Wahrheit* and as a "metacritical" rewrite of, or commentary on, *Werther*; see for example Anz 163. Since this critical path of Lenz's—and Büchner's—quasi-oedipal conflict with Goethe is well traveled and does not bear immediately on my discussion, I will not pursue it further here.

and a possible suicide attempt in Switzerland, Lenz had been sent by a friend to Oberlin's parsonage for care. Büchner's text recounts, seemingly from within the cognitive frenzy and sensory overload of Lenz's mind itself, the young playwright's intensifying downward spiral over the course of his stay. The text's "plot" closely follows Oberlin's own testimony-like report on Lenz's sojourn, which Büchner utilized extensively in drafting his narrative: Lenz arrives in Waldbach, makes numerous attempts at self-harm, frightens Oberlin's family with his disordered behavior, and is eventually sent by the overwhelmed Oberlin to Strasbourg for more thorough treatment. Furthering the aesthetic practice he established with his first play *Dantons Tod* (*Danton's Death*), Büchner incorporates extensive unmarked citations from Oberlin's text: As Richard Sieburth notes, "Of the slightly less than ten thousand words of Büchner's *Lenz*, about one-eighth are directly lifted, without attribution, from the Oberlin manuscript" (afterword 196). To this "experiment in intertextuality" (Sieburth, afterword 196), Büchner adds Lenz's inner life—harrowingly empathic depictions, or, more precisely, *imaginings*, of Lenz's terrifying mental disarray and overwhelming emotional and aesthetic experiences—as well as substantial, freely invented passages on Lenz's encounters with nature, religion, and art that appear nowhere in, or are only briefly suggested by, Oberlin's report. These additions, as we will see, are especially crucial to the concerns of this chapter.

Significantly, two of the most important moments in *Lenz*—the famous *Kunstgespräch* or "conversation about art," inspired perhaps in part by the historical Lenz's *Anmerkungen übers Theater* (*Remarks on the Theater*, 1774) but largely invented by Büchner himself, and the traumatic failed revival of the dead child, greatly expanded in detail and consequence from Oberlin's passing reference—thematize the combination of (sometimes extreme) empathy with the problematic of death's relationship to life, resurrection, and uncanny reanimation.[25] Signaling its centrality, the *Kun-*

---

25. On Büchner's likely lack of source for the *Kunstgespräch*, see Holub 37; on the similarity of some of Lenz's aesthetic positions in the conversation with the historical Lenz's *Anmerkungen übers Theater*, see Pörnbacher et al. 542–45n144.

stgespräch is the longest and most self-reflexive scene in Büchner's text, while the failed resurrection attempt forms a turning point marking the intensification of the docufictional Lenz's descent into "madness." What do the intersections in these scenes tell us about the anxieties and stakes, not only of *Lenz*, but of Vischer's *Über das optische Formgefühl, Einfühlung*, and the ambivalence of their historical positioning?

Büchner's own historical positioning is ambiguous. The years in which he wrote, as I have noted, witnessed the struggle between vitalist and *naturphilosophische* conceptions of nature as a "unified[,] ... single, active evolving substance" (Merchant 102) and the rise of a materialist science that reduced life to the byproduct of chemical and physical processes: the culmination of what Merchant calls the "death of nature" (193). By the middle of the nineteenth century, German thinkers faced an increasingly materialist understanding of nature as "a system of dead, inert particles" (Merchant 193) and of the human body as "fragmented," "composed of separate organic systems ... dominated by involuntary reflex activity" (Crary 76). Büchner's brother, the physiologist Ludwig Büchner, would himself publish one of the mid-century's most uncompromising materialist attacks on vitalism, the scientific bestseller *Kraft und Stoff* (*Force and Matter*), in 1855. Yet the shift from *Naturphilosophie* to materialist science was not a clean break following Johannes Müller's rejection of Schelling around 1830 (Roth 10–11). Rather, conflicting streams of scientific thought continued to contend with each other throughout Büchner's life and afterward (Roth 9), a situation that the neuroanatomist Büchner—well versed in the diverse scientific theories of his day and, as Yvonne Wübben points out, seen more as a scientist than as a dramatist during his lifetime (111)—knew and "lived."

The Lenz of Büchner's narrative speaks like a classic *Naturphilosoph*: "All things were imbued with an indefinable harmony, a note, a bliss that in higher forms of life became more pronounced, more resonant, perceiving the world with a greater variety of organs" (27). And, in "Über Schädelnerven" ("On Cranial Nerves"), the 1836 trial lecture Büchner delivered as a condition of assuming a teaching position in comparative anatomy at the University of Zurich, Büchner himself sounds the same: "The entire bodily existence of the individual . . . becomes the manifestation of a primordial law, a law of beauty, that brings forth the highest and purest forms according to the simplest plans and lines. Everything, form and matter, is . . . bound to this law. All functions are its effects" (336–37). As Büchner goes on to claim, all sense faculties develop genealogically from a single "common feeling" (*Gemeingefühl*) in the simplest organism; brain nerves are simply a "more perfect form" (*vollkommnere Form*) or "modifications at a higher exponential level" (*Modifikationen in einer höheren Potenz*) of the sensory nerves—that is, of the types of nerves bound by Müller's law of specific nerve energies ("Schädelnerven" 340). As is well known, one of the most significant influences on the trial lecture was the renowned *Naturphilosoph* Lorenz Oken, president of the University of Zurich and a member of Büchner's dissertation committee, who would send his son to the only class Büchner was able to teach before Büchner's untimely death.[26]

Roth is ambivalent about how fully Büchner adhered to the *naturphilosophische* tradition (278, 388), writing that the author's position in nineteenth-century science remains unclear (12). John Reddick maintains that, like the nineteenth century's frequently hybrid science itself, it is impossible to assign Büchner either to the "empiricist-materialist-realist" or to the "speculative-idealist" camp (*Georg Büchner* 25). Helmut Müller-Sievers goes so far as to argue that we must not regard the trial lecture's Oken-like, *naturphilosophische* stance as an accurate reflection of Büchner's scientific views at all: Facing political persecution at home, Büchner was, in Müller-Sievers's reading, desperate to secure both job security and personal safety from the Swiss institution whose president he sought to impress (*Desorientierung* 52). Indeed, important strands of Büchner criticism have understood Büchner as a materialist, even nihilist, writer.[27] Intriguingly, just five months before delivering the trial

---

26. See Knapp and Wender 360–63 as well as Reddick, *Georg Büchner* 3–28, especially 10–14. On Büchner as a possible *Naturphilosoph*, see Schings, Guillemin, and Walker, "'Ach die Kunst!'"

27. See for example Viëtor; cf. Reddick, *Georg Büchner* 12, 25.

lecture, Büchner wrote to his publisher Karl Gutzkow that "our age is purely *material*" ("An Karl Gutzkow" ["Letter to Karl Gutzkow"] 258). Perhaps, as Otto Döhner (130) and Daniel Müller Nielaba (7) contend, Büchner's rhetoric most closely resembles that of his influence and advocate Müller, who aimed to defend vitalism and *Naturphilosophie* but ended up advancing materialism. Or, just as plausibly, it represents an anxious dialogue, hesitation, or oscillation between the two—or more—perspectives. As Roth puts it, "Was Büchner a researcher inclined toward *Naturphilosophie*, a figure of the transitional period from *Naturphilosophie* to the 'exact' sciences, a herald of the dialectical-materialist method? Or do we need to find other scientific-historiographical categories in order to determine his position?" (12).

The docufictional Lenz, though clearly grounded in the facts of his biographical model's life, might be seen as a literary-historical embodiment of the transitional period we have been tracing: a quintessentially "mad poet" deracinated from this trope's "home" in the meaning-supplying holism of Romanticism, his formal strategies of representation resurrected and altered in the lens of early realist science—his own uncanny double, so to speak. From one perspective, Lenz's experience of his physical environment—"He stretched out and lay over the earth, he burrowed into the universe" (*Lenz* 5)—recalls elements of the Romantic past (or what would have been the past from Büchner's historical standpoint, although it was the future for the biographical Lenz): the "affective, pantheistic . . . fusion of the soul with nature" (David Morgan 321) of the aesthetic period immediately preceding Büchner's own. More significantly, however, *Lenz* destabilizes Romantic thinking and points toward the uncanny and "pathological" aspects of late nineteenth-century *Einfühlung*.

The pathological and uncanny are, of course, also fundamental aspects of much Romanticism, and Büchner's engagement with his Romantic inheritance is complex. Yet among the clearest indications that, despite Lenz's repeated "fusions" with "the universe," we are not on the exultant ground of Novalis's "person with an organ for nature" are the text's subversions of its own Romantic legacy. Far from causes of bliss or transcendence, the fusions of Büchner's Lenz are more typically sources of terror. Rather than reveling in the privileged Romantic phenomena of darkness and night, Büchner's Lenz fears them. In despair after failing to resurrect the dead girl, he looks up at the emblematic Romantic image of the moon and finds only a "silly" satellite "hanging there, ridiculous" (55). Most importantly, his "madness" is not "romanticized": It is not celebrated as "frohlokkender [sic] Wahnsinn" (jubilant madness), as Hölderlin put it at the very beginning of the period ("Brot und Wein" ["Bread and Wine"] 320–21), or, as might be the case in a different sort of Romantic text, mined for purely "aesthetic" horror; it does not "further a plot" or "stand for." It is dragged screaming, so to speak, into a blank material world where its meaning, if it is to have one, is not pregiven but must be sought—or imposed. And if Lenz is a ghost of his Romantic self—a ghost, that is, of his self as it might have been represented a generation earlier by, say, Eichendorff or Hoffmann—the entire *Lenz* narrative is also a ghost: one that haunts Vischer's theorizing in advance. Central to this haunting are Lenz's intersubjective empathy and, especially, his proto-Vischerian *Einfühlung*: his struggles to find, or project, uncanny "life" in a growing maerialist age. Like the "resurrection men" or body snatchers of old, however, his efforts may only turn up cadavers—and the uncanny feelings and fears attendant on reanimating them.

Pathologies of Empathy

Lenz is a figure for radical empathy in Büchner's text. His association with Christ goes beyond his failed resurrection attempt and the two Dutch paintings he praises in the *Kunstgespräch*: the Rembrandt pupil Carel van Savoy's (or Savoyen's) *Christ and the Disciples at Emmaus* and an unidentified image of a woman "sitting in her room, prayer book in hand," "holding service at home" because she "had not been able to go to church" (*Lenz* 35). Moved by intersubjective fellow-feeling, compassionate identification with others' suffering, pity (including, perhaps, pity for himself), or an excess of amorphous and overwhelming affect—or all of the above—Lenz undertakes a "hysterical" imitatio Christi, a sometimes-panicked translation of empathy into a series of real or imagined prosocial rituals at a collective scale.[28] Preaching a guest sermon for Oberlin, he is comforted that he "could offer sleep to various eyes tired from crying and peace to tortured hearts, that he could show the way to heaven to existences tortured by material needs, all these muffled sorrows" (21–23). In his theory of art, formulated in the *Kunstgespräch*, he proclaims that "one has to love mankind in order to penetrate into the unique existence of each being, nobody can be too humble, too ugly, only then can you understand them" (33). And, in figuring himself as *Agnus Dei, qui tollis peccata mundi,* he even outdoes God Himself: as he tells Oberlin, "As for myself, were I almighty . . . , if I were, if I could no longer put up with all this suffering, I would just save, save everyone" (73–75). Yet, to paraphrase *Othello,* Lenz loves not wisely but too well: His excessively empathic "feeling with" the "sorrows" of the congregation, "mankind," and "everyone" nearly destroys him. In a strange step-by-step process of desiccation and petrification, for example, the pain of the congregation, along with "divine woe" itself, washes through him in the form of the church hymn, becoming or merging indistinguishably with his own emotions; the combined affect then drains from him as literal liquid. Finally, as the narrative voice "pulls back" from the interior of his psyche, past a portrait-like image of his face to a (figurative) moonlit "landscape painting," the entire procedure transforms him into a "fossilized" aesthetic object:

The [hymn's] voices began again:

Burst, O divine woe,
The floodgates of my soul;
May pain be my reward,
In pain I love the Lord.

The pressure within him, the music, the pain, shook [Lenz] to the core. The universe was an open wound; it caused him deep nameless pain. . . . He was alone, alone! Then the springwaters gushed forth, tears poured

---

28. Sieburth's translation reads, "[Lenz] felt deep quiet pity for himself"; Büchner's original is rather more ambiguous: "Er empfand ein leises tiefes Mitleid in sich selbst" (22–23).

from his eyes, he crumpled into himself, his limbs twitched, it was as if he needed to dissolve, . . . his head sank onto his chest, he dozed off, the full moon hung in the sky, his hair fell over his temples and face, the tears clung to his eyelashes and dried on his cheeks, he now lay there alone, everything peaceful and silent and cold, and the moon shone the whole night through, above the mountains. (23)

It is in the realm of aesthetic empathy, however—empathy with forms and objects—that the "pathologies" of Lenz's uncanny transformations are most clearly visible and most strikingly prefigure the implicit anxieties of Vischer's *Einfühlung*. Like Vischer's "scanning" observer, Lenz feels himself into the forms of the inanimate world, animating and ensouling them. Mountains, storms, and other features of the environment fuse, in the text's empathic, frequently unlocalizable narrative voice, with Lenz's own body, thoughts, and emotionl states. Like Vischer's observer "guided by kinesthetic imagination" or "carried away by fleeing clouds" (101), Lenz mentally-physiologically "mobilizes" and is affectively "carried away" by what his, and Büchner's, wildly dynamic metaphors and personifications paint as the sensory overload of nature: "Sometimes when the storms tossed the clouds into the valleys and they floated upwards through the woods . . . and the clouds galloped by like wild whinnying horses and the sunshine shot through them and emerged and drew its glinting sword on the snowfields so that a bright blinding light knifed over the peaks into the valleys . . . he would feel something tearing at his chest, he would stand there, gasping, body bent forward, eyes and mouth open wide" (5). Lenz experiences the corporeal and psychical isomorphism with the contours of the world—the reciprocal alignment, in feeling, of two realms of form—that Vischer will identify as the structural skeleton of *Einfühlung*: "He was convinced he should draw the storm into himself, contain everything within himself, he stretched out and lay over the earth, he burrowed into the universe" (*Lenz* 5). As he tells Oberlin, "It must be an endless delight to feel moved by the unique life of each and every form; to have a soul for stones, metals, water and plants; to take in every being in nature into oneself" (25–27). But it is "a pleasure that gave him pain" (5), and, as we see, the pain side often dominates. In the slide of the narrative's famous opening passages into free indirect discourse, for example, indicated by the swerve-inducing interjection of *but* and the repetition of *so*, Lenz "becomes" the natural world, "objectif[ying] himself in [the] spatial forms" (Vischer 92) of the oppressively overcast sky and lethargic fog: "The 20th, Lenz walked through the mountains. Snow on the peaks and upper slopes, gray rock down into the valleys, swatches of green, boulders, and firs. It was sopping cold, the water trickled down the rocks and leapt across the path. The fir boughs sagged in the damp air. Gray clouds drifted across the sky, *but* everything *so* stifling, and then the fog floated up and crept heavy and damp through the bushes, *so* sluggish, *so* clumsy" (3, my emphasis). Like Vischer's kinesthetic-aesthetic empath, Lenz "move[s] in and with the forms" (Vischer 101) in a way that engages not just his body's "immediate processes of sensation" (Altieri 2), both felt and imagined, but also what Altieri would call the entire affective spectrum of feelings, moods, emotions, and passions (2): versions of the "mental activity" that Vischer will see as inseparable from physiological processes and somatic states (99). And although it seems that Lenz exemplarily "project[s] [his] own life into the lifeless form" (Vischer 104), the origin, vector, and locus of experience are again in fact not so clear. In terms of Spinoza's *affectus*, the "ability to affect and be affected... implying an augmentation or diminution"—here, diminution—"in [the] body's capacity to act" (Massumi, notes xvi), it is uncertain *what is affecting what*. In Lenz's feeling of the form—the bidirectional exchange or mutual "possession" of subject and object, in which form and feeling are inseparable—it is impossible to determine which came first: the sagging boughs, stifling sky, and sluggish fog, or Lenz's sagging, stifling, and sluggish state of mind. As Vischer will write, "Only ostensibly do I keep my own identity although the object remains distinct. I seem merely to adapt and attach myself to it as one hand clasps another, and yet I am mysteriously transplanted and magically transformed into this Other" (104). And when form is no longer perceptible—when night and darkness come—Lenz, too, fears dissolving into formlessness: "He was seized by a nameless anxiety in this emptiness, he was in a void" (7). As Vischer argues, "The perception of exterior limits to a form can combine in some obscure way with the sensation of my own physical boundaries, which I feel on, or rather with, my own skin" (98)—except that here there is no form, and thus no skin.

Lenz anticipates the dangers of *Einfühlung*, the pathologies and fears embedded in the rhetoric and imagery of Vischer's treatise. In an extreme version of the phenomenology of such observations by Vischer as "in rooms with low ceilings our whole body feels the sensation of weight and pressure" (98), Lenz is viscerally assaulted by his physical surroundings: "The landscape was making him anxious, it was so narrow he was afraid he would bump into everything" (*Lenz* 65). For the hyper- or "pathologically" empathic Lenz, the apparent limits of "external" forms do not just, as Vischer writes, "combine in some obscure way with the sensation of [his] own physical boundaries" (98). Rather, the "overpowering solid planes and lines" of the Vosges Mountains "address [Lenz] in loud tones" (19) or blur into unusual sensory experiences—the apprehension of abstract geometrical forms or combinations of feeling and form— of the type that might interest sensory physiology and psychological aesthetics: "Everything blended into a single line like a wave rising and falling between heaven and earth, he felt as if he were lying beside an endless ocean that was gently rocking up and down" (41). Lenz's synesthesia, a privileged Romantic trope (and, in Büchner's narrative, an uncanny reminder of the distance traveled between Romanticism's triumphant universalism and Lenz's "pathology," between Romanticism's "mad poet" and Büchner's), represents a particularly intense and specific manifestation of that "peculiar confusion of our own stimulation with the thing that produces the stimulus" (Vischer 108) that we know from Lenz's "so sluggish, so clumsy" fog.[29] It is also, as Büchner the scientist would have known, a neurological phenomenon, one that would soon be investigated experimentally in Germany's psychological-aesthetic laboratories and come to be seen as the "sensory pathology à la mode" by the end of the nineteenth century (Brain, *Pulse* xxxii). And, as a means

---

29. On Büchner's depiction of "madness," Romantic representational traditions, and the aesthetic production of the uncanny, see also Wübben 97.

of making mountains "speak," it is another way to animate "dead" form.

Büchner had read the work of the early French psychiatrist Jean-Étienne Esquirol, who explained hallucinations as the activity of brain regions functioning in isolation (Wübben 104–7); he was of course familiar with the *Handbuch* of his intellectual benefactor Müller. As Müller had argued, all sensory perceptions, including everyday "reality," nocturnal dreams, artistic visions, and hallucinations (such as the fictionalized Lenz's auditory phantasms), arise on the same physiological continuum and can be explained by the "inner energies" of the nerves and sense organs of what Crary calls the "defective," "prey to illusion" body (Müller-Tamm 39–44; Crary 92). Thus, when Lenz wrestles with pathological distortions in his experience of the relation of space to time—"He could not grasp why it took so much time to clamber down a slope, to reach a distant point; he was convinced he could cover it all with a pair of strides" (3)—he simply embodies a more extreme version of Müller's "normal" developing child who "has as yet no idea of proximity and distance" and who would thus "necessarily recognize no difference in the size of the field of vision, whether it looked into a tube closed at one end, or through an open one upon an extensive landscape" (*Elements of Physiology* 353).[30] Indeed, Lenz's "madness" forms a bridge to what, in their less extreme forms, Vischer, *Einfühlungstheorie*, and the coming psychophysiological turn in aesthetics will identify as universal human processes. As Guyer writes in his *History of Modern Aesthetics*, "A feeling of complete unity in our experience of what would otherwise be considered physical properties of an object and of our emotional response to it is not just a feature of empathy but is a defining feature of aesthetic experience as such and what makes empathy paradigmatic for aesthetic experience" (394). And, as Christian Neuhuber contends, representation in *Lenz* "is bound to the conditions of a *pathological, or*, as the case may be, *radically aesthetic* mode of perception that has been processed by literary means" (40, my emphasis).

---

30. The quotation is from volume 2 of Müller's *Handbuch*, which appeared after Büchner's death; however, Büchner would have been familiar with Müller's general thinking on these matters from volume 1, which he cites in his dissertation.

Lenz's excesses of proto-*Einfühlung* are, like aesthetic empathy in *Über das optische Formgefühl*, inseparable from images of the uncanny and demonic. They encompass not only repetitive, seemingly automatic or out-of-control behaviors and "manifestations of insanity" that evoke uncanny feelings of "mechanical processes at work behind the ordinary appearance of mental activity" (Freud, "Uncanny" 935) but also Lenz's self-figuration as the ultimate demon, "Satan himself": "It seemed to him as if he alone existed, as if the world lay only in his imagination, as if there were nothing but himself, . . . Satan himself; alone, tormented by his imaginings" (71–73). Indeed, as Lenz goes from identification with Christ to identification with Satan, "possessing" the world through demonically subjective projection ("as if the world lay only in his imagination"), Oberlin's maids fear that Lenz himself has *become possessed* or animated by demonic forces (72–73). Significantly, both Müller' law of specific nerve energies and Büchner's own Zurich trial lecture shed physiological light on how this possession might work. Müller's law, as we recall, states that "a uniform cause . . . generates utterly different sensations from one kind of [sensory] nerve to another," such that "electricity applied to the optic nerve produces the experience of light, applied to the skin the sensation of touch," and so on (Crary 90). And, as Büchner argues in "Über Schädelnerven," brain nerves are a "more perfect form" or "modifications at a higher exponential level" of the sensory nerves (340)—that is, of the nerves governed by Müller's law. If this is the case, might we not ask whether the same external causes or energies (say, electromagnetic radiation) that produce "the experience of light" in the optic nerve could likewise produce the *experience of thought* in the *brain nerves* that are, according to Büchner, the "more perfect forms" or "modifications at a higher exponential level" of the sensory nerves themselves? Lenz's disordered thinking thus becomes a function of *too much empathy*, if empathy is conceived here as a "taking in of" rather than a "projection onto" the external world: Too much of the world's energy "gets in," overwhelming the brain nerves. Just as staring directly into the sun disordered Fechner's vision, directly absorbing the total stimulus field of the "outside" world disorders Lenz's mind. The senses (here, the brain as an extension of the senses) are, as Crary emphasizes in his account of Müller, subject to "manipulation" and "derangement" (92–93)—or, to put it differently, *possession*. In thus juxtaposing Lenz's self-assessment as "Satan" with the external positions of Oberlin's maids, Müller's law, and Büchner's trial lecture, we find both directions of our bidirectional model of empathy: Lenz is "mad" (and empathic) because he projects (himself into) the world ("as if the world lay only in his imagination") *and* because he "takes in," and thus falls under the capturing, deranging, and "possessing" sway of, too many outside forces.[31]

Radicalizing the uncanny aspects of empathic processes, Lenz takes both intersubjective empathy and *Einfühlung* to extremes: "If he thought about another person, or vividly pictured them, it was as if he became that person" (*Lenz* 69). More than half a century after Büchner, Theodor Lipps, the first to substantially unite *Einfühlung* with a theory of intersubjective empathy, would supplement Vischer's notion of self-projection with the concept of motor mimicry. Writing of a potentially Lenz-like "becoming another person," Lipps explains,

> I *see* another's arm stretched out. Let the manner of stretching have something perceptibly free, effortless, confident, proud about it. . . . Now I feel . . . a striving. And perhaps I actualize this striving. I imitate the movement. . . . Let us now, however, . . . assume that this imitation is *involuntary*. This will be all the more the case the more that I, observing, give myself over to the observed motion. And conversely, the more the imitation occurs involuntarily, the more I am, observing, *wholly* in the observed motion. However, if I have fully given myself over to the observation of the movement, then I am, concomitantly, fully removed from *what* I am doing, e.g., the movements that I actually carry out, the processes in and of my body; I know nothing more of my *outer* imitation. . . . In sum, with my feeling of activity, I am now wholly in the [other] moving form. . . . I am transported into it. I am, as far as my consciousness is concerned, wholly and completely identical with it. . . . This is aesthetic imitation [*ästhetische Nachahmung*]. And it is at the same time aesthetic empathy [*ästhetische Einfühlung*]. ("Einfühlung, innere Nachahmung" ["Empathy, Inner Imitation"] 190–91)

---

31. On Lenz's "possession" by the "external" world, see also my discussion of Wübben below.

For Lipps, this "aesthetic imitation" or "aesthetic empathy" (*ästhetische Einfühlung*) is an "inner imitation" (*innere Nachahmung*)—a term he borrows and adapts from Groos—that occurs inside the body and mind of the observer, in the observer's spontaneously felt and reprojected resonance with the actions of the other: "I feel myself active in . . . the figure that performs the motion, and in this figure feel myself striving to carry out and completing precisely *this* motion" ("Einfühlung, innere Nachahmung" 191). Or, as Edward Titchener will put it in his introduction of the term "empathy" to English-speaking audiences, "I not only see gravity and modesty and pride . . . in the mind's eye, but also feel or act them in the mind's muscles" (181). However, in another manifestation of "pathological" *Einfühlung*, Lenz "externalizes" Lipps's and Titchener's inner imitation, projection, and motor mimicry, rendering these specular processes disturbingly *spectacular* and exposing them as uncannily compulsive and out of control: "Once [Lenz] was sitting next to Oberlin, the cat lying across from them on a chair, suddenly his eyes locked into a stare, he fixed them upon the animal, then he slowly edged out of his chair, as did the cat, bewitched by his gaze, horribly frightened, bristling with fear, Lenz hissing back at it, his face horribly contorted, the two going at each other as if in desperation, Madame Oberlin finally getting up to pull them apart" (*Lenz* 69–71). Here again we find that "central projection, exchange, and return" through which *Einfühlung* "takes on a [strange, uncanny] life of its own" (*eigenartiges Leben*), "looks at its second self as it sits reshaped in the object," and "intuitively"—or "full of foreboding" (*ahnungsvoll*)—takes this double "back to itself without knowing why" (Vischer 108, *Formgefühl* 27). We likewise find those opaque, automatic, uncanny processes that suggest "magical" transformation or "demonic" possession. Here, however, Lenz is possessed not by literal demons, as the maids believe, but by *Einfühlung*.

In so tightly interweaving the pathological, the aesthetic, and the empathic, *Lenz* suggests that its protagonist is *less* pathological, or that Vischer's *Einfühlung* is *more* pathological, than either appears at first glance. Indeed, what *Lenz*'s proleptic staging of *Einfühlung* points to is the *uncanniness of empathy*, a performance of *Einfühlung* not forcibly sequestered from the pathological, as Vischer's treatise anxiously proposes in its attempt to draw a "strict distinction between purely aesthetic and pathological behavior" (99), but rather *largely coinciding with it*. We find an implicit form of this understanding between the lines of Wilhelm Mayer-Gross's brief 1921 comments on *Lenz*. Without mentioning Freud directly, Mayer-Gross enthusiastically notes the relation of Lenz's attempt to raise the dead girl with "the primitive world of magic!" (890)—a resonance, coincidental or not, with a key component of the uncanny Freud had explicated in his famous essay just two years before Mayer-Gross's remarks ("Uncanny" 945–50).[32] More overtly, Mayer-Gross writes of the "feeling of the uncanny" (*Gefühl des Unheimlichen*) that Büchner's fictionalized Lenz senses "arising within him" (890). Without naming Vischer or Lipps, he frames Lenz's pathologies in terms familiar from *Einfühlungstheorie*: Lenz engages in the "*projection* of all [his] heavy, depressive experiences into the landscape" (890, my emphasis). Most importantly, Mayer-Gross tacitly links uncanny *Einfühlung* with pathology itself: Lenz's perceptions lead to his "feeling that the environment has been changed" (*das Gefühl der Veränderung der Umwelt*) (890), and presumably not for the better. By "empathizing" (*sich einzufühlen*) with Lenz's feeling of the uncanny (890), Mayer-Gross's argument suggests, Büchner *empathizes with Lenz's (pathological, aesthetic) empathy*, assuming, in a sort of transitive uncanniness, some of that pathology for himself. Other nineteenth-century crossings of the aesthetic and the pathological remain ambiguous: If some of the century's psychological-aesthetic experiments on sensory phenomena like synesthesia appeared to normalize what had earlier been viewed as pathological experience (Lanzoni, *Empathy* 73–74), others seemed determined to inscribe the pathological (or at least the highly ethically questionable) directly into the norms of scientific praxis itself. As Crary notes, Müller's student Dubois-Reymond "seriously pursued

---

32. Freud writes that "an uncanny experience" occurs when "primitive beliefs which have been surmounted," such as the belief in "magic," "seem once more to be confirmed" (945–50). Lenz's unsuccessful resurrection attempt of course fails to "confirm" the so-called primitive belief; however, the very attempt, especially coupled with the mood created by the text's narration of Lenz's mental state, moves the scene into the realm of the uncanny.

the possibility of electrically cross-connecting nerves, enabling the eye to see sounds and the ear to hear colors" (93).

Feelings of the Form

Before returning to the concerns with which this chapter began—resurrection, uncanny reanimation, and their relation to the anxieties of *Einfühlung* in the materialist unconscious of a post-vitalist age—let us first look briefly at some of the most striking instances of the intersection of feeling and form in *Lenz*: the formal mechanisms of narrative voice and compositional strategy, both central to the text's performance and elicitation of empathy. It is practically a truism that Büchner, both on the page and off, is one of the greatest exemplars in German literary history of what will come to be called intersubjective empathy. As Patrick Fortmann writes, reflecting overwhelming critical consensus, Büchner's texts "side with those who suffer, who are marginalized in the social order, silenced in the political arena, and crushed by the forces of history. To them and their lives, Büchner's writings turn with radical empathy, seeking human dignity amidst the turmoil of poverty and pathology" (16).[33] Büchner's empathic commitments extended far beyond his docufictional worlds: as a *Vormärz* revolutionary, he exposed the economic misery of Hesse-Darmstadt's rural poor and called for the overthrow of the duchy's repressive government, narrowly escaping prison and torture through self-exile in France. Like Büchner himself, the historical Lenz was a radical playwright whose thematically experimental works embody groundbreaking literary concern for the socially marginalized; it is therefore unsurprising that Büchner chose him as a subject and model. Indeed, the *Lenz* fragment represents a mise en abyme of empathy: Büchner empathizes intersubjectively with the historical Lenz, whose fictionalized ava-

---

33. Among the vast amounts of critical literature on Büchner and empathy (understood in its nontechnical sense as interpersonal fellow-feeling rather than *Einfühlung*, and often referred to as *Mitleid*, *Mitgefühl*, compassion, etc.), see for example Schings and Walker, "'Ach die Kunst!'"

tar empathizes (that is, is rhetorically constructed by the text as empathizing) both intersubjectively and aesthetically with the beings and objects he encounters in Büchner's tale. The narrative thus stages Büchner's attempt to "resurrect" the Sturm und Drang dramatist as an "object" by means of formal literary mechanisms, to "reanimate" or render the (imagined) psyche of the long-dead playwright stunningly "alive" through these mechanisms, and to "save, save" (*Lenz* 75) the misunderstood writer from the lingering shadow of his literary contemporaries' misconceptions, just as the fictionalized Lenz "animates" natural phenomena and attempts to "save" and "resurrect" human others in the fragment's diegesis.[34] That is, Büchner's fragment is a self-reflexive allegory of the relations of resurrective empathy, both interpersonal and *Einfühlung*, to aesthetics: both "knowing through the senses" and the formal mechanisms of literary art.

Of course, all narrative empathy, or audiences' empathy with fictional characters—a subspecies of interpersonal empathy, and, when the characters are based on once-living people, a way of completing a text's resurrection of the dead—takes place by means of form. Without the world-creating words, temporal flow, and synchronic-diachronic arrangements of text on the page or narrative in the ear, all of which are formal structures or "events" (or parts of formal structures or events), there would be no fictional or docufictional characters to empathize *with*. What is striking about *Lenz*, however, is the especially high degree to which the text's famed elicitation of narrative empathy is mobilized by form: by processes, largely pioneered by Büchner himself, that conspicuously announce themselves as "formal." Thus, even outside those moments when Büchner's narrative anticipates or proleptically resonates with Vischer's later understanding of *aesthetic* empathy (with its emphasis on forms and objects), *interpersonal* empathy in *Lenz* also works largely in terms of form—and in a manner that likewise evokes the

---

34. On the importance of the resurrection motif to Büchner, see Reddick, *Georg Büchner* 28; Müller-Sievers, *Desorientierung* 101; and Sieburth, afterword 168. On Büchner's "salvation" of Lenz from the incomprehension and hostility of his contemporaries, including Goethe, see Neuhuber 85–86.

sorts of anxieties that will be implicit in Vischer's concept of *Einfühlung* itself.

Critics have long noted the two most arresting formal features of *Lenz*: its free-floating or unlocalizable narrative voice and its pervasive use of unattributed citations, largely from Oberlin. As Müller-Sievers writes, the use of these formal techniques renders us unable to answer the question "Who speaks?", resulting in a "complete ... disorientation of narrative perspectives and speech axes in *Lenz*" (*Desorientierung* 11). In Lenz's opening walk through the mountains, for example, Büchner's narrative voice—an unprecedented blend of authorial narration, "psycho-narration," and *erlebte Rede*, frequently regarded as the first instance of free indirect discourse in European literary history—"feels itself into" *Lenz feeling himself into* the "so sluggish, so clumsy" fog, bringing readers uncannily close to the suffering wanderer's experience (or, more accurately, creating this experience through an act of poiesis, establishing it by means of self-projection).[35] Here, as Müller-Sievers writes, "at no time can we be sure as readers whether we are reading the description of a landscape or the echo of a landscape in Lenz's disordered mind" (*Desorientierung* 155). Or, as David Horton puts it, it is nearly impossible to "distinguish between free indirect discourse and omniscient, authorial ... analysis," raising the "basic question" of "from whose perspective we are experiencing the processes of the text" (35, 42). In a fusion of feeling and form, Büchner's intersubjective empathy with the historical Lenz, the fictionalized Lenz's *rhetorically* created *Einfühlung* into the physical forms of the mountain scene, and our narrative empathy with the textual Lenz (and with *his Einfühlung*) *become one* through the formal narrative techniques of the text—its voice.

Unattributed citations function similarly in the narrative, scrambling and fusing the text's loci of enunciation and experience. As Müller-Sievers writes, "Fundamentally, there hovers over every sentence, every word in Büchner the suspicion that it may not be by

---

35. On "psycho-narration" as a narrator's direct stating of a fictional character's conscious or unconscious feelings, see Dorrit Cohn, *Transparent Minds*. Cohn's term for *erlebte Rede* or free indirect discourse is "narrated monologue."

him" (*Desorientierung* 8). And, although Müller-Sievers cautions against what he sees as too-easy comparisons that frequently read Büchner's citational technique in terms of his skill as a dissector without doing enough to justify this association with science (*Science* 69), it is difficult not to see Büchner's formal practice of splicing and interweaving source texts—"creating history for a second time," as he wrote to his parents in 1835 ("An die Eltern" ["Letter to His Parents"] 244)—as a sort of "resurrection work" that resonates with the uncanny "laboratory reanimation" we discovered in some of Vischer's descriptions of *Einfühlung*: "[Scanning] sets out to analyze the forms dialectically (by separating and reconnecting the elements). . . . Its movement . . . is accompanied by an impelling animation of the dead phenomenon, a rhythmic enlivening and revitalization of it. . . . To chaotic 'Being' I called 'Become!'—and my Summons brought Light and behold, it was Good" (94). Büchner assembles and reanimates the doppelgänger of history through the cutting, dismembering, and suturing of sources, a suggestively appropriate activity for a poet-anatomist who grew up in the shadow of Darmstadt's Castle Frankenstein.[36] Müller-Sievers, too, sees Büchner as a sort of "resurrection man"—here, not a body snatcher who supplies exhumed corpses for dissection but a writer who causes figures from the past to "rise again" (*auferstehen*) through citation (*Desorientierung* 101). Most significant, however, is perhaps the way the compositional or form-strategy of Büchner's unmarked citations might, like his use of free indirect discourse, be reframed in terms of empathy. The citations, seamlessly interwoven into Büchner's own narration without quotation marks so that it is impossible to tell where a given voice or experience begins or ends, are another way one thing, feeling, or form is taken into or "uncannily" turns into—"is mysteriously transplanted and magically transformed into"—another.

---

36. The historical Castle Frankenstein is located on the outskirts of Büchner's home city of Darmstadt. The novel *Frankenstein* did not appear in German until Heinz Widtmann's 1912 translation. It is unclear whether Büchner knew Shelley's text and, if so, whether he encountered it in one of its English editions (1818 and 1831) or, perhaps more likely, in its 1821 French translation.

Two of the most intriguing readings of form in *Lenz* are provided by Müller-Sievers and Yvonne Wübben. As Wübben points out, in the nineteenth century, Büchner was viewed primarily not as a literary writer but as the author of the anatomical dissertation *Mémoire sur le Système nerveux du Barbeau* (111); correspondingly, Müller-Sievers sees Büchner's scientific writing, particularly the relation of form to content in the *Mémoire*'s analysis of the nervous system of the barbel, as paradigmatic for what happens in Büchner's writing overall (*Desorientierung* 9). Müller-Sievers undertakes a deconstructive reading of Büchner's dissertation, with its frequently noted division into a "descriptive part" and a "philosophical part." The descriptive part ostensibly strives toward a synchronic or spatial understanding of the barbel's nervous system, while the philosophical part focuses on the nerves' evolution through time; both parts ideally work together to provide a holistic account of the fish's neuroanatomical development.[37] As Müller-Sievers argues, on its surface, the *Mémoire* attempts to present the barbel's nervous system as an example of the sort of *naturphilosophische* thinking championed by Goethe and by Büchner's Zurich benefactor Lorenz Oken, including the notion that the animal's skull is a "metamorphosis" of its "lower" vertebrae along a "temporal axis of growth and being" (*Science* 76–78). However, the attempt to present a unified picture of the fish's development by means of the supposedly corresponding descriptive and philosophical sections of the dissertation fails. The two sections are in fact "incompatible" (*Science* 78), and both must rely on a quasi-Derridean supplement to make sense: "In the descriptive half, the [synchronic] space of anatomical presentation must be oriented through [diachronic] writing, while in the interpretative section the temporal [diachronic] concept of the Ur-type [of the vertebrae or nerves] must be presented as a table—that is, in a spatial-schematic [synchronic, atemporal] form"

---

37. The exact relations of synchronic (paradigmatic) vs. diachronic (syntagmatic) processes vis-à-vis the descriptive and philosophical parts of Büchner's dissertation seem to vary or perhaps reverse poles over the course of different versions of Müller-Sievers's presentation of his reading (cf. *Science* 83–87 and *Desorientierug* 10, 93–99); the overarching conclusions of the analyses remain the same.

(*Science* 87). This internal fracturing in the formal structure of Büchner's presentation unintentionally—or perhaps intentionally—destroys the *naturphilosophische* idea of holism the *Mémoire* had at first glance seemed to promote: "The ideal of an identity between description and interpretation, which *Naturphilosophie* had proclaimed against 'mechanistic' science, is shattered in Büchner's text"; "Whether this is a passive cracking or an active destruction must remain undecided" (*Science* 87).

For our purposes, perhaps the most significant conclusion Müller-Sievers draws from what he sees as the collapse of synchronic and diachronic processes in Büchner's science—the collapse, that is, of Saussure's paradigmatic and syntagmatic axes or of Jakobson's metaphoric and metonymic poles into each other—is that the collapse illuminates or calls for the emergence of a new tropic strategy or element of *form* in Büchner, "something like metonymic metaphors and metaphoric metonymies" (*Science* 88).[38] This form is the *quotation*, both metaphor and metonymy at once. As Müller-Sievers explains, "Understood literally, citation is a metaphor, indeed in a way metaphor's material primal form, to the extent that in citation, a block of existent text is transferred into a different context; [but] taken metaphorically, citation is a metonymy in Jakobson's sense, insofar as it is integrated into the syntagm of the guest text" (*Desorientierung* 99). This combined metaphoric-metonymic logic of the quotation becomes the driving logic of Büchner's literary project overall, as well as its chief formal feature and *ductus* (*Science* 88; *Desorientierung* 97–107).

Müller-Sievers interprets the *Mémoire*'s failure of holism and the rise of the quotation form in Büchner as consequences both of the breakdown of the Romantic belief in the unity of nature and metaphor (*Science* 88) and of the larger problem of the search for literal and figurative "orientation" that had obsessed eighteenth- and nineteenth-century maritime navigation, science, and philosophy (*Desorientierung* 10–11); in this context, Büchner's "disorienting" use of unattributed citations qua form reflects not only his inability to orient himself in existing scientific, literary, and philosophical

---

38. Cf. Saussure 837–40 and Jakobson 1074–78.

paradigms but also the "possibility that [he] may joyously affirm a language freed from the bonds of nature and from the compulsion toward representation" (*Science* 89). However, as I suggested earlier, Büchner's "disorientation" might just as plausibly be read as an anticipation of the uncanny stakes of aesthetic empathy: Müller-Sievers's account of "metonymic metaphors and metaphoric metonymies," too, evokes the transformations, transplantations, and exchanges, as well as the ultimate collapse of self-other binaries, that will characterize and haunt Vischer's later formulation of *Einfühlung*.

Wübben links her discussion of form in *Lenz* more directly to feeling and empathy. Drawing on a tradition that goes back at least as far as Mayer-Gross, whose phenomenological readings understood both the "empathy" (*Einfühlungsfähigkeit*) and the "objectivity" of *Lenz*'s depiction of mental illness in terms of the text's "aesthetic form," especially the fragment's "breathless succession of sentences and words" (Mayer-Gross 890; Wübben 266), Wübben analyzes the correspondence between the increasing incidents of parataxis in Büchner's narrative and the acceleration or worsening of Lenz's illness: "The text already performs several psychopathological aspects, such as the compulsion to keep moving, at the level of its sentences. Additionally, the crisis announces itself through the frequent appearance of symptoms—in terms of rhetoric, through repetitions" (Wübben 40–41). As Wübben points out, *Lenz* thus follows the pattern of proto-psychiatric textbooks of Büchner's day, at least some of which also mirrored the course of the illnesses they described through repetition, parataxis, and other formal devices (41–43). Most important, perhaps, is the merger of feeling—interpersonal and aesthetic empathy—with form: "feeling ourselves" as readers into Lenz's experience by means of the bodily, mental, and affective states provoked by the narrative's racing sentences and images of manic motion, so that we too, like Lenz, are compelled, at least in our minds, to "jump around madly" (Wübben 86–87). Indeed, in a section of Mayer-Gross's 1921 remarks on *Lenz* that Wübben does not discuss in detail, Mayer-Gross even exhorts readers to "read [*Lenz*] aloud" (*laut . . . lesen*) because this bodily, respiratory, and sonic engagement with (or *Einfühlung* into) the text's *form*—its "breathless succession of sentences and words"—will best allow readers to "uncannily" (*unheimlich*) see *in that form itself* the "breakdown of a person" (890).[39] *Lenz*'s other numerous depictions of extreme mental suffering through psycho-narration and free indirect discourse have a similar effect: The "virtual" Lenz, manifested as textual form, becomes the *real* cause of readers' distress. As Julian Schmidt, one of the most well-known nineteenth-century theorists of German realism, already wrote in an 1851 review of Büchner's posthumous work, *Lenz* so effectively places the reader into the "tormented soul" of its protagonist that "our own world spins in a fever-dream" (qtd. in Reuchlein 91). Or, as Müller-Sievers puts it, reading *Lenz* becomes, through linguistic form, "an experience of insanity" (*Desorientierung* 149).

In an analysis that resonates with earlier concerns of this chapter, Wübben ties the fictionalized Lenz's compulsive behaviors to the narrative's grammatical form, particularly the text's use of the pronoun *es*, which frequently "takes over" the subject position of Büchner's sentences (84–87). As Wübben argues, formulations such as "es drängte ihm in der Brust" (he felt a tightening in his chest) (*Lenz* 2–3) position Lenz as himself "taken over" by impersonal forces, his madness an effect of what she calls "active nature" (*wirkende Natur*) (84), or nature as a controlling outside agency: "The world seems . . . to work in [Lenz] (not on him), so that we get the impression he would hardly be able to free himself from it and establish a difference between his interior and the world" (85). This "active nature," which Wübben links to vitalist thinking (90), represents a sort of malevolent or demonic *Naturphilosophie*: a "conflation of world and self" in which Lenz is "imprisoned" (*verhaftet*) or "unfree" (85). Like the overwhelming energy of the world that disorders the cranial nerves in my earlier discussion of Büchner's "Über Schädelnerven," Wübben's "active nature" deranges Lenz, resulting in "compulsive activity not channeled through the will" (Wübben 87). And although Wübben understands the disordering union of "active nature" and "madness" as replacing earlier models that conceived of insanity as possession (90), we might in fact

---

39. In this, Mayer-Gross resonates with the conception of *Einfühlung* developed by Vernon Lee, which I discuss in chapter 2.

read this union as suggesting just that sort of possession we have previously identified as one of the uncanny, bidirectional features of Vischer's *Einfühlung*—the kind of possession represented most explicitly in *Über das optische Formgefühl* by Vischer's description of the devil "tak[ing] possession of a corpse" outside any possible questions of will, "caus[ing] it to behave as if alive" (106). This is another way *Lenz* anticipates the covert anxieties of the *Einfühlung* Vischer overtly promotes. But in what way is Lenz a "corpse"? Let us investigate this question by turning to *Lenz*'s simultaneously triumphant, catastrophic, and uncanny rhetoric of resurrection, as well as to the relation of this rhetoric to art. This constellation opens a window onto the stakes of empathy and aesthetics, and aesthetic empathy, in a materialist age—and onto our concluding discussion of Vischer's strange, "demonic" allegory of *Einfühlung* as the devil's reanimation of the "corpse of a beautiful girl recently hanged."

"What I Demand in All Things Is Life," or, Resurrection on Demand

"What I demand in all things is life, the potentiality of existence," Lenz declares at the beginning of the *Kunstgespräch* (29). The famous conversation about art, largely invented by Büchner himself and sometimes viewed as the first programmatic statement of German realist aesthetics, is, underscoring its importance, the longest single scene in the narrative; in it, Lenz develops a theory of art many critics have taken as ventriloquizing Büchner's own.[40] As Lenz-cum-Büchner explains,

> The writers who were purported to offer up reality had no idea of what it was, even though they were more bearable than those who wanted to transfigure [*verklären*] it.... The good Lord has without a doubt made the world as it should be and there is no way we can scratch together anything better, our sole goal should be to imitate [*nachzuschaffen*] him

---

40. See, for example, Holub 38 on the *Kunstgespräch* as the possible beginning of German realist aesthetics and Heinz-Dieter Weber 73–74 on Lenz as a mouthpiece of Büchner's own aesthetic principles in the conversation.

in a small way.... We need not then ask whether it be beautiful or ugly, the feeling that whatever's been created possesses life outweighs the two and should be the sole criterion in matters of art. (28–29)

On its surface, the *Kunstgespräch* announces "life" as its primary value. If this is indeed the dawn of realism, the text seems preemptively to reject or leapfrog past the kind of "transfiguration" (*Verklärung*) that will come to dominate German poetic realist practice later in the century, arguing instead for a rawer mimesis of the living world.[41] For Lenz, the forms of nature do not appear to be "found wanting," as Vischer ominously writes in *Über das optische Formgefühl* (117), nor does artistic beauty stand, as Hegel maintained, "higher than life" (Hegel 4). Indeed, even the mimesis that Lenz calls for, as critics have pointed out, is not a "naïve realism" or passive reproduction, like Vischer's "mere" photographic "seeing" (*Sehen*).[42] Rather, Lenz's proposed "imitation" or *Nachschaffen* exhorts us not simply to copy the world but, echoing the sense of the originary biblical creation—"Am Anfang schuf Gott Himmel und Erde" (In the beginning God created the heavens and the earth)—to *create (life) after* "the good Lord" (*ihm nachzuschaffen*). This "Nach-Schaffen" is not only temporal (*nach*, "after") but *analogical*, to "create after" in the sense of "to follow the example of" or "to act in the manner of": in short, to emulate. In this way, an artist might arrive at what Anna Guillemin calls "vitality" (141)—the creation of aesthetic figures that "surge" and "swell" with "muscle" and "pulse," as Büchner's Lenz puts it (33)—or, as Sarah Kofman writes in a different context, imitation not of nature alone, as in traditional conceptions of mimesis, but of *nature's creative force*, the "divine gift ... made by nature itself of its own power to create": what Aristotle called "productive," rather than "reproductive," mimesis ("Resemblance" 222).

It is unsurprising, then, that resurrection forms the backbone of the *Kunstgespräch*. In the concluding part of the conversation, Lenz famously discusses two Dutch paintings he claims "make nature so

---

41. On poetic realism and transfiguration, see for example Holub 195–201.
42. On Lenz's aesthetics as different from naïve realism, see Walker, "Two Realisms" 102.

utterly real to [him]" (33): a version of the disciples' recognition of the risen Christ most scholars take to be Carel van Savoy's *Christ and the Disciples at Emmaus* (ca. 1650, a painting Büchner knew well from his visits to the Großherzogliches Museum in Darmstadt) and a second painting of a woman sitting at her window, holding an improvised church service at home.[43] Lenz's unelaborated comment that "only" these two paintings "made the same impression on [him] as the New Testament" (33–35), as if the philosophical or artistic need for an impression "like that of the New Testament" were somehow required or self-evident, already places the *Kunstgespräch* in the general frame of the resurrection problematic. The Savoy painting clearly depicts the aftermath of the Western world's most triumphant resurrection; the second painting, as Guillemin points out, represents the historical consequence, ongoing effect, or "devotional reenactment in . . . memory" of the first (147), thus confirming the continued existence of the resurrective lineage. Lenz-cum-Büchner even "resurrects" Savoy's painting itself, commanding it to rise in an aesthetic rebirth within the larger narrative. As scholars have noted, Lenz's discussion of *Christ and the Disciples* significantly exceeds the bounds of traditional ekphrasis. In describing the canvas, Lenz not only transforms its synchronic surface into active, temporal narrative: He also makes substantial changes both to Savoy's image and to its textual source, the biblical account in Luke 24:13–32.[44] When Lenz begins his discussion of the painting by describing *written* text ("When one reads of how the disciples went forth, all of nature immediately lies within these few words," 35), we might assume he is simply summarizing the gospel narrative before coming to the image proper. However, he soon mentions a "solid red streak on the horizon" (35) that appears neither in Savoy's picture—an interior scene—nor in Luke 24. Rather than "passively" mimetic, ekphrastic reproduction, we find active "re-creation" of both of Lenz's textual sources in terms of the com-

---

43. On Savoy's *Christ and the Disciples at Emmaus* (also known in English as *Supper at Emmaus*) as a model for the first painting Lenz describes, see Neuhuber 65; Viëtor 168; and Sieburth, notes 156. On Büchner's likely repeated and "intensive" viewing of the Savoy painting in Darmstadt, see Pörnbacher et al. 547n145.

44. See for example Holub 57–59 and Neuhuber 65–66.

mon "impression" they made on him. Lenz's discussion of the paintings, and of *Christ and the Disciples* in particular, becomes a self-reflexive allegory of the resurrective potential of art, an "emblem" of the (re-)creative project shared by the text, its protagonist, and its author. In what we might call the *text's* imitatio Christi, the narrative qua artwork "sees itself" as the compassionate and life-bestowing Christ, recognizing its own power to resurrect Lenz by means of a complex web of intersubjective and aesthetic—that is, formally mediated—empathy.

This celebration of successful resurrection through empathic art, however, is not as straightforward as it seems. Rather, like Vischer's *Einfühlung*, it is shot through by multiple anxieties. Already the opening of the *Kunstgespräch* calls the efficacy of the resurrective model of art into question. In a frequently discussed passage, Lenz describes having come upon two peasant girls sitting on a rock, one helping the other put up her hair. Moved by the scene's "life," Lenz remarks, "One wishes one were a Medusa's head in order to turn a group like this into stone and call everybody over to have a look" (31). As Robert Holub points out in an influential reading of the scene's deathly implications for aesthetics, "Capturing life in art unavoidably involves a removal of art from life because the nature of aesthetic reproduction is representation in lifeless appearances. . . . The artist, in endeavoring to imitate God, ends up as his antipode: whereas the Lord supposedly breathed life into humankind, the artist, like the Medusa, must make life cease. The second creation is simultaneously the destruction of the first creation. Imitation turns into annihilation" (55–56). Here, unlike in Shaftesbury's famous image of the artist as a "second Maker . . . under Jove" (Shaftesbury 93), the aesthetic gaze becomes, as in the final chapter of *Über das optische Formgefühl*, an act of violence, the artist an anti-Pygmalion.

Art's turning life into death is not the only anxiety that haunts the *Kunstgespräch*'s deployment of resurrection, as a closer look at the role of Savoy's painting in Büchner's narrative reveals. As Lenz part describes, part invents, and part supplements *Christ and the Disciples* in his own gloss on the biblical story, "Shadowy night is falling, a solid red streak on the horizon, the road half in darkness, a stranger [Christ] approaches [the disciples], they talk, he breaks bread, in their simple humanity they recognize who he is and the divine suffering in his features speaks to them distinctly" (35). Similarly, as recounted by Büchner's narrator, Lenz's arrival at Oberlin's parsonage at the beginning of the text conspicuously evokes the "plot," imagery, cadences, and tone of Lenz's narrativization of the painting several pages later. As in Lenz's description of Christ's arrival in Emmaus, Lenz's own entry into Waldbach unfolds in dreamily dissociative, elision-filled parataxis (7–9). Like Christ, Lenz walks as a "stranger" through the darkness and joins others at a table; like Christ, he is first taken for someone else ("[Oberlin] took him to be a journeyman"); finally, he, too, is "recognized" (9). As in Savoy's image, "curls of . . . hair [fall] around" his face, and, mirroring Lenz's description of the painting, the "suffering" in his *own* features—here, the twitching of his eyes and mouth—also implicitly "speaks distinctly" to those whom he joins (9). In a striking instance of what I have called the confusion of the origin, vector, and locus of experience, both Savoy's painting and Lenz's description of it "propagate backward in time" through the text to shape, colonize, or form a template for the narrator's own depiction of Lenz—or have preexisted this depiction to begin with.[45] Put otherwise, Büchner creates an "art-Lenz" that already imitates other art: The figure's imitatio Christi is quite literal (or quite literally figural). As in Vischer's metaphorical and temporal subordination of the bodily act of "scanning" to the aesthetic modes of sketching and sculpting, *art*, not "nature" or "life," is revealed to have been the hidden object, origin, and model of the resurrection allegory from the start. The second painting about the home church service confirms this model: Lenz's description of the fictional canvas either "allude[s] to the genre paintings of Nicolaes Maes" (Sieburth, notes 156) or, as the editors of the Münchner Ausgabe of Büchner's complete works argue, summarizes a scene from Ludwig Tieck's 1800 *Kunstmärchen* "Leben und Tod des kleinen Rotkäppchens" ("Life and Death of Little Red Riding Hood") (Pörnbacher et al. 547n146). Even Müller-Sievers's unique reading of the *Kunstgespräch*'s paint-

---

45. On the resemblance of *Lenz*'s initial depiction of the lighting of Waldbach to a painting, see also William Collins Donahue 118.

ings, which attempts to break out of the traditional scholarly framing of the scene in terms of the tension between life and death (*Desorientierung* 164), might be understood in terms of the model of the primacy of art, and, especially, of art's material basis—its "matter." As Müller-Sievers argues, Dutch Baroque painting, with its focus on physical objects and on the materiality of paint, "in a way paints painting itself" (169); it therefore, I would argue, discovers *art*—and art's material substrate—as its *arché*. Whether this substrate or "matter" is living or dead must concern us here.

As Lenz declares in the *Kunstgespräch*, "What I demand in all things is life, the potentiality of existence, and that's that; we need not then ask whether it be beautiful or ugly, the feeling that whatever's been created possesses life outweighs the two" (29). His tone anticipates the veiled desperation of *Einfühlung*'s projection of "life" into inanimate form. As Vischer writes, "What are space and time to me?.... What are all those forms to me through which the red blood of life does not flow?.... Where there is no life—precisely there do I miss it.... Yes, we miss red-blooded life, and precisely because we miss it, we imagine the dead form as living" (104). This is less a projection than a *willing* of vitality, followed by the maniacal cry "It's alive!"—what we might, modifying Aristotle, call not "productive" but *frantic* (or Frankensteinian) mimesis. Yet Lenz's demand for life "in all things" quickly becomes acceptance of the more tentative and subjective "feeling that whatever's been created possesses life" and even of the entirely *subjunctive* "potentiality of existence" (*Möglichkeit des Daseins*) (28–29)—an ambiguous formulation that suggests not only the potential inherent *in* "existence" but also the possibility that something *could*, but has *not yet* (and perhaps may never), come into being, as if existence itself did not quite exist. And, as Lenz's language makes clear, this slippage into ambiguity and reduced expectations regarding "life" is not limited to art but encompasses the *entirety of existence*, including the natural world: "in *all* things"; "*whatever's* been created." That is, the *Kunstgespräch* communicates not only an aesthetic but also a larger historical and existential anxiety. If *Lenz* explores what it means for art to attempt to resurrect the dead, then the narrative's rhetorical unconscious also raises the more unsettling question of whether, in a soon-to-be post-vitalist, increasingly materialist age, art is perhaps the only thing left "alive." Put otherwise, is there evidence of life outside the artistic act?

The *Kunstgespräch* underlines this anxiety, not in the "Medusa's head" passage about art's turning life into stone, but in inverse passages about *life itself being art*, somehow already dead. As Lenz states, "The writers and painters I prefer are those who make nature so utterly real to me" (*Der Dichter und Bildende ist mir der Liebste, der mir die Natur am Wirklichsten gibt*) (32–33). His superlative formulation ("am Wirklich*sten*," "in the *most* real way") raises the question of how a "second maker," a writer or painter, can "give nature" (*die Natur geben*) in a way that is "more real" than the way nature is already "given"—and why Lenz needs nature to be "made utterly real to him" in the first place. Why, that is, is "real" nature in need of being "made real"? Despite Lenz's repeated declarations of belief in the primacy of "life" and its metonym, "nature," one wonders if the text's focus on the "arts" of resurrection, both literal and figurative, in fact suggests a *lack of faith* in life: the life of the natural world. That is, the arts of resurrection are themselves *made necessary* by the prior "given" of a lifeless object-world, a "dead nature" that, as Vischer will put it in *Über das optische Formgefühl*, is "always found wanting" (117) after all. When Lenz laments, "Now so dead," "dead! Dead!" (51), he is referring diegetically to his feelings; however, in the light of Büchner's own liminal position between *Naturphilosophie* and materialism and of the related scientific divisions that will frame Vischer's work, it is also this death of nature he laments. This is a world in need of a second breath or aesthetic supplement to "(re)animate" it, to "project life into the lifeless form" or—more even than Lenz's desire to "have a soul for stones" (*Lenz* 27)—to (re)equip stones with souls. *Einfühlung*, one of the "arts of resurrection," as practiced in advance by Lenz and later formulated by Vischer, is this supplement. It is also, however, as Lenz's anguish reminds us, inseparable from the materialist trauma of the dead world. Sometimes, there is no resurrection on demand, or resurrection is traversed by uncanny anxieties and ambivalences. Lenz's spectacular and traumatic failure to resurrect the dead girl—an event that, significantly, secures his descent into "atheism" (55)—is the uncanny double of the *Kunstgespräch*'s apparent celebration of "successful" resurrection.

The Materialist Unconscious, or, Empathy with the Devil

In an evolving zone of the epistemic divergence, forking, or bifurcation of mid-nineteenth-century German science that will shape the intellectual context of the realist age, resurrection and its empathic underpinnings split in, and *as*, Büchner's text—or, perhaps better, are superimposed onto each other, presenting two versions of the same text as seen from different angles. Indexing both transcendent victory and traumatic catastrophe, their figures are Savoy's risen Christ on the one hand—an allegory of Büchner's "risen" or "successfully" resurrected Lenz—and the narrative's "unrisen" dead girl on the other. Despite the demand for "life in all things," the girl, like other "things" in the post-vitalist object-world, remains stubbornly dead: for we are living in a material world, and she is a material girl. Unlike in Vischer's account of the dialectics of scanning, Lenz's summons to "Arise and walk!" (*Lenz* 53) does not "bring light," and behold, it is *not* good (cf. Vischer 94). As we have seen, the failed resurrection turns Lenz into *Satan*—the protagonist of Vischer's own allegory of *Einfühlung*'s reanimation of a dead girl almost forty years later.

Lenz's failure to raise the girl points to more than just *Büchner's* possible anxiety, latent in the scene, about the potential limits of his own artistic powers. Rather, the failure is the shadow of Büchner's *successful* revival of the dead Lenz, the penumbra cast by the ambivalent aura of resurrection in a secular, materialist age. As the *Kunstgespräch* shows, even successfully resurrective art, as well as the dream of art as "realer" life—perhaps especially the dream of art as realer life—is predicated on death. Perhaps even more significantly, however, the failed resurrection haunts the text as the uncanny shadow of anxiety—and guilt—thrown by the narrative's projects of empathic reanimation and projective *Einfühlung*: the anxiety and guilt, that is, of "success;" of the empathic, aesthetic, and revivifying gaze's having indeed become, in a materialist world, "divine." As Oberlin warns Lenz, to outdo Christ is "blasphemy" (75). Lenz's atheism immediately following the failed resurrection attempt might itself be read not only as his tacit acknowledgment of the "triumph" of a "cold and imperturbable" materialism ("A song of hell triumphant was in his breast"; "He made his way cold and imperturbable through the uncanny darkness," 53, 55) but also as his (self-)punishment for having outlived nature's god.

Thus we find in the text the longing for a living world and the fear that there is only a dead one: one that can only "return," if at all, as the product of necromantic "arts" whose own status is ambivalent. As Kofman writes in "The Melancholy of Art," the "fascination produced by the uncanniness of art is the same fascination that is provoked by the corpse" (209). Accordingly, not only in the figure of Lenz but also in Büchner's figuration of artistic activity overall and Vischer's later construction of the universal aesthetic-empathic observer, we find a fragmented subject: one simultaneously encouraged to cocreate "nature" or the world, frightened by the onus of assuming this godlike role, and troubled by the uncanny command to resurrect "dead material" (Vischer 106), to reanimate a nature seen as dead. Viewed in this context, *Lenz*'s successful resurrections might, paradoxically, be uncannier than its unsuccessful one. Put otherwise, the twin poles of the bifurcation I have outlined—Savoy/Büchner as Christ, Lenz as "Satan"—reveal themselves to be in some sense one. The character Lenz's resurrection attempt fails because it is "demonic," but the narrative *Lenz*'s resurrection attempts are demonic *insofar as they succeed*.[46] To understand this paradox, let us turn in conclusion to that other demonically successful resurrection from later in the materialist age: the devil's forced or violent reanimation of the hanged girl in *Über das optische Formgefühl*—the unconscious, as it were, of Vischer's conceptualization of *Einfühlung*.

Lenz's attempt to raise the dead girl might be seen as a philosophical forerunner for, or anticipatory interpretive comment on, the

---

46. On the relation of Lenz's failed resurrection attempt to the "demonic," see also Holub 50.

more elaborate and uncanny resurrection scene from Vischer's central "Feeling and Emotion" chapter: the dancing skeletons, walking dead, and demonically reanimated corpse of a "beautiful girl recently hanged" (or, to translate Vischer's German literally, "the beautiful corpse of a hanged girl" [*die schöne Leiche eines gehenkten Mädchens*]). As Vischer writes of *Einfühlung*, "We are ... reminded ... of stories of the spontaneous resurrection of a corpse [*die unwillkürliche Wiederbelebung eines Leichnams*, literally the "involuntary" or "automatic re-animation of a corpse"] and the many legends that tell of skeletons engaged in nocturnal dances and the dead walking abroad. In medieval legends the devil takes possession of a corpse and causes it to behave as if alive—for instance, the tale of a Parisian nobleman whom the devil seduced by animating the corpse of a beautiful girl recently hanged [*der schönen Leiche eines gehenkten Mädchens*]" (106, *Formegefühl* 23).

The passage is a parable of the functioning, stakes, and ambiguity of aesthetic empathy in a time of shifting conceptions of nature. The description, with its crowning image of the reanimated hanged girl, emerges from Vischer's discussion of empathic projection and kinesthetic imagination, two fundamental activities of *Einfühlung* (exemplified in the paragraph preceding the resurrection scene by the previously discussed cliff that "seems to lunge out" at us "as if affected by a passion," its "static form ... empathetically felt as if it could move freely" [105]). Vischer frames the resurrection scene by distinguishing between "organic" and "inorganic nature" and thus, presumably, between the living and the dead (106). However, the distinction he draws soon collapses, and not, as in *Naturphilosophie*, in favor of the universally living. Vischer draws on an example from Theocritus—the Greek poet's comparison of a "lion's leap to a piece of wood under tension that 'slips from the wheelwright's grip and whizzes through the air'"—both to reaffirm the difference between organic and inorganic nature and to demonstrate how the latter can serve as a metaphor for the former (106). The motion of the piece of wood, Vischer writes, is "so strongly and convincingly felt" (*mitgefühlt*) that it appears "as something endowed with a soul"; it is therefore "easy" (*um so leichter*) for Theocritus to use it as an image for the lion's "path and speed of movement"—as Vischer puts it, "the expression of a particular [living] organ" (*Organäusserung*) (106, *Formgefühl* 23, translation modified).[47] The metaphor, however, is just an expedient supplement: Theocritus, Vischer assures us, is "not setting inorganic nature above organic nature" (106).

Beyond its dizzying "hall of metaphors" effect, or the adoption of Theocritus's metaphor as itself a metaphor for *Einfühlung*, Vischer's rhetoric introduces first a vertiginous slippage between the organic and the inorganic, then an insistent slide toward death. The vehicle of Theocritus's metaphor already complicates the border Vischer attempts to maintain: As part of a fallen tree, wood is at once organic *and* dead. And although Vischer's description of the wood's movement as "exclusively mechanical and blind" (106) seems to wish to solidify the plank's position on the side of death, his language conspicuously evokes the sorts of "automatic" actions we have repeatedly linked with the uncanny, and thus with the *inability* to differentiate between the living and the dead. Approaching the ambiguity from the other side, Vischer's insistence that the motion of the "inorganic" wood provides a fitting metaphor for organic action (the lion's leap) places death back in the lead: As in Lenz's *Kunstgespräch*, dead nature, expressed in the likewise "dead" form of Medusa-frozen art (metaphor), is better suited to "signifying" (*Bezeichnung*) (23) the lion's movements than the actual actions of the living thing itself. The supplement, that is, has replaced the thing. Finally, Vischer seems to understand both inorganic *and* organic nature as "soulless"—that is, dead at the core. "The further we descend into nature," he writes, "the coarser it becomes, and the more easily it can be symbolized. Its forms are patchwork—dead material" (106). Here, the distinction between "organic" and "inorganic," "living" and "dead" nature, disappears, and, along with it, apparently the

---

47. Mallgrave and Ikonomou translate loosely here when they write that the "mechanical and blind movements" of the wood may "later serve as something endowed with a soul, the more so the more closely they resemble a particular organ" (106). Vischer's passage should read that the wood's "forms of motion, ... as something already endowed with a soul, can all the more easily serve later to more precisely signify the particular expression of an organ" (*dass [die Bewegungsformen] nachträglich als etwas bereits Beseeltes um so leichter zur näheren Bezeichnung einer specialen Organäusserung dienen können*) (*Formgefühl* 23).

presumption of a salient difference between the two: Vischer uses only the singular term "nature," now seen as "patchwork, dead material." Despite Vischer's claim that Theocritus does not "set inorganic nature above organic nature," the logic of Vischer's own presentation does just that: As so often in *Über das optische Formgefühl* and *Lenz*, "living" nature is teleologically subordinated to the dead, "resurrected" nature from which the images used to figure the living are drawn. As Vischer contends, "After I have... dissipated my strength on nature, it can now serve as a resurrected symbol for everything organic" (106)—or, to render the original more faithfully, "After I have... dissipated my strength on nature, it can now, *as a resurrected thing* or *as resurrected nature [als eine auferweckte] provide similes for everything organic [Gleichnisse für alles Organische abgeben]*" (*Formgefühl* 23). And, of course, to be resurrected, something must first be dead—or perhaps killed.

The reanimated corpse of the "beautiful girl recently hanged" is the image of this dead, resurrected nature, as well as this nature itself. To rephrase Nietzsche, writing in *The Gay Science* not quite ten years after *Über das optische Formgefühl*, nature is dead, and we have killed it—and resurrected it (in, and as, a discourse suited to a materialist age).[48] As in Vischer's descriptions of Theocritus's flying wood and his discussions of *Einfühlung*'s strange, foreboding "life of its own" (*eigenartiges Leben*) (108, *Formgefühl* 27), the girl's resurrection as "symbol" renders her an uncanny set of automatic processes, of "mechanical and blind movements" that "behave as if alive"—"die unwillkürliche Wiederbelebung eines Leichnams," the "involuntary" or "automatic re-animation of a corpse" (106), the corporeal automaton, the art-machine. Here, the scene's empathically animating eye becomes a violent intervention, takeover, or assault that suggests rape or sexual violation—the devil's forceful appropriation of the girl's body—and that ends with a second image of sexualized violence: the demonic seduction of the observer. Indeed, the empathic-aesthetic gaze explicitly evokes necromancy, necrophilia, and the work of reanimation as a blasphemous, diabolical, or desecrating force—the empath-artist not as God but as

---

48. Cf. the "God is dead" passages of *The Gay Science* (181–82).

devil, Lenz's "Satan": "Devils enter into a corpse and cause it to behave like a living being" (*Teufel [fahren] in eine Leiche und [lassen] sie [sich] gleich einem Lebenden benehmen*); "the devil seduces a nobleman in the beautiful corpse of a hanged girl" (*der Teufel [verführt einen Edelmann] in der schönen Leiche eines gehenkten Mädchens*) (106, *Formgefühl* 23, my translation).

The anxiety, guilt, and desire of this imaginary are articulated through a series of uncanny doublings, ambiguities, and overdeterminations. The scene is both violently and erotically charged, but it is disturbingly difficult to assign or limit either the violent or the erotic charge to any specific one of the scene's components. What is "beautiful" here: the previously living girl or, as Vischer's German reads, her dead body itself ("die schöne Leiche," the beautiful corpse)? Are her killing and resurrection a desecration, or, in some way, the text's *desire*—or both? No sooner does the hanged girl appear than Vischer's rhetoric becomes, in the very next paragraph, conspicuously sexualized: "There is in imagination a prompt stimulation and pulsation (immediate sensation) and a successive enveloping, embracing, and caressing of the object (responsive sensation), whereby we project ourselves all the more intensively into the interior of the phenomenon" (106). And Vischer writes on the same page as this eroticized "feeling of the form" that he must first "dissipate [his] strength on nature" before resurrecting "her"—a formulation that evokes, at minimum, a squandering or exhausting of energies, if not, as the context just as readily suggests, a type of depleting orgasm.

The undead hanged girl remains an ambiguous, fetishistic reminder of the uncanniness of *Einfühlung*, especially when aesthetic empathy bears the burden of revivifying the world. Nature, deanimated by materialist epistemology, is figurally revived (as science, as art, as aesthetics). She may dance as a "symbol" for "everything organic" but cannot escape her uncanny status as the subject of a necromantic spell or the victim of a judicial—that is, a juridical, epistemic, paradigm-shifting (or paradigm-shift-contingent)—murder. Indeed, we might wonder whether the devil's seduction "in" her beautiful corpse—the spell, as it were, of *Einfühlung*—consists in making the treatise's reader (or author) feel that the murder never took place. Accordingly, the girl's reanimation—a violent, demonic possession that itself diabolically seduces—blurs the border between seducer and seducee. Not only is the girl both the victim of the devil's reanimating possession and the agent—or at least the vector—of the nobleman's seduction: In keeping with the scene's overall uncanniness, the late nineteenth-century *viewer* evoked by the passage— himself, by virtue of this very position, perhaps already the materialist "hangman"—is further split, doppelgänger-like, into nobleman and devil, the one being seduced and the one doing the seducing. Put otherwise, the empathic artist or artistic empath is the devil who seduces himself. His empathy, we might say, is empathy *with* the devil.

"Selig scheint es in ihm selbst"

Before leaving the founding document of *Einfühlung*, let us look briefly at one more matter at stake in the uncanniness of empathy— one that seems to call into question the very possibility of empathy itself. This is what I have called the problem of the origin, locus, and vector of experience: a problem that repeatedly troubles the narrative voice of Büchner's text and the logic of Vischer's argument. Indeed, the centrality of this problematic to the question of empathy is announced by the very first words we read in *Über das optische Formgefühl*: an epigraph consisting of the notoriously ambiguous final verse of the 1846 poem "Auf eine Lampe" ("To a Lamp"), a Keats-like ekphrastic meditation on a hanging lamp by the post-Romantic poet (and Vischer's family friend) Eduard Mörike. As the verse states of the poem's titular lamp and exemplary aesthetic object, "Was aber schön ist, selig scheint es in ihm selbst" (*Formgefühl* ii)—a line with an array of contradictory meanings.

The ambiguity stems in part from the polysemy of one of the line's key words. As the famous 1951 debate between Martin Heidegger and Emil Staiger underscored, the German "scheinen" means both *lucet*, "to shine," and *videtur*, "to (merely) seem," "to appear."[49] "Selig"—both "blessed" and "blissful"—is both adjective and adverb

---

49. Heidegger read the word as *lucet*, Staiger as *videtur*; see Staiger, Heidegger, and Spitzer.

("blessedly," "blissfully"). Thus, from one perspective, the line states that "What is beautiful [*Was aber schön ist*] *radiates* or *shines* blessedly in itself [*in ihm selbst*]"; from another perspective, "What is beautiful (only) *seems* or *appears to be* blessed in itself." The line's unusual formulation "in ihm selbst" introduces further ambiguity. The phrase might be a rare variant of the common German reflexive *in sich selbst* (in itself), as I use it above; however, it also evokes a distinctly personal, subjective, even living referent—"in *him*self" (*in ihm selbst*). The line, then, simultaneously means that "what is beautiful shines/radiates *and/or* seems/appears blessedly/blissfully in itself *and/or* in himself," in the eyes of an observer. The syntax of the verse might even be parsed as "What is beautiful, however [*Was aber schön ist*], is that 'it' seems to be blessed/blissful and/or shines blessedly/blissfully in itself/himself"—whatever the "it" may be in this case. The line thus paradoxically fuses ontological qualities with "mere" appearance, "intrinsic" aesthetic properties with experiences dependent on an observer for their "truth," Kant's *Ding-an-sich* with his *Erscheinungen*. Like the *Critique of Pure Reason*, then, the epigraph points to the questions "Where is experience?" "Where is aesthetics?" "Where is 'life' or 'animation'?"—and, ultimately, "Where is empathy?"

Matters are further complicated by the verse, not cited by Vischer but doubtlessly known to him, that immediately precedes the enigmatic line quoted in the epigraph: "Ein Kunstgebild der echten Art. Wer achtet sein?" (An artwork of the authentic form. Who notices [*achtet*] it?).[50] In addition to investigating the semiotically rich and potentially contradictory relationship between the notion of a "Kunstgebild," literally a "formation of art or artifice," and its modifier "der echten Art," "of the *authentic* form or *true* type" (with this modifier's possible pun on the English "art"), we might ask: Who "notices" or "achtet" this form indeed? If perception ("noticing") and empathy, both aesthetic and interpersonal, are aspects of the challenge of relating to another (an Other)—*achten* also means "to regard," "to respect," "to esteem"—then both processes, perception and empathy, seem necessarily to be functions of the broader

---

50. The translation here is Scott Horton's.

structuring framework of subject and object. Indeed, it is from the assumption of this very subject-object dichotomy that many of the perils we have associated with the uncanniness of *Einfühlung* and intersubjective empathy—the danger of colonizing or possessing another, the fear of being possessed by that other, the risk of the loss of other or self—arise. Yet it is exactly this dichotomy that the locus problem of early *Einfühlungstheorie* calls into question. The "who" of the "noticer" is just as dependent on the "noticed" as vice versa. Neither term has independent or inherent existence, or, indeed, existence at all, apart from the other. Both are functions of a larger field relation—what Vischer calls an "indivisible whole" (109)—whose "parts" (an inaccurate term here) are groundless.[51] In an ironic "solution," there is no need to "solve" the meaning of Mörike's "in ihm selbst," for there *is* no "ihm selbst"—nor *another* "selbst." But if unmasking the subject-object framework as, from one perspective, an illusory construct eliminates (or at least reduces) many of the potential "pathologies" of empathy, it also effectively eliminates both *Einfühlung* and intersubjective empathy themselves, at least as the terms are conceptualized in their traditional, dualistic sense. If there is no self and no other, then there is no one to empathize, nor anyone—or any *thing*—to empathize *with*. Recall Vischer's pivotal formulation of *Einfühlung* to which we have returned throughout this chapter: "Only ostensibly do I keep my own identity although the object remains distinct. I seem merely to adapt and attach myself to it as one hand clasps another, and yet I am mysteriously transplanted and magically transformed into this Other [*in dieses Nichtich versetzt und verzaubert*]" (104, *Formgefühl* 20).

---

51. Here I draw on the Madhyamaka thought of second-century CE Indian philosopher Nāgārjuna, including his explication of *śūnyatā* (emptiness), understood at its most basic level for the purposes of this study as the absence of "inherently existing things" or "intrinsic nature." See Siderits and Katsura 1–10; cf. also the neuroscientist Francisco Varela's account of Madhyamaka philosophy: "By definition, something is independent, intrinsic, or absolute only if it does not depend on anything else; it must have an identity that transcends its relations.... Nothing in our experience can be found that satisfies this criterion of independence or ultimacy.... Causes and their effects, things and their attributes, and the very mind of the inquiring subject and the objects of mind are each *equally* codependent on the other" (224).

Vischer's German for "Other" here is *Nichtich*: not simply "Other" but literally "not-I," "not-self," or even "nonself"—a transformation that leaves the locus of experience precisely nowhere. In the words of a song that "resurrects" the question of (re)animation that has given form to our discussion of *Einfühlung* in Vischer and Büchner, "Thought you were praying to the resurrector; turns out it was just a reflector" (Arcade Fire, "Reflektor"). In the subjectless and objectless nonlocus of empathy, however, it is a reflector with no one looking into it—except another reflector.

2

ADALBERT STIFTER

Resistances of Form and Feeling

> But without doubt it is [the readers] who truly "write the book into the book" and rejoice because they feel their own living heart beating there. . . . We *can* not, after all, ever give the other something of ourselves, only a faint beginning; he then works out its details and loves us when he is good—and hates us when he is no good himself.
> —STIFTER, LETTER TO MÖRNER, SEPTEMBER 1851

Appearing on the literary scene shortly after Georg Büchner and responding to similar anxieties about the rise of the materialist world, Adalbert Stifter charted a different path in *Einfühlung*'s implicate order. His own engagement with bodies, forms, and objects, including the body of the text itself as a logical or affective "object," anticipates, like Büchner, Robert Vischer's protophenomenology and kinesthetic imagination. But, outpacing Vischer, it also takes things in directions that evoke the later, more profoundly somatically focused

Einfühlungstheorie of Vernon Lee and the questions of other minds, artificial intelligence, and virtual reality that will become important for subsequent thinkers of the blurry border between aesthetic and interpersonal empathy. Indeed, Stifter's writing opens up a space for implicit philosophical speculation and possible affective "escape" at the intersection of emerging *Einfühlung*, intersubjective empathy, feeling, and form.

At first glance, Stifter seems the literary and ideological antipode of Büchner. Although he composed his first novellas while Büchner was writing his dramas and began publishing these stories in 1840, three years after Büchner's death, stylistic and political chasms appear to separate the conservative Austrian master of prose and champion of "moderation" from the revolutionary German playwright who, had he lived, would have been eight years Stifter's junior. Despite their apparent distribution on opposite sides of the Biedermeier-Vormärz divide, however, the two writers are, as scholars have acknowledged, in many ways intellectual kin. Both struggled to navigate the emergence of a nascent realist aesthetic amid the fragments, remnants, or ghosts of Romanticism; both registered, in another variation of Helmut Müller-Sievers's "disorientation," the ongoing decline of previous epistemological paradigms for situating oneself in the world, such as *Naturphilosophie*, vitalism, and religious faith.[1] As Martin and Erika Swales write in their seminal *Adalbert Stifter: A Critical Study*, Stifter's work "is part of a strand in German culture . . . that takes in Georg Büchner's anguished reckoning with materialist thinking" (224). Despite his insistence on the sovereignty of a Christian cosmic order, we find in Stifter's fiction a "sense of futility" that evokes the pessimism of Schopenhauer (also a contemporary) and "the notion, anticipating Darwin, that the world, the universe, may not be a divinely underwritten and sustained creation, but simply a self-sufficient mechanism, revolving in endless cycles of destruction and recreation" (Swales and Swales 14).

---

1. On Stifter and Büchner's similarly "desperate" sense of God, see Ragg-Kirkby 76–77. On the complexity of Stifter's "realist" engagement with Romanticism, see Begemann, *Welt der Zeichen*, especially chapter 4, "Der unleserliche Text: Romantische Entromantisierung in *Der Hochwald*" (164–209).

Mathias Mayer, in *Adalbert Stifter: Erzählen als Erkennen (Narrating as Knowing)*, notes that Büchner and Stifter both belong to an "existentially unsettled" generation whose loss of "transcendence" can only be compensated to a limited degree by the rise of the natural sciences (9–10); W. G. Sebald contends that "the dissolving of the [nineteenth-century] metaphysical order corresponds to the harrowing realism that pervades the entirety of Stifter's work, in which perhaps merely 'looking at' the world is meant to salvage something of its previous meaning" (18). Helena Ragg-Kirkby perhaps goes furthest in her study *Adalbert Stifter's Late Prose: The Mania for Moderation* when she argues that "beneath the surface of [Stifter's] Biedermeier solidity is a vision of fracture, emptiness, meaninglessness not only more radical than that of any other nineteenth-century author, but more radical than the vision of any twentieth-century author because there is such a disjuncture between text and sub-text. Stifter simply leaves the future behind" (11).

In the realm of the sciences, too, Stifter and Büchner exhibit similarities, if not in profession, then at least in interests and sensibilities. Although Stifter did not, as he had initially wished, pursue an academic career in physics, he maintained a lifelong interest in this and related fields (Coen 65). As historian of science Deborah R. Coen points out, Stifter's writing, with its recurrent focus on natural and geological phenomena, participated in the Habsburg Empire's emerging discourse on climatology, atmospheric science, and geophysical scale and "embedd[ed] the earth sciences in Austria's literary canon" (67). Stifter's contemporary, the Austrian philosopher F. T. Bratranek, compared Stifter's "microscopic" attention to the minute nuances of mind and emotions to the work of a "physiologist [detailing] the emergence of psychic life from its elements" (Selge 15). In *Organismus und Gesellschaft: Der Körper in der deutschsprachigen Literatur des Realismus (Organism and Society: The Body in the Literature of German Realism)*, Silke Brodersen reads both Bratranek's metaphor and Stifter's own "preference for the small and material" (24) in terms of the mid-nineteenth-century rise of physiology as a research field. As Brodersen contends, both Stifter's narrative techniques and Bratranek's comparison reflect mid-century physiology's new understanding of the human being as a collection of disparate cells, nerves, and tissues organized into systems "networked" with "material nature" (23–25); she therefore implicitly links Stifter's thematic concerns and formal *ductus* to the conclusions of Johannes Müller's physiological *Handbuch*. The narrator-protagonist of Stifter's most famous novel, the 1857 bildungsroman *Der Nachsommer* (*Indian Summer*), is notably both an amateur scientist and an aesthetician; Stifter's first story collection, *Studien* (*Studies*, 1844–1850), evokes in its title and in the narrative tone of many of its novellas the scientifically detached gaze and voice whose recording of even especially pleasurable and painful events with a distance approaching dispassion has been an ongoing source of these tales' uncanny fascination.[2] The novellas in his later cycle *Bunte Steine* (*Many-Colored Stones*, 1853), each named for a different mineral, clearly call to mind a naturalist's collection, again underscoring Stifter's "attempt to assimilate to the undertaking of the artist that of the 'Forscher' [researcher]" (Swales and Swales 224).

Büchner's publisher Karl Gutzkow maintained that Stifter's early stories were "particularly modern" precisely because of their "poetic-scientific view of the cosmic whole" (qtd. in Mathias Mayer 26). However, Stifter's relationship to "the modern" is notably complex. Critics have long noted his supposed rejection of the not specifically scientific aspects of modernity, especially the realms of politics, social conflict, and industrialization; this is typically seen as a retreat from engagement with the hard realities of a changing Europe into an atemporal or retrograde utopia of "cozy idylls," "the virtues of the agrarian world" (Swales and Swales 220–21), "provincialism," "narrowness," and "psychological and social naivety" (Walker, "Two Realisms" 133). The tone-setter here was Eric Auerbach, whose highly influential *Mimesis* (1946) cast German realism as a whole in an especially negative light. According to Auerbach, German realism "yielded no subject matter for a realism so generally national, so materially modern, so intent upon an analysis of the emerging destiny of European society, as the realism of France" (516). Stifter's characters in particular supposedly lived "in a world with hardly a trace of historical movement" (518).

---

2. See Mathias Mayer 25–26 and Swales and Swales 118–19, 151–55.

More recent criticism has begun to break this mold. Hans Höller, for example, reads the curated and conserved objects in Stifter's "utopias" not as forms of historical escapism but as instrumentally "useless" and therefore unco-optable Adorno-style aesthetic alternatives to the alienation of mass production and commodity capitalism (255–56). Mark G. Ward ("Self-reflexive Discourse") and John Walker ("Two Realisms") argue that German realism of Stifter's variety represents a covert philosophical critique of the linguistic, ideological, and discursive construction of "reality" rather than a blunter treatment of the "external" socioeconomic world of the type called for by Auerbach. And Ragg-Kirkby makes the case for Stifter's late prose in particular as a sort of radical, protomodernist experimentation, albeit less a willingly chosen one than one that compulsively expresses Stifter's struggle against "the abyss" (74): "His style becomes so radically other and ultimately dissolves into the kind of extreme obliqueness that will only be anywhere near matched almost a century later by Beckett or Ionesco" (115).

In *The Antinomies of Realism*, Fredric Jameson argues that the novels of George Eliot and Gustave Flaubert may each be thought of as a unique "laboratory experiment which poses a distinct form-problem" (156). In keeping with Ragg-Kirkby's emphasis on Stifter's stylistic experimentalism, Stifter's own fascination with science, and his fusion of the nuances of feeling with unusual or experimental varieties of prose form, it might be fruitful to extend Jameson's metaphor to Stifter himself: to view his texts, that is, not as regressive fantasies but as strange, even futuristic "laboratory experiments" or narrative machines designed to measure the limits and implications of affect and empathy, both interpersonal and aesthetic. Indeed, in a broad figural sense, Stifter's novellas are no less laboratories for investigating the effects of affect and emergent *Einfühlung* than were the workrooms of his contemporaries Fechner, Müller, and Helmholtz or the psychological laboratories to appear in Germany a generation later. And, like the labs that would become central to psychological aesthetics, Stifter's narratives are sites of aesthetic theory "in practice": They, too, test problems of formal representation and the intersections of empathy, feeling, and form to a striking degree. The experiments they conduct, though different from Büchner's in genre, style, and overt politics, are, as Ragg-Kirkby suggests, no less radical than his. Surprisingly, some of their content may even be, at least in part, progressively rather than conservatively political—if (this time unsurprisingly) covertly and ambivalently so.

The novellas I analyze in this chapter might be read as being about resistance or resistances, or indeed as *forms of resistance*—resistances of feeling channeled through form, or resistances generated by the intersections of feeling and form. In one case, *Turmalin* (*Tourmaline*), what is being resisted is our expectation of unproblematic *access* to empathy and affect through human beings and artistic form; in the other, *Der Hochwald* (*The Mountain Forest*), the seeming ideological commitments of the narrative itself, which are significantly challenged by the affective charge of the text's formal features. The two novellas represent, then, "formal" cases of resistance and empathy, respectively *ex negativo* and "in excess." *Der Hochwald* helped propel Stifter to popularity when its journal version appeared in the well-known Austrian literary almanac *Iris* in 1841; the more commonly read, only lightly revised book version, which I draw on in this chapter, appeared in volume two of *Studien* in 1844. Stifter wrote the enigmatic, much less popular and less well received narrative *Turmalin* in 1848 but did not publish it until 1852, when it appeared under the title "Der Pförtner im Herrenhaus" ("The Doorman in the Manor") in the literary yearbook *Libussa*. He substantially revised the text for its 1853 inclusion in *Bunte Steine* in order to, as the Swaleses put it, "heighten [its] strangeness" (173–76).[3] It is on this *Bunte Steine* version that I primarily draw, as the revised text makes the resistances performed by the convergence of the novella's plot and its experimental form more explicit. Indeed, since *Turmalin*'s overt, and overtly experimental, thematizing of empathy, feeling, and form helps bring *Der Hochwald*'s more cryptic, ambivalent, but perhaps even more radical "empathy experiment" into focus, I shall treat the two texts in reverse chronological order. Ultimately, these early realist texts from the geographical and temporal periphery of

---

3. On the publication history of *Turmalin* and *Der Hochwald*, see Mathias Mayer 40–48 and 129–34.

German *Einfühlungstheorie* reveal what else was inchoate in the broader "cloud" that would in a few decades precipitate *Über das optische Formgefühl*—and show how Stifter's aesthetic praxis, rendered differently legible by the twentieth-century thought with which I place it in dialogue, radicalizes and transcends what Vischer would soon offer.

Turmalin: Feeling and Form

As Karen J. Campbell notes in "Toward a Truer Mimesis," her perceptive analysis of *Turmalin*, it is impossible to capture the effect of the novella's strangeness in summary (576–79). The story zigs and zags, setting up expectations and subverting them. Descriptive detail accumulates in profusion, while explanatory detail is in short supply. Lacunae and abrupt transitions abound; crucial turning points are elided; key occurrences are visible only at their margins, in the lead-up to and aftermath of moments of crisis. Phrases like "an appreciable time had again elapsed since this incident, when something else of significance took place" (*Tourmaline* 128) become an ongoing leitmotif in the text. With one exception, major characters remain unnamed throughout the narrative, while minor or even absent figures receive names. Feelings, even passions, that one would expect to dominate the story's representation of its frequently heart-wrenching events are presented from a weird, almost telescopic distance, mentioned with offhand disregard as if they were significantly less important than the narrative's lengthy descriptions of an apartment's layout or furniture. The solutions to "secrets" that the reader has in most cases already easily guessed are withheld for especially protracted lengths of time, as if the text's "revelations" really *were* ones, while true mysteries—the motivations, whereabouts, and fates of key figures, for example—go unexplained. At one point, the text introduces a detailed subplot about a professor living in a decaying manor—a subplot with suggestively Gothic-Romantic, oneiric, and even proto-Kafkaesque overtones—only to leave the relation of this plot to the main storyline unexplored and entirely implicit. In apparent "realist" deference to verisimilitude, but in a move that feels, amid the text's general opacity, conspicuously contrived and "unrealistic," the story changes time periods and narrators midway through, from a *pluralis majestatis* authorial Stifter stand-in to a first-person intradiegetic housewife who ostensibly knew the other main characters of the tale.[4] Any attempt to synoptically reassemble the fractured *syuzhet* into a coherent fabula inevitably misses the text's uncannily dissociated or mechanical affective tone and flattens the story's *ductus*—or, more precisely, erases its interface between *ductus* and plot: the feeling of its form. It is a profoundly self-reflexive story of problems of aesthetics, feeling, empathy, and theatrical performance whose repeated depictions of fissures in these four concerns at the diegetic level are mirrored by correspondingly disjunctive narrative strategies at the level of form—the structure of the text as a whole.

With apologies to the first version of *Wilhelm Meister*, we might think of *Turmalin* as 'Adalbert Stifters theatralische Sendung' ('Adalbert Stifter's Theatrical Mission'). In the novella, a quartet of characters bound either directly or indirectly by the idea of theater become "actors" in a figurative four-person play we might call "Empathy Experiments" or "The Theater of Empathy."[5] The notion of theater provides an ideal framework for an experiment on empathy, including empathy's paradoxes, limitations, and gaps. The logical form of (traditional) theater—the simulation of emotion, the performance of feeling as form—already raises theoretical questions about the relation of "real" to "virtual" emotion, along with corresponding questions about the relation of interpersonal and aesthetic empathy to the real and simulated affective spheres. The praxis dimension of theater—actors' empathic identification with

---

4. Stifter was in fact told by a female friend, the actress Antonie von Arneth, about the historical events on which *Turmalin* is loosely based: the abandonment of the famous Viennese actor (and Arneth's stage colleague) Joseph Lange by his wife Aloisia Weber, Mozart's sister-in-law; see Mathias Mayer 129 and Luke 16. Stifter distributes the historical Lange across the novella's figures of the Rentherr and Dall. On *Turmalin*'s reputation for opacity, see Geulen 136 and Swales and Swales 173–76.

5. See also Geulen, who views three of the novella's four main characters (father, daughter, and the actor Dall) as parallel figures united by the theme of art (140–41).

roles, audiences' empathic identification with actors—further complicates these questions. Significantly, one of the four key figures in *Turmalin*, a central catalyst for the novella's plot and the only major character to receive a name, is the famous and "brilliant" actor Dall, whose "magnificent performances" (*Tourmaline* 109–10) or theatrical presentations of the "form" of feeling produce what we might call overwhelming "empathy effects": "Accounts still survive of certain great moments at which [Dall] completely transported the spectators, filling them with the uttermost excitement or the uttermost dread, so that they felt they were no longer in the theater but in real life and awaited the further outcome with anxiety" (109).

Interwoven with Dall's actions is a bizarre and sentimental story seemingly tailor-made to arouse readers' narrative empathy, or at least pity and terror: a story, however, strangely attenuated by the novella's distancing and disjointed form. The unnamed "Rentherr" (man with a private income), friends with Dall and himself an artistic dilettante, lives in Vienna with his younger wife and infant daughter, both unnamed. After "some considerable time" in the friendship, Dall "finally . . . began a love affair with his friend's wife and continued it for a while" (*Tourmaline* 112). The wife confesses the affair, then abandons both her husband and Dall, never to be seen again; the Rentherr takes his daughter and likewise vanishes. Years later, he reappears as a shabby street musician accompanied by the girl, who now suffers from both physical and developmental disabilities: a "horrifying" oversized head, presumably macrocephaly or hydrocephalus, such that "one could not take one's eyes off it" (119), and the inability to fully grasp and process emotional states. As the unnamed housewife-narrator—also a friend of Dall's and "very devoted" to the theater (129)—explains, picking up the tale years later, the girl had been repeatedly forced by her father to write identical descriptions of the same traumatic scenes, at once biographical and melodramatically theatrical, over and over again: "How one day [the Rentherr] shall lie dead in [his] coffin and they will bury [him]," and "how [the girl's] mother wanders about the world in the torment of her heart, and how she dare not return, and how in the end she does away with herself in despair" (141). But, as the narrator points out, the girl shows "not a trace of any understanding of the meaning of death, or of wandering about in the world and doing away with oneself in despair" (145). Even after she discovers her father's body after his fatal fall from a ladder and informs the neighborhood of his death, she continues to ask when he will "come back" (138). The narrator pieces together the obviously telegraphed evidence and identifies the dead musician and disabled girl as the long-missing Rentherr and his daughter. In the story's final pages, the housewife and her husband take in the girl and "normalize" her, teaching her "household" or, as Stifter puts it, "women's work" (*weibliche Arbeit*) (140, *Turmalin* 163). Based on the instructions of a doctor friend, they also improbably make the girl's head "smaller and shapelier and her features more flexible, better defined, and more expressive" through "a course of iodide baths" (146).

One of the most crucial figures linking theater, feeling, form, *Einfühlung*, and intersubjective empathy in the text is the girl herself—Dall's uncanny double, as it were. As the housewife explains, the girl speaks "in the purest literary diction, but what she said was scarcely intelligible. Her thoughts were so strange . . . that her whole speech might have seemed feeble-minded if parts of it had not nevertheless been very intelligent" (132). Similarly, the girl's writings might have been "stories or poems if they had contained any intelligible thought or if there had been any discernible rhyme or reason or continuity in the text. . . . Her expressions were clear and incisive, her sentences correct and well constructed, and her words, although senseless, were noble and lofty [*erhaben*]" (145, *Turmalin* 167). The girl, that is, is no content and all form. The housewife tests the, as it were, senseless sublimity of this form by "reading aloud, in an emphatic and declamatory tone, sentences from poets or other writers" (145); like an actor, the girl imitates the prompts and is soon giving "semi-dramatic performances of extracts from the finest masterpieces of our national literature" (145). Again, however, when "questioned . . . further on the work from which she had recited a passage" and "asked . . . about its content or meaning or form," the girl "did not understand what one was talking about" (145).

From one perspective, as Eva Geulen writes, the daughter is a figure for the aesthetic processes of Stifter's text itself: "The physiognomy of the child is as distorted as the [novella's] narration"; "distorted body and distorted narration are mirrored for their part in the girl's strange, meaningful, and yet incoherent writings" (137). The daughter thus takes her place among the narrative's conspicuous inventory of self-reflexive "allegories of writing," to adapt Paul de Man, that the relatively small number of critics commenting on this text have reliably pointed out—the girl's "talking" jackdaw that speaks, as it were, in "unintelligible" words (132), her dilettante father's excessive collection of artistic implements (musical instruments, easels, writing desk, and so on), and, of course, the eccentric melodies the Rentherr plays on his flute, that, like the story's narration, "diverge from all that one normally calls music" (121): "The most fascinating thing was that when he had set off on one course and begun leading the listener's ear along it, what came was always something other than what one expected and had the right to expect, so that one always had to start afresh and follow him in some new direction, until in the end one was involved in a confusion that might almost have been described as demented" (121–22).[6] More problematically, the daughter also joins a long line of female Stifter protagonists whose bodies, especially when disabled, racialized, or physically divergent from nineteenth-century gender or beauty norms, become the objectified sites for negotiating aesthetic questions.[7]

Most importantly, the girl is a figure for the text's experimental inquiry into the interface of feeling, form, and empathy. In her, feeling is pure form: she formally performs expressions of feeling (such as the housewife's literary-theatrical prompts) without being able to grasp their content herself, or she composes texts with whose semantic and emotional content she cannot identify, even when it is *her own* (such

---

6. See Campbell; Schiffermüller; Geulen 137–39; and Swales and Swales 179–81.

7. Think, for example, of Ditha in *Abdias*, whose disability (blindness) ties her to a particular set of "Romantic" aesthetic questions (preference for the night, synesthesia); these in turn intersect with her Jewishness to provide possible antisemitic motivation for the text to kill her (see Metz, "The Jew as Sign"). *Turmalin* criticism has not escaped the problems of enlisting the disabilities of the Rentherr's daughter as figures for the text's dis-figuration or de-formation: Schiffermüller's analysis, for example, while clearly reading the daughter as embodying "psychotic" language arising from her *father's* failure to integrate her into a Lacanian symbolic order, nevertheless characterizes the daughter's body as "monstrous" (224–27).

as her repetitive descriptions of autobiographically relevant traumas). Her function, that is, is to *represent the representation of feeling as pure formalism*. Her presence in the text asks, in an uncannier, more penetrating and philosophically wide-ranging way than does the case of Dall (whose implications can be more easily "contained" within the restricted, socially "comprehensible" space of theater), whether there is a difference, or a way to tell the difference, between "real" feeling and its formal simulation. She is likewise the site where intersubjective and aesthetic empathy or *Einfühlung* meet: She asks what it means to "feel oneself into" another person if that other is only known as pure form or formalism, a virtual effect. In this sense, she anticipates Vischer's object-world, Theodor Lipps's wedding of *Einfühlung* to interpersonal empathy, and Alan Turing's famous thought experiment about artificial intelligence, to which I will return momentarily. But since her "acting," like Dall's, also has real-world effects on those around her, she is simultaneously the locus of ethical questions: questions, that is, of the possibility of knowing, responding to, and being "affected by" "other minds" and of self-other relations more generally.

Adalbert Stifter's *theatralische Sendung*

As Susan Lanzoni writes, "It is appropriate to think of empathy with theatrical tropes, given that taking on the role of the other is one of its many definitions" (*Empathy* 15). Fritz Breithaupt points out that empathy has long been closely, perhaps paradigmatically, "intertwined" with theater and notes the many "stage effects" that heighten "both empathy and aesthetic experience": "The spotlight of the theater lightening [sic] glows on the skin of the actors, gives special relevance to all their actions and emotions and makes them appear more true than things that do not happen on stage.... Stages generate or trigger empathy. Once someone stands on a stage people are invited to take his or her perspective and to co-experience his or her imaginary or real situation.... Empathy is for us a stage experience" ("Empathy and Aesthetics" 57–58). Indeed, as Georg Braungart reminds us, Lessing's *Hamburgische Dramaturgie* (*Hamburg Dramaturgy*, 1767–1769) and *Theatralische Bibliothek* (*Theatrical Library*, 1754) had already proposed, long before the similar theories of Fechner, Karl Groos, and William James, that an actor's physical "mimicry" of the outward expressions and bodily postures of an emotion—a sort of "corporeal empathy" or intersubjective empathy through *Einfühlung*, through the achieved isomorphism of *forms*—can cause that same emotion to arise in the actor's own mind and body (55–57).

All four of *Turmalin*'s main characters are united by the trope of theater, none more obviously than Dall, in whom explicit and implicit theories of acting take, as it were, center stage. His performances, as I have noted, have profound empathy effects on his audiences, taking over or "possessing" their emotions, blurring the borders between the virtual and real, and "filling [spectators] with the uttermost excitement or the uttermost dread, so that they felt they were no longer in the theater but in real life and awaited the further outcome with anxiety" (109). But Dall is also *taken over by* his roles. As *Turmalin*'s first narrator tells us, "He was what he acted," "really was the person . . . portrayed" (110). Or, as Geulen writes, "Reality and art, role and life converge without differentiation on the surface of the actor's body" (140). This merger of actor and part seems, at first glance, a striking example of exceptional narrative empathy—Dall's with his roles—that in turn arouses exceptional narrative empathy in viewers. It also seems the very opposite of the Rentherr's daughter, who "does not understand what she is talking about" when "questioned on a work from which she has recited a passage" (*Tourmaline* 145). However, the details of Dall's empathic "performance" reveal a different picture, exposing subterranean problems of empathy, or empathy as a problem.

Right from the beginning, the origin, vector, and locus of Dall's empathy—to return to a problem that troubled Büchner and Vischer—is strikingly unclear. As the first narrator explains, "A great connoisseur of such matters once said that Dall did not arrive at his interpretations of his roles by artful reflection and preparatory training, but that if a part suited his personality [*Wesen*] he would live himself into it [*daß er sich in dieselben . . . hineingelebt habe*] and then rely on his temperament to suggest the appropriate behavior to him at any given moment" (109–10, *Turmalin* 131). The language of this description of Dall's approach to his roles—"living himself into them," *sich in dieselben hineinleben*—conspicuously prefigures the rhetoric of Vischer's *Einfühlung*. If Vischer's term leaves us uncertain how much of "sich einfühlen" is isomorphic "contouring" with what is already present in the other and how much is self-projection, Dall's *sich hineinleben* seems to suffer from no such ambiguity: Dall's "others," even if only textually existent, are costumed versions of himself, subsumed within his "personality" or "Being" (*Wesen*). As the narrator states, Dall is incapable of performing roles with which he does not already identify: "This explains why, if he could not live himself into a part, he was quite unable to act it at all, even badly" (110). His starting point is less the mental and emotional life of a real or imagined other than the already existing contents of his own "Being," which this other must "suit" (*seinem Wesen zusagen*) (131)—or, to capture an additional meaning of "zusagen," to which the other must "consent." Dall, correspondingly, must in some way already "be" the part, such that he is not in a traditional sense *acting*: "In this way he did not act his part but really was the person it portrayed" (110). Put otherwise, Dall's performances subordinate *form* ("the part") to *content*: his own personality or "Being," living out his feelings onstage in real time.

Dall's acting anticipates late twentieth-century simulation theories of mind and intersubjective empathy: "ego-centric methods" that "use [oneself] as a model for the other person's mental life" (Stueber, section 2.1). According to simulation theory, one draws on one's own psychological states as the basis for imagining the mental states or "mindedness" of others, a form of empathic perspective taking that, according to some scholars, owes the roots of its theoretical elaboration to Vischer's successor Lipps and presages the techniques of Method acting (of which Dall's approach might be considered a protoform). As Lipps will argue, what we observe, experience, or assume about others' mental states ultimately constitutes a series of "metaphors" for our own self-experience; like Lipps and the Method actors, then, Dall must first "create" the "others" with whom he empathizes.[8]

---

8. See chapter 3 below. On the simulation theory of empathy, see Goldman. On the roots of simulation theory in Lipps's thought, see Debes 295n26. On the relations among simulation theory, empathy, and acting, see Gallagher and Gallagher.

The effects of Dall's "simulation-empathic" self-projection into fictional forms on *audiences* who are compelled, through these "roles that are not roles," to empathize with *him* are tellingly violent: They end with his (figuratively) taking not theatrical but *bodily* parts from *actual* others. Here, "consent" (*zusagen*) to Dall's "Being" is *forced*: He "ravishes" or, literally, "violently pulls" his spectators (*hinreißen*), "filling them with the uttermost excitement or the uttermost dread, so that they ... awaited the ... outcome with anxiety"; he "drives" (*treiben*) their "souls" to "the deepest shocks" (*zu den tiefsten Erschütterungen*), to "fear and horror and joy and ecstasy" (109–10, *Turmalin* 131–32). Like Vischer's demonically empathic resurrector, Dall "animates" (*belebte*) society and "gives it emotions" (*gab ihr Empfindungen*) (110, *Turmalin* 132)—or, more accurately, *inflicts* animation and emotion, a process not that different, at the extreme end of its affective "life," from seduction, assault, and death. The Rentherr compares the actor's violently eroticized empathy effects on his theater audience with Dall's affair with the Rentherr's wife, figuring both as "dramas" in which traditional tropes of sexual and emotional "surrender" take on ever more sinister connotations of externally imposed corporeal loss and dismemberment: "It had been inevitable that she should succumb [*fallen*] to Dall. ... She had lost her heart to him, just as on any evening at the theater he stole the hearts of thousands"—as Stifter's original reads, "Sie habe an Dall fallen müssen, ... sie habe ihm das Herz gegeben, wie er es Tausenden an einem Schauspielabende aus dem Leibe nehme" (literally, "just as he took the heart out of the bodies of thousands") (113, *Turmalin* 134). The Rentherr's rhetoric leaves ambiguous the amount of consent versus coercion in these figuratively bloody matters of the heart: When the narrator dispassionately states that Dall "finally"—the word suggesting that this was simply the expected thing to do—"began a love affair with his friend's wife" (112), the lines of force, imposition, and assent are entirely unclear.

The Rentherr, though not a professional actor, is likewise linked to the theater, and not only metonymically through his friendship with Dall. After his fall into poverty, he "performs" by playing his flute at inns for food and alms, presenting himself in his conspicuous Werther-esque blue-and-yellow "costume." When confronting Dall about his missing wife, he repeatedly approaches the actor with the same ritualistic, theatrical gestures: "[He] knelt down in front of [Dall], folded his hands, and begged him for his wife" (114). He maneuvers about his original apartment's bizarre hall of celebrity portraits on mobile couches set on "Rollen" (127)—"small wheels," but also "roles," a theatrical pun that the Swaleses (183) and Geulen (140) point out.

The celebrity hall of the Rentherr's first apartment, its walls "completely pasted over with portraits of famous men," such that "at no point was there even a hand's-breadth of the original wall to be seen" (*Tourmaline* 106), is especially significant in this context. The aesthetics of this space, to which we are introduced at the very beginning of the narrative, along with the Rentherr's obsession with celebrity overall, already place us in the arena of intersubjective, if conspicuously "perverted," empathy. Here, as often in literature, architectural space becomes psychic space. The celebrity gallery, around which the Rentherr moves on his "small wheels" or wished-for "roles," scrutinizing every image, becomes the locus for what Breithaupt calls "vampiristic empathy": an "extreme form of emotional identification" associated with such aberrations of interpersonal empathy as stalking and obsessive fandom (*Dark Sides* 205). As Breithaupt argues, radical fans engage in acts of "obsessive observation," "ritualized stagings of observation that can create an imagined closeness": "The fan or stalker sees in or projects onto the object of their obsession a perfection (whether real or not) that they lack in their own lives" (*Dark Sides* 211). In *Turmalin*, the Rentherr not only ritualistically observes and projects onto but also quite literally "possesses" the other—indeed, the "complete set" of others. As the narrator tells us, "As to the fame of the men in the pictures, it did not matter to their *owner* what their occupation had been and in what profession their fame had been gained, he simply *possessed* so far as possible *the complete set of them*" (106, my emphasis). Seen differently, of course, it is the Rentherr himself, the unnamed dilettante, "lacking something in his own life," who is "possessed"—bound by his obsessive identification with his "objects," the shadow celebrities.

If the celebrity hall is a space of perverse interpersonal empathy, it is also, conspicuously, a space of modernity. Indeed, the narrator's description of the Rentherr's indiscriminate consumerism and indifference to the content of his celebrities' fame anticipates Walter Benjamin's critique of the cult of the movie star under capitalism—a cult that "preserves not the unique aura of the person but the 'spell of the personality,' the phony spell of a commodity" (Benjamin, "Work of Art" 231). As Breithaupt contends, not only will the rise of mass media in the late nineteenth and early twentieth centuries "transform the nature of fame and fandom" into something more obsessive and pathological: "Our age's fascination with empathy" will itself be "connected to our heightened engagement with media" (*Dark Sides* 212–13). The Rentherr's celebrity image inventory stands on the cusp of this age of obsessive, commodified, and mediated empathy, heralding it: As Geulen remarks, the picture-covered walls of the Rentherr's apartment recall the commodity-hawking advertising posters whose emergence Stifter describes in an earlier collection of essays about Viennese urban scenes (142).

Most strikingly, perhaps, as a site for producing both art (the Rentherr's musical instruments, scores, and papier-mâché figures) *and* empathic spectatorship—and particularly as a site that, in allowing the viewing of the celebrity images, literally houses the staging of empathy as *spectacle* (from Latin *specere*, "to look")—the Rentherr's apartment is likewise a type of *theater*: a still-life theater of static pictures or forms, and thus something on the border between intersubjective and aesthetic empathy. In this theater, the Rentherr is both audience and performer. He performs identification with the mediated images he spectates: images that, while immobile, nonetheless "move" him (indeed, move him around the room) with their empathy effects. I will return to the further implications and significance of this hall of images and its relation to "the modern" later in the chapter. For the moment, let us simply underscore the figural connection between the Rentherr and his theatrical-celebrity friend Dall, tellingly the only other character in the story who observes the celebrity portraits (he in fact regularly visits the Rentherr's apartment to do just that [111]). When Dall "finally" begins his affair with the Rentherr's wife, the transference makes "tropic" sense: The friends have always already, as it were, been "feeling their way into each other."

Regarding interpersonal empathy, Dall and the Rentherr seem suspended between hyperempathy and empathy's lack. In contrast to his overidentification with the famous men, the Rentherr appears terrifyingly detached from his own daughter. In the wake of Dall's affair with his wife, he forces the girl to "script" the imagined scenes of his death and her mother's suicide again and again, unconcerned with, or perhaps desiring, the potential (re)traumatizing effect on her psyche: "When [she] said: 'Father, I've described that . . . many times already,' he would answer: 'Then describe it again'" (141). From another perspective, it is *precisely through* this compulsory traumatic reinscription that the Rentherr attempts to *produce identification* with his daughter, or to induce her empathic identification with him: indeed, to craft a sort of "absolute" experiential identity between them. It is a mental version of the famous body-inscribing torture machine in Kafka's "In the Penal Colony," which produces not the interpersonal but the social identification of the condemned man with the law that is, literally, repeatedly engraved on his body. In a lineage that can be traced back to the beginning of the story, the Rentherr's "stage direction" of his daughter's proliferating texts becomes another version—a continuation and variation—of the obsessive empathy work of his excessively multiplying celebrity images. Dall's acting, for its part, is all about himself, and outside the theater he also seems unable or unwilling to imagine or feel the Rentherr's feelings in their alterity. Or, "living himself into" a real-life version of the role of Don Juan, or into the Rentherr himself, he identifies so much with these "parts" that he sleeps with his friend's wife.

But what of a seemingly less ambiguous case? As Denis Diderot famously and perhaps counterintuitively argued in *The Paradox of Acting*, a great actor should have *no* "real identification" with his parts: He should indeed have an actual "lack of feelings" (Kofman, "Resemblance" 223–24). In this sense, the Rentherr's daughter—apparently unidentified with the pieces she "performs," and even, it seems, with her own emotional knowledge—may be a "greater" actor than Dall.

Insofar as the daughter's writings and theatrical recitations are divorced from the "inhabited" content of their messages (lived autobiographical feeling, intellectual understanding of a text), they become pure surface, pure sound, pure formalism—to adapt Campbell's formulation, "truer mimesis." The "truth" of this mimesis, however, is logically problematic: It is veridical only in an abstract sense, detached from experiential confirmation by its "responsible" first-person consciousness. This formalism serves both to resist and to solicit different types of empathy, intersubjective and aesthetic. On the one hand, the daughter's purely formalist discourse throws up a wall against interpersonal empathy or others' attempts to "feel with" her: Her feelings are so virtual that even *she* can't feel with *herself*. Like a performer in Brecht's Epic theatre, her nonidentification with her "role" is well positioned to produce anti-empathic "alienation effects" in her metaphorical audiences.[9] On the other hand, precisely this formal wall solicits *aesthetic* empathy or *Einfühlung*. Indeed, the concept of *Einfühlung* itself was at least in part Vischer's response to formalism, as represented by the aesthetics of Stifter's older contemporary and possible influence Johann Friedrich Herbart (1776–1841).[10] In his *Lehrbuch zur Einleitung in die Philosophie (Introduction to Philosophy*, 1813), Herbart maintained that aesthetics should exclude emotions, intellect, and "content" and instead concern itself only with "elementary relations of lines, tones, planes, [and] colors" (Mallgrave and Ikonomou 10–11). In the case of the dramatic monologues and writing exercises of the Rentherr's daughter, the equivalents would be elementary relations of signifiers, syntax, and acoustic phenomena. Vischer explains that *Über das optische Formgefühl* arose from his father Friedrich Theodor Vischer's critique of Herbart's notion of "form without content" (89). As the younger Vischer contends, "There can be no form without content"; therefore, those forms that are seemingly "devoid of emotional life" must be "supplied with emotional content that

---

9. Cf. Brecht, "Short Description of a New Technique of Acting."
10. As state school board supervisor for Upper Austria, Stifter may have been influenced by Herbart's theories on educational psychology during the time he was revising *Turmalin* for publication in *Bunte Steine*; see Arens 111–17.

we—the observers—unwittingly transfer to them" by means of *Einfühlung* (89). Thus the girl's purely formal or "aesthetic" mode of experience makes her something like an "object," the ideal target of *Einfühlung*'s projective activity.

Stifter's relation to "the object" as a component, even a producer, of narration is complex. His practice of meticulously "scrubbing" the original, journal versions of his stories of emotional or "subjective" content before republishing them as book versions in his novella collections is well known (Mathias Mayer 25–26; Swales and Swales 118–19, 151–55). This method progressed to the point of the (attempted) complete erasure of narrative voice in Stifter's later stories—"the reproduction of exterior views without commentary" (Begemann, *Welt der Zeichen* 208), or, as pioneering Stifter scholar Hans Dietrich Irmscher put it, "gegenständliche Darstellung" (262): not just "objective representation" but, more radically, representation *as if from the side of an object*. How does the perfectly, but uncannily, mimetic "virtual reality" the Rentherr's daughter-as-object creates complete, reframe, problematize, and transcend the empathy experiments we have seen thus far in *Turmalin*? For this, we will need the concept of the *empathy machine*.

Empathy Machines

Shortly after the Rentherr's death, the housewife-narrator has a strange encounter with the man's daughter that will prove central to our understanding of the girl's relation to feeling, form, empathy, and theater. After the girl has explained how her father died, the narrator accompanies her back to the man's apartment. As the narrator recounts, "When we arrived in the basement room, [the girl] asked where her father was. I was in some embarrassment, as I had supposed that she knew that her father was dead, since she had used that word herself" (138). On the diegetic level, of course, the girl's uncomprehending use of the word "dead" indexes her neurodivergency or developmental disability, perhaps a result of her macrocephaly. On the level of the text as a signifying machine, however, the daughter's "objective" "performance" of language and (lack of) comprehension represents the novella's most sophisticated empathy experiment: one that "tests" a series of hypotheses about *Einfühlung* and intersubjective empathy at the site of aesthetics or form, and one that has real-world effects on the housewife-narrator. Here, the daughter herself becomes a "machine," or, more precisely, an empathy machine. As Grant Bollmer writes, "*Empathy machine* refers to any attempt to make sensible to oneself the emotional experience of another via technology, often with the goal of inhabiting another body. This term has regularly been used to describe virtual reality (VR), as VR, at least ideally, permits one to see through another's eyes, embodying their experiences, thus 'empathizing' with them" (63). In the case of the Rentherr's daughter, the technology is the girl's written and spoken words, as well as, from a certain perspective, the girl herself. She is the "other" whose emotional experience is to be "made sensible" to the housewife-narrator. But, strikingly, the girl is also *Other to herself*. Her own experience must be "made sensible" to *her*; she is herself the "other body" she may come to "inhabit." To follow this empathy experiment, we must bracket readings of the daughter that rely on psychological-realist, psychoanalytic, neurodivergency, or disability studies frameworks; ironically, we must also suspend reader response or "empathic" approaches to what would be the girl's traumatic suffering were she "real." Rather, we must focus on the girl's role as a "mechanism" in the text's machinery or as a performer in its semiotic "play."

Before undertaking this bracketing, let us turn for a moment to some other possible understandings of the daughter's role in the text. Despite its emphasis on the girl's lack of identification with her own mental and emotional experience, the narrative does at times equip her with externally observable and "motivated" affective responses that align with "neurotypical" expectations. After the narrator's second attempt to make the girl understand that her father's death means that he will never "come back," for example, the daughter finally begins to "weep bitterly" (138). Here, the girl's initial difficulty processing the situation and eventual display of emotion potentially correspond to psychologically realistic depictions of post-traumatic response, physical and developmental disability, neurodivergence, the unique and individual expression of grief, or the struggle to negotiate the expectations of an ableist world, among other possibilities. Yet the text's conspicuously extensive, repeated, and self-reflexive descriptions of the daughter's "dis-identified" affective presentation in her writings and recitations point to the substantially figurative dimension of her portrayal.

Psychoanalytically, the novella might be read as a "ghost story" about trauma and repression in which the living girl herself comes to embody or house the ghost. The Rentherr "haunts" his daughter and transmits his "actor trauma" to her; her written repetition of autobiographically painful scenes and vocal performances of "theatrical" texts, incomprehensible to her but clearly decipherable by an outside observer, are Freudian condensations and displacements of Dall and of the repressed effects of the Dall affair on her father and family.[11] The girl's claim that she "could no longer think of what had gone before [*es hatte alles Frühere vergessen*]" (141, *Turmalin* 163) and the fact that "she never spoke of anything except the room in the basement" (141)—a figurative locus, that is, of the unconscious—are marks of this repression. Even her physical disability might be read in this context as "symbolic" of the trauma to which she has been subjected. And, tellingly, when city officials arrive to open the Rentherr's original abandoned apartment, they find that the pendulum of his clock "had stopped and the hands pointed immutably to the same hour" (116–17), as if marking the time of a bomb blast or irremediable trauma.

To return to our bracket, however: Long before giving her "semi-dramatic performances of extracts from the finest masterpieces of our national literature" (145), the Rentherr's daughter enters the text as a "theatrical" figure, repeatedly put on display for "audiences." As an infant, she is adoringly watched by her parents as she lies in a proscenium-like crib presided over by a gilded, curtain-holding angel—already, as it were, onstage (108). Later, now macrocephalic, she becomes a "spectacle" to those who see her: The

---

11. I am indebted to my students Marcus Blackburn, Dylan McDonald, and Yabing (Sylvia) Sun for stimulating conversations about the nature of trauma, ghosts, and haunting in *Turmalin*; in particular, I thank McDonald for his felicitous phrase "actor trauma." See also Weitzman and Schiffermüller on the Rentherr's traumatizing of his daughter.

housewife-narrator must struggle to "avoid the crowd and get the girl away from the stares and exclamations of surprise which the sight of her unusual head ... provoked" (135). From another perspective, however, it is precisely the housewife who most subjects the girl to observation. From the beginning, the housewife's uncannily insistent, almost fanatical desire to "help" the girl makes this narrator an exemplary and unsettling figure for spectatorship and surveillance. Her very first act in the text is to follow the unknown father-daughter pair on the street to "find out something more about [them] or have a closer look at them" (120). In keeping with the "laboratory side" rather than the theatrical side of the daughter's spectacular visibility, the housewife transforms the girl into an "observable" experimental subject or lab animal. She uses doled-out sweets to lure the girl out of and back into her underground apartment as needed, then "scientifically" describes the daughter's reactions as though they were pieces of empirical evidence calling for interpretation: "[The girl] snatched at [the biscuit], ate it, and the features of her huge face expressed obvious pleasure [*einen augenfälligen Schein von Freude*]"; "She ate [the apple] with every sign of satisfaction" (132–33, *Turmalin* 155). Indeed, the narrator "trains" the girl through behaviorist mechanisms: "I repeated this procedure several times in the course of the day, partly in order to ... accustom [the girl] to a change in her situation and to allow her a semblance of freedom, so that she would not feel constrained and become recalcitrant and unmanageable" (139). Like Benjamin's actor in the age of mechanical reproduction, the daughter is "subjected to a series of tests": The narrator herself tests the girl by theatrically reciting the famous literary passages and waiting to see whether the girl will imitate them (145).[12]

Most crucially, however, the girl—viewed, again, not as an "actual," if fictional, person with a disability but as a device in the text's signifying economy—becomes an "art machine" or "empathy machine," a sort of "artificial intelligence" into which various commands have been input and whose programs she must execute. As

---

12. Cf. Benjamin, "Work of Art" 228–29; there, it is the motion picture camera that subjects the screen actor to a series of optical tests.

Ada Lovelace, author of the first computer algorithm, wrote of Charles Babbage's prototype punchcard computer in 1842, ten years before the publication of *Turmalin*, "The Analytical Engine has no pretensions to *originate* anything. It can do *whatever we know how to order it* to perform" (qtd. in Turing 450). The girl's theatrical and laboratory spectacle, that is, is intimately linked to what we might call her *performance of mindedness*, as well as to this performance's reception.

Mindedness—the assumption and confidence that, like ourselves, other people inhabit a conscious subjectivity—brings us to the central concern of the daughter's figuration. In his seminal paper "Computing Machinery and Intelligence" (1950), Turing asks whether, in an "imitation game," machines could behave so indistinguishably from humans that a human interrogator questioning two respondents—a computer and another human being, both hidden by screens—would be unable to tell from the printed answers alone which of the two respondents was human (433–36). Put slightly differently, could a computer's behavior trick a human into believing in the machine's mindedness, and, if so, is there any reliable way to differentiate between "real" mindedness and its (supposed) imitation? In a sense, the spoken words and written texts of the Rentherr's daughter, particularly as described by the housewife, represent just such a "Turing test."[13]

The housewife claims that the daughter speaks "in the purest literary diction" but that her words are still somehow "scarcely intelligible"—except when they are not: "Her whole speech might have seemed feeble-minded if parts of it had not nevertheless been very intelligent [*verständig*]" (132, *Turmalin* 154–55). She insists

---

13. Of course, Turing's "imitation game" differs from the housewife's interaction with the Rentherr's daughter in at least three important respects. First, Turing's game relies not on two players but three: the interrogator, the human respondent, and the machine respondent. In *Turmalin*, the housewife is the interrogator, and the girl is both respondents in one: a human whose responses appear to be "pure," machinelike imitation. The missing third player would be a human fully self-identified with her own experience. Secondly, the narrator has direct interaction with the daughter, who is not hidden behind a screen. Finally, of course, Turing's game involves an actual, not a metaphorical or tropic, machine.

that she must translate "the sense" of the girl's words into "our language or style of speech, because her own sequence of thoughts would not be intelligible" (133). Yet without the preexistence of this very intelligibility in at least some form, translation itself would be impossible. The housewife likewise says of the girl's writings that "the expressions were clear and incisive, the sentences correct and well constructed"—but nonetheless continues to characterize these texts as "senseless" (*sinnlos*) (154, *Turmalin* 167). A certain paradox seems to be at work here: It is very difficult to get a handle on what the girl's words are actually *like*. On the one hand, the narrator calls them "scarcely intelligible," in need of translation into a more comprehensible mode of communication, indeed "senseless"; on the other hand, the "expressions are clear and incisive," the "sentences correct and well constructed," and the overall meaning certainly "sensible" enough to permit translation into, or at least interpretative description within, the narrator's discourse. In what sense, then, are these verbal and written texts unintelligible, and what is the distinction between an intelligible and an unintelligible text?

The problem is compounded by the narrator's seamless conflation of the girl herself with her textual output. As the housewife states, apparently referring both to the daughter and her texts at once, "There was not a trace of any understanding of the meaning of death, or of wandering about in the world and doing away with oneself in despair, and yet these melancholy themes were the sole content of the girl's writings" (145). Here, the narrator's assumption that the *girl* does not understand or "feel" the meaning of her father's anticipated demise or her mother's imagined suffering—a potentially reasonable conclusion based on the girl's initial uncomprehending response to her father's actual death—slides into the rhetorical, metonymic assertion that, despite their "melancholy themes," the girl's *texts* do not understand. But texts do not "understand" in any case, and, as far as the *narrator's* understanding of *them* is concerned, their "sole content" transmits a quite intelligible message that the housewife easily receives and retransmits to the reader: "One day I [the Rentherr] shall lie dead in my coffin and they will bury me," and, "Your mother wanders about the world in the torment of her heart, ... dare[s] not return, and ... in the end ... does away with herself in despair" (141). The "melancholy themes" *are* the texts' "meaning," at least grammatically; the relation between this communicable, grammatical, "objective" meaning and "lived" understanding takes us back to mindedness—and our Turing test.

Theory of mind, "the ability to understand others as being minded, as having desires and beliefs that may differ from one's own" (Bollmer 66)—or, as the case may be, desires and beliefs that are *like* one's own—has been a part not just of theories of intersubjective empathy but also of the theorization of *aesthetic* empathy at least since *Einfühlung*'s heyday. As Meghan Marie Hammond contends, Lipps was the first to suggest that *Einfühlung* "might be used to deal with the conceptual problem of other minds" (73), and, as Bollmer writes, paraphrasing Lipps, "my understanding of another's mind is based on visible"—that is, in Alexander Baumgarten's sense, aesthetic—"evidence from the body of another, and my ability to grasp what another is feeling comes from the judgments that I make about what I imagine I would feel given what I can see about another" (73). Indeed, there is controversy surrounding Bollmer's last point about judgment and imagination: Lipps's *Einfühlungstheorie*, anticipating mirror neurons, might be read as arguing that *simply seeing* the physical actions of another—the movement through space of another's form—instantaneously generates an "automatic embodied resonance" that allows us to "experience (not just imagine) the same thing that the other person experiences" (Gallagher and Gallagher 779–80).[14]

In the case of the Rentherr's daughter, it is not the girl's body but her words—a prosthetic body, as it were, and a more abstract kind of form—that convince, or fail to convince, the housewife that the girl is "minded" and lead her to make empathic inferences about the girl's knowledge and affective states. If the girl's written words and theatrical recitations ultimately seem to the housewife-narrator mere simulations of lived meaning, this is at least in part because *another* of the girl's speech acts, or speech "acts"—an earlier utterance whose performance by the girl was, for the narrator, indistin-

---

14. On the many early debates about whether empathic access to another is automatic or analogically inferred, see Debes 313 ff. and Hammond 150–51.

guishable from the narrator's perception of this performance as "real"—had already "tricked" the narrator into a mistaken understanding *before* she encountered the girl's melancholy writings and enthusiastic declamations. This is the use of the word "dead" we have already noted: "When we arrived in the basement room [the girl] asked where her father was. I was in some embarrassment, as I had supposed that she knew that her father was dead, since she had used that word herself" (138). It is the disappointing of this understanding, the revelation that it had been in error, that conditions the narrator's conflation of girl and text.

The housewife's intersubjective feelings for and about the girl are substantially generated and mediated by the girl's function as pure form or formalism, her role as the "mechanical" producer of (mere) verbal and written "forms" (textual templates) of feeling. The narrator's sympathy for and empathy with the girl thus become a sort of *Einfühlung*, a self-projection into an object (the girl as textual form broadly understood). In this sense, the Rentherr's daughter anticipates the object-world that will come to dominate Vischer's conception of *Einfühlung*: his placing of objects, despite his claim that only love for his fellow humans makes projection into objects possible, at the very center of his theoretical system. In *Turmalin*, a human being can become (or become figured as) an object; in *Über das optische Formgefühl* and *Einfühlung* more broadly, feeling oneself into objects takes pride of place—even, in Lipps, becomes a model for thinking about how to relate empathically to other human beings—because, in a materialist age, the object, and also what we could logically call the object-form of relations, reigns.

Ultimately, in this empathy experiment, it doesn't matter whether the girl is "minded" or not: She can still produce what I have called "empathy effects." What is crucial here is, first, the housewife's *reception* of the girl (that is, her initial conviction, before learning to read the girl's "performance," that the daughter's understanding of death is genuine), and, second, the fact that empathy *does things on its own*, functions mechanically—is a machine. Unlike the replicants in *Blade Runner*, the girl herself does not need to experience the reality of her feelings (or the sense of the texts she reproduces): Their content can still be transmitted in a meaningful way to others, for whom it becomes effectively "real." Thus, in a sort of anti–Epic theatre that ironically arises *despite* the actor's nonidentification with her role, a virtual version of empathy is installed in the workings of early realist literary mimesis. The "reality" of the situation, however, at least until the narrator figures out what is going on, is more like Roland Barthes's "reality effect," and thus closer to "unowned" Massumian affect than to any actual emotional content. To borrow and alter the language of Barthes's famous discussion of the *effet de réel*, the daughter's words "finally say nothing but this": *we are to be felt* (by the girl's observers); "it is the category of ['empathy'] (and not [the words'] contingent contents) which is then signified" (cf. Barthes 148: "Flaubert's barometer, Michelet's little door finally say nothing but this: *we are the real*; it is the category of 'the real' (and not its contingent contents) which is then signified").

Empathy and the Erasure of Difference

The figure of the housewife-narrator has received less critical attention than Dall, the Rentherr, and his daughter, yet she is an equally important player in *Turmalin*'s theater of empathy. Her relation to the novella's "in-world" theater, however, is unique. Unlike the other characters, she enjoys the stage from a position of comfortable recreation and middle-class patronage, stopping by a friend's house with her husband after a Burgtheater performance to relax, take refreshments, and trade opinions about the piece they have just seen (120). This relation to the theater reflects the housewife's overall "bourgeois" role in the text's larger ideological web. Despite her spectator position with regard to the literal theater, she is at once the director and lead actress of a secondary (power) play unfolding alongside the narrative's other dramas—one in which pragmatic "empathy" kills Romanticism.

The housewife is the story's most overtly realist character, entirely lacking the fantastical elements that characterize the Rentherr and his daughter. Although clearly domestic according to the gender norms of her day (cleaning house, caring for her children), she is a powerhouse, almost to the point of self-parody, of effective hyper-efficiency in the realms of practical utility and the business of the everyday. She rapidly takes charge of the rescue and "rehabilitation" of the daughter, marching uninvited into the middle of the authorities' investigation of the Rentherr's death and speedily mobilizing an army of maids, city officials, and local personalities—as well as her husband—to secure the girl's protection. She is likewise a figurative detective (uncovering the mystery of the missing Rentherr), experimenter, and scientist, "testing" and "training" the daughter in numerous ways. In all these interventions, she appears ahead of her time, an activist or even a protofeminist, far from the stereotype of Stifterian misogyny, at least superficially. Additionally, she seems to embody the text's most healthy version of interpersonal empathy, or, more precisely, sympathetic altruism: Once she learns of the girl's plight, she springs into action, sparing no resource of time, effort, or money to assist her. But the picture is not so simple. The eagerness and ability of the housewife and her husband to "help" the daughter already have something excessive, mechanical, and therefore uncanny about them. The husband visits literally "every office in Vienna that had even the remotest connection with money or assets of any other sort" on the girl's behalf (143); he eventually assumes guardianship of the total stranger. The housewife organizes each step of the girl's resocialization like an "amateur social worker" (Campbell 578). It is difficult not to sense something monstrous in the way the pair, especially the wife, makes it their business to manage all aspects of the girl's case: The couple's relentless good cheer, limitless extra time, and apparent inability to become exhausted, no matter how many draining tasks they perform, are conspicuous and unsettling. And the actual content of the housewife's help is questionable as well.

As ethical theorist Nel Noddings contends, the incursive projection of Self into Other associated with *Einfühlung* might be thought of as a "peculiarly rational, western, masculine way of looking at 'feeling with'" (28). Bollmer draws on metaphors of incorporation rather than penetration but similarly conveys some of the strongest critiques of empathy, both aesthetic and interpersonal, when he writes that empathy "absorb[s] another's body and experience into one's own," only "acknowledg[ing] the existence of the Other insofar as it can become assimilated into the same" (71). What is instead needed, he maintains, is "radical compassion," an "ethical stance" that is "about the potentials of *not* understanding another, of *not* feeling what they feel, in a way that does not negate or ignore the experience of another but is open to it, even if it can never fully grasp it" (71–72). The daughter's inner experience, "impenetrable" and unknowable, resists both the masculinist and absorptive empathic modes; it therefore invites us to ask whether the housewife's interventions, despite their "peculiarly rational, western" nature, might in fact represent such an alternative approach to caring not based on problematic models of empathy, if only by default. The housewife does, after all, fully engage in attempting to help the girl even though she does not and cannot *understand the girl's understanding* of her own experiences. Still, the process begins with the "trick" or illusion of understanding generated by projective *Einfühlung* into the empty vessels or pure forms of the daughter's words, the effect of the "empathy machine" represented by the girl: "When we arrived in the basement room [the girl] asked where her father was. I was in some embarrassment, as I had supposed that she knew that her father was dead, since she had used that word herself" (138). And if it later seems that the housewife, upon considering the daughter's writings, implicitly "acknowledges that the affective does not inhabit all bodies equally and ... does not move through all bodies similarly" (Bollmer 74), it is only this assumption of affective and cognitive similarity, or indeed identity, that allows the narrator to insist that the girl shows "not a trace of understanding" of her own suffering—that her words are "senseless" (145). Put otherwise, the narrator, pragmatically pushing past all resistance, is projecting or "penetrating"— in Noddings's terms, "masculine"—after all. She will *declare* the daughter "senseless," and what she does not understand, what is senseless to her, she will *make* into a particular type of sense.

This is the domestic, and domesticated, sense of the mid-nineteenth century's gendered labor order, of which the housewife herself is, ironically, the agent and enforcer. There is no need for the surrogate father figures of husband, state, or society to show the daughter her "proper place" when the female but patriarchally socialized narrator—tellingly, Stifter's only substantial use of a female narrative voice (Mathias Mayer 129)—so easily steps into that role. Not long after she and her husband take the daughter in, the housewife conspicuously notes that "although the words [the girl] used were so well chosen and correct and so well arranged, even if her train of thought was often hard to follow, she had nevertheless not the slightest knowledge or conception of any kind of household work [*weibliche Arbeit*, literally "women's work"]" (140, *Turmalin* 163). Here, the strange legibility-illegibility of the girl's language becomes inextricably linked to the difficulty of locating her position on a grid of nineteenth-century gendered labor coordinates— an ambiguity the narrator takes it upon herself to resolve. This "resolution" likewise "resolves," or at least forcibly attempts to resolve, the tension between fading Romanticism and rising realism that pervades the novella.

On one level, *Turmalin*, with its allusions to the Gothic (the mad musician and his "deformed" daughter), the detective story (the mystery of the missing Rentherr), and the fairy tale (the girl who learns domestic tasks by living with a "strange" woman), evokes the templates of familiar Romantic texts. The housewife first hears the Rentherr's weird flute music while walking by moonlight, a conspicuously Romantically overdetermined scene (120–22). The Rentherr dresses like Goethe's Werther, technically a Sturm und Drang figure, but a clear progenitor of the Romanticism to come (119). The daughter's nodding and "talking" jackdaw (132) recalls the nodding and talking magic bird of Tieck's *Der blonde Eckbert* (*Blond Eckbert*), one of the earliest German Romantic novellas and *Kunstmärchen*. But if the text positions the girl and her father as Romantic figures, or at least as figures for an aesthetic past (the daughter is introduced wearing a "sleevelss cloak . . . almost like a toga," 119), this past is marked as something "sick," an aesthetic to be overcome. The girl's head is "pathologically" oversized, the bird's speech "unintelligible, distorted, and scarcely . . . human[like]" (132), the Rentherr's music "almost . . . demented" (122). The father and daughter are thus prime examples of the Biedermeier "outsider" or *Sonderling*, the eccentric, Romantic-aesthetic holdover in a rising realist age. The Rentherr and his flute playing in particular recall the melancholy fiddler and his "Katzenmusik" (charivari) from the 1848 novella *Der arme Spielmann* (*The Poor Musician*) by Stifter's fellow Austrian Franz Grillparzer, one of the most well-known representations of the *Sonderling* motif in German-language literature. Tellingly, the housewife, on first seeing the strange epigonal couple pass by, assumes that they are going to the "hospital church" (119–20), a double site of secular and spiritual healing. And if the first two-thirds of the novella stages an intertwining of Romantic genres, the housewife-narrator's "education" of the daughter to economically profitable, gender-normative labor—"[the girl] took to weaving carpets, rugs, and similar articles [that people] . . . were always very willing to buy" (147)—transforms the text into a realist demystification or "anti-Märchen."[15]

As in an archetypal fairy tale collected by the Brothers Grimm, a girl in crisis goes to live with an unrelated woman and learns domestic tasks. But, in a reversal of generic expectations, *Turmalin*'s girl is removed from, rather than placed into, social isolation; her new host and teacher is not a witch but an avatar of pragmatic "usefulness"; and the spinning (or, rather, weaving) she masters produces not magical golden thread but actual, no-nonsense "gold"— currency, legal tender. The domesticated beneficiary of the housewife's relentlessly rationalizing "help," the daughter concludes her trajectory in a literally dis-enchanted world, released from the "spell" of the Rentherr's Romantic "song" (the etymological roots of *enchantment* mean a spell cast by song, from the Latin *incantare*, "to bewitch," and *cantare*, "to sing"). As if to give physical form to this transformation, the girl's head tangibly shrinks as she is "cured" of the spell of the Romantic—as the narrator succeeds in replacing her "wild, fragmentary, indeed almost uncanny education," the literal and figurative "flute music" of the Rentherr, with "simple, coherent, and intelligible thoughts" (146, 169, translation modified). Put otherwise, the girl's disenchantment is complete when she *spinnt*, "spins thread," but no longer *spinnt*, "is crazy"— the German *spinnen* means both. For the housewife-narrator, empathizing with, *imagining* that she empathizes with, and ultimately

---

15. Cf. Büchner's more well-known use of the grandmother's nihilistic anti-Märchen in *Woyzeck* (252).

deciding she *cannot* truly empathize with—which effectively means the same thing as "feeling *herself* into"—the girl erases this other's Otherness and difference.

Empathy Machines Revisited: Hidden Pictures; Ambivalent Aesthetics

Sarah Kofman argues that "only a machine can be truly devoid of all feeling, ... and therefore only a machine can rigorously imitate nature and be a perfect portraitist" ("Resemblance" 224). But what type of machine, and what type of portraitist? As Jonathan Crary writes, nineteenth-century industrialization saw the rise of "a new kind of sign": "potentially identical objects produced in indefinite series" (12). The most important of these was the photograph, first popularized by the daguerreotype in 1839 and made truly "serial" by the introduction of the calotype paper negative process in 1841. As Crary explains, "Within this new field of serially produced objects, the most significant, in terms of their social and cultural impact, were photography and a host of related techniques for the industrialization of image making. The photograph becomes a central element not only in a new commodity economy but in the reshaping of an entire territory on which signs and images ... circulate and proliferate.... Photography is an element of a new and homogeneous terrain of consumption and circulation in which an observer becomes lodged" (13). And, as art historian Krzysztof Pijarski notes, "the fact that [literary realism] is historically a nineteenth-century phenomenon and that it appeared around the same time as photography is very telling" (148). Indeed, Stifter's first story was published in 1840, one year after the appearance of the daguerreotype.

Despite the historical overlap between the rise of realism and the rise of photography, photographs and cameras are rarely depicted directly in canonical German realist texts. Hegel had already "condemn[ed] the strict imitation of nature as ... sacrilegious, demonic, and unworthy of spirit because it is the work of a pure, technical skill rather than that of a truly creative power" (Kofman, "Resemblance" 224). The German realists followed suit. As Kathrin

Maurer points out, "Karl Gutzkow, Theodor Storm, and Theodor Fontane, to name but a few, regarded the photographic reproduction of reality as an offense against what they viewed as the essential function of art" (63). Charles Baudelaire, writing "perhaps the most famous nineteenth-century critique of photography" (Pijarski 148) in his *Salon of 1859*, just a few years after the publication of *Turmalin*, argued that realist art had "declared war on the imagination" (Pijarski 148) by wishing to depict "the universe without man" (Baudelaire, qtd. in Pijarski 149). As Pijarski summarizes, "The suggestion that is made here is clear: . . . The painter-realist is somebody who strives for a certain *automatism*, as if he were himself a machine. In the same way, photography, as it is inhuman, can only record reality, but not interpret it. As a mechanical, *automatic* thing (and thus working on its own) it is a representative of the destructive forces of modernization: progress and industry" (149). Stifter himself took a decidedly negative view of photography (Maurer 68), and it is precisely the "forces of modernization: progress and industry," that, according to many scholars, he endeavored to fight in his supposed textual "utopias."[16] Ironically, nineteenth-century writers' "negative reactions to photography . . . were of the same kind as the arguments against the 'realists' [themselves] . . . : creating a perfectly accurate picture of reality does not necessarily translate to understanding it . . . ; it means that we remain on the surface of things" (Pijarski 148).

Photography is never overtly mentioned or represented in *Turmalin*. Indeed, the novella's historical setting "long ago" (*Turmalin* 105) makes it unlikely that actual photographs could appear in the text: Based on Stifter's probable use of the Enlightenment-era Viennese actor Joseph Lange as the inspiration for Dall (Luke, introduction 15–16), it is reasonable to place the novella's plot in the second half of the eighteenth century. However, the narrative installs a covert discourse of photography, and particularly of photography as serial or "machine" reproduction, below its surface. This already

---

16. Maurer maintains that despite Stifter's skepticism toward photography "as an aesthetic medium," he was "nevertheless . . . drawn to the new possibilities of representation that it provided"; see "Close-Ups" 72.

begins with the Rentherr's hall of proliferating celebrity "portraits" (106), or, as Stifter's original puts it, "Blätter von Bildnissen"—"pages of likenesses," "pages of images," or "sheets of paper with images" (*Turmalin* 127). Even if we disregard the narrative's likely eighteenth-century time frame in favor of an internal chronology based on the dates of the novella's composition, daguerreotype and calotype photography would only appear around the beginning of the story's final decade—that is, decades after the diegetic events in the celebrity hall. However, in the light of the daguerreotype's explosive spread as a portrait medium in the 1840s and especially the growth of serially reproducible paper photographs around 1850—the time, in other words, of *Turmalin*'s composition, revision, and publication—we might wonder whether, in a productive flash of anachronism and extradiegetic conflation, the Rentherr's "likenesses" could register for *Stifter's audiences* as photographs. That is, the highly popular but expensive (and therefore less collectable) daguerreotype portraits of the 1840s and the more easily accessible paper photographs of the later 1840s and early 1850s—the kind of mechanically reproducible objects that, at least in theory, could appear as copious "sheets with likenesses" on a "wall of images"—might merge in a contemporary reader's mind into the undifferentiated signifier "photography." Benjamin, for example, underscores in his "Kleine Geschichte der Photographie" ("Small History of Photography") the mid-nineteenth-century association of the reproduction of human likenesses with photography: "The actual victim of photography became ... the miniature portrait. Things developed so fast that already around 1840 most of the countless painters of miniatures became professional photographers, at first only on the side, but soon exclusively" (293). The Rentherr's position in the middle of such an implicitly "photographic" field of "spectacular," serially reproduced commodities heightens his association with a perilous modernity—with mimetically "accurate" but machinelike, uncomprehending, and surface-level "realist" aesthetics (cf. Pijarski 148–49)—and with the problem of possession, both material and psychological. To recall Crary's point, "The photograph becomes a central element not only in a new commodity economy but in the reshaping of an entire territory on which signs and images ... circulate

160   Chapter 2

and proliferate. . . . Photography is an element of a new and homogeneous terrain of consumption and circulation in which an observer becomes lodged" (13).

As *Turmalin*'s most striking examples of perfectly reproductive but uncomprehending "technology," the Rentherr's daughter and her "serially reproduced" narratives and declamations continue the novella's subterranean figuration of photography, here displaced from a visual to an oral/aural and written register. As suggested in the previous chapter, the modern rise of *Einfühlung* might be read, at least in part, as a *resistance* to modernity: that is, as a means, ironically arising out of developments in modernity itself (neurophysiology, materialism), of preserving an albeit ghostly, uncanny, or "demonic" version of holistic "life" against a world of dead objects. In a different understanding of resistance than the ones we have previously considered, the Rentherr's daughter emerges here as *modernity without the resistance*—not just an object but a "mass" object, or at least the producer of ones. Simultaneously uncomprehending, "spectacular" (like a photograph, *to be looked at*), and indefatigably (re)productive, she is an uncanny medium or, to paraphrase Benjamin, a "mechanical reproducer"—and thus a perfect site to stage the nineteenth century's (and Stifter's) anxieties about the potential dangers of an emergent realist, "photographic" aesthetic. Her speech and writing are not Vischer's "scanning" but rather his mere "seeing," "the simple reproduction or photographic impression of the object on our retina" (Vischer 93)—in her case, the simple reproduction or photographic impression of *feeling* on the *form* of her voice or text. The novella even goes so far as to immerse the girl in "iodide baths" (146) like a daguerreotype plate being sensitized for exposure: a detail invented, like the Rentherr's portrait hall and the girl's written "Turing tests," specifically for the revised *Bunte Steine* edition of the narrative, and thus an indication of the importance of these "photographic" features to Stifter's signifying economy.[17]

---

17. A daguerreotype plate must be sensitized by iodine fumes to create the silver iodide surface required for photography; technically, then, early photographs required not a liquid but a "fume bath." Additionally, iodide baths may be used to

Kofman, paraphrasing Plato, writes of the uncanniness of rigorous mimesis that "resemblance . . . can be situated neither in the place of being nor in the place of nonbeing"; it is "an unwonted and ambiguous presence, which is also the sign of an absence and belongs to an inaccessible elsewhere—hence ungraspable and diabolically deceptive. Resemblance upsets all the categories that clearly distinguish between model and copy, life and death" ("Resemblance" 220–21). Even if we do not consider the Rentherr's daughter "diabolically deceptive," like Vischer's empathic reanimation of the hanged girl, but rather only deceptive *in effect*, we might still conclude that the "formal" doppelgänger of her mimetic "art," as Kofman writes in a different context, undermines "the entire system of metaphysical oppositions on which philosophical discourse on art"—and, I might add, "on 'Being'"—"classically depends: the opposition between art and nature, sensible and intelligible, form and content, surface and depth, appearance and reality, signifier and signified, and so forth" (Kofman, "Melancholy" 205). Thus the initial apparent opposition between the Rentherr's daughter and Dall dissolves. If, in a reversal of Dall's "Method acting," the girl's performances abolish content in favor of form, both "actors" end up in the same place: with the poles of art and reality collapsed into each other and thus equally erased, like *Einfühlung*'s illusory binary self and other of the previous chapter.

Turmalin stages an ambivalent experiment about the relations of empathy and aesthetics, feeling and form. Theater itself, a binding trope of the novella, becomes the form of the experiment being run—an experiment on the limits, gaps, and paradoxes of empathy. At first, the text seems to be about limit cases of intersubjective empathy as allegorized by theater: actors' empathy with parts, audiences' with actors, observers' with developmentally disabled subjects *figured* as actors (the Rentherr's daughter), and, if playing oneself is a role, the daughter's with herself. However, this inquiry into

---

treat goiters. However, since the girl's medical condition is an enlarged head rather than an enlarged neck, the image of the iodide bath, with its reference to a chemical intimately associated with early photographic production, retains its suggestively figurative function.

intersubjective empathy is inseparable from questions of form, or the question of our ability to feel with or feel into what presents as *pure formalism*: the formal simulation of feeling, or what we might call the "logical form" of theater itself.

The text is ambivalent about its central figure of the Rentherr's daughter. On the one hand, it sets her up as a figure for an almost Herbartian "contentless" aesthetic. If, for Herbart, aesthetics is purely formal or formalist, then "the perfect aesthetic frame of mind" is, as the girl's often seems to be, "a state of absolute indifference" (Mallgrave and Ikonomou 10–11). Or perhaps the girl's feelings, like those of the novella itself, are "present" in "virtual form," just as the text performs its own affective content virtually, spread across its dispassionate surface, in the gaps and swerves of its experimental narrative form. It "acts" affect obliquely; we must work to fill in the seemingly absent feelings between the lines. Or, again, the girl's formalism functions metaphorically as a sort of Turing test, anticipating artificial intelligence and asking whether there is a way to tell the difference between real and simulated emotion and mindedness—"resemblance," as Kofman would put it, "deceiving" the housewife-narrator into the illusion of understanding and empathy. Finally, the daughter's performance of feeling as form makes it almost inevitable that attempts at intersubjective empathy with her will become *Einfühlung*, the projection of an observing self into an aesthetic object. Thus the narrative is about the feeling of its own forms, as well as about its characters' feelings about the forms with which they diegetically engage.

Turmalin likewise remains suspended between fear and fascination regarding the daughter's mimetic aesthetics. The daughter is a "spectacle" of reproduction, a "machine" uncanny in its ability to produce effects, both empathic and aesthetic. Ultimately, she and the novella for which she is the most representative figure open up an experimental space for asking certain philosophical and ethical questions. In the decades of the mid-nineteenth century when materialism and the "object world" were on the rise—the decades, that is, when people, too, might start to be seen as "objects" of the sort that Vischer will make the center of his form-based *Einfühlungstheorie* a generation later—how can we be sure that we are indeed accessing "other minds"? And what do we do when we do, or do not, "access" them? How do we relate to, and treat, these others whom the epistemic currents of the day invite us to objectify?

Der Hochwald, the second Stifter text we shall investigate, is an even more ambivalent empathy experiment, for it works against itself. Even as its content tragically or melodramatically punishes characters with whom the reader narratively empathizes, its form, especially its rhythms, syntax, and punctuation, "embodies" intensity and affect in the Massumian sense, anticipating a corporeally focused, post-Vischerian *Einfühlung* that holds out hope for the "escape" of these characters from the novella's overtly oppressive gender order. It is to this text that I now turn.

Der Hochwald: Divided Loyalties, "Colliding Forms"

As *Der Hochwald* approaches its catastrophic conclusion—catastrophic in the triple sense of disastrous, marking the resolution of a tragic plot, and potentially reversing a text's ideological investments—we encounter a scene of divided loyalties, both a character's and a narrator's, that opens a window onto this strange novella's embodiment of empathy and affect, intensity and form. The young Bohemian Austrian noblewoman Clarissa von Wittinghausen, sequestered by her father from the dangers of the Thirty Years' War in an uncanny forest safe house, has just exchanged impromptu engagement vows with her secret lover Ronald, errant and incognito son of the Swedish king and thus high-ranking royalty on the enemy side. In a mixture of authorial and psychonarration, the narrator transmits and critiques Clarissa's shifting feelings about Ronald, her younger sister Johanna, and the sisters' septuagenarian caretaker Gregor, the latter two of whom have also been hiding with Clarissa in the forest retreat before Ronald's disconcerting arrival. I cite the passage in its entirety:

> Strange is man, and stranger is his heart. How uniformly the days in the forest had passed one after the other before Ronald's arrival! Every day the same colors, the same voices, the same solemnity, and on the lake

the same still air, so that it had sometimes seemed they were bored; – now a surfeit, indeed a *shower* of bliss had come over Clarissa's heart, streaming out from that incomprehensible feeling through which the Creator binds the two sexes, that they blessedly serve His ends – but nevertheless she did not feel blessed, indeed, she felt as though those earlier monotonous days had been happier than the current ones, and as though she had esteemed and loved herself more then. – She looked back almost with melancholy at how she had walked through the places in the woods with Gregor, with Johanna, chatting innocently, herself as innocent as her sister and the old man, both of whom had so beautifully believed in her, then in the evenings talking [*kosend*] and teaching and falling asleep with Johanna, for whose simple heart she had been the treasure and riches of this earth – – and now: she carried a heavy sweet feeling in her heart, leading away from the two figures at her side, otherwise beloved by her, and seeking a stranger, and seeking the increase of her own bliss. – – O holy gold of the conscience, how quickly and beautifully you punish the heart that begins to grow selfish. (96–97)

The divided loyalties here are not only personal and political but also *narratological*. On the one hand, the passage is a prime example, channeled through the narrative voice, of Stifter's notorious and oft-noted hostility toward excess, passion, and desire—especially, in a predictable patriarchal fusion of all of the above, *female* agency and desire.[18] Despite the extreme security measures taken by Clarissa's father Baron Heinrich and his appointed agent Gregor, Ronald has managed to find the hidden sanctuary. The star-crossed couple's sudden betrothal will lead Ronald to race to the sisters' castle to attempt to convince the approaching Swedish troops to leave its remaining inhabitants, including the girls' father and their brother Felix, unharmed; an outraged Heinrich, however, will launch an attack that ends up causing not only his own death but also the deaths of Felix and, ironically, Ronald himself. The sisters are about to return from their "protective" exile to a scene of burned-out castle ruins and familial extinction; after years of childless spinsterdom, they will disappear into unmarked graves. The

---

18. On Stifter's hostility toward passion and desire, see for example Merker 127–28; on his policing of female desire and agency in particular, see Downing 41–90. For a counterargument positing Stifter's unconscious attraction to passion, see Reddick, "Mystification" 69.

narrator, telling the tale from the standpoint of Stifter's 1840s, knows all of this, and makes a point of blaming Clarissa—and, by extension, "woman"—for it.

On the other hand, despite the narrator's attempts to make the novella conform to an "Eve-in-the-garden" template, the text, like the biblical story itself, presents ample evidence, even on the purely diegetic level, for a significantly more complicated picture. Clarissa, to be sure, had hidden her love for Ronald from her family and compatriots (albeit without knowing that he was a Swedish prince); however, Ronald likewise hides his feelings for Clarissa from Gregor, his old friend from incognito hunting forays, thereby delaying the lovers' meeting and increasing their danger from the approaching troops. Gregor makes no attempt to determine why Ronald wishes to speak with Clarissa before simply refusing his entrance to the sanctuary, thus similarly obstructing the couple's meeting and increasing the difficulty of reaching the girls' castle in time. Baron Heinrich had long ago hosted the undercover Ronald as a guest at the castle (ironically the roots of the affair with Clarissa), and Gregor himself had shown Ronald the spot that would one day become the site of the forest retreat, thus allowing the Swede to locate the sisters in hiding—again without knowing Ronald's true identity or how the site would be used in the future. Ronald's father, the Swedish king, had forced his son to distance himself from Clarissa, hindering any earlier movement toward interpersonal or international understanding. The Swedish troops, for their part, had not even intended to attack Castle Wittinghausen: The Austrians ambushed them as they passed a nearby town, inciting them to revenge. Finally, it is Baron Heinrich himself who, without seeking clarification or understanding, angrily launches the assault on Ronald when he sees his erstwhile houseguest approach the castle (with, as the reader knows, an offer of protection)—the assault that leads to his own, his son's, and the young Swedish prince's death. Passion, along with stupidity, blind chance, a nihilistically indifferent universe, and the sadistic machinations of plot, may indeed play a role in the novella's cascading series of disasters—but it is as much, if not more, *male* passion as female.

Most importantly, however, the narrative voice of the long passage cited above is not only ambivalent but in fact strikingly radical in its assigning of liability. Intertwined with blame, the narrator articulates an exonerating understanding or exculpatory empathy with Clarissa. For how can one's "heart" be truly "selfish" when it is simply obeying the "incomprehensible," perhaps even irresistible, "feeling through which the Creator binds the two sexes, that they blessedly serve His ends"? Indeed, it would seem that the narrator's deeper quarrel is not with Clarissa but with God. The Swaleses devote considerable attention to this paradox, both in Stifter's text and in the larger context of Christian thought, without resolving it: They conclude that *Der Hochwald* is an "early" and "flawed" work "that does not fully succeed in transforming irresolution . . . into the tensions of a consistent dialectical illumination" (57). Whatever the case, the text's "irresolution" points to the culpability of a transcendent patriarchal principle: If there is a critique of passion here, it is simultaneously a critique of passion's *author*, the "divine" patriarch. When, early in the novella, Johanna links the as yet unseen Ronald with rumors of a mysterious "marksman" or "poacher" (the German word "Wildschütze" may suggest both) in the woods, describing him as a sort of malevolent cupid ("This man only has to fire his rifle, and he will always hit the one he is thinking of," 14), Clarissa's reply is a revealing anti-theodicy: "How could God, the all-powerful lord of the universe, allow such evil miracles if He wants us to go on trusting how He has arranged the world, this trust being after all our duty and our joy?" (15). From one perspective, the entire text might be read as a shattering of the trustworthiness of "the Father" and his earthly avatars, an unveiling of the fact that this trustworthiness, its claim to moral authority, has been flawed from the start. But this shattering, or, perhaps more accurately, *liquifying* ("a surfeit, indeed a *shower* of bliss had come over Clarissa's heart, *streaming* out from that incomprehensible feeling"), exists in constant tension throughout the text with the counteracting forces—or, better, *forms*—of patriarchal order, exemplified by the novella's excessive proliferation of social and physical structures, patterns, and practices meant to figuratively and literally "channel" the sisters' flows: patriarchal, dynastic, and (ethno-)national marriage expectations; Baron Heinrich's sequestering of his daughters in the impenetrable retreat, as much an attempt to remove them from the sexual economy overall as to protect them from the region's marauding military forces (Downing 87–88); the girls' mazelike path through the forest, riding in the "narrow carryable prison" (*das enge tragbare Gefängnis*) of the sedan box (42); the geophysical features of the sanctuary site, with its sentinel cliffs and defensive lake; and, finally, the architectural layout of the safe house itself, in which the "chambers assigned" to the girls are "frighteningly similar [*bis zum Erschrecken ähnlich*] to the ones they had inhabited in [Castle] Wittinghausen" (43).[19]

Forms, Caroline Levine writes, "make order"; they are thus "the stuff of politics" (3). Just as significantly, forms can "collide" with each other (18–19): "Aesthetic and political forms may be nested inside one another," each "capable of disturbing the other's organizing power" (16–17). As Levine argues, "The form that best captures the experience of colliding forms is narrative" (31), and narrative voice is indeed the most pervasive "form," broadly conceived, of Stifter's text. We have already seen something of this voice's internal division or *self*-collision in the suspension, discovered in the long passage above, between blame and exoneration. There is another way, however, that forms collide within the broader structure of the novella's narrative voice. Inseparable from—at times supporting and enabling, at times pulling against—not only the text's individual discursive statements but, more importantly, its overall ideological "messaging" or investments, we find *Der Hochwald*'s rhythms, punctuation, and syntax, the "formal" pulse of its *ductus* or the "surfeits" and "showers" of its textual "body," allegorized in the long passage by the marker of the double dash, " – – " (97). We will encounter stronger and more relevant examples throughout the text.

Innigkeit: Intensity and Affect, Empathy and *Einfühlung*

Clarissa's "surfeit, indeed *shower* of bliss" and the text's corresponding pulses bring us to the intersection point of intensity and affect, empathy and *Einfühlung*—the feeling of (and into) the text's form.

---

19. On the "frighteningly similar" rooms, see also Downing 58–59.

The cited passage, like the novella as a whole, is permeated by affect in its broad sense: Seigworth and Gregg's "inventory of shimmers," micro-nuances of feeling, or bodily "capacities to act and be acted upon" (Seigworth and Gregg 1). As Seigworth and Gregg write, "Affect is in many ways synonymous with force or forces of encounter," but not simply with "especially forceful" or traumatic force (2). Rather, "it is quite likely that affect more often transpires within and across the subtlest of shuttling intensities: all the miniscule or molecular events of the unnoticed" (2). In *Der Hochwald*, we find *both*: in the long passage alone, "seeming" boredom, a streaming shower of bliss, "incomprehensible" and "heavy sweet" feelings, "almost" melancholy, Clarissa's subjunctive sense "as though" things had been happier in the past, and of course the "forceful" or traumatic force of the encounter with Ronald. In one sense, the novella might be said to be *about* affect capaciously defined, with Stifter indeed, as F. T. Bratranek maintained, the "physiologist [detailing] the emergence of psychic life from its elements" (Selge 15).

However, as the "surfeit" and "shower" of "bliss" suggest, *Der Hochwald* is also about affect in Massumi's more specific sense: an undifferentiated flow of felt "intensity" as opposed to fixed, named, and personally "owned" emotions, "corresponding to the passage from one experiential state of the body to another and implying an augmentation or diminution in that body's capacity to act" (Massumi, notes xvi). For Massumi, affect is "equated with" intensity itself ("Autonomy of Affect" 88) and is an unreified, "asubjective," "asignifying" energy (Shaviro, *Post-Cinematic Affect* 3), both bodily and trans-bodily, that remains, as Massumi puts it, "unassimilable" or "autonomous" ("Autonomy" 88). As Massumi writes, *emotion* is "subjective content, the socio-linguistic fixing of the quality of an experience which is from that point onward defined as personal. Emotion is qualified intensity, the conventional, consensual insertion of intensity into semantically and semiotically formed progressions, into narrativizable ... function and meaning. It is intensity owned and recognized ("Autonomy" 88). *Affect*, on the other hand,

> is autonomous to the degree to which it escapes confinement in the particular body whose vitality, or potential for interaction, it is. Formed,

qualified, situated perceptions and cognitions fulfilling functions of actual connection or blockage are the *capture* and closure of affect. Emotion is the intensest (most contracted) expression of that capture—and of the fact that something has always and again escaped. Something remains unactualized, inseparable from but unassimilable to any *particular*, functionally anchored perspective. That is why all emotion is ... disorienting, and why it is classically described as being outside of oneself, at the very point at which one is most intimately ... in contact with oneself and one's vitality.... Actually existing, structured things live in and through that which escapes them. Their autonomy is the autonomy of affect. ("Autonomy" 96–97)

Or, as Steven Shaviro puts it, "subjects are overwhelmed and traversed by affect, but they *have* or *possess* their own emotions" (*Post-Cinematic Affect* 3).

In the light of Massumi's distinction, Clarissa's transition from a surfeit and shower of bliss to her "not feeling blessed," "looking back almost with melancholy," "as though earlier days had been happier," "as though she had esteemed and loved herself more then," cuts two ways. It is the passage from affect to, or back to, the "confinement" of emotion, yet one whose hesitantly subjunctive nature—"*as though* earlier days had been happier," "*as though* she had esteemed and loved herself more then," "looking back *almost* with melancholy"—reveals the trace or "autonomic remainder" (Massumi, "Autonomy" 85) of affect itself. As Massumi contends, "The escape of affect *cannot but be perceived, alongside* the perceptions that are its capture" ("Autonomy" 97). Before, during, and after her betrothal and other emotional and physical "captures," Clarissa is continuously *leaking affect*—as is Stifter's text.

Intensity was an object of philosophical and scientific concern in Stifter's day: As Crary points out, in the law of differential sensitivity formulated by Stifter's contemporary Gustav Fechner, which Fechner would publish in his 1860 *Elemente der Psychophysik*, "human perception became a sequence of magnitudes of varying intensity" (146). Massumi's equating of affect with intensity evokes what is perhaps the most prevalent term for, and mode of, affective intensity in Der Hochwald: *Innigkeit*, one of Stifter's favorite words in the novella, and one that appears with striking frequency in both its nominal and adjectival forms in connection with Clarissa or the

Wittinghausen sisters. A word with a notably extensive range of meanings, *Innigkeit* spans the semantic spectrum covered in English by such diverse concepts as inwardness, intimacy, mutuality of feeling, *excessive* intimacy, sincerity, devotion, poignancy, heartfelt depth, fervency, ardency, ardor, and indeed *intensity itself*. *Turmalin*'s translator David Luke, for example, renders Stifter's *Innigkeit* as "intensity" (105, *Turmalin* 126), and philosopher David Farrell Krell, in a discussion of Hölderlin, writes that "*Innigkeit* suggests the intensity of ecstasy, of standing outside onself": "amicable and intimate, yes—but also intense to the point of ecstasy" (notes 226). Just as Massumi declares, then, that "for present purposes, intensity will be equated with affect" ("Autonomy" 88), we may state that, for present purposes, *Innigkeit* will be glossed, though not without residue, as intensity. Almost immediately after Clarissa and Johanna's initial appearance in the text, the term occurs four times in the space of less than a page. Clarissa tells Johanna that there are "joys in the world so fierce that they can break our hearts – – and sufferings of such intensity [*Innigkeit*] – – – oh, they are so intense [*innig*]!! –" (12). Johanna responds by rushing to her sister and kissing her "inexpressibly tenderly [*unsäglich zärtlich*] on the mouth"; in reply, Clarissa likewise kisses Johanna "twice quite intensely [*innig*] on her childlike lips" (13). The girls then engage in conversation whose "fundamental tone" or "tonic note" (*Grundton*) the narrator describes as "Innigkeit" (13)—a linking of intensity with musical terminology that recalls the performance mark *innig* popular on Romantic scores of Stifter's day. On the one hand, *Innigkeit* here is a nameless (*unsäglich*) flow of intensity, excessive and undetermined. Like Massumi's affect, it marks the space of unspecified, perhaps unspecifiable experience (" – – – "; "!!"): In semiotic terms, it is a contentless slot. From another perspective, however, the content, or at least the "Grundton," of this experience may perhaps be, if not specified, then gestured toward and *worked with* after all.

If the content of the narrator's discourse cannot decide whether it wants to blame Clarissa or exonerate her—if it remains suspended, that is, between compassionate understanding or "virtual" intersubjective empathy and a cruelty that goes beyond even what Breithaupt, in a different context, calls "empathic sadism," "sadistic and violent behavior ... performed for the sake of exciting empathy," "evoked and enjoyed," as we will see later in this chapter, "even (or perhaps especially) when the other is suffering" (*Dark Sides* 161–62)—then the text's *form* nevertheless invites us to *aesthetic* empathy, particularly to a somatically based *Einfühlung* that correlates our own bodily responses as readers with bodies *in* the text (notably Clarissa's) and the body *of* the text: its cadences, rhythms, punctuation, and syntax. This aesthetic empathy is different than the call to projection and objectification we encountered in *Turmalin*. Rather, *Der Hochwald*'s formal features provide "affordances" (to speak with Levine) for linking the novella to a post-Vischerian *Einfühlungstheorie* that retroactively illuminates Stifter's text, revealing ways in which the text's granular form "collides" with its ideological content or "ideational form." This is the corporeally focused empathy theory of the German-influenced British aesthetician Vernon Lee, with its emphasis on the sensations of heartbeat, circulation, breath, and the real and imagined movements of the reader's body. In this linking, feeling and form, affect and intensity (*Innigkeit*), intersubjective and aesthetic empathy, and human and textual bodies become networked.

This networked reading of *Der Hochwald* helps us understand the fraught and mutually destabilizing relationship between, on the one hand, the female protagonists' "caughtness" in the demands of patriarchal societal and familial structures and, on the other, the possible "escape" offered by the intense affective energies of the body, as articulated by the sisters' *Innigkeit* and the stylistic form of Stifter's prose. Stifter's original publication venues were periodicals and literary almanacs, with their customary audiences of women and children; *Bunte Steine* indeed explicitly advertised itself as a "festival gift" for "young readers" (front matter and 16). This dual female and juvenile readership, equivalently feminized and metonymically exchangeable in the nineteenth-century imagination, formed, at least from a patriarchal perspective, an ideal public for the "womanly" genre qualities—abundantly on display in *Der Hochwald*—of melodrama, sentimentality, and, as some of the meanings of *Innigkeit* would have it, heartfelt intimacy and ardor. It likewise provided the desired social and bodily targets, both inside and outside the text, for "discipline," interpellating surveillance, and ideological education; that is, for an anti-Massumian "fixing" in multiple senses of the term.[20] But *Der Hochwald*'s audience, in its presumed and feared "wild" and unruly nature, also constituted a "dangerous" ground—a ground with cracks—for subversion, be-wilderment, and escape, again both outside the text and between its lines.[21] As Massumi writes, "When the continuity of affective escape is put into words, it tends to take on positive connotations. For it is nothing less than *the perception of one's own vitality*, one's sense of aliveness, of changeability (often signified as 'freedom')" ("Autonomy" 97).

Like the narrator's feelings about Clarissa, *Der Hochwald*'s dominant descriptive mode is divided: in this case, between grand, panoramic, and "sublime" displays of eye and word and their seeming opposite, the proliferation of minute descriptive details and formal techniques of syntactic or punctuational delay, with their corresponding bodily stops, pulses, and flows. Read together with Massumi and Lee, the novella's deployment of idiosyncratic punctuation, repetition, spaces, and rhythms forms an "inventory of intensities" that suggests a proto–affect theory. Placed in further dialogue with eighteenth- and twentieth-century thought—influential and strongly gender-coded theories of the beautiful and sublime well known in Stifter's day, as well as Julia Kristeva's notion, structurally related to affect theory, of a feminine-marked "semiotic chora" of bodily stases and movements underlying language—we find Stifter's text to be "about" the relation of empathy and *Einfühlung* to the gendered voice and gaze. We find the text's "body," that is, to be a gendered body. If, as Adorno argues in *Ästhetische Theorie* (*Aesthetic Theory*), "intensity" is a quality "ceded by the many to the totality, . . . [which], as it were, refunds the power accumulated in it back to the detail" (279), then sublime "totality" and "beautiful" detail occupy the same aesthetic space, and we arrive at two

---

20. On the surveilling and disciplining of women in *Der Hochwald*, see Downing 41–90, especially 58–60 and 82–88.

21. On "bewilderment," "the wild," and the "queer" body (here in twentieth-century thought), see Halberstam.

"gendered" ways of reading the body of Stifter's text. We discover a "parallel Stifter" operating alongside the traditionally patriarchal figure this author is often taken to be: a Stifter whose formal fascination with the "small" (Seigworth and Gregg's "miniscule or molecular"), the *innig*, and the rhythmically pulsing and breathing body constitutes an aesthetic that the patriarchal norms and socially constructed gender discourses of the mid-nineteenth century might characterize as "feminine"—the body of the text as female body.

Of course, any attempt to "recuperate" Stifter for a sort of *écriture féminine* must be undertaken with caution, and not only because of the author's presumed "biological sex" and patriarchal reputation. Reading Stifter's discourse in terms of a female poetics of the body runs the double risk of falling into gender essentialism, the sad patriarchal tradition of reducing "the feminine" to *nothing but* body, or both. The risk is compounded by drawing on concepts like Kristeva's semiotic chora, with its definitional connection with the maternal body and lingering, if perhaps oversimplified, associations with gender essentialism. Indeed, venturing onto the terrain of the body and gender at all risks becoming caught in a perilous semiotic web of alternatingly, shiftingly negatively and positively coded binaries and reifications, not the least of which are the essentializing signifiers "masculine," "feminine," and "gender" themselves. As I read *Der Hochwald* alongside Kristeva, Massumi, and Lee, then, attempting to uncover whether a parallel Stifter might exist alongside, within, and against the patriarchal constraints of the text's narrative voice, my use of the terms "feminine," "masculine," and "gender" reflects not an ahistorical or ontological understanding of genders (or "gender") as truly existing "things" with fixed, inherent qualities but rather the social construction and coding of gender in (largely patriarchal) discourse. Correspondingly, the manifestations of the "small," the "bodily," and the *innig* I explore are not inherently, physically or metaphysically, "feminine," although they have often been used as markers for a *posited feminine* in patriarchally dominated linguistic and social practice (just as the capacity for violence is, of course, not inherently masculine, although the *practice* of *systemic* violence has, in Western cultures, largely been orchestrated by people constructed and coded by those cultures as "male"). Ultimately, *Der Hochwald*, in its ambiguously gendered textual embodiment of empathy, is, rhetorically, both "masculine" *and* "feminine": It simultaneously empathizes with, becomes, *and* destroys its female protagonists.

The dialectic of constraint and escape structures Stifter's text: thus the usefulness of Kristeva's concept, to which I will return below, of alternating bodily stases and flows—mobile prelinguistic energies recurrently, temporarily arrested by the social constraints mediated by the body itself (in Kristeva's case, the maternal body), then repeatedly turned loose again in the somatic circuit, in endless cycles. The Wittinghausen sisters are intermittently moved, channeled, obstructed, and detained by the story's physical settings and social systems; eventually, they are erased from the narrative itself. From another perspective, however, their very concluding disappearance from diegetic and "authorial" knowledge might be read as a figure for their escape from the visual, narrative, and discursive regimes that dominate the novella's plot and strive to control, order, or surveil them: It might be seen, that is, as a "higher-order" textual performance of empathy with the women's plight. As Levine writes, "Forms do organize us, but on a daily basis we are organized at once by multiple social, political, biological, and aesthetic rhythms, each imposing a different order and following a different logic. They do not work together, and so in the end are not able to impose a single coherent order on experience" (80–81). Or, as Massumi states, "Actually existing, structured things live in and through that which escapes them" ("Autonomy" 96–97). To explore how Stifter's "structured things" live through "that which escapes them," we must ask how the text's flows of empathy and *Einfühlung*—to the extent that they are, like affect, "unfixed" qualities, "forms" with no "positive content" of their own—are linked in the novella less to content than to form (or at least as much to form as to content), less to the "interpersonal," about which the text seems ideologically divided, than to a fusion of *Innigkeit*, bodily intensities and surpluses (both human and textual), and stylistic *ductus*: the narrative's lexical lists, syntax, tempo, and orthographic-punctuational features. Yet, importantly, even and perhaps especially when they resist the patriarchal ideologies of their day, Stifter's empathy experiments, like Vischer's, are also problematically complicit with what they resist.

Affect Engines: Cruelty

A chief site of this complicity is the narrative's cruelty. Let us visit this briefly before turning to the concerns above. If the largest or macro-forms of the novella are the narrator's voice and the temporal unfolding of the plot—the actual words used and the methodical placement of one descriptor and event after another, a disciplined process that is both agonizingly diachronic and meticulously synchronic, like carefully arranging pieces on a diegetic chessboard—then there is little doubt that this union of voice and plot has as one of its most prominent effects the torturing of both the story's characters and its readers. Indeed, in its production of feeling, we might view this formal union as an *affect engine* whose activation or revving up places readers in a state of profound agitation. Even beyond the specifics of its (from one perspective) tragic ending, the narrative is marked by affective excess—another of the text's many articulations of "intensity"—that manifests either in the form of "too much" or, paradoxically, "too little." The novella is both too hot and too cold, bringing readers exceptionally close to its female protagonists through the passionate arousal of narrative empathy, then zooming out again to an almost nihilistic distance and indifference, spitting us out or casting us ashore, as it were, in a sort of narrative shipwreck. The text begins with sweeping forest vistas, lengthy descriptions of the present-day Wittinghausen castle ruins that will form the setting of the embedded seventeenth-century plot, and evocations of the passage of great geological and historical time, thus thematizing its own interweaving of the synchronic and diachronic. After the death or disappearance of all the major characters we have "loved," so to speak, it ends the same way: Vast and plodding nature reclaims the sites of both "safe house" and castle; "westward lie the immeasurable woods and are silent, lovely and wild as in the past" (118). The narrative painstakingly, even excruciatingly, builds identification with the Wittinghausen sisters over six chapters, only to traumatize and "delete" them in the seventh, a seemingly prime example of Breithaupt's "empathic sadism," or "creat[ing], encourag[ing], wish[ing] for, or tolerat[ing] a scenario in which someone else is placed in danger or made to suffer, precisely in order to feel empathy with that person, now cast in the role of the victim" (*Dark Sides* 170). Yet, as I have noted, the text likewise reveals the indivisible coexistence of multiple images of empathy in the same rhetorical time and space: The sisters' disappearance is simultaneously their escape from the novella's literal and figurative patriarchal maps, and the micro-forms of the novella's *ductus*—its cadences, punctuation, and syntax—invite *Einfühlung* into the similar "autonomy" of Clarissa's affective intensity. In each of these gestures, then, the novella fractally repeats the sense of one of its main recurring motifs: the image of the Wittinghausen castle viewed through an unstable telescope, both remote and close-up, at once crystal clear and uninterpretable, perhaps destroyed and perhaps intact.

Taking pleasure, empathic or otherwise, in tragedy is an enigma not easily explained.[22] Aristotle, beyond his famous discussion of pity, fear, and catharsis, established the recurrent framework for many Western treatments of the problem when he traced the enjoyment of all artistic subjects, painful ones included, to a supposedly "innate" human "delight" in imitation or mimesis (*Poetics* 6–11, 1448b–1449b). A little less than a hundred years before *Der Hochwald*, Edmund Burke, in his 1757 *Philosophical Enquiry into the Origin of Our Ideas of the Sublime and Beautiful*, counterintuitively argued that we enjoy others' suffering more even in *actual life* than in fictional tragedy because this "delight" secures our bonds of sympathy and altruism with people whose misery and needs we might otherwise turn away from. We do not, however, "wish" this suffering on others, and our enjoyment of it is "blended with no small uneasiness" (41–44). Schiller's later concept of the "pathetically sublime" furthers Aristotelian ideas of artistic representation, combining them with the necessity of resistance: "Suffering can become aesthetic . . . only when either it is a mere illusion and fabrication or (in case it had happened in reality) it is presented, not immediately to the senses, but to the imagination"; in "tragic art," this suffering must be accompanied by "an image of the *resistance* to the suffering, in order to call into consciousness the mind's inner free-

---

22. See Breithaupt, *Dark Sides* 163–70. For a different approach to "ambiguous" aggression and empathy in (other) Stifter, see Barbara N. Nagel 80–88; cf. Nagel also on affect, form, and the roots of "flirtation, passive aggression, and domestic violence" (1) in German realism.

dom" (Schiller 159–60). Presumably channeling Schiller, Lipps maintained that we "aesthetically" enjoy representations (not real-life instances) of others' misfortunes because these depictions allow us to feel the "humanity," strength, and life force of the other, even or especially as the other struggles against and succumbs to his fate: "There is ... no more powerful way to make the positive in man vivid to us and allow us to experientially feel it [*miterleben*] than through its negation. And this negation lies in misery, adversity, despair, destruction.... This alone is the way in which the suffering, ... the appalling and the horrible that we reject and deem ugly in everyday life, can, in artistic representation, become beautiful, that is, an object of aesthetic pleasure" ("Einfühlung und ästhetischer Genuss" 114).

Lee's influence, the pioneering play and empathy theorist Karl Groos, builds on Aristotle's mimesis, Kant's notion of aesthetic disinterestedness, and Schiller's *Spieltrieb* (play drive) when he explains our pleasure in tragedy as a subset of his famous "inner imitation"—in his view humankind's "noblest form of play" and an internal state of "freedom" one can enter and leave at will (*Einleitung* 170–77). Here, "feelings of displeasure lose ... a great deal of the painfulness they would possess if they occurred in earnest" (*Einleitung* 171): "We only allow our mind [*Seele*], not our body and mind, to be shaken by aesthetic feelings, since in complete aesthetic pleasure our consciousness lives more in the observed object than in our own body"; "In this process the mind can be placed in tremendous agitation, but this agitation lacks, as it were, the friction and impact with the material world" (174). Breithaupt proposes a model of tragic pleasure as empathy "with an exit strategy—the tragic ending" (*Dark Sides* 167). As he writes, "Because of empathy's relationship to the phenomenon of self-loss, it follows that the observer ... will seek out catalysts for empathetic identification that control, soften, or *limit the timespan* of self-loss.... The object of their identification is sure to meet their end, allowing the viewer to return to themself. Tragedy, then, offers quite the deal to the viewer: Not only can they experience a particularly profound and moving spectacle but they then get to exit the experience at the end" (167–68). Some argue that simply being moved is itself the point, a position that resonates with the directions in affect theory that foreground intensity, the capacity to be "acted upon," or "force or forces of encounter" as central components in aesthetic experience.[23] Classicist Malcolm Heath concludes bluntly that "the experience of tragic emotion is pleasurable in itself" (xlii), quite apart from any edifying function. However we approach the nexus of tragedy, pleasure, empathy, and ethics in *Der Hochwald*, we might concur with Breithaupt that "the tragic" might be seen as "a particularly strong drug for exciting emotions in individuals": a drug "released by observing the suffering of another" and, at least potentially, "only very loosely coupled, if at all, with concern for the other's ... well-being" (*Dark Sides* 165). "In this formulation," Breithaupt concludes, "the audience's excitement is tragedy's final purpose, which has led some critics, like Jean-Jacques Rousseau in *Lettre a M. D'Alembert sur les spectacles* (1758), to reject tragedy entirely" (165).

The "drug" of empathic sadism is strongly at work in *Der Hochwald*. Not only does the novella on one level effectively consist of an extraordinary number of scenes of interpersonal empathy: It also strives both to generate a singular level of narrative empathy in the reader and, "perversely," to use this empathy to wound audiences. The text repeatedly portrays Clarissa and Johanna as sharing an unusually strong emotional bond, a mutual understanding and closeness mirrored by their intertwining physical actions. The sisters share a bedroom, pray simultaneously in identical window niches, kiss recurrently, "fuse" in mutually absorbing conversations, and generally display exceptional sensitivity to each other's feelings and thoughts. Recalling Spinoza's *affectus* or "ability to affect and be affected" (Massumi, notes xvi), Johanna is literally moved to tears, "the most violent sobbing," by Clarissa's crying (76). Baron Heinrich, too, understands his daughters with almost uncanny (and ominously regulatory) empathy: He has the girls' rooms in the forest retreat constructed as nearly exact doubles of the ones they had occupied in Castle Wittinghausen, and the sisters subsequently find "everything ... furnished in the most carefully planned way; not

---

23. Cf. Seigworth and Gregg 1–2 and Breithaupt's discussion of Menninghaus (*Dark Sides* 166).

even the tiniest detail, often seldom taken notice of by men, but of great value to girls, was missing here, and every day they discovered anew that their father had often anticipated and arranged for things that they themselves had not yet thought of" (50).[24]

The novella's plot similarly comprises a conspicuous string of what Breithaupt, in a different context, calls "empathy triggers": diegetic occurrences that arouse emotional responses in the reader, such as characters' expressions of affective states, romantic and erotic experiences, situations that lay bare "the pressures and opportunities of the other," and "decisive," "intense" moments when someone "has to act, has to choose"—especially in ways that "affect [their] well-being" ("Empathy and Aesthetics" 46, 54–56). Clarissa and Ronald's high-stakes betrothal, with its extravagant expressions of passion and intense pressure to make immediate, life-altering decisions, is a striking example of this phenomenon. Will Clarissa commit to the secret marriage despite Johanna's disapproval and her father's lack of knowledge? Will Ronald succeed in intercepting the Swedish troops before they raze the castle? As Breithaupt writes, we "imagine the horror in due course, wishing that the moment before would last forever or would give way for another scenario that we know will not come" ("Empathy and Aesthetics" 50). In particular, anticipating what will become the central metaphor of *Turmalin*, *Der Hochwald* deploys "stage effects": empathy-generating techniques that, like a theater stage, promote a heightened state of attention and encourage readers to "observe the situation carefully, . . . reflect on the situation of the protagonists . . . , and . . . analyze their emotions" (Breithaupt, "Empathy and Aesthetics" 57). The novella repeatedly portrays Clarissa and Johanna as framed by a figurative "proscenium arch," as if on a stage, or, in a closely linked trope, as actual paintings.[25] At the beginning of the embedded plot, the doors to the sisters' bedroom fly open like theater curtains; "stage directions" provide present-tense

---

24. On Heinrich's furnishing of the rooms as control of his daughters, see Downing 59.

25. On their way to the forest retreat, for example, the girls peer from the "frame" of their sedan box window "like two pictures of angels" (35). On the common nineteenth-century association of theater with painting as "sister arts," see Smith 344–45.

instructions for the "actors" ("The older one ... sits ... on a sort of day bed on which she has spread out numerous papers ... through which she searches"); the balustrade windows form a "frame" (*Rahmen*); and the sky "stretches" (*spannt sich*) behind this "proscenium" like a backcloth (9–11). Continuing this theatrical subtext, in the silence after the sisters first hear Ronald's mysterious singing in their supposedly impenetrable retreat, they "are afraid to move, as though the *scene* were not yet over" ("als sei die *Szene* nicht aus") (74, my emphasis). And the improvised exchange of vows that follows transforms the forest clearing in which it occurs into "a stage," "a court house," "the theater," or "politics" (Breithaupt, "Empathy and Aesthetics" 57): as Ronald declaims, "Let this meadow ... be the betrothal-hall, and all that surrounds us witnesses" (90).

But perhaps *Der Hochwald*'s most striking empathy engine is its *cruelty*—the calculation with which it solicits emotional investment in the Wittinghausen sisters, then wields this investment to "move" the reader (one might say, wields this investment against the reader). The novella goes out of its way to portray Clarissa and Johanna as especially kind, attractive, lovable, and caring in their heartfelt devotion to each other and their father. The girls laugh endearingly as they dress and chat merrily as they embroider, united both in feeling and in the novella's ambiguous syntax: Stifter's frequent use of definite articles as a sort of "collective" possessive ("the heart," "the childlike tongue," "the eye" instead of *her* heart, *her* tongue, *her* eye) often makes it difficult to determine whether the text is describing one daughter or both at once. The sisters' shared room is "holy and pure, like a church" (16), the girls themselves "angels" (23). When differentiated, Johanna especially is presented as profoundly innocent (*unschuldig*) (11, 71), and the narrator's voice takes on the flavor of this innocence as it slides toward free indirect discourse: "One sees how the young soul, untouched by pain and passion, still looks out so guilelessly eager from the little windows [of her eyes], for the world is just so [*gar so*] big and splendid" (10). The text seems almost to delight in intensifying its moments of cruel irony. The baron explains to his daughters "with what effort and care the forest nourishes and nurtures the smallest of its flowers" (20); even "the weakest little blade of grass can flourish [there] undisturbed"

(19). The sisters en route to their "safe house" are surely just such flowers. At the conclusion of the chapter describing their disorienting arrival in the forest retreat, the narrator sentimentally and melodramatically exclaims, "Good night, you dear lovely frightened hearts, good night!" (44). The narrator even literally commands us to love the girls: "Our hearts must love them more than all the wisdom of the wise" (16).[26] When the caretaker Gregor thus forebodingly remarks that the sisters are "two lovely forest flowers; it would be a pity if they came to ruin" (32), the "stage" is set for the story's destructive conclusion, and the reader's anticipatory, empathic dread is ratcheted to an extreme.

During this conclusion, the text continues to twist the knife. Distant Castle Wittinghausen, viewed through the telescope from the forest retreat, first appears "so serene and so dear ... and so unharmed" (52)—as the narrator cries in intersubjective empathic fusion with the sisters, "Oh how beautiful, how friendly!" (52)—then as a pitilessly scorched and roofless ruin, ironically standing beneath a "brilliant, cheerfully sparkling" sky (104). Upon arriving at the ruins, Clarissa will sob that it was she who, through her hidden love for Ronald, "slew her father and brother" (114); the sisters' family friend Bruno, an Austrian knight who secretly pines for Clarissa, will, despite his supposed "pity" (116), nevertheless insist on admonishing her that "if [she] had been more trusting of everyone from the beginning, the final catastrophe most likely would also not have occurred" (111). The narrator makes sure we are aware of Clarissa's "lovely form" beneath her black mourning dress (110) and describes the anguished Johanna as "beautiful like a dead angel" (114); Clarissa becomes a "fair creature perishing before Bruno" (116), and the sisters' tears flow "abundantly and as if of their own accord, gently-sweet even, like the last blood of a slain creature" (115). In its apparent reveling in this sort of excess, the novella's conclusion becomes misogyny, empathy sensationalism, and grief porn at once.

---

26. Due to the ambiguity of the German *sie* (them/she), this is one of the moments in which it is unclear whether the narrator means one sister or both. Johanna has been the main subject of the passage, but the paragraph concludes with a reference to the "*two* beautiful faces" of the girls (16, my emphasis).

Der Hochwald's strategies of intersubjective, narrative empathy are thus intermingled with cruelty. The text's *Einfühlung*, however, is of a different order.

A Body in Motion, or The Mime of the Beholder

A critical truism holds that the opening passages of a literary text establish the "law" of the text. The opening of *Der Hochwald*—one of the most extensive and detailed nature descriptions in German literary history, and a depiction that strikingly anticipates Vischer's *Über das optische Formgefühl*—establishes this novella's law as *Einfühlung*. Already in the story's first paragraph, we read that the forest "draws its band of darkness westward, . . . striving forth to that border knot where Bohemian land collides with Austria and Bavaria"; there, a profusion of mighty ridges "shot against each other and thrust a rough massif upward," "deflect[ing] . . . the course of the mountain range" (3). The land "gently rises"; the range "meanders"; a "rock-wall theater soars vertically up" (4–5). The descriptions might have been written by Vischer himself: "A cliff appears to stand at attention and squarely face us; we therefore read spiritual *defiance* into it. Its projecting angle seems to lunge out as if affected by a *passion* (impatience, curiosity, anger)" (Vischer 105). Or, as Lipps will observe, "When we look at a line, we 'create' the line . . . by following it from point to point with our eyes" (Benjamin Morgan 35). The question of the origin, vector, and locus of feeling that we encountered in Vischer's and *Lenz*'s engagement with form also appears in *Der Hochwald*'s opening. The narrator twice locates an "eye" in the landscape: the "uncanny eye of nature" (*unheimlich Naturauge*) formed by the forest retreat's alpine lake and the "tender, open eye" of the Moldau River valley (6). Both these ocular images inside the text's observed world are themselves conspicuously specular: The lake is a "monstrous black glass mirror," and the river shines with reflected sunlight (5–6). The images thus suggest a mirrorlike exchange between viewer and environment, self and "object." Gazing at the "melancholy-beautiful" (3) landscapes, which, as their eye imagery reveals, *gaze back*, makes the *narrator* melancholy; likewise, the landscapes "look melancholy" because the narrator *is* melancholy, and so on in an infinite loop whose origin is, as in Vischer and Büchner, unclear.

Especially, however, *Der Hochwald*'s opening passages prefigure Vernon Lee's account of aesthetic empathy from her 1913 introduction to psychological aesthetics, *The Beautiful*:

> *The mountain rises.* What do we mean when we employ this form of words? ... Of course nobody imagines that the rock and the earth of the mountain are rising, or that the mountain is getting up or growing taller! All we mean is that the mountain *looks* as if it were rising. The mountain *looks*! Surely here is a case of putting the cart before the horse. No; we cannot explain the mountain *rising* by the mountain *looking*, for the only *looking* in the business is *our* looking *at* the mountain. ... The rising of which we are aware is going on in us. ... The *rising* of the mountain is an idea started by the awareness of our own lifting or raising of our eyes, head or neck, and it is an idea containing the awareness of that lifting or raising. (61–64)

As Lee continues, paralleling Stifter's descriptions (with which she was most likely not familiar) and Vischer's explanations (which she knew secondhand through Lipps), "lines meeting one another may conflict, check, deflect one another"; "along with the empathic suggestion of the mechanical forces experienced in ourselves, will come the empathic suggestion of spiritual characteristics [in objects]: the lines will have aims, intentions, desires, moods" (*The Beautiful* 80).[27] Or, as she puts it in an earlier essay's discussion of the relations among *Einfühlung*, feeling, and form, "We attribute to these lines not only balance, direction, velocity, pace, rhythm, energy, but also *thrust, resistance, strain, feeling, intention, and character*" (53); "the succession of moments attributed to the co-existing qualities of ... form *is the succession of our impressions*; ... the activity we

---

27. Lee appears to have had no knowledge of Vischer when she began her own psychological aesthetic studies. However, she absorbed similar ideas from the work of Vischer's contemporary and possible influence Hermann Lotze, particularly his *Microcosmos* (1856–1864, English translation 1885–1888); see Guyer 432. By at least 1907, Lee had learned of Vischer's central ideas, most likely through Lipps's work; she mentions Vischer briefly in her 1907 essay "Aesthetic Empathy and Its Organic Accompaniments" (46).

speak of is *ours*" ("Aesthetic Empathy" 51). And, in a moment that proleptically summarizes both the main thrust (and tropic vocabulary) of Vischer's *Einfühlungstheorie* and the materialist death of nature that Vischer and Büchner struggled with, the narrator of *Der Hochwald* states that the sisters and Gregor "stood silently for a moment [in the forest], their human hearts seemed to feel the solemnity and peace empathically [*die Feier und Ruhe mitzufühlen*], for there is a decorum, I would say an expression of virtue in the countenance of nature, not yet touched by human hands, before which the soul must bow, as to something chaste and divine, – – and nevertheless it is finally just the mind alone [*doch . . . zuletzt wieder die Seele allein*] that projects all its inner greatness outward into the simile of nature [*hinaus in das Gleichnis der Natur legt*]" (35). We are reminded here of Vischer's argument, discussed in the previous chapter, that nature, "resurrected" by human *Einfühlung*, can "provide similes [*Gleichnisse*] for everything organic" (106, *Formgefühl* 23). It is not, however, where Lee corresponds with *Über das optische Formgefühl* but where she goes beyond it that her work most sheds light on *Der Hochwald*, for Lee's own theory of *Einfühlung* and *Der Hochwald*'s opening frame constitute a remarkable staging of somatically centered empathic projection and exchange that, even more than Vischer's, places the body in the text and the text in the body—and sets this joint body in motion.[28]

It would be impossible to capture the dizzying effect of the novella's multipage opening (3–9) without reproducing the text in its entirety, like a Borgesian map that equals its territory. The narrator's "camera eye" avant la lettre swivels through all points of the compass, cinematically panning and tilting, tracing the sharp twists of a mountain range and the supple turns of a river, now pulling back to reveal extensive horizon-line vistas, now zooming in to ex-

---

28. For an earlier (2010) discussion of the production of motion effects in *Der Hochwald*, see Strowick. Strowick's analysis focuses primarily on the "active gaze" (273) rather than (as in my reading) the totality of the body and its responses. Strowick does not explicitly address questions of *Einfühlung*; however, her interest in Stifter's syntax and "the motion of description itself" (273) resonates with my own, and her conclusions implicitly support my understanding of Stifter as a precursor to later formulations of *Einfühlung* (see Strowick 277–78).

amine the erosion-smoothed contours of individual rocks on the ground. It deliriously switches angles mid-sentence from a panoramic overview of a distant valley seen from the Wittinghausen castle ruins to a "shot" of those same ruins now glimpsed as a tiny cube from the floor of the valley that has just been described; it finally explores the ruins from the phenomenological perspective of a wanderer—the narrator, but also, "empathically" fused with him and addressed in the second person, the *reader* ("*your* astonished and bewildered gaze," 8, my emphasis)—climbing about the tumbled walls at human scale. The frame's palpable sense of optical and physical (indeed, by the conclusion of the sequence, full-body) motion—a grove of spruce trees "aborbs us," the narrator-cum-reader is exhorted to "turn his gaze," "walk through" the forest, and so on (4–9)—is matched by similarly conspicuous temporal motion: The chief locations of the story, introduced here in the novella's narrative present, have already fulfilled their roles in the narrator's "personal past" (wandering around the ruins as a young man, "dreaming a part of the double-dream of youth and first love," 3), but are yet to come in his analeptic récit of the Wittinghausen sisters' tragedy. The opening's final scene and segue to the plot "proper" melds the two forms of motion:

> And now, dear wanderer, when you have fully satisfied your gaze, come with me two centuries into the past, in your mind erase the blue flowerbells . . . and dandelions from the ruined masonry . . . ; instead strew white sand all the way up to the outer wall, place a sturdy beech door in the entrance and a roof on the tower, able to withstand any storm, . . . divide the rooms, and adorn them with all the beloved household effects and glitter of domestic comfort – then, when all is as it was in the days of happiness . . . – – climb with me the central staircase to the second floor, the doors fly open – – – Do you like the lovely pair? *It is the daughters of Heinrich von Wittinghausen* in whose house you find yourself – . (9)

Historical and geological time can be "rewound," run not only forward but backward, through the "technology" of narrative.

As Benjamin argues in "The Work of Art in the Age of Mechanical Reproduction," "The history of every art form shows critical epochs in which a certain art form aspires to effects which could be fully obtained only with a changed technical standard, that is to say, in a new art form" (237). Stifter's swooping narrative "camera," rapid shifts in scale, and fast-motion, time-traveling reconstruction of the castle, with its culminating "dolly shot" through the girls' self-opening doors, clearly go beyond the mid-nineteenth century's theater and photographic technologies to foreshadow cinema, if not the first-person-player point of view or avatar-in-landscape effects of video games and virtual reality. The reverse-time-lapse restoration of the castle, for example, anticipates the famous transition from frame to embedded narrative in James Cameron's film *Titanic*, in which the sunken wreckage of the doomed ocean liner rebuilds itself into the pristine ship of its maiden voyage as the camera pans over it; similarly, *Der Hochwald*'s "single-shot" sweep across the landscape from wide-angle panorama to extreme close-up brings to mind Peter Jackson's diving camera in his film adaptation of *The Lord of the Rings: The Fellowship of the Ring*, in which our point of view spirals down vertiginously from an expansive aerial prospect of the Isengard landscape through the vertical flues of the orc forges to the very sparks flying from the villains' anvils. *Der Hochwald*'s rapid changes in scale as the narrator's camera eye shifts from long shots of far-reaching landscapes to close-ups of individual rocks and plants likewise evoke the satellite camera zoom function of Google Earth. The gyroscopic motion of the reader's body and eye within the novella's environments and her dynamic participation in "erasing the flower-bells," "strewing white sand," "placing the door," and "dividing and adorning the rooms" in the castle suggest the actions of an individual playing *Minecraft*, navigating an open-world video game like miHoYo's *Genshin Impact*, or wearing a virtual reality suit and headgear.

The importance of bodily motion, both real and imagined, to early theories of aesthetic empathy cannot be overstated. As Lanzoni writes, Vischer's *Einfühlung* already "entailed ... the projection of implicit movements in a perceived line, shape, or architectural form" ("Introduction" 289). At the apex of the age of psychological aesthetics, Edward Titchener, translator of *Einfühlung* into English, concluded that "imagined movement comprised the core of [aesthetic] empathy" (Lanzoni, *Empathy* 60). As Lanzoni explains, "At Titchener's Cornell laboratory, empathy was defined ... as a mental image of bodily movement, what he called the kinesthetic image" (*Empathy* 9–10); *Einfühlung* thus "joined the optical with the kinesthetic" (60). Nearly seventy years earlier, *Der Hochwald*'s "kinesthetic images" spectacularly prefigure this fusion. Indeed, they suggest even subtler and more comprehensive forms of embodiment that go substantially beyond the gaze and imagination—and that are inseparable from *form* and *literary style* as a broader somatic interface. To understand what is at stake in this interface and in the centrality of the body overall, including the gendered body, to *Der Hochwald*, let us turn more closely to Lee, who likewise went beyond Vischer, Lipps, and Titchener to bring new dimensions of corporeality to psychological aesthetics.

Perhaps best known for her novels and short stories of the supernatural, Vernon Lee, the pen name of Violet Paget, was an independent intellectual who published over forty books on topics ranging from art history through travel literature to literary criticism. Her writings on psychological aesthetics—a combination of original theorizing, interpretation of qualitative empirical data, and conclusions reached through scholarly exchange with major figures in the field, including Lipps—helped popularize the concept of empathy in the English-speaking world (Guyer 426–37). Starting approximately in 1895, before having read Lipps's work, Lee partnered with her research collaborator and lover, the Scottish artist Clementina (Kit) Anstruther-Thomson, to conduct a series of highly nuanced observations of their own bodily responses as they viewed paintings, sculptures, architecture, and objets d'art in European museums, churches, and galleries. The pair thus stood in a long line of scientific and aesthetic self-experimenters in the realm of sensory physiology, albeit without the self-destructiveness of a Fechner or Müller. Lee and Anstruther-Thomson focused especially on variations of proprioceptive and interoceptive sensations and motions such as adjustments of balance, eye movements, heartbeat, circulation, respiration, and muscular contraction. As Lee later explained the experiments, "All the real truth in the *Einfühlung* hypothesis is connected with the subjective existence of the work of art, that is to say, with the idea of it which we make for ourselves; an idea made up in part of our experiences of life and activity; I would venture to specify even further, made up in part of the experience of movements of our own body" ("Aesthetic Empathy" 59). These movements, Lee writes, are caused by "those great organic processes, cardiac, respiratory, equilibratory, and locomotor" ("The Central Problem of Aesthetics" 78). As Benjamin Morgan summarizes Lee's argument, "Art's effects resonate in a specific body with muscles and lungs," not, as Lipps had contended, "in an abstract subject" ("Critical Empathy" 37). Lee's literary criticism, too, written before or concurrently with her work on psychological aesthetics, attends carefully to the "muscles and lungs," pulses and rhythms, or, as we might put it, the *form body* of language and its *feeling*—what she calls the "mysterious essence" to be sought in language's "movement, as *pace and weight, impact and rhythm*" (*The Handling of Words* 132).[29] As Benjamin Morgan explains, Lee was "interested in what it would mean to empathize [aesthetically] with language," in "how a reader might somatically respond to linguistic patterns" (44)—or, to use Vischer's terms, how one might *feel oneself* or *feel one's way into* language. Morgan elaborates: "When Lee empathizes with literature, she feels the movement of the syntax" (46–47). Lee's literary criticism, then, conceptualized "the bond between reader and writer" in a way "akin" to her "visual aesthetics" of the—moved and moving—body (Lanzoni, "Practicing Psychology" 351).

What type of moved and moving body was this? Lee's chief German influence Karl Groos, with whom she maintained a twenty-eight-year scholarly correspondence (Petraschka, "Future Way" 297–98), had argued that aesthetic form always involved at minimum "internal" or mental motion: For form to become perceptible at all, the mind had to "build" it "kinetically," in "successive pieces," so to speak, through "inner imitation," or the sequential abstraction of appearances from the mass of raw sense data (Groos, *Einleitung* 100–106). This discernment of form was likewise linked

---

29. Lee's *The Handling of Words* appeared in 1923; however, most of the essays it contains were originally written and published at the same time as her work on *Einfühlung*. Lee had also published earlier work on the link between language and bodily responses; cf. Benjamin Morgan 44.

both to feeling and the body. As Groos writes, following the famous James-Lange hypothesis that physiological changes precede the mental perception of emotions, respiration, circulation, and digestive processes create "internal organ sensations" that make the experience of emotion possible and interact with forms or objects in the world, helping us perceive them (Groos, "Das ästhetische Miterleben" 161–66; Petraschka, "Future Way" 302). Our emotions are not solely the result of these processes, but "the 'detour' through the sensations of the internal organs [is] necessary" ("Das ästhetische Miterleben" 167). Importantly, Groos notes that the mental, internal motions or "inner imitation" central to his theory can at times also result in *external* motion, the bodily imitation of what is perceived (*Einleitung* 86–87).

Lee substantially expanded and radicalized Groos's positions. She at first maintained that *Einfühlung* in fact *required* actual bodily motion—muscle contractions, alterations of posture, and movements of the lungs—for an observer to perceive an art object. In his "Das ästhetische Miterleben," for example, Groos discusses Lee's argument, formulated with Anstruther-Thomson, that the body must "mimic" the poses of a sculpture in order for the sculpture to be fully "seen"; he cites the pair's report of breathing in front of a pitcher to imitate and feel the object's form, the inhalations and exhalations paralleling the pitcher's narrowest and widest points (175–77). Not only did Lee engage deeply in hands-on, experiential exploration of the relation of the body, its motions, and its feelings to the perception of form, thereby anticipating present-day directions in cognitive science and "embodied aesthetics" (Prinz 331); she also "tried to construct an image of herself as a hybrid between a philosopher/scientist and an artist/poet" (Petraschka, "Future Way" 298)—an endeavor not unlike Stifter's own. By the end of the first decade of the twentieth century at least, the lines of influence between Groos and Lee had become a two-way street: Groos's "Das ästhetische Miterleben" of 1909 clearly draws on and takes seriously Lee's work (177–79).

Lee and Anstruther-Thomson published the results of their gallery experiments as *Beauty and Ugliness* in 1897; they thus came to Lipps's—unfavorable—attention. The criticism was mutual: In her 1907 essay "Aesthetic Empathy and Its Organic Accompaniments," Lee accused Lipps of being a "metaphysical" thinker who "absolutely refus[ed] to entertain ... the participation of the body in the phenomenon of aesthetic Empathy" (60). As Müller-Tamm explains, Lipps believed that only a mental, nonspatial "I" could be projected onto external things (244); he was particularly skeptical of what he called the "cult of bodily sensations" (Lanzoni, "Practicing Psychology" 344). Later, after absorbing more of Lipps's ideas, Lee modified her claim that empathic response depended on "actual *muscular sensations* and ... *objective bodily movements*" rather than "mere *ideas* of a motor kind" (Lee, "Central Problem of Aesthetics" 89); in the revised 1912 edition of *Beauty and Ugliness*, she consequently demoted concrete physical movements to secondary phenomena that *accompanied* the "direct, primary" act of mental projection Lipps had championed as the core of *Einfühlung* (*Beauty and Ugliness* 153–54). However, she "never fully rejected aspects of a bodily inflected understanding of empathy" (Lanzoni, "Practicing Psychology" 332), "steer[ing] a course," as it were, between the "extremes" of asserting *Einfühlung*'s dependence on literal corporeal motion and belief in the projection of a "disembodied ego" (Prinz 334). As Lee writes, "Both hypotheses are, as I have constantly repeated, in all probability necessary for a complete and physiologico-psychological explanation" (*Beauty and Ugliness* 154). For Lee, the body remained "a node where the formal properties of any art—color, sound, depth, syntax—intersect" (Benjamin Morgan 47). Lee and Anstruther-Thomson saw in their work "nothing at variance with the trend of philosophy since Kant" (*Beauty and Ugliness* 236); however, as Paul Guyer concludes, "one might suggest that it is only with [Lee's exceptional emphasis on the bodily dimension of aesthetic experience] that the century-long grip of idealism on aesthetic theory began to be loosened" (434).

In *Der Hochwald*'s opening passages, we find marked points of contact with Lee's thought. The "*pace and weight, impact and rhythm*" of the frame's language (Lee, *The Handling of Words* 132) transmit a palpable sense of movement and corporeality. Like the rest of the novella, the frame contains a striking number of sentences whose form stages a conspicuous performance of "muscles and lungs." Lengthy hypotactic blocks, independent and dependent clauses separated by commas, conjunctions, and relative pronouns, accumulate and "stride" in resolute strings, many of them a quarter-page long; these alternate with stuttering paratactic fragments, often divided by semicolons, dashes, double dashes, and even, as we have seen, triple dashes, mirroring or acting in tandem with the breaths, pulses, pauses, and muscular exertions of the reader's body, and constituting parallel movements in the text's "body." The pulses stop and start; the breath slows down, speeds up, spreads, and expands into the story's described landscapes—into space. The imagined gaze follows suit: "Your marveling and bewildered gaze wanders over many, many green mountain peaks floating in the sunlight's woven haze, and passes then beyond them into a blue band of veiling mist – . . . until the eye finally meets the tremendous halfmoon that girds the horizon: the Noric Alps" (*Hochwald* 8). "Now," as Anstruther-Thomson writes in a section of *Beauty and Ugliness* that evokes Stifter's narrative technique, "as the breathing works in closest connexion with the eyes, this widened way of seeing is necessarily accompanied by a widened way of breathing . . . and the respiratory expansion inevitably produces a general sense of expanded existence" (190–91). The body responds to the text, but, as Lee and Anstruther-Thomson argue, bodily responses also *create* our *feeling of the text as form*, generating a *shared body*. As they explain in the passage that forms the epigraph to the present study, "The subjective pattern of our perceptive feelings and the objective pattern of the form perceived are one and the same phenomenon differently thought of"; the "notion of external form" is "in a way executed, or, to use a convenient word, *mimed*, by the beholder" (*Beauty and Ugliness* 227, 236).[30]

Lee's thinking moves beyond syntax, rhythm, and "prose prosody" in the strictest sense to include larger patterns of movement within semantics, structure, and form: "It is the complicated pattern

---

30. Regarding language, Lee's conception of the relations among form, movement, and feeling is complex and not without internal tensions. In *The Handling of Words*, for example, she describes the movement of language as being both "in the thinking and feeling of the Reader" and "obedient to the thinking and feeling of the Writer" (132).

of stresses put not upon syllables, but upon suggestions; the pattern of insistence, of slurring, of hurrying, of binding together, of imperceptible approach or sudden attack, of dwelling on and drawing out, of letting go and breaking off, of reiteration and syncope; all woven together by a pace solemn or swift, lingering or light, but whatsoever it be, informed by some great unifying rhythm" (*Handling of Words* 132). Even if *Der Hochwald* does not have a "great unifying rhythm" but multiple competing rhythms, Lee's observations on textual form can help us visualize and feel the larger "shape" of Stifter's narrative as a whole: its succession of accelerations, decelerations, repetitions, elisions, and moments of concealment or intensity. Lee's comments likewise resonate with Seigworth and Gregg's discussion of affect as what they call "form of relation": "A rhythm, a fold, a timing, a habit, a contour, or a shape comes to mark the passage of intensities (whether dimming or accentuating) in body-to-body / world-body imbrication" (13). Form here is an affective structure, as Brinkema would argue: "Affective force works over form" (37). Stifter's double and triple dashes point to that in form which moves form to its limits, that which cannot be "fixed" by words and "escapes" the linguistic economy of the text—the "mysterious essence" in language's movement (*The Handling of Words* 132), and, relatedly, the intensity of affect. The dashes similarly index the energetic starts and stops that will come to characterize Kristeva's bodily, pre- and protolinguistic semiotic chora. As Groos writes in "Das ästhetische Miterleben," breath is the most important corporeal component in the "inner imitation" that constructs form, and feeling or affect truly come into their own with the movement of the breath, in the starting and stopping, expanding and contracting motion of the diaphragm (177–78): "This is where feelings first seem to me to take on"—as Groos quotes Hermann Lotze and as Stifter will also put it—"'vibrant *intensity*' [*Innigkeit*]" ("Das ästhetische Miterleben" 168, my emphasis).[31]

---

31. Without using the words "Innigkeit" or "intensity" themselves, Braungart's discussion of Groos makes a good implicit case for Groos's having theorized a poetics of intensity; cf. *Leibhafter Sinn* 107–14.

Vast and Minute: Gendered Economies of Word and Gaze

Der Hochwald's movement of language, shared body of text and reader, and intensity of affect (*Innigkeit*) are *gendered*. To begin to shed light on these matters, let us first look briefly at another area in the novella where form and feeling meet: the recurrent aesthetic categories of the sublime and the beautiful, represented in the text by Stifter's copious descriptions. Both historically and in *Der Hochwald*, the two aesthetic categories seem to enact a gendered agon.

At minimum, Stifter knew Kant's influential theory of the sublime through his friend, benefactor, and fellow Bohemian Forest native, the Austrian physicist Andreas von Baumgartner (Häge 68–69). Centered on the titanic struggle of the human subject to grasp the "absolute magnitude" of infinity (the "mathematical sublime") or transcend the destructive powers of nature (the "dynamical sublime"), the two manifestations of Kantian sublimity entail, first, the momentary suspension of our "vital forces" in the face of such seemingly superior "mights," then the triumph of human reason over them: over, that is, the related limitations of body, senses, and imagination. Here, it is not nature or infinity itself that is sublime, but reason's ability to master them through "supersensible" ideas and moral action, a "power in us greater than nature." Immeasurable magnitudes, immense physical spaces, and overwhelming natural forces, phenomena that are literally "in-comprehensible" or unable to be brought into a unity by the senses or imagination, are merely catalysts for arousing reason's truly "superior" or sublime power in the mind (Kant, *Kritik der Urteilskraft* [*Critique of Judgment*] 164–91).

Commentators have frequently viewed the Kantian sublime as a "masculinist" mode, deeply entwined with patriarchal ideologies of control, including control of forces coded as feminine in Western discourse.[32] This mirrors, at least from one perspective, the ideational content of *Der Hochwald* as a patriarchal text. The sisters' exile in the forest retreat, with its hypertrophic accumulation of security measures (impassable cliffs, paths blocked by engineered rockfalls, bulletproof rafts, builders sworn to secrecy), might be read

---

32. See for example Freeman's *The Feminine Sublime*.

not only as a reasonable attempt to ensure the young women's safety in wartime but also as an opportunity to regulate or control their sexuality, especially Clarissa's: an attempt to sequester them from "inappropriate" men and to preserve "proper" familial and national lines.[33] When telling his daughters they must move to the retreat, Baron Heinrich vehemently denies rumors that a mysterious marksman or poacher is haunting the woods (22). Even if Heinrich is not consciously aware of Clarissa's secret love for Ronald—who, of course, the "Wildschütze" turns out to be—or of Ronald's Swedish identity, the character of the baron seems to come equipped with an "unconscious" fear of his daughter's being "poached." The forest retreat's bedrooms, frighteningly "uncanny" doubles ("bis zum Erschrecken ähnlich," 43) of the girls' rooms at Castle Wittinghausen, evoke an artificial habitat and its aura of containment and surveillance; the equally surveillant device of the telescope, through which Clarissa and Johanna repeatedly view their home castle, binds the sisters to the otherwise distant "law of the father," now made ever present and active through the work of the scope (Downing 82–88). The baron already scripts his daughters' desires by deciding on all the forest house's supplies and activities—establishing their "scope," as it were—in advance: As I noted earlier, "Everything was furnished in the most carefully planned way, not even the tiniest detail . . . was missing here, and every day [the girls] discovered anew that their father had often anticipated and arranged for things that they themselves had not yet thought of" (50; cf. Downing 58–59). And, as we have seen, the story's conclusion, at least at first glance, especially follows a patriarchal, even misogynistic, logic: The narrator appears to blame Clarissa's passion or desire for the catastrophic final battle, sending the message that an entire family, perhaps even the entire male state order, can be taken down by a single woman's, as the text puts it, "selfishness" (97).

Given this pervasive patriarchal atmosphere, it is perhaps unsurprising that the novella's visual and verbal economies seem permeated by allusions to the Kantian sublime, with its rhetoric of impossible magnitudes and monumental forces that the power of reason,

---

33. Cf. Downing 41–90.

typically coded male in Western patriarchal discourse, must battle for "phallic" mastery. We find in the text "immeasurable" vistas, "streaming into your eyes and almost overwhelming them with splendor" (8); "boundless" stars (102), a favorite Kantian image for the infinite; recurrent terms such as "Unmaß" or "Übermaß" ("an immeasurable amount," "a monstrous amount," "an amount beyond scale"); the endless forest; the immensity of geological time; and the ethical challenges in extremis of danger and war, among other examples.

From another perspective, however, the text runs counter to its own patriarchal impulses and their "sublime" correlates. To begin with, it is the *sisters* who survive the Wittinghausen calamity—not dead, like the male members of the family, but living alone together, off the surveillance grid, and perhaps, weirdly, *forever*: "The sisters lived on [in the castle ruins], both unwed.... That [they] grew very old was known even until the most recent times ... but no one knows their grave" (117). The baron is introduced as a "ruin of powerful masculine strength and greatness" (17): a prefiguration, that is, of his soon-to-be-destroyed castle and male line. Word and gaze, stereotypical sites of attempted patriarchal mastery, are likewise destabilized by conspicuous blind spots in seeing, saying, and, sense. Already the opening frame gives us a vision thwarted, undermined, or wounded by what it beholds: When "you" climb the pile of rubble to peer out the ruined castle's third-floor window, the "immeasurable view" does not just "stream into your eyes, almost overwhelming them"; it literally nearly *smothers* or *crushes them to death*—"erdrücken"—with its radiance ("eine unermeßne Aussicht, strömend in deine Augen und sie fast mit Glanz erdrückend," 8). Despite repeated, indeed excessive, attempts at descriptive precision, the frame's narrated "seeing," with its multiple shifts in perspective, opens onto optically confusing space, or, despite recurrent references to the cardinal directions, yields a vertiginous disorientation: "Your astonished and bewildered gaze" (8). Alternatively, narrative at first *outstrips* vision—"The point from which one can *almost see* as much of the course of [the river] *as is here described*, is a ruined castle" (7, my emphasis)—before succumbing to a similar fate: "An *unsayable* amount of dearness and melancholy dwells in this sight" (9, my emphasis). And if these limitations in senses, imagination, and narratability are still potentially compatible with the Kantian sublime, for Kant posits *reason* (*Vernunft*) as the supreme faculty that can triumph over the "merely" sensual vastness or "magnitude" of just such limitations, then the text denies this supposedly sovereign faculty its victory as well. The story's catastrophic conclusion, as well as the caretaker Gregor's inability (or unwillingness) to comprehend that the catastrophe has taken place, are framed as a failure of reason itself. As Gregor insists after he and the sisters have viewed the ruined castle through the scope but do not yet know the fate of its inhabitants, "I tell you, nothing has happened, because it *would be too unreasonable* [*weil's zu unvernünftig wäre*]" (106, my emphasis).[34] Indeed, if there is a "sublime" in *Der Hochwald*, it is less Kant's than Burke's, whose earlier understanding of the term highlighted not reason's apotheosis but obscurity, pain, and the *inability* of reason to master "the terrible."[35] As Burke writes, "Whatever is fitted in any sort to excite the idea of pain, and danger, that is to say, whatever is in any sort terrible, or is conversant about terrible objects, or operates in a manner analogous to terror, is a source of the *sublime*; that is, it is productive of the strongest emotion which the mind is capable of feeling" (36). Perhaps even more significantly, Burke's sublime has been read as an aesthetics of *intensity*: As Jean-François Lyotard points out, "For Burke, the sublime was no longer a matter of elevation (the category by which Aristotle defined tragedy), but a matter of intensification" (591).

Running alongside the masculinist mode of the sublime in *Der Hochwald*—indeed, perhaps even subordinating it—is the equally familiar aesthetic category of the beautiful. Evoking for Burke the small, the bounded, the delicate, the colorful, and the gently varying (*Philosophical Enquiry* 102–7), the beautiful has traditionally been

---

34. For a different, non-Kant-related discussion of the incomprehensibility of the view through the telescope and the failure of the novella's characters to interpret the "signs" of what they see, see Begemann, *Welt der Zeichen* 195–206.

35. See Burke 54–59, 73–79, 119–23, and 131–34. Although Burke's conception differs substantially from Kant's, Burke's sublime is—at least on the surface—also associated with characteristics stereotypically coded "male" in patriarchal discourse and, like Kant's, evoked by power, vastness, and infinity: see *Philosophical Enquiry* 36–40, 59–65, 66–68, and 83–114.

linked to "the feminine" in modern Western aesthetics, as Burke's own problematic feminization of the category in the *Philosophical Equiry* underscores.[36] As problematic as this linkage is, with its complicity in the construction of patriarchal, hierarchical gender codes and binaries, it is nonetheless instructive for an understanding of *Der Hochwald*. From within the framework of nineteenth-century gender discourse, the "feminized beautiful" gives us another way to position the novella's image inventory and narrative voice. Here, the story's word and gaze—the form of its descriptions—are not sweeping but *minute*. The narrative's nature depictions just as often present a cascade of micro-details as they do majestic vistas; their shimmering miniature canvases anticipate the conspicuously "anti-sublime" valorization of "the small" that will come to characterize Stifter's preface to *Bunte Steine*: "The blowing of the wind the trickling of water the growing of the grain the rocking of the sea the greening of the earth the shimmering of the stars I consider to be great: the grandly arriving storm, the lightning bolt that splits houses, the tempest that drives the waves, the fire-spitting volcano, the earthquake that lays waste to the lands I do not hold to be greater than the above phenomena, indeed I take them for smaller, because they are only the effects of much higher laws" (Vorrede 8).[37] *Der Hochwald* lavishes extraordinary attention on the tiniest, most delicate features of the forest plants, animals, and weather conditions ("now a curious shrub showered with odd glowing red berries, or now ... the beautiful brightly colored fungi ..., or now a sunbeam suddenly breaking around a corner,

---

36. Burke writes that the "beautiful," (supposedly) "feminine" qualities of "smallness," "weakness," and so on help generate feelings of love that cement social bonds; however, these qualities are "of less dignity" (100) than their masculinized, "sublime" counterparts, as they evoke "what submits to us" (103) and are "nearer to contempt than is commonly imagined" (61). Kant's treatment of the beautiful as evoking "disinterested" aesthetic pleasure, or pleasure free from desire and from any logical concepts about what the "purpose" of the aesthetic object could be (*Kritik der Urteilskraft* 115–67), is more narrowly focused and therefore less relevant to *Der Hochwald*.

37. The idiosyncratic lack of punctuation in the preface is Stifter's. His skeptical listing of "volcanoes" and "earthquakes" among the "not great" phenomena seems a direct dismissal of Kant's preferred images for the "dynamical sublime" in the *Critique of Judgment*.

setting the bushes before it on strange green fire and luring silver sparks out of invisible little forest streams," 29–30); it painstakingly portrays the sisters' clothing, their household items, domestic activities, nuances of feeling, and, of course, the girls themselves, all glowing as if under a nimbus of wonder and charm.[38] Even Baron Heinrich's meticulous care for household details might be read not as patriarchal control but as a practice of "the beautiful" or "the feminine"; the "womanly" eye with which he outfits the forest retreat might correspondingly be understood as a self-reflexive allegory of Stifter's own narrative technique: "Everything was arranged with the greatest attention; not the tiniest detail, often seldom noticed by men, but of great value to girls, was missing here" (50). Hebbel had famously criticized Stifter for his concentration on the small (Mathias Mayer 365); Stifter wrote the preface to *Bunte Steine* in direct response to Hebbel's comments. In the light of nineteenth-century patriarchal thought, however, it is useful to recognize the extent to which Hebbel's critique was a gendered, masculinist one, and Stifter's countersublime aesthetics (or, more precisely, the nonsublime elements of his divided aesthetics) at least a potential poetics of the feminine.

The ambiguity and possible self-reflexivity of the baron's relation to domestic details, along with the text's deployment of detail more generally, uncover additional tensions within an already agonistic scene: They trouble the novella's ideological point of gender identification. As Naomi Schor asks regarding the gendering of the detail in the wake of literary realism, "Does the triumph of the detail signify a triumph of the feminine with which it has so long been linked? Or has the detail achieved its new prestige by being taken over as masculine, . . . ceasing to be connoted as feminine at the very moment when it is taken up by the male-dominated cultural establishment?" (144).[39] The questions find a possible answer in Clarissa's suggestively sexualized, incremental appropriation of the tele-

---

38. For a discussion of the "beautiful" apprehension of the world in Stifter in terms of the possible traversing of the narrator's realist discourse by the "Romantic" points of view of diegetic characters, see Preisendanz; on perspectivism in Stifter more broadly, see Begemann, *Welt der Zeichen* 173–74.
39. Cf. Barbara N. Nagel (14), who also notes part of Schor's passage.

scope belonging to the Wittinghausen family friend and unsuccessful suitor for her hand, the knight Bruno—an instrument that serves as a key metonymy of the father's controlling gaze, "law," and phalloculocentric power:

> Clarissa kneeled . . . before the tube and moved it and moved it; she saw immediately that it was a disproportionately better one than her father's, but she couldn't find anything with it. Everything stood conjured frighteningly clear and close in front of her, but it was all utterly strange. . . . – – she touched the screw to lengthen [the tube] – then she guided it along the edge of a dark band [of trees] – suddenly a soft cry – trembling in the circular frame of the miraculous glass stood the whole paternal house, tiny and delicate, as if painted, yet with its walls, oriels, and roofs astonishingly distinguishable. (51–52)

Here we see a gradual assumption and apprehension (from Latin *prehendere*, "to lay hold of," "to take with the hand")—a literal, figurative, and ultimately *figural* grasping—of conventionally male-coded vision, along with a technical, sexual, and ideological "adjustment" of this vision into something, as it were, "disproportionately better." At first everything is confusing, strange, and frightening, but in the end Clarissa, in a moment of orgasmic intensity whose proprietary bodies remain—importantly, as we shall see—unspecified (*the* lengthening tube, *a* soft cry), transforms "phallic" seeing and patriarchal law at once. The vast panoramas and immeasurable distances become the diminutively bounded "beautiful" or "picturesque"; the castle becomes a tiny, delicate, and circularly framed painting with clearly distinguishable—that is, "feminine"—details: the domestication of the sublime. Later, Johanna also wants to turn "the father's house" (*das väterliche Haus*) *around*: She "expressed the childish wish to be able to see it from the other side" (53). As an alternative, the girls turn the phallic *scope* around to view the castle's double, the "sequestering" and social-order-imposing forest retreat, through the telescope's miniaturizing end, rejoicing "when their house, tiny like the head of a pin [*Stecknadelkopf*], lay miles away out there, and the lake like a little glass table next to it" (53). The pin-and-table imagery, recalling the "needles and sewing things" (*Nadeln und Nähzeug*) the baron supplies as a "womanly detail" to the forest house (47), poetologically links (that is, *stitches*) the father's aesthetic practice—and thus also the authorial "weaving" of the form of Stifter's text (from Latin *texere*, "to weave")—to these traditionally feminine activities and implements. The scene immediately following the sisters' reversal of the scope and the shrinking of the castle to the sewing table conspicuously finds the girls "cutting and sewing and altering all of their fabrics and clothes" (53). Indeed, images of sewing and embroidering—figurative *textual* "weaving"— repeatedly mark the sisters' representation in the novella.[40] Even the scope, in its "orgasmic" transition from phallic or patriarchal instrument (or figure for patriarchal instrumentalization) to agent of the castle's feminization, moves sensually across a treeline figured as clothing: The "edge of the dark band" of trees that Clarissa guides the scope along ("dem Saume eines dunklen Bandes entlang," 51) is also a "seam" or "hemline" (*Saum*). If these scenes are not quite a "burial" of the masculinist economy, as when the money that Baron Heinrich had set aside to secure the survival of the Wittinghausen family line after the war disappears into the conspicuously feminized "womb of the earth" (*Schoße der Erde*) beneath an equally symbolic "image of the mother of God" (*Muttergottesbild*) (45), they are nonetheless a significant relativizing, "rewriting," and reorganization of "the father's house." They raise questions both about *Einfühlung* and about covert intersubjective empathy: about *whose* body the text is empathizing with, and what sort of empathic body the *reader* is figured or imagined as having.

Chora

The novella's ambivalence about sight reflects the ambiguity surrounding this sense in the nineteenth century. Not only did midcentury developments in neurophysiology, including Müller's law

---

40. For a detailed analysis of the imagery of cloth and sewing in *Der Hochwald*, see Begemann, *Welt der Zeichen* 180–81 and 199–203. Begemann also interprets these metaphors as figures for the poetological dimension of the text as semiotic "cloth" or "textile"; however, he does not read this dimension in terms of gender.

of specific nerve energies, displace vision from the supposedly objective or "transparent" realm of "immediate knowing," represented by "the mechanics of light and optical transmission" (Crary 70), to what Crary calls "the unstable physiology and temporality"—the "cloud[ed] over" subjectivity—"of the human body" (70). The widespread acceptance of Müller's law itself helped sever sight from the other senses, especially touch; it thereby "unloosen[ed] . . . the eye from the network of referentiality incarnated in tactility and its . . . relation to perceived space" (Crary 19). Both developments worked together to pave the way for what Pijarski calls the "sovereignty of sight in modernism" (164).

It is precisely this emerging sovereignty that *Der Hochwald* works against by insisting on a spectrum of full-body, proprioceptive and interoceptive feeling and experience of the type that will become central to Groos's, and especially Anstruther-Thomson and Lee's, conception of *Einfühlung*—kinesthesis, cardiac rhythm, breath: the pulsions of corporeality.[41] These bodily processes find their analogue in the novella's form as cadence, the alternation of hypotaxis and parataxis, the distribution of dashes, the bursts and nerve plucks of punctuation, and the diaphragm-pauses of (sometimes extra) white spaces *around* punctuation (that is, around dashes): Lee's "handling" of (not just) "words," or what aesthetic philosopher Susan L. Feagin might understand as a *phenomenology of style*. As Feagin argues in her work on empathy, two processes (in our case, the body and Stifter's text) must be "structurally similar, in relevant aspects" (149) for one of them to simulate the other: "It is the structural properties of a process"—that is to say, formal properties—"that account for, at least to some extent, the affective or phenomenological 'feel' of [an] experience, and hence for the types and degrees of understanding one may have" (151). (This seems a slightly less unconditional version of Lee and Anstruther-Thomson's assertion, in *Beauty and Ugliness*, of equivalence between "subjective pattern of feeling" and "objective pattern of form.") Prose style, imagery, alliteration, sentence length, and punctuation are all significant examples of these

---

41. On the centrality of full-body aesthetic experience to Anstruther-Thomson, see Benjamin Morgan 39–40.

structural properties; they are thus important contributors to an experience's "affective or phenomenological 'feel'" (Feagin 156).

Take, for example, the single protracted sentence, almost three hundred words long, that forms the penultimate sequence in *Der Hochwald*'s third chapter, "Waldhaus" ("Forest House"). A series of richly descriptive, metaphorical examples of how the Wittinghausen sisters "appear as fairy tales for the wilderness marveling at them all around" (54), the sentence exhibits an almost metrically hypnotic, somatically throbbing structure. The rhythmic reoccurrence of the conjunctions "oder" (or), "und" (and), and "wenn" (when), often in the anapestic combination "oder wenn" or the even more heartbeat-like iamb "und wenn," separates six strongly hypotactic blocks of text, the first three especially long, dense, and languorously incantatory (with their strings of progressive verbs), the final three shorter and increasingly accelerating. A caesura of double dashes—a marked pause—before each "oder wenn" further separates the three earlier, longer blocks from each other; the first two of these blocks are likewise split in the middle by a single dash followed by "so" (then), giving them the feeling of "when-then" statements or call-and-response, and tangibly decelerating the tempo. The occurrences of "and when," and then simply "and," begin to multiply as the syntactic pace speeds up, leading into the final three blocks. A sudden colon brings the rapidly accelerating flow of text to an abrupt halt just before the last lines of the sentence; after this fleeting suspension, the final block—a conclusion, as it were, to the entire sequence of metaphors and conditionals—races dizzyingly toward the closing period, its velocity accentuated by two more "ands" in the space of a mere five lines (54–55). The entire sequence, which could be formally mapped thus, with the number of asterisks indicating the relative lengths of the sentence's six text blocks, here separated by slashes—

(1) Wenn . . . – so . . . **/
(2) – – oder wenn . . . – so . . . ***/
(3) – – oder wenn . . . , und . . . **/
(4) – und wenn . . . , und . . . */
(5) , und wenn . . . , und . . . */
(6) : so . . . , und . . . und . . . *

—is a remarkable example of Lee's "movement [of language and body], as *pace and weight, impact and rhythm*" (*The Handling of Words* 132).[42]

Or consider the astonishing final sequence of the chapter, directly following the sentence just described. Here, the notes of Clarissa's harp resound like a bodily "pulsebeat" (*Pulsschlag*) through the "sleeping midnight air" of a quiet full moon night, "playing" the woods like a corporeal instrument, summoning the animals, and creating new melodies and feelings (indeed, new *capacities* for feeling) that are unable to be represented, repeated, or defined—that escape, as it were, semantics and mimesis: "It was no different than as if a new feeling [*Fühlen*] moved gently through the whole woods, and the tones were as if the forest here and there stirred a ringing limb [*als rühre er hie und da ein klingend Glied*], – the roe emerged, the slumbering birds nodded on their branches and dreamed of new heavenly melodies that they will not be able to sing tomorrow, – and the echo at once tried to babble back the golden riddle" (55–56). Immediately after this merger of heartbeat, sound, and silence, we find the further fusion of speed and slowness, human and more-than-human action,[43] sensed and unsensed motion, heard and unheard sonority—a protocinematic time lapse whose almost Rilkean alliteration and assonance are difficult to capture in translation, ending in ecstatically punctuated bursts of intensity:

---

42. For readers who wish to get a partial sense of the pulsing rhythm of this remarkable sentence, I reproduce portions of its beginning and ending here, untranslated: "Wenn sie zum Beispiele an dem See saßen, lange weiße Streifen als flatternde Spiegel ihrer Gewänder in ihn sendend, der gleichsam seine Wasser herandrängte, um ihr Nachbild aufzufassen – so glichen sie eher zwei zart gedichteten Wesen aus einer nordischen Runensage, als menschlichen Bewohnern dieses Ortes – – . . . oder wenn sie in der bereits milder werdenden Herbstsonne auf ihrer Wiese am Rande des Gerölles saßen, . . . die schönen Hände ineinander gelegt, wie zwei Liebende, . . . : so ist es, als schweige die prangende Wüste um sie aus Ehrfurcht, und die tausend kleinen Glimmertäfelchen der Steinwand glänzen und blitzen nur so emsig, um einen Sternenbogen um die geliebten Häupter zu spannen" (54–55).

43. The phrase "more-than-human" stems from Abram; see *The Spell of the Sensuous*.

> And when the harp was long silent, ... – – the night still listened [*horchte noch die Nacht*]; the moon standing directly above draped long beams into the spruce branches, ... – meanwhile the weight and curvature [*Wucht und Wölbung*] of the earth, unfelt and unheard by its inhabitants, stormed toward the east, – the moon was hurled into the west, the old stars along with it, new ones rose in the east – – – and so on and on, until finally amidst them below on the forest rim a pale milky light-strip bloomed – a small fresh breeze nudged the treetops – and the first morning-cry burst from the throat of a bird! – – –. (56)

These passages inscribe the text in the reader's body, but also the reader's body in the text. Fleshly body and textual body resonate or pulse together, speed up and slow down as one to create the reading experience—Lee's collaborative feeling of the text's form. This sense of a common body verifies *Einfühlung* as something not only seen but also heard, performed, and, perhaps most importantly, *felt*. We find a single phenomenological body: The night-human-text "listens," the moon-human-text "drapes its beams," and so on. It is a global, libidinal haptics, as when Clarissa lengthens the telescope tube with her touch, then guides it along the edge of a "dark seam," provoking a "soft cry": the hand literally *affecting* the eye and *effecting* a shudder (of persons or things), "trembling in the circle of the miraculous glass" (51–52). One again recalls here Spinoza's *affectus*, or the body's "ability to affect and be affected" (Massumi, notes xvi). Even Vischer, while privileging sight as the first key factor he discusses when theorizing *Einfühlung* (seeing vs. scanning, the isomorphism of eye and observed object), does not limit vision to the eye alone but distributes it across the whole sensorium: nerve vibrations that "travel through the entire person," for example (115), or rhetoric that figures the eye in terms of the hand. Like Vischer's "real and intimate connection" of hand and eye (94), Clarissa's, and the text's, full-body engagement mobilizes an erotic, corporeal, and—in the case of Clarissa and *Der Hochwald*—affective event, here a transpersonal and transobjective one. Drawing on a different nuance of Stifter's German in the harp scene, it is "as if new feeling moved gently through the ... woods, and the tones were as if the forest here and there touched [*rühre*] a ringing member [*Glied*]" (56, my emphasis). Here, the forest feels *moved*, both physically and emotionally *touched*: indeed, moved to *touch itself*. Significantly, the text deploys the same verb, "rühren"—literally "to touch," "to move" in a physical sense, but also "to affect the emotions," to "stir the feelings" in an intimate, intense, heartfelt (*innig*) way, to "touch with feeling"—for both the scope and harp scenes, suggesting a corresponding likeness between the two scenes' "tones." This is why the "proprietary" or bodily "owner" of the orgasmic cry of the scope scene remains unspecified: The *common* body spasms, or the text we were initially led to believe would be traditionally, patriarchally scopophilic—phalloculocentric—spasms at its own release into more comprehensive bodily presence. This expansion, indexed by dashes, can be an expansion into the "unfixed," the "uncaptured" (as in Massumi's affect), or into nonpatriarchal, even counterpatriarchal space.

The spasms, rhythms, and cries of the preceding passages, in a sort of family resemblance that extends their resonance with Massumi's affect and Lee's understanding of the somatic dimensions of art, proleptically call to mind Kristeva's concept of the *semiotic chora* from her groundbreaking 1974 study *Revolution in Poetic Language*. As Kristeva makes clear, "semiotic" here does not mean the functioning of signs, signifiers, and symbols in propositional discourse. Rather, the semiotic chora—from *khóra*, ancient Greek for "mark," "space," "place," or "region," and a term Kristeva borrows from Plato's *Timaeus*, where it designated a receptacle or third space between the intelligible and the sensible—is a preverbal matrix of rhythmic energy pulses anterior to, but necessary for the acquisition of, language: the bodily beats *beneath* language, or, as Kristeva puts it, "an essentially mobile and extremely provisional articulation constituted by movements and their ephemeral stases" (*Revolution* 25). As Kristeva argues, "discrete quantities of energy move through the body" of the infant or "subject who is not yet constituted as such," forming a "chora" that "precedes and underlies figuration . . . and is analogous only to vocal or kinetic rhythm" (26). Like the cardiac, respiratory, and muscular motions that, for Lee, cocreate the work of art, the "drive charges," "energy flows," and "affect pulses" of the chora (Margaroni 85) are both motile and regulated by recurrent starts and stops. In the chora, the movement of unconscious drives is temporarily halted by the physical and social constraints of the symbolic order within which the developing subject is embedded, only to overcome these "stases" provisionally, flow again, be halted temporarily once more, and so on (*Revolution* 27–28). Through its rhythm of alternating flows and stases, the chora is the "place where the subject is both generated and negated" (28), or transiently and incompletely congealed and dissolved. The chora thus serves as an embodied testament to the subject's lack of "fixed" unity and ongoing potential for resisting reification, even after further symbolic inscription. Although the chora precedes and provides the "innate precondition" for language, it continues to exist within and beneath language as a sort of "inborn basis" or "physiological memory": an "enigmatic" and, as Kristeva writes, "feminine" space "underlying the written . . . , irreducible to its intelligible verbal translation" (29). The intermittent movements of this space burst out in the rhythms and "primary processes" (condensation, displacement, absorption, and repulsion) of literature, "marking discontinuities" in "the various material supports . . . susceptible to semiotization: . . . phonic (later phonemic), kinetic, or chromatic units and differences" (28–29).

Some strands of scholarship have critiqued this notion of a "feminine space underlying the written" as reinforcing a biologically essentialist understanding of gender, the masculinist conflation of "woman" with "body," or a limiting mapping of the feminine onto the maternal. And indeed, Kristeva describes the chora as profoundly oriented toward the maternal body, which, she contends, "mediates" between the "symbolic law organizing social relations"—identified as a rule as patriarchal in the psychoanalytic traditions in which Kristeva writes—and the chora's drive flows (*Revolution* 27).[44] In *Der Hochwald*, the Wittinghausen sisters, whose mother dies ten years before the start of the main plot (17), effectively act as the "maternal body" for each other: The text frequently places them in "mother-daughter" configurations, as when we see them "resting,

---

44. For an overview of critiques of the chora and its relation to language, including claims that the concept is gender-essentialist or, conversely, not essentialist *enough* (that is, that it reduces "actual" women to abstract signifiers for alterity or excess), see Margaroni 79 ff. and 94–95.

Johanna's head with its childlike curls in her sister's lap, and Clarissa bent over her with clear, lovingly maternal eyes" (55). In this sense, the sisters' bodies become what "mediates" (for each other) "the symbolic law organizing social relations": that is, their father's law. However, as Maria Margaroni argues in opposition to essentialist interpretations, Kristeva's "feminine space" might itself be understood as "social": social, however, in "collision" (Levine) with the text's other, patriarchal, socially and physically ordering forms. The maternal body, Margaroni writes, itself represents a "socially experienced situation of alterity"; the chora consequently makes possible the reclamation of "what has (culturally at least) formed part of female experience for both male and female subjects" (96). If Margaroni's reading risks exemplifying the opposite extreme from gender essentialism, it nonetheless follows Kristeva in understanding the chora as a complex *interface* between physical and cultural factors. Somatic and sociohistorical forces intersect and interact with the chora, such that "its effect . . . is *transverbal* (moving through and across logos) and *transhistorical* (alongside, opposite to and in the margins of history)" (Margaroni 84). Or, as Kristeva writes from the opposite starting point, "Our discourse—all discourse—moves with and against the *chora* in the sense that it simultaneously depends upon and refuses it" (26). In its imbrication with the constraints of the social, the bodily experience of the chora thus has a conspicuously political dimension. To understand the relevance of this dimension, as well as of related dimensions in Massumi and Lee, for Stifter's narrative and its engagement with gender, *Einfühlung*, and intersubjective empathy, let us return to *Der Hochwald*'s articulation of *Innigkeit*—the name the novella gives to its nameless flows of feeling, affect, and intensity.

As I pointed out at the beginning of the chapter, the term *Innigkeit* first appears in *Der Hochwald* in connection with the Wittinghausen sisters, where, almost immediately after the girls' introduction, it occurs four times in the space of less than a page. Clarissa inaugurates the concept when she tells Johanna that there are "joys in the world so fierce that they can break our hearts – – and sufferings of such intensity [*Innigkeit*] – – – oh, they are so intense!! –" (12). When

Johanna kisses Clarissa "inexpressibly [*unsäglich*] tenderly on the mouth" (12–13), the inexpressibility of her tenderness another of the text's previously noted gaps in language or saying, Clarissa responds by kissing Johanna "twice quite intensely [*innig*] on her childlike lips, *in whose unconscious swelling beauty she took pleasure like a lover*" (13, my emphasis). The sisters then engage in rhythmic, "choric," intermittently stopping and starting speech whose affective "keynote" is *Innigkeit*: "They spoke about many more things, then were silent – then they spoke again, but always the fundamental tone remained the intensity"—or intimacy, fervency, or ardor: the *Innigkeit*—"of two siblings who dearly love each other" (13).

The concurrence of the rapid fourfold repetition of *innig* or *Innigkeit* with the introduction of the sisters and their "flowing" feelings links the term not only with the feminine but also, strikingly, with female desire: indeed, with desire *for* the feminine and desire *figured as* feminine. As if echoing *Innigkeit*'s fourfold repetition, the four factors—the flows of desire, affective intensity, the feminine, and desire for the feminine—merge into one. And even though Clarissa first uses the word *Innigkeit* when evoking the unnamed and as yet diegetically unintroduced Ronald (her exclamation about "joys and sufferings" occurs amid the sisters' discussion of a song Clarissa had learned from the incognito prince, here only described as "the one who composed the song," 11), the *narrator* quickly applies the term to the *girls' relationship itself*: Ronald remains, at least at this point in the text, a secondary and occulted factor. Indeed, it is the sisters who are first figured as lovers: Clarissa "takes pleasure like a lover" in the "unconscious swelling beauty" of Johanna's lips (13). When the baron leaves his daughters' room after a brief appearance, the *Innigkeit* that had been temporarily interrupted by his presence and authority (though ever covertly there in the text's "other" form, its punctuation and syntax) resumes its flow, albeit slightly "constrained," to use Kristeva's term, by the trace of the symbolic law he represents: "*Just one single time*, when he was gone, had the sisters embraced and pressed two, three hot kisses [*heiße Küsse*] on each other's lips" (25, my emphasis). Later, the autumn forest and its sun-pierced fog themselves become *innig*—"more beautiful and intense [*schöner und inniger*] than all the colors of spring and summer"

(96)—as do a host of other phenomena not explicitly labeled with the term, but clearly represented as intense, even "intense to the point of ecstasy," as Krell translates the term (notes 226). As foreshadowed by the context of Clarissa's initial use of the word, these phenomena come to *include* Ronald, whose hypersentimental, "ecstatic" masculinity might, from one perspective, be read as suggestively *feminine*. Although his flowing locks of blond hair (78), eyes swimming with tears (86), and other "feminizing" physical and affective markers might be read as recalling the *masculine* ideals of certain strands of *Empfindsamkeit* or Romanticism, Ronald's gendering also takes on other important implications for the novella's *Einfühlung* and interpersonal empathy I will return to shortly.

A frequent companion to *Innigkeit* in the text, and a fitting counterpart to this difficult-to-translate term, is *Unsäglichkeit* (unsayability)—a word that will be central to our discussion of Rilke, metaphor, catachresis, and empathy in the next chapter. The kisses that Johanna places on Clarissa's mouth are "unsayably tender" (*unsäglich zärtlich*) (13), and, after the concluding battle, the knight Bruno believes that the tears of the sisters' "intensely deep pain" (*inniger Schmerz*) will bring a relief that is "unsayably [*unsäglich*] sweeter and more salutary than all of their previous dull surrender" (115). In the conversation in which she introduces the word *Innigkeit* into the text, Clarissa uses images of "mists" and "lightning bolts" to figure those "intense" (*innig*) feelings that "people have mistakenly called passions" (12). As representatives of something misnamed, these images already link the *innig* to the unsayable, or at least to the incorrectly said. As the narrator puts it late in the tale, uniting the *innig*, the affective, and the unsayable, the novella's characters pulse with "speechless emotion" (*sprachlose Gemütsbewegung*)— movement (*Bewegung*) of the mind and feelings (*Gemüt*) so intense, or being moved so intensely, that one cannot speak (91).

This speechless emotion makes its perhaps most significant and "intense" appearance at the end of the novella's second chapter, "Waldwanderung" ("Forest Trek"). The sisters have finally arrived at the forest retreat, the festive welcoming dinner has ended, and the baron, after wishing his daughters a peaceful first night, has once again left their chambers. "And now," the narrator tells us, "when the door was locked, as though an obstacle [*Hemmnis*], as it were, had violently held it back until now, the flood [*Flut*] broke loose: the girls plunged [*stürzten sich*] into each other's arms, sheltering [*verbergend*] heart on heart, indeed almost burrowing [*vergrabend*] into each other, and pressing the tender seal of their lips against each other, as hot [*heiß*], as ardent [*inbrünstig*], as painfully sweet [*schmerzlich süß*] as two star-crossed lovers [*unglückselig Liebende*]" (43). As in the semiotic chora, an "obstacle" had temporarily halted the surge of the girls' "boundless" (*unbegrenzt*) (35) feeling for each other; this "ephemeral stasis" (Kristeva, *Revolution* 25) now dissolves, and the flows of *Innigkeit*, intensity, and affect, as well as of female desire and desire for the feminine, move unimpeded. This is again a full-body experience—not only, or even primarily, of the gaze but of touch, balance, breath, and heartbeat: "In the foreboding confusion no foothold [for the girls] but their reciprocal warm lips, devoted eyes, and pounding hearts" (43). The scene takes place outside the range of the "in-world" male gaze, literally "behind closed doors," as another of the text's blind spots in vision and knowledge—but not, importantly, in a blind spot for the narrator (or Stifter). It is, of course, a scene of the "intimacy [*Innigkeit*] of two siblings who dearly love each other" (*Hochwald* 13), but it is also, with its intensity, conspicuous eroticization, and escalation of the novella's ongoing figuration of Clarissa and Johanna as lovers, *more*: the "escape of [Massumian] affect," and perhaps of the sisters themselves; the pulse of the chora against the constraints of patriarchal social order; and a way to *undiscipline, de-subjectivize,* or *de-frame* the body, especially the female-coded body, in the realist age. As Adrienne Rich describes what she calls the "lesbian continuum," or the "range—through each woman's life and throughout history—of woman-identified experience," the concept encompasses more than "simply the fact that a woman has had or consciously desired genital sexual experience with another woman": Rather, it "embrace[s] many more forms of primary *intensity* between and among women, including the sharing of a rich inner life [and] the bonding against male tyranny" (1528, my emphasis). The sisters' retreat evokes fear, but also vibrates with possibility, the potential for transformation and flight. Consider the (at least) two ways, the negative and the adventurously positive, that the narrator's free indirect depiction of the girls' new life can be read: "Then it is true: home, the good paternal house, is surrendered and lost, all their previous life cut off, they themselves drawn like active players [*Mitspieler*] into a colorful fairy tale, everything new, everything foreign, everything strange and threatening – in the foreboding confusion no foothold but their reciprocal warm lips, devoted eyes, and pounding hearts" (43). Like the doppelgänger rooms of the forest house, the text becomes its own double—a sort of Foucauldian heterotopia that promises as much liberating movement as encroaching menace or stultifying surveillance.[45] From a certain perspective, it might even be possible to see this movement, along with its related *Einfühlung* and intersubjective empathy, as something resembling what Margaroni, in her reading of the chora, calls a "permanent revolution of the feminine" (96).[46] Stifter, or his narrative voice, shares (in) this movement: His text empathically makes the trek or "migration" ("Waldwanderung") into this forested space.

Stifter the Woman?

To return to the larger question of form in the novella, broadly conceived: Who is the narrator of *Der Hochwald*? On the one hand, we find a voice we have heard repeatedly: one whose melodramatic sentimentalism and sometimes overwhelmingly apodictic, gnomic tone ("Our heart must love [the sisters] more than all the wisdom of the wise," 16; "Devotion is bashful, like love," 11) is a mask for patriarchal sadism. This is the voice that condemns Clarissa and blames her (and, by extension, "woman") for the text's conclusion:

---

45. On heterotopias, or set-apart spaces that simultaneously reflect, interact with, and subvert the repressive measures of the larger society, see Foucault 175–85.

46. The Swaleses note the eroticized or sexualized intimacy of the Wittinghausen sisters but otherwise make no interpretive comment (56–57); Reddick reads the intensity of the sisters' relationship as Stifter's way of introducing passion, which he otherwise purportedly rejects, "under the disguise of 'legitimate' relationships between members of a family" ("Mystification" 69). Most critics overlook or ignore the scene of the sisters' affective "flood," making it a true "blind spot."

"O holy gold of the conscience, how quickly and beautifully you punish the heart that begins to grow selfish" (97). On the other hand, we discover the "choric" voice of ecstatically flashing stops and starts, floods and flows, "moving" blocks of text, dashes and triple dashes: the formal index of Massumi's escape of affect, Lee's "pace and weight, impact and rhythm" or oneness of "subjective pattern of perceptive feelings and objective pattern of form perceived," Clarissa's intensity or *Innigkeit*, and the sisters' pounding hearts and pulsing bodies. The telescope, then, particularly after the sisters' intervention, may be self-reflexive in ways that go beyond suggesting the obscurity of Stifter's text and the difficulty of interpreting what is "seen" in the novella (Begemann, *Welt der Zeichen* 195–206): The scope additionally points to the possibility that the narrative's "scope" or "perspective," as it were, has been "adjusted" or taken over, through the combined linguistic-formal and full-body path of Lee-like *Einfühlung*, by "the feminine."

Just as striking as Clarissa's transformation of the scope is the metamorphosis brought about in *Ronald* by the intensity of his love relationship with Clarissa: a relationship that, significantly, doubles, copies, or reproduces key aspects of Clarissa's bond with Johanna. As I have noted, the text repeatedly figures the *sisters* as lovers; indeed, the most "intense" description of the girls' *Innigkeit*, the surging torrent of their first night in the forest retreat, with its "hot," "ardent" kisses, overtly compares the siblings to "star-crossed lovers" (45), thus making the parallel to Clarissa and Ronald's forbidden wartime affair explicit. Reddick notes that the narrator uses the same word, "Kinderlippen" (childlike lips), in connection both with Ronald's desire for Clarissa and Clarissa's desire for Johanna: As he animatedly writes without drawing the conclusions we are drawing, Clarissa "responds to her sister's 'Kinderlippen' as Ronald responded to her own!" ("Mystification" 69).

The text had already introduced Ronald with signifiers for affect, intensity, flow, and the feminine: his "beauty" (78); "flood" of curly blond hair, tellingly similar to Johanna's (78); his "raptures" (*Entzücken*) (84), "bloom of tenderness" (*Schmelz von Zärtlichkeit*) (82), and "ocean of feeling and soul" (*Meer von Gemüt und Seele*) (84); his interactions with Clarissa, "namelessly, inseparably exchanging fervor for fervor [*Glut um Glut*], bliss for bliss" (84). Now, at his "wedding" in the forest clearing, Ronald truly begins to pulse with affect. In a scene that lexically and syntactically recalls the sisters' earlier flowing embrace, he and Clarissa "plunge [*stürzten sich*] into each other's arms, so tightly clasping and clinging to each other [*umschlingend und klammernd*] that his blond curls flow down onto the velvet of her shoulders" (87). Together, Clarissa and Ronald "shudder" or "tremble" in a "surfeit of feeling," "zitternd vor Übermacht des Gefühles" (87).

But perhaps the most significant part of the scene is Clarissa and Ronald's empathic body exchange—put otherwise, the moment when Ronald becomes a woman. As he exclaims to Clarissa amid a now familiar flood of italics, dashes, and double dashes, "You are my breath and my pulsebeat" (85): That is, her body *takes over for his* those somatic functions that Lee and Anstruther-Thomson saw as comprising the common body of observer and art, and that evoke the rhythmic stops and starts of Kristeva's semiotic chora. Relatedly, the forest becomes a "womb" (*Schoß*) (89), a maternal body, in which Ronald hears a "heartbeat": "On this meadow, at this lake is the heartbeat of the forest, it seems to me that I must hear it" (81). Finally, as Ronald muses to Clarissa, "I do not know whether this magic of transformation emanates from you or from the woods – I feel as though I were another [*ein anderer*]" (89). The formulation anticipates the language of Vischer's later definition of *Einfühlung*: "Only ostensibly do I keep my own identity although the object remains distinct.... I am mysteriously transplanted and magically transformed into this Other" (104). Here, the Other into whom Ronald is transformed is not an object but *Clarissa herself*. Although Ronald also wishes to "transplant" himself into Clarissa (or, more precisely, to have her take, like Dall from his audiences in *Turmalin*, "the soul from [his] body, so you can see how I love you," 87), the text, significantly, only records Ronald's permeation by *Clarissa's* body: She is "his breath and his pulsebeat" (85). The scene ends with the aforementioned "speechless emotion," "speechless movements of feeling," or "speechlessly being moved" (*sprachlose Gemütsbewegung*) (91): The betrothal, with its at least potentially mappable or narrativizable emotion, becomes the social-symbolic "constraint" alongside which the "escape" of "unsayable" affect can occur. As Massumi writes, "Emotion is ... the conventional, consensual insertion of intensity into ... narrativizable ... function and meaning," while affect "remains ... inseparable from but unassimilable to any particular, functionally anchored perspective.... [The autonomy of] actually existing, structured things ... is the autonomy of affect" ("Autonomy" 88, 96–97). The exchanges, transformations, and escapes of the betrothal scene enact in miniature the larger empathic and gender exchange of the novella itself: the change, through pulses and flows, to a feminine body of the text.

The text consists of allegories for this change. Think, for example, of Clarissa's harp, which, with its rhythmic "Pulsschlag" (pulsebeat) (55), becomes the somaticized instrument of a female Orpheus. As in the myth, the animals emerge to listen to the music and, at least in *Der Hochwald*'s version, witness the creation of a new world. It is as if the harp's tones themselves are the "kinetic energy" (*Wucht*) that "hurls the moon into the west" and forces "the first morning-cry from the throat of a bird!" (56). As pure sound, intensity, and beat, Clarissa's "divine melodies" (*Himmelsmelodien*) exceed complete "capture" by discourse—a point hyperbolically underscored by the fact that even the birds cannot reproduce them (56). As Luce Irigaray reminds us in a different context, Plato had originally spoken of two forms of mimesis, the "imitative" form we might associate with discursive language (and the mimetic mode of literary realism) and a "productive" form linked with *music*: "It is doubtless in the direction of, and on the basis of, that [musical] mimesis that the possibility of a women's writing may come about" (*This Sex* 131). This is the "choric" modality of, as it were, a female "Stifter," whose name can mean "founder" or "originator."[47] The Wittinghausen money or symbolic order is buried beneath an image of the *mother* of God in the "womb of the earth" (*Schoß der Erde*) (45): patriarchal signification nested within the maternal body; text embedded—*em-bodied*—in the chora.

---

47. On Stifter's possible covert "female" coding, see also Metz, "Eine eigentliche Durchdringung" 324–25.

Most significant, however, is the text's form *as* chora—the rhythm of beats and pulsions, flows and interruptions, dashes and conjunctions that marks the text's *Innigkeit* or intensity, indexes the escape of its affect, and becomes a second economy or second narrator alongside and inside its language.[48] Unlike in *Turmalin*, where an overtly female narrator serves covertly patriarchal ends, *Der Hochwald* installs a covert female narrator "in" the body of the text, resisting through *Einfühlung* and undercover interpersonal empathy the novella's overt patriarchal agenda. Like Ronald, the narrator of *Der Hochwald* exchanges bodies with the feminine—or, more accurately, we see that this exchange had always already taken place. In the "pace and weight" (Lee) of its form, the text empathizes *with and as* the body: that is, *with and as* what the patriarchal gender discourse of Stifter's day coded as the feminine. This empathy does not entirely displace or replace the text's cruelty: *Der Hochwald* still tortures and toys with its readers and female protagonists, and, at least on the surface, "erases" these protagonists from the diegetic scene. Yet in the "intense" feeling of its form, something "remains unactualized" or "escapes," "inseparable from but unassimilable to [patriarchy's] functionally anchored perspective" (Massumi, "Autonomy" 96, modified).

Writing a quarter century before Vischer, Stifter anticipates important problems and implications of aesthetic empathy; though an approximate contemporary of Büchner, he also prefigures the "postlife" of *Einfühlung* along a different path, foreshadows different conclusions about its stakes, or points to different possibilities in its implicate order. These include speculation about the challenges of knowing, identifying with, and empathizing with others who may only appear to us, in a materialist "object world," as "artificial intelligences" or purely "formal" effects (*Turmalin*) and the potential for resisting (possibly one's own) dominant ideologies through "intense" and comprehensive bodily *Einfühlung* into textual form, as

---

48. On the possibility of a text's containing a concealed "second narrator" whose voice, once decrypted, contests that of the more overtly audible narrator, see Cohn, "The 'Second Author' of *Death in Venice*."

in Vernon Lee's theories (*Der Hochwald*). The latter possibility, at least, seems a more optimistic direction for *Einfühlung* than Büchner and Vischer's uncanny anxiety. As reading Stifter with Lee, Massumi, and Kristeva suggests, *Einfühlung* can move beyond Vischer's conceptualization because it has the capacity to become a proto–affect theory, a channel of *Innigkeit*.

Stifter's interest in formalism (the Rentherr's daughter in *Turmalin*, the striking punctuation and syntax of *Der Hochwald*) and in the unsayability and escape of affect (*Der Hochwald*'s punctuation and syntax again) opens up an additional dimension in what will become Vischer's understanding of *Einfühlung* in terms of metaphors of self-other (subject-object) identification and exchange. For problems of adequate form, challenges of expressibility, and questions of what may "escape" correlation are themselves what is jointly at stake in self-other identification and exchange (that is, *empathy*) and metaphor, or *empathy conceived of* as *metaphor*. This is the problem of catachresis. In the past two chapters, we have explored *Einfühlung*'s birth and prehistory. In the final chapter, we attend to its zenith and aftermath. For the modernist poet Rainer Maria Rilke, student of Vischer's successor Theodor Lipps, empathy is inseparably linked with the mechanisms of catachresis or "bad" metaphor. It is to him that I now turn.

3

BAD METAPHORS

Catachresis and Coercion in Rainer Maria Rilke

"I have seen all sorts of eyes, of that you can be sure: never again such eyes. Those eyes needed nothing external, it resided within them. Have you heard of Venice? Good. I'm telling you, those eyes would have seen Venice into this room so it would have been here like this desk. . . . Do you see him?" he barked at her. And suddenly he seized one of the silver candelabras and shone it blindingly into her face. Abelone remembered that she had seen him.

—RAINER MARIA RILKE, *THE NOTEBOOKS OF MALTE LAURIDS BRIGGE*

Wie wenn . . . .
   (bin ichs zu sagen denn imstande?)
Sieh: diese Augen lagen da: Gewande,
ein Angesicht, ein Glanz ging in sie ein

als wären sie – – ja was? – –:
        der Canal Grande
in seiner großen Zeit und vor dem Brande –
———————————————
und plötzlich hört Venedig auf zu sein.
        —Rainer Maria Rilke, Gedichtkreis für Madeleine Broglie

The age of Theodor Lipps, fin-de-siècle Europe's most prominent theorist of aesthetic empathy, was the age of the heyday of *Einfühlungstheorie*. It was also the beginning of *Einfühlung*'s merger with interests we might more typically assign to intersubjective, not aesthetic, empathy. Not only was Lipps the first to think *Einfühlung* and intersubjective empathy together, combining in a single theoretical framework the former's focus on feeling oneself into aesthetic forms and objects and the latter's concentration on the relation between one's own feelings and those of other people (Hammond 72–74). Lipps was also, as Hammond points out, the first to suggest that empathy "might be used to deal with the conceptual problem of other minds" (73)—a possibility we saw prefigured and problematized in Stifter's *Turmalin*. Accordingly, in keeping with the trends of the period and the importance of Lipps to the concerns of this chapter, I do not differentiate as strictly and frequently between *Einfühlung* and intersubjective empathy in the following readings as I generally did in earlier discussions of Vischer, Büchner, and Stifter.

If *Turmalin*, and, in a different way, *Der Hochwald*, wrestled with the problem of knowing, empathizing with, and feeling into others *as form* in an increasingly "objectifying" (becoming-object) world, it might be tempting to read Lipps's efforts to blend *Einfühlung* with intersubjective empathy as an attempt to slow or arrest this objectifying process. However, Lipps's labors did not end up reversing or softening the previous century's growing transformation of life into a "thing." Rather, his unique theory of projection might be said to have taken another step toward using feeling and form to erase the distinct life—and thus possibly to increase the "thingness"—of the other.

For Lipps's former student Rainer Maria Rilke, the problem of form *is* the problem of other minds. The form in question is bad metaphor. Here, Rilke does not just adopt but adapts, goes beyond, and resists Lipps. If Lipps's metaphors were bad because they replaced the other with the self (a point I will return to shortly), Rilke's are "bad" because they are either *coercive* or *inadequate*, and sometimes both at once. The logic of their form is one of catachresis. This logic, too, opens onto questions of objects, other minds, and other minds *as* objects, but it suggests or anticipates a vision of "the object" that differs substantially from the one posited by the materialism of nineteenth-century thought. This object, more akin to the present-day understanding of object-oriented ontology, has significant, even possibly salutary, ramifications for the intersection of aesthetics and empathy.

A year after the turn of the twentieth century, Rilke became riveted by a Viennese case of child murder. The twenty-five-year-old writer was soon to become, with the publication of his landmark collection *Neue Gedichte* (*New Poems*, 1907–1908), the German-speaking world's foremost poet of empathy with animals and inanimate objects (Fischer 183–84). He had just returned from long trips to Russia and an extended stay in the northern German artists' colony of Worpswede, gathering new creative impulses in both places; a year later, he would move to Paris and, under Rodin's influence, write "Der Panther" ("The Panther"), the first of the "thing poems" composed for *Neue Gedichte*. Rilke's middle period was about to begin: the period of sustained poetological reflection and artistic production that would mark a radical change in his style, give rise not only to *Neue Gedichte* but also the groundbreaking experimental novel *Die Aufzeichnungen des Malte Laurids Brigge* (*The Notebooks of Malte Laurids Brigge*, 1910), and signal Rilke's emergence as one of the great voices in German modernism. 1901, then, was a "moment between," a period of incubation and incipient transformation, the cusp of wide-ranging shifts in Rilkean, and European, poetic practice. It is on the threshold of these developments that we find the young author consumed by an obscure and grisly Viennese "true crime" court case, the silence surrounding whose "injustice" had, as Rilke put it, "afflicted [him] like a lie" (Zinn 1381).

The Vienna courts had sentenced a young newspaper delivery man, Joseph Ott, to death for killing his son Pepi, who was four or five years old. In a gruesome turn, Ott had disposed of the body by dismembering it and burning it piece by piece in his family's stove. The details of the crime were disputed. Ott maintained that he had attempted to lance an abscess on his son's body, found the child the next morning dead of natural causes, and burned the corpse in a panicked attempt to avoid investigation. The prosecution dismissed not only the father's version of events but also, according to Rilke, alternative explanations and extenuating circumstances that might have reduced Ott's murder charge or mitigated his death sentence: the possibility, for example, that Ott had accidentally killed his son while trying to perform the amateur medical operation, the impact of the delivery man's tenuous mental and physical health on his actions under stress, and so forth. It is against these failings in the application of the law, but also, just as vehemently, against the court's transformation of the trial into a cheapened, sensationalistic spectacle, that Rilke protests in an open letter to the controversial political journalist Maximilian Harden, editor of *Die Zukunft*, the same influential Berlin journal in which Lipps would publish his essay on *Einfühlung* as "objectified self-enjoyment" five years later. But, as a closer reading of Rilke's letter reveals, the poet's protest is as much about the Ott case's problematic strategies of representation, its misuse of language and rhetoric, as about its outcome. As Rilke writes, the prosecution's closing argument is "simply tagged on and could also fit nicely at the end of a completely different trial" ("Offener Brief" ["Open Letter"] 490). The argument, Rilke sarcastically notes, "does not fail to mention Egypt and 'the most dim and distant antiquity'; it includes all the tried and tested"—that is, clichéd—"phrases of the past twenty years from the 'majesty of death' to the 'tragedy in retribution'" (490). Indeed, the prosecutor's rhetoric recalls the "style of trashy literature" (*Kolportageromanstil*) (491). The witnesses "talk like people for whom words are cheap" (483), and even the external newspaper accounts of the case are "poorly narrated" and "light and sloppy in tone" (482). It is perhaps not surprising, then, that Rilke describes the case as afflicting him "like a lie"—a conspicuously linguistic offense. The misuse of language is dangerous and leads to catastrophic consequences: Ott's death sentence and Rilke's fear that children captivated by the lurid reporting will "play hanging," with fatal results (492). But it is also, for the poet, an outrage in its own right. Apart from Ott's alleged crime, the *court's* crime against *Ott*—the prosecution's ill-fitting categories, summaries, and classifications (491), or its unfortunate *signifiers*—is an *aesthetic* one. For, as Rilke puts it, "every crime, *like every work of art*, is a singular case" ("Offener Brief" 491, my emphasis). Put otherwise, Rilke's letter to Harden, which itself takes on the rhetorical style or aesthetic (generic) form of a defense attorney's summation, becomes a *Plädoyer* against *bad metaphor*.

It is puzzling, then, that in 1906, deep into the composition of the *Neue Gedichte*, Rilke turns to bad metaphor himself to make his poetic "case." The scene of the crime is his *Gedichtkreis für Madeleine Broglie* (*Poem Cycle for Madeleine Broglie*), one of the princess-paramours with whom he would fall in and out of love throughout the years.[1] In the third section of the cycle, cited in this chapter's epigraph, Rilke compares eyes, presumably Broglie's, not to an ocean, lake, or pool but to Venice's backward-S-shaped Grand Canal:

> As if....
>   (am I capable of saying it?)
> See: these eyes lay there: raiment,
> a face, a shine went into them
> as if they were – – well, what? – –:
>   the Grand Canal
> in its glory days before the burning –
> ————————————
> and all at once Venice ceases to be.
> (196)

The conceit, whose weirdness is underscored by the speaker's question "Bin ichs zu sagen denn imstande?" (Am I capable of saying it?), the somewhat frantic extended rhyme sequence "imstande-Gewande-Grande-Brande," and the labored modifying phrase "in its glory days before the burning" (*in seiner großen Zeit und vor dem Brande*), which, in Rilke's German, sounds as though it was

---

1. Cf. Torgersen 197.

chosen at least in part simply to sustain the ongoing rhyme on "-*ande*," is just one among the poem cycle's long chain of spectacularly bizarre and (borderline or actually) catachrestic images: *This mistress's eyes are, indeed, nothing like the sun.*

The question of the significance of differences among the various formal figures for, and grammatical expressions of, comparison is complex. For Aristotle, in addition to its typical meaning as a direct comparison between two things that, unlike simile, does not use the words "like" or "as," metaphor could be understood as encompassing "all figures of speech that achieve their effect through association, comparison, and resemblance"; in this view, "figures like antithesis; hyperbole; metonymy; simile are all species of metaphor" (McArthur et al. 395).[2] Some theorists argue that metaphor and simile function in fundamentally different ways; that metaphor cannot be "reduced" to simile (Cohen 1–3; Kurz 21–22). The technique of analogy and the grammatical form of the subjunctive, as in Rilke's formulation "als wären sie – –: / ja was? – –: / der Canal Grande" (as if they were – – well, what? – –: / the Grand Canal), introduce additional complications. For the purposes of this chapter, I treat all figures, techniques, and grammatical structures of comparison that do not obviously express a literal association as, broadly speaking, metaphorical. I therefore as a rule use the overarching term *metaphor* to refer to all these devices and relationships. This is partly for the sake of stylistic efficiency, but also because I am in many cases more interested in the larger modes and effects of what I am broadly calling metaphor in Rilke than in differences among more strictly defined tropes and techniques: The larger modes and effects, I believe, can tell us much about Rilke's performance of metaphor's relation to empathy. By *modes* I refer here to questions of the content and word choice of imagery, the relations of vehicle to tenor, and the "fit" of imagery to its context; the issue of catachresis or bad metaphor belongs to this general category. By *effects* I refer to relations between image and reader, such as the question of coercion, to which I will return.

---

2. In the original source, the words "figures of speech," "antithesis," "hyperbole," "metonymy," and "simile" are capitalized.

It might seem at first glance odd to enter Rilke's corpus through the portal of two such apparently minor texts as the "Offener Brief an Maximilian Harden" and the *Gedichtkreis für Madeleine Broglie*. However, as so frequently is the case with Rilke, the seemingly minor or obscure is at the same time often profoundly *poetological*: a self-reflexive articulation of aesthetic theory and practice. These "minor" texts, then, open a striking window onto Rilke's larger artistic processes and body of work. In the case of the Harden letter and the Broglie cycle, the window opens onto Rilke's relation to the interfaces of metaphor and empathy, feeling and form.

It is not a metaphor to say that Rilke was Lipps's student. Lipps, chair of the Department of Philosophy at Munich's Ludwig-Maximilian University and the most influential champion of Vischer's *Einfühlungsästhetik*, deepened, expanded, and popularized Vischer's ideas, helping make the projection theory of empathy the dominant approach to aesthetics in the German-speaking world of the late nineteenth and early twentieth centuries. In 1896 and 1897, during Rilke's time as a student in Munich, Lipps was Rilke's professor for foundational courses on aesthetic theory (Corbett 20–24). Lipps's book *Raumästhetik und geometrisch-optische Täuschungen (Spatial Aesthetics and Geometrical-Optical Illusions)*, in which he laid the groundwork for his conceptualization of aesthetic empathy, appeared in the summer of 1897, just at the end of Rilke's studies with him. His more exhaustive volumes on aesthetics, which explicate his understanding of *Einfühlung* in detail, would appear between 1903 and 1906, contemporaneously with Rilke's work on the first volume of the *Neue Gedichte*.

Rilke's middle period largely coincided with the apogee of *Einfühlungstheorie*, and, from a certain perspective, the poet's writing during that time might itself be seen as the culmination and apotheosis of *Einfühlung*. The *Neue Gedichte*, with their striking attempt to depict how animals and objects are experienced in human consciousness, seem to provide ample evidence of Rilke's proximity to Lipps's understanding of aesthetic empathy. Indeed, philosopher and poet Luke Fischer notes that "the majority of interpretations of Rilke's animal poems" from the *Neue Gedichte*—interpretations with which he disagrees—read these texts either as examples of empathic projection in the Vischerian or Lippsian vein or as "humanistic" subjectivism, anthropomorphism, or outright solipsism (231–32, 183–84).

But Rilke was also writing at the beginning of the *end* of empathy theory, when, in 1908, the year volume 2 of the *Neue Gedichte* appeared, Wilhelm Worringer, another of Lipps's former students, would publish his landmark dissertation *Abstraktion und Einfühlung*, the study that would posit the supposed counterpole of "an aesthetics which proceeds not from man's urge to empathy, but from his urge to abstraction," to finding "beauty in the life-defying inorganic, in the crystalline . . . , in all abstract laws and necessity" (Worringer 4). Worringer's book, the reception of which was immediate, widespread, and largely ecstatic, went on to become one of the most reprinted theoretical works on German modernism: a manifesto, as it were, of the emerging Expressionist movement and a retroactive elucidation of Cubism (Corbett 163–67). Of course, as many have later noted, Worringer's thesis rests on a misreading of *Einfühlung*: Lipps in particular, whom Worringer discusses extensively in his book, had argued for the centrality of "empathizing with" or "feeling oneself into" precisely *abstract forms themselves* (Maskarinec 13, 59). Tellingly, Rilke's own aesthetic practice walks an ambiguous line between empathy and abstraction. The object and animal poems of *Neue Gedichte* might indeed be read as exemplary cases of "feeling oneself into," yet they are also master classes in the manipulation of the "abstract" rules and nonrepresentational conventions of the sonnet form: "crystalline" rhyme, meter, caesura, and enjambment. The eponymous narrator of *Malte Laurids Brigge* experiences striking—indeed, often terrifying—levels of empathic identification with, or self-projection into, suffering others (a neurologically impaired man stumbling down a Paris street, the abjectly poor urban "outcasts" or "Fortgeworfene"), but he is equally taken by the figurative potential of the flat, stylized, icon-like, and emotionally distancing imagery of playing cards.[3] Even Malte's famous description of a gutted building, in which Rilke's narrator identifies with the exposed interior of a Paris apartment house in the process

---

3. See Rilke, *Malte* 27–29, 47–52, 137–38, and 157–65.

of demolition ("I recognize all these things here, and that is why it enters me so readily: it is at home in me," *Malte* 34), fuses empathic projection—the conflation of the opened or "autopsied" house with Malte's own metaphorically eviscerated body and mind—with what we might think of as a perceptual formalism: The architectural forms of the house's "innards" are not only Vischerian analogues of the organic forms of Malte's bodily interior but also a vision of the gutted dwelling as an abstract, Kandinsky-like geometrical assemblage of lines, shapes, and colors ("here and there [the paths taken by illuminating gas] bent around quite unexpectedly ... and ran into the colored wall and into a hole that was black and ... ruthlessly punched out," *Malte* 33). The "geometrical" backward S of Madeleine Broglie's Grand Canal eyes perhaps partakes of this representational abstraction as well: a Cubist face (shortly) avant la lettre.

This chapter explores the question of bad metaphors in Rilke in two senses of the word: on the one hand, the inadequate, unsuccessful, or unconvincing metaphor, or the eccentrically bold but forced, strained, or "coerced" metaphor—what we might broadly call catachresis (from the Greek *katakhrésthai*, "misuse" or "abuse")—and, on the other hand, the *ethically* bad metaphor; the metaphor capable of exerting coercive force in the world, or the metaphor with, ironically, *literally* dangerous, injurious, or insidious consequences. I am particularly interested in the instances where the two senses, the formal and the ethical, come together; where the forcing of language becomes a forcing of others—where the coerced metaphor becomes, as it were, a *coercing* metaphor. As Paul de Man notes in *Allegories of Reading*, this sense of coercion is central to at least parts of Rilke's poetic project: "Rilke not only claims the right to state his own salvation but to impose it ... on others. The imperative mode that often appears in his poetry ('You must change your life' ...) is not only addressed to himself but asks for the acquiescence of the reader" (24). And, as de Man implies without using the term, this coercion is mysteriously intertwined with the question and functioning of *empathy*—in de Man's interpretation, with readers' projective belief (that is, their "empathically" projective belief) that

Rilke would have had empathy with *them*: "Many have read [Rilke] as if he addressed the most secluded parts of their selves, . . . allowing them to share in ordeals he helped them to understand and to overcome" (20).

Already in the two texts that introduce this chapter, we see the nexus of metaphor and coercion—the "coerced-coercing" metaphor. It is evident in the hackneyed rhetoric of persuasion of the prosecutorial speeches described in the Harden letter (and in Rilke's own equally dubious, sarcastically hectoring responses for the "defense"), as well as in the forceful "infliction" on the reader of the Broglie cycle's ocular Grand Canal image, which, significantly, not only strong-arms the recipient into *seeing* like the *speaker*—think here of *Malte*'s Count Brahe in this chapter's epigraph, thrusting the candelabra blindingly into Countess Abelone's face and screaming "Do you see him?"—but also unleashes massive destructive power. As we read in the Broglie cycle, the image of eyes as the Venetian canal erases, destroys, or annihilates the *actual* Venice in an instant ("And all at once Venice ceases to be"): catachresis as nuclear weapon, or, if one prefers a less disturbing metaphor, the Death Star firing on Alderaan. Thus we have on the one hand the power of coerced-coercive metaphor to "make one see," on the other hand the power of such metaphor to *make things disappear*—precisely because one has "seen" so hard.

It is likely not insignificant that the problem of "saying," of "unsayability"—the place where metaphor meets the inexpressibility or ineffability topos—is central to the thematics of the Broglie cycle, just as questions of (in)adequate expression and (un)fathomability (for example, of Ott's crimes) are central to the Harden letter. For, in attempting to circumvent problems of expression through catachresis, or to battle bad metaphor with more bad metaphor ("Am I capable of saying it?"), both texts attempt to force the reader to "see the unsayable," which is to see the *unseeable*: to see "like me," or, in empathic terms, to *feel like me*. This is a more violent version of what philosopher Ted Cohen identifies as "a leading aim of . . . metaphor-makers": "the communication of some feelings they have about the subjects of their metaphors, and the often-hoped-for inducement of similar feelings in those who grasp their metaphors" (6). Put otherwise, catachresis, as coerced-coercive metaphor, is a sort of forced empathy.

Questions of coerced and coercing metaphors, of forced seeing and erasure, are already present in Lipps's theorizing of empathy. Rilke's textual practice stands in dialogue with these elements but does not incorporate them wholesale. Instead, it ultimately asks how the simultaneous and contesting feelings of coercion and rhetorical "failure" evoked by bad metaphor introduce paradoxes that can have not only negative but also potentially restorative consequences for our relations with an "Other." It asks, that is, how the form of bad metaphor at the smaller and larger textual levels of individual "inadequate" images, strained formulations, internally conflicted themes, and problematic movements of argument complicates *Einfühlung* and intersubjective empathy, perhaps helping us negotiate ethical problems these concepts have involved since Vischer and Lipps. Here, Rilke's very catachreses save his texts from the presumption of direct or even adequate correlation with their "objects"—a potential, if still imperfect, protection of the space of the Other. In this reading, bad metaphor paradoxically emerges as a *good* defense against the self's possession of (or by) the Other, and perhaps also as the basis for an ethics based on aesthetics. Let us trace this emergence from Rilke's empathic obsession with the 1901 Ott case, through the "disastrously" catachrestic language of unsayability in the Broglie cycle, to the perils of Lipps-inflected empathy and metaphor-making in Rilke's poetological identification with non-Western others, to Rilke's own self-transformation into a Vischerian "dead object" of *his own* empathy, and finally to Rilke's anticipation of something like present-day object-oriented ontology, with its recognition of the inevitability of bad metaphor in any encounter with another.[4]

---

4. The concept of metaphor also plays a central role in Müller-Tamm's understanding of projection, including its subset, *Einfühlung*, as an early parallel to structuralist linguistics. In her reading, which recalls Crary's analysis of the "arbitrary signification" of the sense-impressions produced by Johannes Müller's specific nerve energies (Crary 90–91), the physiological phenomenon of perception becomes a series of "arbitrary" translations that point to a "metaphorizing of perception" or "fictionalization of reality" (Müller-Tamm 11–12). Müller-Tamm does not treat Rilke's works or the multivalent implications of "bad metaphor" specifically.

Crimes of Taste

The case beneath the case in Rilke's Harden letter is a crime of aesthetics and representation. It is, in other words, a formal problem. As Rilke writes, the prosecution's closing argument, like the conclusion of a bad student paper, does not follow organically from the body of the trial itself. It also includes twenty years' worth of clichés. The witnesses' words are "cheap," the newspaper accounts of the proceedings "poorly narrated." The categories (*Kategorien*) (491) organizing the court's rhetorical strategies, and thus the moves of the argumentation and the discursive articulation of the crime itself, are simplistic and inadequate—a failure of the courtroom "genre." The entire trial resembles a sensationalistic spectacle. As Rilke sardonically states, "The esteemed State Attorney ... has just discovered a way to sum up a whole series of crimes under a common name perfectly suited to the style of trashy literature: 'How to Murder Children'" ("Offener Brief" 490–91). Bad form leads to bad feelings: Rilke's outrage and the inappropriate frivolity of the participants in the trial.

The letter, however, is also a case of the *problematic of empathy*, one that Rilke does not simply observe or describe but formally enacts.[5] On the most obvious level, the letter is a document of Rilke's interpersonal empathy with the alleged murderer Ott; on a secondary level, it is an exposé of the *lack* of empathy toward Ott on the part of the witnesses, public, and court. Crucially, in its combination of free indirect discourse, psychonarration, and the imaginative re-creation, or simply creation, of extenuating "facts," the letter becomes both a journey into Ott's (fictionalized) mental state *and* the rhetorically—aesthetically—sophisticated "defense speech" the defendant never got. Beginning with a lengthy and sympathetic account of the pressures of poverty on the Ott household, the letter merges writer, reader, and Ott himself in a conspicuous performance, and solicitation, of empathic identification: "The best father," Rilke's voice tells us, "bur-

---

5. Little secondary literature exists on the letter; however, one of the few examples, Judith Ryan's one-paragraph discussion in "Rilke's Early Narratives," links the letter both to Malte's "attempts to empathize with the pathological figures he meets in ... Paris" and to questions of "how narrative emerges out of persuasive prose" (71).

dened with small children, with all their wants and needs, would come to know... moments of impatience. On top of all these daily demands came the fact that one day little Pepi developed an abscess" (486). After the child's death, "the father is gripped by insane terror. Unexpectedly, accountability crashes down on him, heavy as a mountain.... In a state of violent agitation only one thing becomes clear to him: that no one may see and examine the dead child; that it—now that it has died anyway—must join the dead as quickly as possible; that it must disintegrate; must dissolve" (486).

The narratological performance culminates in a remarkable series of passages that deserve unpacking at greater length. Rilke begins by proposing that "even if Ott did kill his child," exculpatory circumstances exist that at least partially exonerate him *if* one "attempts to imagine"—that is, empathize with—the father's "condition" or "state of mind" on the night of the deed (488). Mimicking the stock moves or formal gestures of lawyerly speech, Rilke paints "pathetic," empathy-inducing pictures of the pitiable Ott's "agitated, trembling hands" (488) and sways the "jury" of readers through rhetorical questions: "In such unusual circumstances, who would not wish to take the nervous, unhealthy nature of this man especially into consideration?" (488). The crux of the exculpatory argument, however, consists of "an uncertain memory... of events from [Rilke's] childhood" (488) that comes to the poet's mind when he learns about the Ott case. What begins as a personal recollection slides quickly into a statement about "nervous children" in general, who, Rilke avers, sometimes attempt to operate on a sick or wounded animal "out of a feeling of strong commiseration [*Mitleiden*]" (488). If the operation goes wrong and "something ugly happens, maybe the animal's bowels spill out," some of these children throw the animal aside and run away (489). Others, however—including, perhaps, the text implies, Rilke himself—"beat the ruptured animal against the wall in rage, disappointment, hatred, and disgust (not out of suffering for the suffering of the animal!) until it is dead" (489). Significantly, it is empathy—"Mitleiden" (commiseration, sympathizing)—that is the first link in the causal chain that leads to harm: children who accidentally maim the animals they mean to help, or, perhaps particularly, children who *purposely* kill the animals they mean to help when their attempts to turn empathy into action fail. In either case, we are confronted here with, to paraphrase Schiller, not "Verbrecher aus verlorener Ehre," criminals due to lost honor, but "Verbrecher aus fehlgeschlagener Empathie": criminals due to empathy gone awry. And, in his explication of his simultaneously autobiographical and allegorical "uncertain memory," *Rilke's* empathy is reserved for those whose *own* empathy produces deadly results.

Conspicuously, Rilke disowns this recollection, however authentic, accurately remembered, invented, or, as Vischer would put it, "artistically reshaped" it may be, as soon as it has fulfilled its function of demonstrating and generating empathy: "I do not wish to offer any commentary about this memory that has arisen" (489). The memory is, in any case, like the inexpressibility topos of the poem cycle for Madeleine Broglie, *unsayable*: "an uncertain memory . . . of childhood events that I can only express in uncertain outlines" (488), "very clear for my feelings, but not close to the words with which I attempt to communicate it" (489). The real point here is to install or transpose the *feeling* of things—of the childhood memory, the accidental-on-purpose but "understandable" killing of the animals, Ott's deed—into the reader *empathically*: "an uncertain memory . . . that I can only express in uncertain outlines, but still in such a way that the sensation that is at stake becomes able to be felt [*daß die Sensation, um die es sich handelt, fühlbar wird*]" (488). Thus, through their coerced empathy with *Rilke's* empathy, the letter's readers or surrogate jurors likewise become "criminals out of empathy gone awry."

Rilke criticizes the aestheticization, or, rather, the *tawdry* aestheticization, the sensationalism, of the trial. Rather than presenting the alleged murder weapon, the knife, for inspection, the court displays an imitation child's skull and a model of Ott's stove "to give the audience the pleasurable creeps" (488). Rather than taking the proceedings seriously, the judge makes ironic jokes, again "for the amusement of the audience" (490). The prosecutor coins dubious catchphrases ("prägt Schlagwörter," 491): He is a bad metaphor-maker. Indeed, for Rilke, the entire trial is a bad metaphor. Miscarriage of language and miscarriage of justice are one: The state attorney "feels himself to be an especially advanced agent of a justice that he *never even allows to speak [nicht zu Wort kommen läßt]*" (491, my emphasis). The "Open Letter," then, is an essay in literary criticism, a judgment of the vulgarity of the style—the verbal forms—through which the *court* passes judgment, a critique of the feeling of the form (and of the feelings generated by the form), a discourse on taste. In that sense, it is a covert descendant of Enlightenment-era philosophical aesthetics, whose own concept of taste was always already a metaphor: the mind's capacity for subtle discernment as an analogue to the mouth's capacity for perceiving and consuming flavors and textures. As Voltaire writes, "Like the palate, [taste] relishes what is good with an exquisite and voluptuous sensibility, and rejects the contrary with loathing and disgust" (213–14). If, then, the Harden letter is a treatise on bad metaphor and bad taste, it is significant that the metaphor that organizes the text, both at the level of content and at the level of rhetoric or "form," *itself* evokes taste, or a grotesque—a "bad"—variant of it: *cannibalism*. And we might say that the metaphor of cannibalism, itself arguably in bad taste, becomes particularly and in multiple senses "bad" when *its taste* is also cannibalistic. Let us explore what this means in practice.

The pivotal occurrence of the cannibalism metaphor, its "primal scene," as it were, is Rilke's description of the aftermath of Ott's decision not to throw his son's dead body into the river:

> An element that can chew [*kauen*] more quickly than earth and better than water had to consume [*verzehren*] this little bloody body [*blutigen Körper*]: fire. And no other fire was there to do [Ott's] bidding than the small flame of his daily stove [*täglichen Herdes*]. Thus he stood before the horrible task of cutting the bites into this narrow mouth [*diesem engen Mund die Bissen zuzuschneiden*], of chopping up [*zerkleinern*] his child and burning him piece by piece [*Stück für Stück*]. And the flame that did him this service could of course not be freed from the duty of warming the paltry daily meal for the living [*das tägliche armsälige Mahl den Lebenden zu wärmen*]. (487)

Like a hub, this image complex extends its spokes throughout the text, structuring the letter's figural inventory and "plot" like a macabre joke. In the very first paragraph of the letter—preparing the way, so to speak, for the image complex's unveiling—Rilke lambastes the press for "cut[ting] the narrative of the trial into tiny juicy bites [*in kleine pikante Bissen*]" with "trash-novel headlines" (482–83) and derides the implied verbal vomitus of "witness statements, objections, and contradictions" coughed up "in fits and starts" by the trial's participants (*stoßweise vorgebrachten Zeugenaussagen, Einwürfe und Widerrufe*) (483). Shortly after his description of the stove scene, Rilke notes that Ott's young daughter Poldi, who was also present at the failed abscess operation, "naturally cannot forget how horrible it was when Father 'cut a piece of flesh out of the little Pepi'": She "sees her father since then entirely in the light of this cannibal gesture [*Menschenfressergebärde*]" (489). Toward the end of the letter, Rilke sardonically writes of the state prosecutor that "one gets the feeling: he . . . has a good appetite" (491). And, most obviously, the entire tone of the letter makes it clear that every aspect of the trial and its representation is, for Rilke, a spectacle "in bad taste": something, like a revolting meal of human flesh, to be rejected (as Voltaire put it) "with loathing and disgust."

It is therefore interesting that Rilke's text, or, more precisely, its intertextuality, its broader form as a web of allusions, itself "cannibalizes" literary tradition, particularly the tradition of literature about cannibals. The letter's depiction of the stove scene, with its suggestion that the child Pepi is in fact being cooked for the family's dinner ("the flame that did [Ott the] service [of burning Pepi's body] could of course not be freed from the duty of warming the paltry daily meal for the living," 487), evokes the myth of Philomela and Tereus, Shakespeare's variation of the story in *Titus Andronicus*, and such popular German folklore as the Grimms' "Hansel and Gretel." More importantly, Rilke's letter gleefully engages in what it criticizes: the "tasteless" reliance on metaphors in bad taste, including metaphors of cannibalism; the sensationalizing of the crime through crimes of representation; the very irony and sarcasm Rilke deplores in the judge; the outré rhetorical gestures he accuses the prosecutor of. For example, Rilke lambastes the judge for such mocking comments about Ott as "precisely for the nervously ill, the dismembering of corpses is really not an appropriate activity" (490);

however, Rilke himself writes in a similarly sarcastic vein of the prosecutor that "he ... doesn't content himself ... with being the most important part of that immaculately functioning machine [of the law].... Heaven protect us: he lives! [*Bewahre: er lebt*]" (491). These sorts of formal characteristics—including this ironic or possibly unconscious self-reflexivity, if you will—are present throughout the text. It is most spectacularly evident in the Grand Guignol or penny-dreadful phrasing of the stove scene, where Rilke's web of "bad" metaphor, personification, and associative displacement "serves up" the dismembered Pepi as a (figurative) family dish: Fire "chews" (*kauen*) and "consumes" (*verzehren*) the boy's "little bloody body," Ott "cuts the bites" into the stove's "narrow mouth," the same cooking flame that burns up the child's corpse likewise "warms the paltry daily meal for the living"—which meal, of course, Pepi has now metonymically "become." When Rilke, repeating language he has used earlier in the letter, once again concludes that the prosecutor has inappropriately, even "criminally," grouped all similar cases together "under the *tasteful* [*geschmackvollen*] title: How to Murder Children" (492, my emphasis), the statement is a syllepsis, simultaneously figurative and literal, at once ironic and, within the web of meaning created by the letter's metaphoric network, *true*. Of course Rilke means that the imaginary title (and actual technique) of the prosecutor's closing argument is precisely *tasteless*, the opposite of *geschmackvoll*. But *geschmackvoll* means, literally, "full of taste"—and the imagined *taste* of murdered children is precisely what the letter, qua Rilke's extended "bad metaphor," is figuratively and rhetorically *about*.

Rilke's objection to the prosecutor's grouping of cases reveals much of what is at stake in the aesthetic politics of the letter. As Rilke writes, the state attorney fails to understand that "it is not a matter of creating categories of crimes ... because every crime, like every work of art, is a singular case, with its own roots, its own growth, with its own unique sky above it that rains and shines over the strange seeds of incomprehensible deeds" (491). Rilke's analogy recalls Nietzsche's similar (and similarly botanical) critique of conceptual categories in "Über Wahrheit und Lüge im außermoralischen Sinne" ("On Truth and Lying in a Non-Moral Sense"), posthumously published two years after the Harden letter. This is not just because Rilke, like Nietzsche, so to speak sees in "nature" no overarching model of a leaf, only individual leaves (in the Harden letter's case, individual crimes), but also because, again like Nietzsche, Rilke recognizes the fundamentally metaphorical nature of "truth."[6] As Rilke's comparison posits, crimes are "like" works of art—that is, figures (similes or metaphors) *for* aesthetic artifacts, or themselves aesthetic artifacts at the interface of figure, form, and feeling. Presumably, then, the representational strategies that "textualize," explicate, and, at least in part, grant meaning to these crimes—criminal codes and "categories," juridical speech, prosecutorial and defense rhetoric, and so on—are correspondingly "aesthetic" discourses. Despite the comparison of crime to art, this is not fin-de-siècle decadence, nor even aestheticism—but it *is* a "case" of aesthetics. Put differently, it was never a matter of removing metaphor from the Ott trial but rather of finding the *right* metaphor. In decrying the unseriousness of the court's rhetoric and instead seeking a *ductus* that might, in theory, arouse pity and terror, Rilke, his insistence on the "singular" nature of crimes notwithstanding, asserts the formal "rightness," for this case, of the *nonsingular*—that is, *generic*—category of *tragedy*. His retelling, and his telling of *others' telling*, of the case are part of this art. That his anthropophagic imagery perhaps instead succeeds in arousing the same feeling of "pleasurable creeps" he denounces in the prosecutor's presentation (488) reveals once again that the letter's apparent battle against bad metaphor is itself bad metaphor. But what does this metaphor *mean*?

Rilke's reliance on the metaphoric field of cannibalism, whether calculated or unconscious, might be approached through the problematic of coercion. In the Ott trial as Rilke tells it, reader and courtroom public are compulsory "consumers," forced or coerced to

---

6. Nietzsche criticizes concepts' "making equivalent that which is nonequivalent": The idea of *leaf* "gives rise to the notion that something other than leaves exists in nature, something which would be 'leaf,' a primal form" ("On Truth and Lying" 877). For Müller-Tamm, Nietzsche's essay supports her understanding of nineteenth-century physiology as, so to speak, Saussurian: Nietzsche's discussion of the transformation of nerve sensations into mental images or "metaphors" parallels the account of arbitrary signification in structural linguistics (*Abstraktion* 181–91). On Nietzsche's influence on Rilke, see Heller 121–77.

"eat," digest, and be affected by a meal that is "bad" in both the aesthetic and the ethical sense. Bad metaphor joins forces with the latent violence, always ready to be deployed, of the court setting: Mesmerized by the tasteless and damaging language of the trial and its press re-presentations, "one doesn't notice that things are moving toward a [possibly unjust] death sentence" ("Offener Brief" 490, my bracketed insertion). It is against this backdrop that we can understand Rilke's intentional or unintentional self-reflexive discourse. For, ironically, the trial's (more specifically, the prosecutor's) juridical rhetoric is not only a source of jurors' coercion—coercion into lack of empathy with Ott—but is itself, paradoxically, a master class in *empathy production*, particularly if we think of "empathy production" here as the production, or coercion, of mimesis, including Rilke's. From one perspective, Rilke's letter is a better defense of Ott than Ott received from his own attorney; from another, it is an uncanny mirror (or cannibalization) of the *prosecutor's* language and tactics. Of the prosecutor's closing argument, Rilke writes that it "erects itself massively before the defendant and screams the rhetorical question at him, 'You nervous man! Did your hands not tremble when you rent the flesh of your child apart piece by piece[?]'" (490). Rilke's "defense" responds with a rhetorical question of its own, in a similarly histrionic register: "How does the esteemed State Attorney know that Joseph Ott did not with tremulous hands consummate [*vollbracht*] the abominable?" (490).[7] The trial sensationalizes; Rilke's mirroring defense makes the cannibalistic subtext of the proceedings explicit, thereby sensationalizing even more. In a sort of willing or unwilling empathic dance, the letter's rhetoric moves with the trial's; to paraphrase and expand Vischer, it moves "in and with the [trial's] forms" (101). Put otherwise, Rilke's "defense" speech *becomes* the prosecutor's, or has in some way *been coerced or compelled to*—it has cannibalized and incorporated it.

---

7. The register of Rilke's verb choice "vollbringen" (consummate) is particularly elevated, dramatic, and (histrionically) biblical: cf. Luther's famous translation of the "consummatum est" (It is finished) verse of Jesus's crucifixion in John 19:30 as "Es ist vollbracht!"

Thus bad metaphor produces more bad metaphor all the way up the line, including the individual images and structuring figure of the Harden letter's proxy advocacy itself. As Rilke drily notes, the prosecutor's closing statement "would work on jurors every time. This time it also worked on the defense" (490). After the prosecutor's "splendid performance," the "speeches of the defense attorneys naturally don't make any impression anymore. Both stand under the influence of the prosecutor" (492). The arguments of Ott's counsel themselves become saturated with ridiculous imagery, inappropriate style, and irrelevant clichés (492). The proliferation of bad metaphor coerces the jurors, and not just the jurors, into making bad *decisions*. At the end of the empathic and mimetic chain that bad metaphor sets in motion, Rilke fears the ultimate disastrous result of the literalization of tropes: that children imitating the trial by "playing hanging"—a type of simile, a game of "like"—will end up dead in reality ("that children play 'hanging' and finally one of them really remains in the noose, heavy, motionless," 492). What Rilke imagines as the adults' likely response to, and refusal to take responsibility for, the catastrophe—"that they do not run away but rather greet each other with dignity and part from each other with solemnity and mutual esteem"—ironically only proves that the "grown-ups" have also been "playing" ("daß Erwachsene gespielt haben," 492). More precisely, the court, press, and public have been performing tawdry theater, tasteless aesthetics, faux seriousness, and a travesty of tragedy: playing, that is, at bad metaphor. And, at least to a degree, so has Rilke himself.

Bad Metaphors

Part of what is at stake in Rilke's poetological game of bad metaphor can be gleaned from the opening lines of his *Gedichtkreis für Madeleine Broglie*, written five years after the Harden letter and in the midst of his work on the *Neue Gedichte*. The cycle begins with a series of formal slippages—slippages of syntax, punctuation, and phonetics—that rapidly become *semantic* slippages, laying the groundwork for the poem's overall thematic field and introducing the specific figures or metaphors, including the larger problematic of bad metaphor, that will dominate the text. "Vergangen nicht, verwandelt ist was war" (Gone not, transformed is what was), Rilke writes at the outset of the cycle's first section, "Widmung" ("Dedication")—"O wie unsäglich selig kehrt es wieder" (O how unsayably blessed it returns) (193).[8] Already the first line is shot through with significant (and, for the poem as a whole, signifying) ambiguity: With no alteration in syntax, the mere shifting of a comma one position or word to the left would transform the entire meaning of the sentence into its opposite, 'Vergangen, nicht verwandelt ist was war'; 'Gone, not transformed is what was.'[9] Thus a purely orthographic revision, nearly inaudible except for small changes in the position of pauses, raises the question of whether things "gone" are indeed "transformed"—or simply *gone*. More significantly, in combination with the verse that follows, "O wie unsäglich selig kehrt es wieder" (O how unsayably blessed it returns), the line asks whether the "transformed" return of a "gone" thing—a comma, say, or something even more "unsayable"—indeed always has a "blessed" effect. Now, primed by the semantic slippage of the first line, we encounter the latent or implicit phonetic slippage of the second—a slippage of near assonance (German *ä/e*) or similar-sounding words, with its corresponding morphemic shifts and reversals of meaning: "O wie *unsäglich selig* kehrt es wieder" → 'O wie *unselig säglich* kehrt es wieder' ("O how *unsayably blessed* it returns" → 'O how *disastrously sayably* or *sayable* it returns,' my emphasis).

This second line fulfills a number of functions. It announces the *Unsagbarkeitstopos* or topos of inexpressibility to which the entire poem, not just its opening section, "Dedication," is indeed dedicated ("O wie *unsäglich* selig kehrt es wieder," O how *unsayably* blessed

---

8. In the citation above, I have omitted Rilke's parentheses around the second verse: "Vergangen nicht, verwandelt ist was war. / (O wie unsäglich selig kehrt es wieder.)" On the multiple meanings of "selig" (blessed[ly], blissful[ly], and so on), see my discussion of Mörike in chapter 1.

9. In the following discussion, I place single quotation marks around altered Rilke verses.

it returns).[10] It opens, through the potential sonant slippage it dangles before us, as it were, like a temptation, the question of a sort of "saying" that is in fact damaging, destructive, disastrous: 'O wie unselig säglich kehrt es wieder' (O how disastrously sayably—or how *disastrously sayable*—it returns). The pair *unsäglich selig / unselig säglich* (unsayably blessed / disastrously sayable) points to a wedge or split in the poem: how the attempt to circumvent the unsayability topos leads to a saying that is not blessed but cursed—a *bad saying*. Put otherwise, catachresis bridges the gap between *Unsagbarkeitstopos* and *unseliges Sagen* (disastrous, unfortunate, or "cursed" saying): The unsayable can only be said inadequately or badly, through *bad metaphor*. Here, resurrection fantasy ("O wie unsäglich selig kehrt es wieder," O how unsayably blessed it returns) becomes something else: as we (almost) read/hear, 'O wie unselig säglich kehrt es wieder' (O how disastrously sayable it returns). Inexpressibility "returns" precisely as bad metaphor: Catachresis is the revenant of the unsayable. Or the unsayable returns as *dead* metaphor, a "bad" resurrection in which the thing resurrected remains, paradoxically, dead (an echo of the problematic resurrections we encountered in Büchner and Vischer). At the end of the Broglie cycle, for example, the image of the "inexpressible" woman Rilke writes about returns as a profile on a coin. Since coins are both frequently used metaphors *and* common figures for metaphoricity itself (Kurz 26; Shell 3–4), the return, after long "circulation," of the princess remains within the bounds of (all too) conventional expression: Her metaphoric resurrection is, as it were, dead on arrival.[11] That the poem seems self-reflexively aware of all of this does not necessarily rescue it.

---

10. The italics in the Rilke quote are mine. On inexpressibility topoi (*Unsagbarkeitstopoi*), see Curtius 159–62. For a thorough discussion of the term, see Richards, especially 32–71. As Richards writes, "In the end [all variations of] the topos never entirely lose the self-conscious rhetoric of [the rhetorical trope of] *occupatio*, where a speaker says, 'Words fail me' and goes on anyway" (48).

11. Cf. also Nietzsche's famous (metaphorical!) image of truth as a "lie" or *dead metaphor* represented by "coins which, having lost their stamp, are now regarded as metal and no longer as coins" ("Truth and Lying" 878).

Bad Metaphors 239

With the *Gedichtkreis für Madeleine Broglie*, a lyric cycle most likely never meant for wider dissemination, we approach a Rilkean theory and praxis of metaphor—and empathy—from the margins. But this margin is, as is often the case, tellingly central. Not only does Rilke's work on the Broglie cycle intersect with his composition of many of the *Neue Gedichte*, with their rich metaphoric language for attempting to express, if not the "inexpressibility," then at least the unique "appearing to human consciousness of," and empathic resonance with, numerous animal, material, and historical-mythical Others. The cycle itself in fact frequently shares the same image inventory that will appear, or has already appeared, in several of the most well known of the *Neue Gedichte*—a re- and pre-cycling of metaphor not unlike the circulation and return of the coin in the last section of the *Gedichtkreis*. In the second section of the Broglie cycle, for example, we read that if the princess "rais[es] [her] hands: then also comes dream, / comes into them like the falling of a ball" (194)—an image that anticipates the much-discussed ball "falling toward the chalice of raised hands" in the closing line of the celebrated 1907 *Dinggedicht* "Der Ball," published in part 2 of *Neue Gedichte* (640). Similarly, the section's imagery of falling petals prefigures nearly identical language in Rilke's sonnet "Die Gazelle" ("The Gazelle"), written, like "Der Ball," one year after the Broglie cycle and published in *Neue Gedichte* part 1 (*Gedichtkreis* 194; "Gazelle" 506). Key parts of the concluding "coin" section of the *Gedichtkreis*, with its highly sexualized lexicon of "rushing," "swelling" flows (199–200), are sketched out in advance (with the gender roles reversed) in Rilke's 1904 poem "Hetären-Gräber" ("Graves of the Hetaerae") (541–42). Most strikingly, and, for the problematic of empathy, most significantly, the "eye" conceit of *Broglie*'s Grand Canal recalls the famous conclusion of "Der Panther" (1902): Objects and experiences "go into" the cycle's canal-like eyes, and "plötzlich hört Venedig auf zu sein" (suddenly Venice ceases to be) (196); in a slight alteration, an image ("ein Bild") goes into the eye of Rilke's panther and "in its heart ceases to be" ("Dann geht ein Bild hinein, / . . . / und hört im Herzen auf zu sein") (505). We might therefore think of the Broglie cycle as a storehouse for the reception and distribution (and, if necessary, hiding) of metaphoric material or a workshop in which the stress limits of figurative language are tested outside the public eye. The *Gedichtkreis* thus may tell us something about the stakes and implications of metaphor-making in Rilke's middle period.

The cycle consists of six parts: the aforementioned "Dedication"; an untitled second section heavily focused on a lengthy succession of metaphors for the concept of "dream"; the central third section, "Fortgehn" ("Departing," "Leaving"), with its pivotal Grand Canal image; an untitled fourth section that plays extensively on the *occupatio* or apophatic tradition of asserting something while claiming not to assert; a fifth section titled "Der Engel" ("The Angel"), a possible anticipation of the famous angelic figure from Rilke's *Duino Elegies*; and the concluding sixth section, "Die Münze" ("The Coin"), with its titular medallion. Each of the sections revolves around the common literary trope of the unsayability of the beloved woman, the inadequacy of language to "speak" her beauty or sufficiently articulate the poet's experience of her. As Rilke writes in section 5, "How helpless is he who with nothing but words / should state how he feels and sees you" (198). Or, as we read at the beginning of section 4, "I have not joined those poets / who announce you or lament / and imagine they name your beauty / when they call it: not of this world" (196)—although the resulting scramble to proclaim the "this-worldliness" of the princess only ends up confirming that she is, indeed, "out of this world": "Is it not [this world] ... / where the almost Unsayable still was not enough / to allow your Being to assemble itself from it all[?]" (197). Broglie is, as it were, *incomparable*, seemingly escaping the representational capacity of metaphor. On her command, an angel "passes her the hours of her life," which she takes from his hands with a sublimely Kantian "greatness without compare" (*Größe ohne gleichen*) (*Gedichtkreis* 199), an absolute quantity, nonexistent *tertium comparationis*, or "quantity as such" that recalls the language of the *Kritik der Urteilskraft* (169). Yet none of this stops the poem from continuing to try to "say" or "compare" the princess in a series of ever more precarious, questionable, and outlandish conceits that would put the metaphysical poets to shame; indeed, outrageous conceits, though inadequate to the task, seem the only way the princess can (not) be said.

She is the gap, so to speak, that motors both desire and a seemingly endless proliferation of strained metaphor: Even the extended angel imagery that contains the assertion of her "incomparable" action is, of course, itself a protracted comparison or trope. From a different perspective, then, the cycle gives "form" to, and transmits the feeling tone of, a frustrating impediment to intersubjective empathy: the inaccessibility to the reader of key aspects of the speaker's experience. Or, to change the lens: What the reader *can* empathize with is the speaker's frustration, recognizable from the related experience of the reader's also having had—and having been unable adequately to communicate—unsayable experiences.

If every saying in the poem is a mis-saying, this metaphoric *hamartia* points to the link of catachresis with *imposed* empathy. The cycle becomes about forced empathy because it is about forced seeing through forced saying—the attempt of coerced-coercing metaphor to make one see "as I do." The language of (bad) metaphor is the language of (inflicted) empathy, and vice versa. *Malte*'s Count Brahe from this chapter's epigraph, forcing his daughter to take dictation for his memoirs (and memories), is again the relevant allegory here: The count is unable to capture his experience in words, Abelone is unable to write the words, and Brahe fears that potential readers will be unable to "see" the images behind the words in any case (*Malte* 109–14). To shed further light on the implications of this problematic, let us take a closer look at some of the cycle's more striking catachreses, figurative eccentricities, and moments of forced seeing/saying.

After an introductory group of verses in which the speaker's memories, presumably of Madeleine Broglie, *begin* as metaphor before "returning" as a list of literal body parts ("Once it was Festival and Devotion and Danger, / ... / and now is face and hand and hair," 193), the dedication moves on to its chief tropic business: transforming Broglie *back into metaphor*, or, more precisely, establishing the metaphoric exchangeability of "woman" and "city" (in this case, Florence), thereby setting in motion an extended figure (Broglie as city/landscape/cosmos) that will continue throughout the cycle—and become the first of the poem's metaphors to go "bad." The speaker asks how a city can "configure," "arrange," or "construct" itself "for the sake of a woman" ("dich auferbaun zuliebe einer Frau," 193). However, in a recollection of the phonetic and semantic slippages of the poem's second verse ("unsäglich selig" / 'unselig säglich'), we might just as easily hear the city "constructing itself" to *become* the beloved ('dich auferbaun *zu einer lieben Frau*'). For this is indeed what happens as the city imagery becomes increasingly anthropomorphized, or the Broglie imagery increasingly "citified." The city's courtyards "stand as if in dances [*wie in Tänzen*] / around the fountains' round structure" (193), while the "Unsayabilty" of Florence's hills ("das Unsagbare deiner Hügelränder") "flows through [Broglie's] bearing and gesture [*Haltung und Gebärde*]" (194)—the conflation of city and woman here reinforced not only through the apostrophic use of "Du" to address Florence but also through the evocation of hips (*Hüften*) by the section's dance imagery ("Tänzen," "Haltung," "Gebärde") and repetition of the alliterative, quasi-assonant H-words *Höfe* (courtyards) and *Hügel* (hills) (194).

That there is already trouble in this metaphor-making is clear: The speaker marks the tenor of the hill image as "unsayable" ("das Unsagbare deiner Hügelränder"), and one wonders what kind of dance consists in "standing still" ("welche wie in Tänzen / stehn bleiben") (193). But the figural complex continues to expand throughout the poem's remaining sections. The progression starts small in section 2 with a Thomas Campion–like "garden in her face" ("I only know how / to sing your praise: . . . / Garden around a house, / in whose windows I saw the heavens," 195), although even here, the imagery rapidly turns galactic in scope: The windows/eyes contain "so much heaven over so much distance" and "what great stars" (195). Soon, however, Broglie's conflation with the city, landscape, and cosmos becomes positively hyperbolic: The river in section 3 "is the way it is so that it may signify her [*damit er dich bedeute*]" (195); the city (this time Venice) "rises up" *as, like, when,* or *in the same way that* Broglie "appears" (to capture some of the range of *wie* in the line "und diese Stadt stand auf wie du erschienst," 195); and "all these things" are "thought up" (by the speaker? by God?) "in order to 'mean' her" ("Weil das alles ausgedacht ist nur: / dich zu bedeuten," 196). Broglie's figural field passes from a simile of the earth ("it is like the earth," 196) to a metaphor of an entire universe containing its own vast eons: The angel of section 5 "expends its many eternities / in [Broglie's] time like a short day" (199). Finally, the speaker seems to acknowledge the limitations of his metaphor factory ("O no, all of that is after all a comparison," 195)—and the comparison quickly comes off its hinges.

The unhinging already begins in section 1. As the speaker says of Florence (the city) in comparison to Broglie, "as your bells go [*wie deine Glocken gehen*], so goes her stride" (193). Here we might ask ourselves: What would this be "like," the city bells "stepping" or "striding," the princess striding "like" the bells? One thinks perhaps of the rhythmic and measured pace, the graceful regularity—but also of great, booming church bells; the cacophony of the bells of many different churches ringing at once; the almost deafening discomfort of standing next to the bell tower on a Sunday morning; the princess stomping through the city with footfalls like the gonging of a monstrous bell, like Godzilla stamping through Tokyo. Would one want to be around this princess? The passage from the conventional through the sublime to the ridiculous continues in section 2, whose enjambed accumulation, in immediate succession, of at least eight metaphors for "dream" is not only a celebration of the creative power of figuration but also a formal index of the inadequacy, the necessity for supplementation or replacement, of any *one* figure—excess saying, that is, as a marker of unsayability. After noting that "dream is" not only "brocade that flows down from" Broglie but also a tree, a passing glow, a sound, a feeling, an animal that gazes into the princess's eyes, an angel that "enjoys" her, a word that falls like a petal or a falling ball, and a "confused piece [of life] in which Vision / and Being bite and weave into each other / like golden animals taken from / the deaths of kings of Thebes," the speaker insists that Broglie "carries all of that," "laden with it as with her hair" ("So wie mit deinem Haar damit beladen") (194). One wonders just how much hair Broglie has, or whether her head is loaded down, à la the Chiquita banana woman, with a basket of trees, animals, angels, balls, and funeral statuary. And if section 2 moves on to the speaker's imagining having seen animals "bathing in Broglie's gaze" and "drinking her presence" (195), section 5 takes this image to its grotesque extreme: The angel that continuously accompanies the princess will never return to his fellows in the heavenly council, "but people will speak of the countenance"—that is, Broglie's—"from which [it] lived and in which it drowned [*an dem ein Engel lebte und ertrank*]" (199). One imagines the angel spinning slowly in the pond of Broglie's face like a dead insect in a pool, its wings sticky and extended. The drinking and bathing animals become angels; the angels become bugs; Broglie's face becomes liquid and huge. As de Man has argued in a different context, "In the most innocent of catachreses"—that is, in bad metaphor or "bad saying"—"something monstrous lurks" ("Epistemology of Metaphor" 21).

The "monstrosity," violent undertones, or destructive consequences of bad metaphor reach their apogee (or nadir) in sections 3 and 6, the midpoint and conclusion of the cycle. Section 3, "Fortgehn," sets itself up as an aubade-like departure ("Sudden leave-taking: being outside in the gray," 195), but it is in fact more of a *return* ("And yet nonetheless, nonetheless now it returns," 196): a return, however, less "unsayably blessed" than "disastrously sayable." In particular, it is the imagery and motifs of section 1 that return, in altered, frequently negative form—an unsettling enactment of the dedication's assertion that "gone not, transformed is what was." As in the first section, memories of Broglie reappear, this time as pain: "And yet nonetheless, nonetheless now it returns: the pain, the pain of the first moment [*des ersten Augenblicks*]" (196). The woman-as-city metaphor returns as well, with Florence now "transformed" into Venice and, in place of dancing hips/courtyards and striding footfalls/bells, bridges that "with decorum . . . / go calmly forth and back in [Broglie's] service" (196). In similarly transformative recurrences (or reversals), rather than the "unsayableness" of the hills flowing through Broglie's gestures, the "gardens" and "distances" of section 3, themselves "returns" of the imagery of section 2, now perform their *own* gestures, "signify" (*bedeuten*) Broglie, and are filled with "meaningful figures" or "tropes" (*deutsamer Figur*): "die Gärten stehn in dunkelnder Gebärde, / die Fernen sind voll deutsamer Figur" (196). This time, however, the chain of saying ends not with the city or landscape "building itself up" for the sake of—or into—Broglie (193) but with Broglie, or her image, tearing the city down: "and suddenly Venice ceases to be" (196).

Even before culminating in the metaphor of eyes as the Grand Canal, the section is powerfully dominated by the eye motif, which from the outset threatens to tip into the overdone. Already in the section's first two lines we read of "sudden leave-taking: being outside in the gray / with eyes smelted [*eingeschmolzen*], hot and soft," 195). Immediately after this moltenly ocular beginning, the speaker expresses the wish or expectation that he will now be able to look directly into "the Real" ("und nun in das was *ist* hinauszuschauen"), followed by the distressed realization that his vision is limited to the metaphorical after all ("O no, all of that is after all a comparison," 195)—a progression that, like the opening pages of Stifter's *Hochwald*, once again underscores the relation between (impossible) seeing and (inadequate) saying. The pain that returns to the speaker in the section is notably "the pain of the first moment" or "Augenblick" (196), presumably the first moment of seeing or being with Broglie. The compound noun *Augenblick* here carries the force of its twin German roots: the amount of time it takes the eye (*Auge*) to take a single glance or complete, as it were, a discrete unit of "gaze" (*Blick*). The movement of this pain itself unfolds as an extended eye conceit. The pain "goes down" and "flies up" like "songs" (*Lieder*) (196), but also like *eyelids* (*Lider*): a homophonic pun on the two indistinguishably pronounced words, and a tropic conflation of poetic speech, lyric, or metaphor itself (songs) with vision (eyelids) that Rilke will later use to great effect in his famous gravestone inscription, "Rose, oh reiner Widerspruch, Lust / Niemandes Schlaf zu sein unter soviel / Lidern" (Rose, oh pure contradiction, delight / of being no one's sleep under so many / eyelids [songs]) ("Rose" 185).[12] The "Unsayable" of section 1 returns as well, this time as the inexpressibility of the "erster Augenblick," of that moment's—or sight's—pain and its transformations (going down, flying up, being "done" like a song, "aus wie Lieder"): "[All of] that was so full of unsayable fate [*unsäglichen Geschicks*]" (196). We thus arrive at the concluding Grand Canal image: the attempt

---

12. The gravestone inscription also puns homophonically on Rilke's first name: "oh *reiner* [Rainer] Widerspruch," "oh *pure* contradiction."

to *say* that "Unsayable," and to make the reader *see that Unseeable*, through metaphor anyway.

After a performatively tentative introduction—the formulation "As if . . . ." with its four hesitant elliptical dots, followed by the topoi of (false) humility and inability ("am I even capable of saying it?")—the section launches into its final metaphoric bid, itself a doubling down on the "eye-and-vision" conceit:

Sieh: diese Augen lagen da: Gewande,
ein Angesicht, ein Glanz ging in sie ein
als wären sie – – ja was? – –:
        der Canal Grande
in seiner großen Zeit und vor dem Brande –
----
und plötzlich hört Venedig auf zu sein.

[See: these eyes lay there: raiment,
a face, a shine went into them
as if they were – – well, what? – –:
        the Grand Canal
in its glory days before the burning –
----
and all at once Venice ceases to be.]
(196)

The linguistic transformation of what is incommunicable about the speaker's experience of Broglie into the "disastrously sayable" ('unselig säglich') image of the eyes as "Grand Canal," a metaphor about which the speaker himself seems embarrassed ("am I even capable of saying it?" "well, what?"), leads to a literally disastrous result: the actual Venice obliterated, stomped out of existence by the poem's preceding row of dashes. "Outside in the gray," indeed, but also "outside in the *horror*" ("draußensein im *Grauen*," 195, my emphasis). Here, catachresis eliminates, or at least seems to eliminate, "the real," a point to which I will return later in this chapter. For the moment, however, let us ask a different question relevant to section 3: *Whose* eyes "lay there as if they were . . . the Grand Canal"? And whose eyes appear at the opening of the section, "smelted, hot and soft"?

A long lyric tradition of poems about women's eyes stands behind any attempt to read Rilke's text: "My mistress' eyes are nothing like the sun." And the cycle's trajectory up to this point, including the first two sections' overriding focus on Broglie, the numerous second-person addresses to her, the explicit descriptions of animals "looking into" and "bathing in" her eyes (194–95), and, of course, the assertion that all the poem's imagery is "only thought up to signify her" (196), strongly grooms—coerces?—the reader to "see" the princess's eyes as the subject of the *Canal Grande* metaphor. Here, the eyes are simultaneously cloth-like "raiment" (barely veiling glory, perhaps) *and* the mirrorlike waterway into which "a countenance" and "a glow" can plunge, like the drowning insect-angel of section 5: "Look: these eyes lay there: raiment, / a countenance, a glow went into them" (196). But of course these could be the speaker's eyes as well: Nothing syntactically prevents this from being the case. It would then be Broglie's clothing, face, and glow that enter the aqueous (or vitreous) "canal" of the speaker's eyeball, blinding him and causing the pain of that first "Augen-Blick." This way of reading the equivocal verses resonates with the section's opening image of "being outside ... with eyes smelted, hot and soft" (195), an image that seems to evoke the speaker's, rather than Broglie's, distress (although even here things are ambiguous: No subject is named to specify precisely *who* is outside with eyes turned, possibly by crying, into ocular slag).

What is at stake in our inability to be certain whose eyes we "see" in these images, and why does it feel less "bad" (and less like a bad metaphor) if the *Canal Grande* eyes are his rather than hers? In either case the image is bizarre, in either case the city is destroyed, and in either case the destruction is caused, or seems to be caused, by the princess. Either the blinding light of Broglie's eyes itself obliterates Venice, or the speaker's seeing of her with *his* eyes—seeing, that is, her sublime and all-replacing radiance—wipes out the city. In fact, the two options are not all that different: In both cases, it is really the speaker's *metaphorical* eyes—his perception or interpretation of Broglie, his seeing her "as"—that annihilates. Underlying, or activated by, both versions of Venice's disappearance, like an element of transformational-generative grammar, is the hoary convention of "only having eyes for" the beloved: the beloved's ability to displace or replace (in effect, eliminate) any other "sight," whether actual or figurative. But the destructive force of the metaphor seems so much less *destructive* when recuperated by that very conventionality—when linked, that is, to the speaker's amorous perception or to the structural positionality, in the poem's symbolic economy, of Broglie as a signifier for beauty, the ineffable, the unrepresentable nature of overwhelming experience, and so on—than when imagined, literally but also catachrestically-metaphorically, as emanating from Broglie's weird eyes themselves, surreally shaped like the Grand Canal, and actively erasing Venice like a sort of radiation or laser. In conventionality ("I only have eyes for you"), catachresis is destroyed like Venice: One type of bad metaphor eradicates another. In the first version of the image (Broglie's eyes as the canal), the speaker forces us, through forced metaphor, to "see like him"; in the second version (the speaker's eyes as the canal), we more conventionally participate in his experience of Broglie. Both versions paradoxically transform catachresis and the incommunicability of another's experience into empathy—like Abelone in the chapter epigraph, we "see" what we cannot see—but one is more revealing. The double image of Broglie's and the speaker's eyes as the canal, two alternatives in one, followed by the erasure of Venice, suggests that the violence implicit in both versions of the metaphor—the violence of being *made* to see like another—is one of degree, not kind.

That this is the case becomes clear in section 6, "Die Münze" ("The Coin"), where the question of "seeing as I do," of "feeling with," "empathy," and "shared experience," reaches its violent, disturbingly gender-inflected conclusion. As the title of this final section suggests, the poem arrives at its conclusion through the image of *circulation* (and the circulation of an image). And if section 3 gives us the apotheosis of the violence of bad metaphor as catachresis, section 6 repositions this violence and "bad saying" as the return of conventionality—of dead, but also still deadly, metaphor. It therefore brings the Broglie cycle's thematic and generic staging of *re-*

turn full circle and exposes this return as indeed a matter of "disastrous saying": 'O wie unselig säglich kehrt es wieder.'

At stake in the return is an allegory of, or figure for, bad saying: the conventional image of a circulated coin, of metaphor itself as a circulated coin—of the circulation and return of Broglie-as-coin *as* this metaphor. The section begins with a figurative return of the dead, the "passing down" or "handing off" of Broglie's numismatically preserved image: "That a coin, princess, would pass along to someone / your profile carved in gold" (199). Of course, the princess is not dead yet, but the metaphor so strongly evokes the archaeological discovery of nobles' faces on ancient currency that one might say it projects the speaker and reader into a distant, post-Broglie future: a "future perfect" in which Broglie herself is now also a perfect image, finally "reproducible," *visually* "sayable," *iconically* capturable and captured without ambiguity or lack, one-to-one. The metaphor already exercises its violence, then, by killing off Broglie before the fact. In this sense, she truly is "selig," a word commonly used in German to refer to the dead ("meine selige Frau," "my wife of blessed memory").

Strikingly, this revenant, all-too-conventional metaphor, or now dead / now sayable Broglie ('selig/säglich'), immediately becomes the site both of radical empathy (here, eroticized empathy) and of radical violence. The "coin" of Broglie is passed to a "great man" (*einen Großen*) (199) with whom the speaker, as it were, "shares" her; the great man in turn becomes, figuratively, sexually charged by the exchange. One result of this "great one's" empathic participation in the speaker's erotic economy is war, rampage, and conquest:

[The great one,] who, when from high above, [Broglie's] splendor
would shoot down into him as from mountains,
would rise [*anwüchse*] and pour himself out [*ergösse*] as if in rage
over the youth of another age:

Ripping young men from the soil of their homes
and (roaring onward in a swollen drive)
calling no home and no refuge sacred any more
and no bounded settlement;

> like foreign tribes bringing sheer distance
> into the feeling and assault,
> and casting all the conquered
> like stars into boundless space – (199–200)

Another result is (momentary) gender scrambling. While the "great man" remains stereotypically (hyper)masculinized and "ejaculatory" throughout his encounter with the princess (he "rises," "rages," "pours himself out," and "conquers" with a "swollen drive"), he is also "inseminated" by a masculinized Broglie "shooting down into him." Unlike in *Der Hochwald*, however, this brief gender exchange does not translate into empathy *with Broglie*, who does not, like Stifter's Clarissa and Johanna, escape "circulation." By the end of the section, the empathic-erotic sharing of Broglie has become an orgy for all, including the (socioeconomically) "not great" ones: "That one day someone should [be able to] create such a song / . . . / the hieroglyph / of your face that you squander on us would have to / endure in a golden coin / and someday be found intact / where one does not expect, with shepherds or with farmers" (200). As the speaker, in anticipation of this universal concubinage, asserts in section 2, "I only know [how] / to sing your praise"—or, as the German original also means, your *price* ("Preis") (195). However, what the multitudes gaze into here, "turned toward the finder as if since forever" (200), is not, as was the case earlier in the cycle, Broglie's "unsayable" face but rather the reproducible (indeed, reproducibly "minted") ekphrastic face of *art*—a figure for art's tropic conventions. Here, the evocation of a "turn" underscores the figure's self-reflexive nature. Not only does the formulation "turned toward" recall the overarching cyclic imagery of "return" that frames the entire *Gedichtkreis*: It also suggests the Greek root of the word "trope," from *trópos*, "turn."

Thus we find the violent power of the speaker/poet *over* the female subject he had originally experienced as violently overpowering and "unsayable." Not only does her return as coin—as metaphor of metaphor, so to speak—seem to proclaim the speaker's own aesthetic mastery of the form, and of her: as he says to her in section 4, in a barely veiled panegyric to his own poetic prowess that summarizes the "real" goal of the cycle, "You golden device [*Gerät*]: /

that ... / ... *a king* touches for a moment [*Augenblick*] / in order to signify *his* elevated soul" (198, my emphasis). There is also the matter of *how* he asserts this apparent mastery: by forcing the princess into prostitution, as it were; by making her generally accessible to an erotics of public reception and comprehension. As a combined literary and financial device, she is the currency that his text can distribute, circulate, and disseminate at will. And, in a reversal or polysemy that betokens the gender politics underlying the poem's concluding metaphorical turns, she ironically becomes less "woman" than a function of the *speaker's* literary-creative "seed": "When from high above your splendor / would shoot down into him as from mountains" (199).

Ultimately, however, the concept of metaphor in the poem, and the coin metaphor itself, remains highly treacherous, not only to Broglie, but to the cycle as a whole. To begin with, section 6's overcoming of the inadequacy of metaphor by the visual or iconic depends on a tautological relationship between word and image. The ability to compose poetry, a verbal or written art, is contingent on the (ostensibly) unproblematically visual or "mimetic" image, the "coin": "That one day someone should [be able to] create such a song / ... / the hieroglyph / of your face ... would have to / endure in a golden coin / and someday be found intact" (200). Yet the coin itself is a visual metaphor *in a written* text, a dilemma underscored by the poem's reference to the pictorio-graphic *hieroglyph* of Broglie's face. And the face that launches the concluding section's war, another circulation or "cannibalization" of (this time Homeric) tradition and literary convention, returns to the "finder" as a conventional image *for metaphorical imagery* whose very circulation was set in motion by other conventions: the inexpressibility topos, apophasis, and so forth. Convention, then—perhaps finally the fate of all metaphor or language vis-à-vis "reality"—can be just as destructive as catachresis. As Wittgenstein writes in *Philosophical Investigations*, "A simile that has been absorbed into the forms of our language produces a false appearance, and this disquiets us. 'But *this* isn't how it is!'—we say. 'Yet *this* is how it has to *be*!'" (41e). Or, even more famously: "A *picture* held us captive. And we could not get outside it, for it lay in our language and language seemed to repeat it to us inexorably" (41e).

Reading Lipps

Before becoming the author of the object and animal poems of the *Neue Gedichte*, Rilke was Theodor Lipps's pupil. The poet studied aesthetics with Europe's most prominent empathy theorist from 1896 to 1897, during the time of the philosopher's early work on *Einfühlung*. Lipps's more extensive treatises on *Einfühlungstheorie* appeared between 1903 and 1906, when Rilke was writing the first volume of *Neue Gedichte* and the *Gedichtkreis für Madeleine Broglie*. The impact of Rodin on this period of Rilke's art has long been noted, as has Cézanne's role in Rilke's thought after the painter's death in 1906. However, the possible place of Rilke's teacher Lipps, the first to theorize *Einfühlung* together with intersubjective empathy, has been almost entirely overlooked.[13] Let us turn then to Lipps to imagine what Rilke might have adopted, adapted, and transcended from the philosopher's thinking, both explicit and implicit, about empathy, metaphor, and the relations between them. We do not have access to Rilke's lecture notes, but Lipps's 1903 book *Grundlegung der Ästhetik* (*Foundations of Aesthetics*), volume one of *Ästhetik: Psychologie des Schönen und der Kunst* (*Aesthetics: The Psychology of the Beautiful and of Art*), whose main principles Lipps may already have been working out during Rilke's student time, might give us an idea of what Rilke could have heard in those Munich classrooms. I have chosen to initiate this speculative journey with the slightly later *Grundlegung* rather than the more precisely contemporaneous *Raumästhetik* (1897), partly because the classroom can be a space not just for presenting already developed ideas but also for discovering and testing new ones, partly because Lipps's conceptualization of *Einfühlung* is more richly fleshed out in the later text. In any case, my goal here is not to prove any specific or irrefutable "history of influence" but to explore the implications of productive resonances and, perhaps, synchronicities.

As historians of empathy have frequently noted, Lipps is generally considered the first to have combined *Einfühlung* in Vischer's strict

---

13. For an exception see Hutchinson, who explores traces of Lipps's thinking in Rilke but does not link his discussion to questions of empathy (92–117).

sense—the process, based in physiology, of "feeling oneself into" the forms of inanimate shapes and objects, experiencing isomorphic resonances between these external forms and the forms of one's own body (both external and internal), and projecting our sense of motion, animation, feeling, and "life" into these objects (or, as we have seen, at times *receiving* our feelings from those objects)—with interpersonal empathy, or attention to the forms, feelings, motions, and emotions of human others. Put otherwise, Lipps was the first to conceptualize already "animate" human others as Vischerian forms. Lipps's initial discussion of *Einfühlung* in the *Grundlegung* leaves little doubt as to which end of the projection spectrum, the "projector" or the "projectee," takes priority in his understanding of empathy: "The 'other' is my *own* personality, imagined and modified according to this other's external appearance and observable expressions of life—a modified 'own self.' The person outside of me, of whom I am consciously aware, is simultaneously a doubling and a modification of myself" (106). Here, Lipps seems to offer a decisive answer to the murky question of the origin, locus, and trajectory of empathy that Vischer's *Optisches Formgefühl* had opened up; he does so at the cost of the subordination, even erasure, of the other. Indeed, not only does Lipps render the other almost entirely dependent on the projecting "self": Even the other's remaining "observable expressions of life" (*Lebensäußerungen*) or "expressive movements" (*Ausdrucksbewegungen*), such as "sounds," "facial expressions," and "gestures," do not actually "have anything to do with" (*haben an sich nichts zu tun mit*) what they seem to express (106–8). As in what will become the simulation theory of empathy, these expressions and movements only "mean" or "signify" (*bedeuten*) "for me" because I have already had similar feelings, expressed in similar bodily ways, in the past (108). Put otherwise, the other's body becomes a collection or generator of *metaphors* for my own experiences, corporeal performances, and psychic states, a figural or tropic process Lipps also sees at work in the aesthetic object: "In the aesthetic object, the sensual is always a 'symbol' of a mental content; it is animated or ensouled [by us]" (96). If this is Lipps's attempt to "use" empathy to "deal with the conceptual problem of other minds" (Hammond 73), it is an approach that leaves the other conspicuously on the margins of the "mind" equation. Lipps's metaphors, that is, are "bad" because they "coerce" the feelings and forms of the other into the service of the self.

But Lipps's further conceptualization of *Einfühlung* also substantially complicates the concept of metaphor, or, more precisely, introduces a new way of thinking about metaphor. If others are figures for our own experience, then this figuration works for Lipps in radically *direct* ways. Lipps chooses as his first and guiding example of this metaphoric-empathic process what he calls "affective sounds" (*Affektlaute*): the sounds through which we spontaneously express "all sorts of affects [*Affekte*], movements of the emotions [*Gemütsbewegungen*], [and] types of inner excitation, such as fear, joy, [and] astonishment" (*Grundlegung* 106). "If I hear a sound," Lipps writes, "similar to the one in which I myself gave voice to my affect, then I find this affect again—not connected to the [other's] sound, but immediately *in* it [*unmittelbar* in *ihm*]" (106). And this "finding" is "more" than a mere "imagining-with" ("*blosses . . . Mitvorstellen*") (106): "I do not just get the idea that the affect underlies the sound, but I *experience* [*erlebe*] this affect. I take part in it internally [*mache ihn innerlich mit*], all the more surely and completely the more I am inwardly fully turned toward the sound. . . . We may grasp this state of affairs . . . straightaway . . . with the concept of 'empathy' [*Einfühlung*]" (106–7). That is, the "metaphor" of the other's body communicates, as Lipps puts it, "immediately" (*unmittelbar*): It is metaphor without mediation (in- or im-mediate, 'un-mittelbar,' 106).

The question of metaphoricity versus immediacy, or metaphoricity conceived of *as* immediacy, introduces challenging confusions and paradoxes: Debes (313 ff.) and others have written about the many early scholarly debates, inspired in part by Lipps, surrounding whether empathy with others is automatic or analogically inferred and whether empathic identification erases or preserves self-other difference. In the *Grundlegung*, Lipps sums up "immediate metaphoricity" in one of his most famous formulations of *Einfühlung*. When we observe another's motions, he argues, our instinctual drive or "striving" (*Streben*) to imitate or repeat these motions is "*immediately bound to*" or "immediately given *in and with*" our optical perception of the motions ("*unmittelbar* an die optische Wahrnehmung *gebunden*," "*unmittelbar in und mit ihr gegeben*"); by virtue of this "givenness" in another's—an Other's— movements and body, *our* striving becomes "*objectified*" ("*objektiviert*," 120, emphasis in original). But this striving nevertheless "does not cease to be *my* striving and to be felt by me as my striving" (120). As Lipps elaborates,

> Precisely this striving of mine I feel in the optically perceived movement.... I feel myself striving *in this* movement, that is, striving for the kinesthetic image of motion [*kinästhetisches Bewegungsbilde*] that corresponds to the movement I have optically perceived, and therefore simultaneously striving toward the movement itself. I feel ... myself striving *in something perceived* [*in einem Wahrgenommenen*] toward the execution of a motion. We designate this fact ... with the name "empathy" [*Einfühlung*]. This empathy constitutes at the same time the *aesthetic understanding* [*das ästhetische Verständnis*] of what is optically perceived. This "empathy" is, as we see, nothing other than the one side, more precisely, the *inside of imitation* [*die Innenseite der Nachahmung*]. (120)

To illustrate this "inside of imitation," a concept that seems to have descended from Fechner's notions of the "interior" (*Inneres*), "interior world" (*Innenwelt*), and "inside" (*Innenseite*) (Fick 51) by way of Groos's "inner imitation" (*innere Nachahmung*), and that may itself have shaped Rilke'e even more well-known conception of "inner space" (*Weltinnenraum*), Lipps turns to a popular image from the last decades of the nineteenth century: the image of the acrobat. As Jacques Rancière argues, the acrobat played an important role in the aesthetic imagination of the late nineteenth and early twentieth centuries (75–91); the image was also, like the concern with interiority, important for Rilke: The fifth of the *Duino Elegies* famously focuses on extended imagery of a family of acrobats. Most critics hold that Rilke's imagery derives from his processing of his impressions of Picasso's 1905 painting *La Famille des Saltimbanques* (*The Family of Acrobats*) and from his personal experience of observing Paris street performers (Ryan, *Rilke, Modernism and Poetic Tradition* 186–88); however, in the light of Rilke's year studying with Lipps, we might also wonder whether Lipps's focus on the observation of acrobats as a prime illustration of *Einfühlung* might also have played a role in the poet's metaphoric inventory. In the *Grundlegung*, Lipps imagines himself gazing at, and identifying with, the acrobat "up there" (*da oben*) (121):

> In such "inner imitation" [*innere Nachahmung*] I do not perform [*vollziehe*] for a second time the movements that the acrobat has carried out. Rather, I directly [*unmittelbar*, "immediately," "in a nonmediated fashion"] carry out and complete [*vollziehe*]—that is to say, internally, or "in my thoughts"—the *acrobat's* movements. I perform the movements—insofar as this "performance of the movments" [*Vollzug der Bewegungen*] is not an outer, but an inner doing [*inneres Tun*]—in the acrobat *himself*. According to the evidence of my immediate consciousness, I am in him [*in ihm*]; I am therefore up there [*da oben*]. I am transferred there [*dahin versetzt*]. Not next to the acrobat, but precisely there where he finds himself [*wo er sich befindet*]. This, then, is the complete meaning of "empathy" [*Einfühlung*]. (122)

Consistent with its ultimate origin not just in Groos's but in Vischer's aesthetic theory, Lipps's "inner" or "inside of" imitation transforms the empathic circuit formed by the body (and mind) of the observer and the body of the perceived other into a perfect work of art. Viewed from the side of the observer, we find "pure" reception of the other's motions. These movements bypass mimesis and even imagination to achieve in the perceiver a representation that is, precisely, *not* a re-presentation. Empathy or *Einfühlung* (the two meanings now combined), the inside of imitation, is, Lipps implies, another word for im-mediate metaphor.

The traces of Lipps's thinking in Rilke are diffuse and difficult to identify with certainty. Yet their possible shadows may prove useful in our understanding of Rilke's own conflation of empathy and metaphor. More than a decade after the end of Rilke's semesters with Lipps, for example, the spirit of the Munich philosopher's aesthetic-empathic concern with affective sound, *Einfühlung* as the inner imitation of another's physical movements, and the status of the other's body as a source of analogies for our own experience still seems to haunt the multilayered fusion of empathy and metaphor Rilke performs in his 1912 essay "Über den Dichter" ("Concerning the Poet"), a concise poetological treatise in the guise of an "exotic" travel narrative. The essay serves as a theoretical pendant to Rilke's middle period of literary production, which had ended with a grave artistic crisis: the author's increasingly agonized post-*Malte* struggle to find his voice as a nascent modernist poet and his subsequent temporary inability to write.[14] If, however, "Über den Dichter" attempts to work through or resolve this struggle by placing the intersection of metaphor-making and bodily *Einfühlung* at the center of its understanding of the larger meaning of lyric poetry, both metaphor and body in the brief text turn out to be especially problematic.

The essay, which mines and reworks Rilke's experiences during his 1911 trip to Egypt, describes the poet's journey up the Nile on a ship rowed by sixteen Egyptian youths. The young rowers must strain themselves considerably to propel the craft up the river: The struggle to pull back the massive oars literally lifts the boys from their seats, and their efforts to call out a sculling rhythm repeatedly end in breathlessness (1033–34). But from time to time, an "unforeseeable intervention that we all felt in the most exceptional way" comes "rhythmically to [the rowers'] aid" and gives them access to "new, still-undiminished areas of power" (1034). For another Egyptian sits at the front of the boat, acting as a coxswain. The man sings out at irregular intervals; his apparently random song, regardless of whether it is vocalized when the crew is exhausted or when they seem filled with energy, always comes, Rilke contends, at just the right time (1034). As Rilke explains, this scene provided him with "a beautiful allegory" (*Gleichnis*) of the "meaning" of poets in relation to "existence" and "time" (1032, 1035):

> In [the coxswain-singer] the forward momentum of our vehicle and the force of what came to meet us continuously balanced each other out, – from time to time a surplus collected: then he sang. The ship overcame the resistance; he, however, the sorcerer, transformed that which could not be overcome into a series of long, hovering tones that belonged neither

---

14. On Rilke's writing crisis, see Prater 175–85; Ryan, "Dead Poets' Voices"; and Ryan, *Rilke, Modernism and Poetic Tradition* 98–100.

here nor there and that everyone drew on in their own way. While [the rowers] engaged again and again with what was nearest and graspable and conquered it, his voice maintained a relationship to what was farthest and tied us to it, until it pulled us. (1035)

Strikingly, the essay is grounded in Lipps's two key catalysts for *Einfühlung*: affective sound and muscular motion. Both find their predicted "immediate" reception in Rilke as he assimilates himself through the "inside of imitation" to the boat's collective "we." The coxswain's singing and the youths' rowing are transmitted straightaway to Rilke's body: "We *all* felt [the singer's intervention] in the most exceptional way" (1034, my emphasis). Rilke speaks of the crew as though he is one of them—empathically identified with them—and of the water's resistance, the "force of that which approached us," as though he is among those overcoming it: "[The coxswain's] song found *everyone* up to the task"; "I don't know the extent to which the constitution of *our* crew communicated itself to him" (1034–35, my emphasis). Here, it is less a matter of "compassionate" intersubjective empathy with the rowers' feelings than Lippsian *Einfühlung* into their (moving) *form*: the exertions of their muscles, the rhythmic motions of their bodies, their sculling chants, and the coxswain's "hovering tones."

In what at first appears a turn from Lipps, the river scene is immediately *re-mediated*: It becomes a metaphor, an "allegory" (*Gleichnis*), for poetry or metaphor-making—a metaphor of metaphor, as it were, and a strangely literal "vehicle" for its tenor (as is well known, metaphor's etymological origin is the ancient Greek *metaphérein*, "to carry or transfer over," as with a boat). Yet on closer consideration, in Rilke's allegory, the implications of Lipps's understanding of the (other's) body as "art"—that is, as a collection of metaphors for "us"—reach their logical conclusion: The other's body becomes *art about art*. Thus, in Rilke's transformation of his "immediate reception" of the other's body into literary discourse, *aísthesis* in Baumgarten's older sense of "knowing through the senses" and the modern meaning of "aesthetics" become one. It is not even necessary for Rilke to have to have first rowed, or even physically sung, in order to "empathize." Rather, it is already an internal, "metaphorical" motion that is at stake: He needs to have *produced poetry* to "see" or "feel" it in the boat's crew.

Importantly, as a racialized and gendered colonial scene, the metaphor of the boat journey as poetry cannot be separated from its own type of "badness." Rilke appears here as a colonial tourist, with art as the commodity brought back from "exotic foreign parts" at the cost of the physical labor, and ultimately the figurative erasure—the erasure through figuration—of subaltern Others. Rilke's gaze transforms the Egyptian crew into "spectacularly" visible objects or animals, like the "things" of his *Dinggedichte*. He "observes" (*beobachten*), "examines" (*untersuchen*), and surveils them (1033); their bodies become sleek, "metallic" exteriors (*metallische Körper*) (1032); *their* eyes, or "animal gaze" (*Tierblick*), as he puts it, are robbed of agency and sight ("most often . . . there was no 'seeing' in their eyes," 1032). They thus become a different and highly problematic version of "pure form."[15] The colonial inventory reaches its simultaneous apogee and collapse when Rilke pushes his bad metaphor too far: into the unsavory realm of Eurocentric revulsion, desire, and, ultimately, internal contradiction and "Self"-destruction. As Rilke writes, a filthily clad helmsman, his hands and feet "intimately" manipulating the "pole" of the rudder, "squats" in the "rear-end" of the ship, his "body not worth mentioning" (*nicht der Rede wert*) (1033). The eyes of the weirdly and abjectly sexualized man, who seems to embody for Rilke what Robert J. C. Young calls "colonial desire," or the "ambivalent movement of attraction and repulsion," the "sexual economy of desire in fantasies of race, and of race in fantasies of desire" in colonial contexts (90), are again figuratively blind—they seem to "drip" (*triefen*) from the man's face (1033). But they are also paradoxically equipped with colonial desire's uncanny transformative power: "[The man] looked as though he could turn one into something repulsive" (1033). As Joseph Imorde has argued, one of the reasons for the popularity of *Einfühlung* in the German

---

15. On colonial tourism and the Orientalist trope of the "foreign Other" as an "object" that can be transformed into importable Western "knowledge," see Behdad.

imperial period was that "the discovery of the self in the other became a reality of colonial power politics" (129). Rilke, though not a citizen of the German Empire, seems with his extended North African journey to partake in the same nasty, "imperially empathic" mode of the zeitgeist. Indeed, as early as his 1898 essay "Über Kunst" ("Concerning Art"), he had conceived of the artist as an "importer" of "strange customs" from foreign spheres problematically coded as "primitive": "[The artist] brings foreign customs with him and demands space for immodest gestures" (431–32). In the "Dichter" essay, however, in the two-way mirror of empathy, the other's eyes, which Rilke had figured as simultaneously blind and Medusa-like, look back at *him*, "turning him into" what his own colonial gaze and "immodest gestures" had *already turned the Other into*, or into what he had already projected from himself: "something repulsive." If, through his "inner imitation" of the Egyptian bodies that he sees as an allegory and source of metaphor—and that he has turned *into* a metaphor for the poetry with which he identifies—Rilke "feels himself" in(to) these bodies, then he feels *himself* as the *abject* body: the body that his own vision has already abjected.[16]

Lipps soon abandons his memorable characterization of empathy as the inside of imitation. The problem for him is the word "imitation" (*Nachahmung*), which, he writes, "shifts the meaning" of what is occurring (*Grundlegung* 122). Rather than imitating, Lipps argues, we internally "experience" (*erleben*), "carry out" (*vollziehen*), or even "consummate" (*vollziehen* again) the movements we observe (say, of the acrobats)—a "virtual reality" that is inseparable from "real" reality: "This constitutes . . . 'inner doing' [*das innere Tun*]. Its reality is an indisputable fact" (*Grundlegung* 122). The only proper term for this inner experience, Lipps contends, is the unglossed neologism *Einfühlung*, unadorned by synonyms or appositives (*Grundlegung* 126–27),

---

16. On abjection as that which destabilizes the borders or imagined bodily and psychic integrity of the "self," often by means of feelings of revulsion and disgust evoked by the "repulsive" phenomena by which the abject is symbolized, see Kristeva, *Powers of Horror* 1–89. In its suspension between casting aside and identifying with a revulsion-inspiring "Other" that is nonetheless inseparable from the self, abjection bears a complex relationship to empathy.

for only this word "excludes... any separation of myself and [the object]" and "signifies complete unity or identity" (192). As Lipps explains, when we lift a stone, we do not feel "our" striving and the stone's or gravity's resistance as separate forces; rather, we experience a singular, unified field of sensation, a "total situation" or "total state of affairs" (*Gesamtsachverhalt*) (*Grundlegung* 182). We may look at this totality from two sides, attributing one force (lifting) to ourselves and another (resistance) to the stone, but this does not reflect our actual *experience*: Any division into "self" and "other" happens retroactively, as an interpretive act (*Grundlegung* 172–82, 122).

With this understanding of *Einfühlung*, empathy, or the union of the two, Lipps takes his place in the development of a genuine phenomenology and transcends, or at least seems to transcend, the subject-object dichotomy that had vexed Vischer's confusing attempts to describe the origin, vector, and locus of *Einfühlung*.[17] More specifically, he transcends the dichotomy by *seeing through its illusory nature*. It is, as it were, the seamless superimposition of "*páthos*" and "*em*," perfect empathy as the transcendence of the binary logic at the root of empathy itself. But Lipps is only ambivalently committed to this phenomenological nondualism: Proclamations of "unity" appear alongside wholesale privileging of the "self," such as the assertion that "the reason for the aesthetic value of anything given to the senses is something 'lying in it,' an interior. And this interior is always me" (*Grundlegung* 159). As he writes in language that is simultaneously Kantian and colonizing, "We possess [things] even more surely by possessing ourselves in them" (*Wir haben [die Dinge] erst recht, indem wir uns in ihnen haben*) (*Grundlegung* 64). Indeed, some of Lipps's formulations of *Einfühlung* sound suspiciously like a threat: "No being and no occurrence in nature escapes our striving to

---

17. Lipps's place in the development of phenomenology is complex. Edmund Husserl was well acquainted with Lipps's turn-of-the-century publications on empathy and adopted the term *Einfühlung* from him circa 1905; conversely, Lipps's developing thoughts on *Einfühlung* were themselves influenced by Husserl's earliest phenomenological writings, the 1901 *Logical Investigations* (Dermot Morgan 291, 277). Additionally, early phenomenologists such as Max Scheler and Edith Stein engaged significantly with, and substantially critiqued, Lipps's theories of *Einfühlung* and protophenomenology; see Dermot Morgan.

empathically put ourselves into them [*uns mitfühlend in dasselbe hineinzuversetzen*]" (*Grundlegung* 163). Thus we arrive back at the concerns that had troubled Vischer's projection theory: relations of "subject" and "object," "possessor" and "possessed."

Rilke's relation to these concerns is complex, and the phenomenological critic Luke Fischer's conclusion that Rilke circumvents the problems of projective *Einfühlung* through a radically "receptive" writing practice that channels not his own "interiority" but "the interior of the [represented] things themselves" (207–8) may be too optimistic.[18] The notion of "receptivity," in any case, opens uncannier dimensions—ones that recall our earlier discussion of the uncanniness of Vischer's subject-object or self-other exchanges in chapter 1, but that introduce new levels to these exchanges as well. For the "Other," the "dead object," to which Rilke is receptive or with which he exchanges himself here is *himself*. To better understand the implications of this uncanny situation for empathy and metaphor, let us follow Rilke to the inside of things: not just to the "inside of imitation" but, as Rilke puts it, to "the other side of nature" (*die andere Seite der Natur*).

The Other Side of Nature

The formulation "die andere Seite der Natur," with its suggestive syntactical similarity to Lipps's "die Innenseite der Nachahmung," stems from Rilke's short prose sketch "Erlebnis" ("Experience"), a piece that Monika Fick calls the "paradigm par excellence for the equilibrium between the 'Self' [*Ich*] with its inwardness [*Innerlichkeit*] and the outside world" (198). Written in 1913, the sketch describes events that occurred in late 1911 or early 1912, shortly after the poet's return from Egypt; it therefore belongs to the same general period of thought that gave rise to the "Dichter" essay. Like empathy and metaphor themselves, the piece, whose title allusively recalls the

---

18. For other examples of the strong tradition of phenomenological Rilke criticism, see Käte Hamburger's seminal "Phänomenologische Struktur der Dichtung Rilkes" and Rochelle Tobias's "Rilke, Phenomenology, and the Sensuality of Thought."

Lippsian terminology of "experiencing" (*erleben*) (*Grundlegung* 122), revolves around the relation of—indeed, the question of the very existence of—"self" and "other." For, in an even more explicit and radical way than in Lipps's acrobat analogies or Rilke's "Über den Dichter," the Other of the "Erlebnis" sketch *is* the Self.

"Erlebnis" is divided into two parts, both originally written as diary entries in 1913 in Ronda, Spain. Part 1, published in the *Insel-Almanach* in 1918, describes a striking experience that took place during Rilke's 1911–1912 stay as a guest of the Princess Marie von Thurn und Taxis at Duino Castle in Italy—the same stay that produced the beginning of the *Duino Elegies*. In the piece, Rilke, conspicuously referring to himself in the third person as "er" (he), wanders through the castle garden, reading a book. He relaxes against the shoulder-high fork of a small tree and soon finds himself "fully sunken into" nature (*völlig eingelassen in die Natur*) (1037), thoroughly "embedded" in it in a state of meditative absorption, an "almost unconscious beholding" (*beinah unbewußten Anschaun*) (1037). Gradually he becomes aware of what feel like subtle vibrations or oscillations emanating from the tree and passing into his body: "He felt he had never been filled with gentler flows [*Bewegungen*], his body was in a manner of speaking handled like a soul [*Seele*] and placed in the position of being able to receive a level of influence [*Einfluß*, literally "flowing in"] that, given the usual clarity of bodily circumstances, actually ought not to have been perceptible at all" (1037). It is after being thus "handled" that Rilke feels he has "arrived at the other side of nature" (*auf die andere Seite der Natur geraten*) (1038). The results are strange ones. Not only does he, so to speak, experience his body "from outside" (Fick 198): His body becomes "exactly like a *revenant*" (*Revenant*) that "stands pure and warily *in him*" (1038, my emphasis), the "him" presumably being larger and more encompassing than his body itself. Correspondingly, he feels more prepared to see long-dead members of the household coming along the garden path than living ones.[19]

---

19. Fick reads Rilke's "other side of nature" as the account of a "death experience" grounded in the spiritualistic practices and the beliefs in life after death of Rilke's day (184–87, 199–200).

After an unspecified amount of time, the altered state fades, and he finds himself back on "this" side of nature. Part 2, not published until 1935 but treating even earlier experiences in Capri, recounts a series of similar events in which things "outside and in his interior [were] there in unison by, so to speak, not breaking on the borders of his body, gathering both [outside and inside] together into one uninterrupted space in which . . . only a single point of the purest, deepest consciousness remained" (1040).[20] In both parts of the sketch, Rilke's heightened closeness to, or apparent unity with, the natural world simultaneously creates a curious feeling of distance: not just a space between "himself" and "himself," as it were, but also, as he puts it in part 2, a "pure, almost shining interstice" (*einen reinen, fast scheinenden Zwischenraum*) between him and the other people he somewhat estrangingly calls "the humans" (*den Menschen*) (1041). In this sense, we do not quite find Fick's "equilibrium" between "the 'Self' with its inwardness and the outside world" (*Sinnenwelt* 198).

Rilke called the piece "in a way the most intimate [sketch] I have ever put to paper" (Zinn 1477). It is curious, then, that he insistently refers to his narrator as "he" rather than "I"—a move that both evokes the logic of the narrative techniques of psychonarration and free indirect discourse and constitutes a telling displacement of the self onto an other, a reading of one's own "intimate" experience through a proxy. Here, however, the Other is the Self, separated from itself by an uncanny spacing. From one perspective, it is not a question of thinking, feeling, or projecting one's way into another (*Einfühlung*), nor is it, as with the Rentherr's daughter in *Turmalin*, a matter of the presumed incapacity to access one's own inner life. Rather, it is the inability to "own" one's own experience unless this experience is *figured as being experienced "empathically*," at the site of an Other. We might think of this as "autobiographical psychonarration" or "autobiographical free indirect discourse." Put otherwise, to be "himself," the narrator must first become the Other

---

20. Part 2 of "Erlebnis," which Rilke had given to Lou Andreas-Salomé as a manuscript in 1919, appeared posthumously in Rilke's *Briefe aus Muzot 1921–1926* (1935); see Zinn 1475–78.

he empathizes with. Or, to paraphrase Lipps, the "he" here is both the observer *and* the acrobat: Rilke's "er" preserves what we might call the "acrobat function" with no need for the external funambulist. From another perspective that I shall explore below, however, we could also say that *alienation from oneself* and *alienation from others* are one.

My description of experience in the piece as being "figured" is intentional: The sketch's narrating "er" is simultaneously a figure or character in the essay's "story," a metaphor or trope (figure) of the extratextual Rilke, and a stylistic device, an element of rhetoric. Indeed, the transformation of Rilke's personal voice into the psychonarrated or free indirect "er" maps empathic (self-)identification onto a recognizable *aesthetic* or formal discourse: the stylings of European prose fiction since the realist period. It is therefore significant, and perhaps unsurprising, that as the text unfolds its performance of simultaneous closeness and distance at the levels of both content and form (rhetoric, narration), it likewise begins to accumulate the "aesthetic" accretion of ever more—and ever more questionable or "bad"—metaphors. These metaphors, microcosms of the dialectic of distance and closeness, cannot be separated from the text's "haunted," "revenant" articulation of the structurally similar phenomenon of empathy, both aesthetic and interpersonal.

The sketch's first explicit metaphor (or, more precisely, simile) already frames the narrator's response to nature in terms familiar from Vischer and Lipps's *Einfühlung*. "Embedded" in the tree and sensing its vibrations, Rilke's body is, he writes, "handled *like* a soul [*Seele*]" and "placed in the position of being able to receive a level of influence that, given the usual clarity of bodily circumstances, actually ought not to have been perceptible at all" (1037, my emphasis). This is *aísthesis* as "knowing through the senses"; however, unlike in Müller's law of specific nerve energies, it is unclear which sense is transmitting the knowledge: "To this circumstance was added the fact that, in the first moments, he was unable to determine the sense through which he received such a subtle and diffuse communication [*Mitteilung*]" (1037). This time affirming Fick's notion of an "equilibrium," the entire body-mind continuum, linked to the world, becomes one singular organ, "everywhere and ever more uniformly filled with the surge [*Andrang*] that returned in strangely intense [*innigen*] intervals [*Abständen*]" (1038). Being this organ and feeling this surge constitute having reached "the other side of nature."

Strikingly, arriving at the other side of nature makes Rilke's body "unbeschreiblich rührend"—"indescribably touching," "poignant," "moving," or "affecting"—to him ("sein Körper [wurde] ihm unbeschreiblich rührend," 1038). This is Spinoza's famous *affectus*, touching and touched, moving and moved, with its "affections of the body by which the body's power of acting," of affecting and being affected, "is increased or diminished, aided or restrained" (Spinoza, *Ethics* 154): Rilke's body is "handled like a soul"; it is "placed in the position of being able to receive a level of influence that . . . ought not to have been perceptible at all." The emphasis on affect, with its pulses, intervals (*Abstände*), and suggestively Massumi-esque rushes, surges, and flows (*Andrang, Einfluß*, 'in-fluence'), is underscored by the appearance of the word *innig* (intense)—a term whose implications we explored at length in the previous chapter. Here, intense affect catalyzes the bifurcating, "spacing," and doubling process. Rilke's own body—in Spinoza's terms "action" and "passion" at once (*Ethics* 154)—becomes the "other" that can "touch" *him*, by which *he* is affected, and with which he empathizes: the "Other" side of nature, indeed.

But if the body here is, in effect, an exquisitely calibrated psychological aesthetic recording device (or, more accurately, a simultaneous receiver and transmitter), a machine for measuring sensory physiology such as might be found in one of Wilhelm Wundt's late nineteenth-century German laboratories, it is one that cannot be extricated from a problematic relationship to textuality: "die andere *Seite* der Natur," "the other *page* [*Seite*] of nature."[21] Indeed, Rilke describes the vibrations he receives from nature as a "Mitteilung," a "message"—that is, as something closely associated with, and figured in terms of, linguistic communication (1037). Rilke finds his essay's own "message" or

---

21. In a related vein, Fick calls Rilke's 1919 essay "Ur-Geräusch" ("Primal Sound"), which memorably speculates about the sounds that might be produced by "playing" the grooves in a human skull with a phonograph needle, a "fanciful . . . approach to sensory-physiological research" (189).

signature rhetorical formulation, "the other side of nature," especially apt and on point, "correct almost completely without remainder" (*beinah restlos zutreffend*) (1038). The formulation "the other side of nature," however, remains in essence a *metaphor* for an *indescribably* (*unbeschreiblich*) moving, touching, or affecting experience (1038), and the internal ambiguity of the seemingly laudatory, but on closer inspection ambivalent, statement "correct almost completely without remainder" points to a lacuna in signification and communication: What does "correct almost completely without remainder" actually *mean*? The ambiguity points, that is, if not to "bad," then at least to insufficient or *gappy* metaphor ("*almost* correct," "*almost* complete," "*almost* without remainder"). Put otherwise, there *is* a remainder, and *something* comes through that gap.

The remainder haunts the text, for it is clear that Rilke's sketch is, to a significant and much more direct degree than Vischer's *Über das optische Formgefühl* or Stifter's *Turmalin*, a ghost story. As Rilke writes, after his remarkable passage to the "other side of nature," his transformed or "handled" body is "only useful any more for standing pure and warily in him [*in ihm*], exactly like a revenant [*Revenant*] that, already living elsewhere, steps melancholically into this thing that has been tenderly laid aside in order to belong one more time, if only distractedly, to the world it once regarded as so indispensable" (1038). Here we find an uncanny return, reversal, and expansion of the rhetoric of resurrection we first encountered in Vischer's figuration of *Einfühlung*. Instead of our needing to re-animate nature, nature is the force that animates *us*—the tree's vibrations turning Rilke's body into a more sensitive organ—but also "kills" us, only to resurrect us again: Rilke's transformation into a "revenant" that returns to inhabit his reanimated body. To adapt Lipps, Rilke is not "in" the acrobats; rather, his "own" body is "in him," like a precarious photographic superimposition or one of Vischer's "dead objects" by means of which a personified *Einfühlung* "looks at its second self as it sits reshaped in the object" and uncannily "takes it back to itself" (Vischer 108).

Rilke's projection of himself into the "other side of nature," along with nature's simultaneous, vibrating projection of itself into *him*— and *both of these* in combination with Rilke's spectral-corporeal "reentry" and his self-figuration through the device and image of the simultaneously "own" and "other" narrative "er"—"ghosts" him, leaving his body both living and dead. It is a situation with a family resemblance to Vischer's and Büchner's aesthetic zombie. Unsurprisingly, as I noted earlier, Rilke's narrator now feels more prepared to encounter deceased members of the Thurn and Taxis household than living ones (1039). As befits the structural logic of both empathy and metaphor—what I have called their dialectic of distance and closeness—objects are both more alienated and less: "Overall he could see how all objects presented themselves to him as more distant and, at the same time, truer" (1039). Significantly, the figure through which this empathic ghost story unfolds is itself again a metaphor (or, more precisely, again a simile), and another problematic one at that. Rilke's "indescribably" affected and affecting body is somehow "exactly like" (*genau wie*) a revenant (1038): a formulation that, both in its predication of indescribability on a *description* and, especially, in the impossibly paradoxical *nature* of that description itself—"*exactly like*," "*genau wie*"—points to the paradox at the very heart of empathy and metaphor. Like Rilke and his "er," they are both the same and not the same, both "self" and "other" at once.

In his 1908 *Abstraktion und Einfühlung*, Worringer would conclude that the two supposedly opposite aesthetic poles of his title were in fact unified by their shared expression of "a common need, which is revealed to us as the deepest and ultimate essence of all aesthetic experience: ... the need for self-alienation" (23). Rilke would read Worringer's book in 1913, the year he wrote "Erlebnis" (Ryan, *Rilke, Modernism and Poetic Tradition* 156). If the metaphorical ghost story of "Erlebnis" suggests Worringer's need for self-alienation, as well as perhaps an idiosyncratically "intra-personal" version of the "objectified," or *objectifying*, "self-enjoyment" Lipps identified as the essence of *Einfühlung* ("Einfühlung und ästhetischer Genuss" 100), Rilke's essay also culminates in *alienation from others*, with concomitantly equivocal or "bad" consequences for *interpersonal* empathy. For Rilke's journey to the other side of nature makes him dead to the mundane world, and the mundane world dead to him. Despite the seemingly *truly* perfect isomorphism of the "form" of the object of his *Einfühlung*, an isomorphism Vischer could only envy (Rilke projects into *himself*), the "feeling" he feels "into" or "with" himself is a potentially dissatisfying wariness, "melancholy," and distraction (1038). And even as his body assumes heightened receptivity to unseen vibrations, it retreats from engagement with visible people and things: "The sudden appearance of a housemate would have shocked him in the most torturous way"; "He looked back at Things [*die Dinge*] as if over his shoulder, and their Being [*Dasein*], which for him had reached its conclusion, took on a keen, sweet aftertaste, as though everything were spiced with a trace of the blossom of parting" (1039). The more Rilke's narrative "er" is "embedded" in nature or "himself"—that is, the more *Einfühlung* "he" embodies—the less intersubjective empathy he feels, and the less connection he senses to his fellow humans, who appear almost like members of another species: "Something softly dividing maintained a pure, almost shining interstice between him and the humans [*den Menschen*]" (1041). Indeed, Rilke claims to have attained his transcendence or "type of overcoming" (*seine Art Überwindung*) not among the bonds and relations (*Bindungen*) of the human world "but rather *out there*, in a spaciousness so little set up in a human way [*in einer menschlich so wenig eingerichteten Geräumigkeit*] that they wouldn't call it anything other than 'the void' [*das Leere*]" (1042, my emphasis). However, unlike the Buddha after his awakening, the post-"Erlebnis" Rilke becomes a teacher whose interventions appear curiously limited in scope, yielding what might seem like an anticlimactic conclusion to part 2 of the sketch: "It was reserved for him to speak to [the people] about joy where he found them too much caught in the contraries of happiness, also arguably [*wohl*] to communicate to them some things [*einzelnes*] from his dealings with nature, things that they missed or only observed in passing" (1042). But in the conspicuous *restriction* of the scope of his interaction with "the human" (including himself), Rilke—the "metaphor of himself" who occupies, or at least has occupied, "the other side of nature"—comes in certain ways to resemble what object-oriented ontologists call the "withdrawn object": an entity that can never fully be grasped, that only presents itself in a radically *limited* way, and that, as object-oriented philosophers Graham Harman and Ian Bogost argue, is another way of talking about *metaphor*.

To the extent that it is also a way of thinking about *bad* metaphor, it has significant implications for the relations between empathy and aesthetics.

Words and Things

Object-oriented ontology (OOO) gives us another way of thinking about aesthetics, empathy, and (bad) metaphor. First articulated by philosopher Graham Harman in 1999, OOO positions itself as anti-Kantian, and thus, implicitly, as against a certain understanding of the "thought-figure of projection" that Müller-Tamm sees as underlying the theory of *Einfühlung*. By some object-oriented philosophers' admission, however, OOO might more accurately be thought of as a radical expansion of key aspects of Kantian thought. We have frequently noted Kant's division of reality into inaccessible "things-in-themselves," never directly perceptible to us, and their "appearances," whose perception can only take place according to the mind's a priori laws for synthesizing sense data. We thus never experience reality "as such," only the reality *imposed on reality* by the pregiven operations of our own mind. Object-oriented ontologists accept this fundamental Kantian split between noumena and phenomena; however, they reject the de facto idealism and anthropocentrism they see as having arisen from its formulation and reception.[22] The problematic result of Kant's "Copernican Revolution," they argue, has been an exclusive focus on the human mind and on humans themselves as the reference points for philosophy and reality: the effective rendering irrelevant of all nonhuman beings, objects, perspectives, and concerns, or all "Other" others. Especially OOO rejects the anthropocentric and idealist implications of what Quentin Meillassoux calls Kantian "correlationism," or the belief that, as Harman puts it, "we cannot speak of the world without humans or humans without the world, but only of a primordial correlation or rapport between the two" (*Object-Oriented Ontology* 56–57). Timothy Morton de-

---

22. The following description of general positions in OOO loosely summarizes Harman's presentation of the movement in his *Object-Oriented Ontology*.

scribes this as "the notion that . . . meaning is only possible between a human mind and what it thinks" (9), such that nonhuman "things" seem to have existence or significance only within the realm of human perception and cognition. In contrast, OOO posits a "real world" of innumerable "objects," from humans to animals to orange peels to cell phones, all interacting with each other on a level playing field or "flat ontology," none more privileged than any of the others. However, like the Kantian thing-in-itself, what OOO means by "objects" is complex.

Drawing on Heidegger's *Being and Time*, OOO understands objects as *withdrawn*: unfathomable entities whose "genuine realities [are] deeper than any of the relations in which they might become involved" (Harman, "Well-Wrought" 196).[23] Like Heidegger's "Being" itself, whose "truth . . . is none of its particular historical determinations—*idea*, *substantia*, *actualitas*, objectivity or the will to power" but "the openness, the free region which always out of sight provides the space . . . for the different determinations of being" (Korab-Karpowicz section 6), "objects" in OOO cannot be reduced to any of their apparent manifestations, functions, or relations, either for humans or each other.[24] As Harman argues, objects "resist all forms of causal or cognitive mastery" ("Well-Wrought" 188); in their essence, they "withdraw from human view into a dark subterranean reality that never becomes present to practical action any more than it does to theoretical awareness" (*Tool-Being* 1). In this sense, OOO is a "speculative realism": It affirms a reality outside the human mind but maintains that, due to the unknowability of this reality in its totality, we can only "speculate" about it—or, in Harman and Morton's terms, approach it *aesthetically*.[25]

---

23. Harman explains that key tenets of OOO arose from his reading of Heidegger's analysis of tools or equipment in *Being and Time* (95–101 ff.); see Harman, *Tool-Being* 10.

24. Critics of metaphysical readings of Heidegger reject what they see as OOO's reification of "withdrawn Being" into an "entity" or substance "behind" what they understand as the relations constituting objects (Kotsko); however, it is precisely the reduction of objects to "relations," especially relations defined exclusively in reference to the human, that object-oriented thinkers seem to wish to combat.

25. This positioning of aesthetics rather than "inaccessible" knowledge or "truth" as the "root of all philosophy" (Harman, *Object-Oriented Ontology* 59–102)

Importantly, objects are as much "withdrawn" from each other—from all other objects—as they are from "the human" (indeed, humans are themselves "objects" in this specifically OOO sense and consequently withdrawn from *themselves*, like Rilke's narrative "er" in "Erlebnis"). An object is only experienced in partial ways by the objects with which it interacts—experienced, that is, in ways that correspond to the "perceiving" objects' modes of "perception." For example, I "see" (experience, interact with) what I call oxygen differently than a rusting piece of iron does: An inexhaustible "object" underlies and enters into the diverse local experiences. And in "my" experience, I never interact with "oxygen," or any other object, in its totality. Put otherwise, objects are effectively infinite, ineffable resources—*mysteries*, so to speak—whose interactions with the human, and with each other, necessarily remain limited and can never "exhaust" each other's "depths" (Harman, "Well-Wrought" 185–87): "No object relates with others without ... distortion" ("Well-Wrought 188); "even inanimate things only unlock each other's realities to a minimal extent, reducing one another to caricatures" (*Tool-Being* 2). Thus, every human perception, as well as every interaction between nonhuman objects, is "haunted by some hidden surplus in the things that never becomes present" (*Tool-Being* 2), like Rilke's "correct almost completely without remainder" metaphor of the "other side of nature." Strikingly, despite its apparent alignment with Kantian correlationism, *Einfühlungstheorie* itself may have anticipated aspects of object-oriented ontology, a possibility that neither object-oriented philosophers nor historians of *Einfühlung* have seemed to explore. As Vernon Lee, for example, writes in *The Beautiful*, her 1913 introduction to psychological aesthetics,

> a *Thing* is both much more and much less than an *Aspect* [of that Thing]. Much more, because a *Thing* really means not only qualities of its own and reactions of ours which are actual and present, but a far greater number and variety thereof which are potential. Much *less*, on the other hand, because of these potential qualities and reactions constituting a

---

aligns OOO with Nietzschean as well as Heideggerian concerns; cf. Nietzsche, *On the Genealogy of Morals* 589–90.

Thing only a minimum need be thought of at any given time; instead of which, an aspect is all there, its qualities closely interdependent, and our reactions entirely taken up in connecting them as whole and parts. (17)

From one perspective—and not just in the way that any poet is—Rilke is a poet of *words*. Indeed, he might be read as a paradigmatic case of the linguistic turn, or the turn toward viewing language as the central factor in the human experience (and construction) of reality. As Rilke writes in the *Ninth Duino Elegy*,

> when the traveler returns from the mountain-slopes into the valley,
> he brings, not a handful of earth, unsayable to others, but instead
> some word he has gained. . . .
> Perhaps we are *here* in order to say: house,
> bridge, fountain, gate, pitcher, fruit-tree, window—
> (199)

The elegy's insights culminate in a series of triumphant (or frantically defensive) linguistic epiphanies: "*Here* is the time for the *sayable*, *here* is its homeland. / Speak and bear witness"; "Earth, isn't this what you want: to arise within us, / *invisible*? Isn't it your dream / to be wholly invisible someday?—O Earth: invisible!" (201–3). As Peter Sloterdijk writes, "In his field, and with his means, Rilke carries out an operation that one could philosophically describe as the 'transformation of being into message' (more commonly, 'linguistic turn')" (20). This turn, in the first quarter century of whose "axial age" Rilke wrote, would soon make language one of the most important twentieth-century subjects of philosophy and the literary arts.[26]

But, as we know from his famous *Dinggedichte*, Rilke is also a poet of *things*. Indeed, as Sloterdijk argues, despite the apparent dualism of the *Ninth Elegy*, things and words do not necessarily constitute for Rilke two separate realms. Rather, Sloterdijk maintains, the combined sphere of "artifices" (crafted or artistic things) and

---

26. Among the linguistic turn "events" contemporaneous with Rilke's literary career were the publication of Nietzsche's "Truth and Lying" essay (1903), Hofmannsthal's "Letter of Lord Chandos" (1902), Saussure's *Course in General Linguistics* (1916), and Wittgenstein's *Tractatus Logico-Philosophicus* (1921).

"living creatures" (the animals that form the other concern of Rilke's *Dinggedichte*) comprises an object-sphere through which a quasi-Heideggerian Being "speaks" (20).[27] What relation might Rilke's "speaking" object-sphere have to the "object" of object-oriented ontology? How might we situate Rilke's poetic production at the intersection of the linguistic turn, the implications of theories of intersubjective and aesthetic empathy, and a way of thinking about "things" that accounts for, or shuttles between, OOO's ontological object (what "is") and our phenomenological reception of this? Heidegger's own interest in Rilke's writings, as ambivalent or critical as it was, might possibly form a transitive *genealogical* bridge between the poet's work and the concerns of object-oriented ontology.[28] A different and even more important type of bridge, however, not only to OOO but also to the linguistic turn and the workings and limitations of empathy, is the concept of metaphor.

The relevance of metaphor to considerations of language and the linguistic turn is clear: As Gerhard Kurz notes, "Metaphor is not a deviation from the normal use of language; it is the normal use of language" (17). But object-oriented ontology, with its notion of objects whose "inexhaustible" realities exceed their specific appearances or interactions "in the form of a hidden surplus" (Harman, "Well-Wrought" 189), likewise evokes the sphere of metaphor: As Harman argues, objects only make contact with each other in "allusive," "indirect," or "vicarious" ways ("Well-Wrought" 187–88), "by way of the fictional images they present to each other" (*Object-Oriented Ontology* 163). Harman writes that he was initially inspired to develop OOO while reading José Ortega y Gasset's essay on metaphor (*Guerrilla Metaphysics* 98), and in *Object-Oriented Ontology*, his systematic overview of the field, he devotes a chapter to situating "the root of all philosophy" in aesthetics, here largely equated with metaphor (59–102). Indeed, Harman's use of words such as "distortion" and "caricature" to describe the contact between objects even suggests incomplete, inadequate, or "bad"

---

27. For an opposing view, see de Man, *Allegories of Reading* 20–56.
28. See Heidegger, "Wozu Dichter?"; Cassedy 216–24; and Stephens.

metaphor. These considerations of bad metaphor return us to the questions of projection, self-other exchange, colonization or possession, and the extent to which human and other "forms" can act as "metaphors of each other" with which this study began.

Ian Bogost elaborates on the importance of metaphor to OOO in his book *Alien Phenomenology, or What It's Like to Be a Thing* (2012). Building on Thomas Nagel's seminal 1974 theory-of-mind essay "What Is It Like to Be a Bat?", Bogost develops the concept of "metaphorism," a term he borrows from the experimental aesthetics of Soviet poet Andrei Voznesensky (*Alien Phenomenology* 66). All entities, Bogost argues, interact with each other by means of an experiential or phenomenological interface that functions analogously to metaphor. Objects "try to make sense of each other through the qualities and logics they possess" (66); specific aspects of one object's withdrawn reality dialogue with specific aspects of another object's withdrawn reality, a process Harman had described as "basking in each other's notes" (Bogost 67). The two objects can only relate to or "see" each other in terms of this interface. Thus objects "make metaphors" of each other: They perceive not what the other "is" but some limited aspect of what the other *is like* (or, more accurately, "is like" *for* the "perceiving" object, for this particular interaction)—a "distortion" or "caricature" (Harman, "Well-Wrought" 188; *Tool-Being* 2), as in the famous story of a group of men in a dark room touching, and thereby perceiving, an elephant as a vine (trunk), tree (leg), boat (body), or rope (tail), respectively. As Bogost puts it, paraphrasing Harman, "Relation takes place not just *like* metaphor but *as* metaphor" (67l)—"it's not turtles all the way down, but metaphors" (84).

One implication of this process is that, as Bogost writes, "centrism is inevitable—whether it be anthropocentrism ... or any other" (80). That is, "the answer to correlationism is not the rejection of *any* correlate but the acknowledgment of *endless* ones, all self-absorbed" (Bogost 78). In this infinite proliferation of Copernican revolutions, the relations of *all* objects to each other unfold within "distorting" constraints that are structurally similar to the limits imposed on the human experience of reality by Kant's categories of understanding. Ironically, therefore, OOO, despite its superficially anti-Kantian stance, ends up reinscribing, and expanding, key tenets of Kantian thought. However, this very reinscription and expansion ideally breaks Kantianism from its anthropocentric shell: The experiences and reality of the nonhuman world are "important" again, and not just "philosophically" (to humans). Whether or not the withdrawn objects of OOO are "larger" in scope than Kant's things-in-themselves, they *appear* larger (and thus, in practice, "are" larger) due to their now recognized and foregrounded participation in "endless" interactions with other, nonhuman objects: They are "of concern" *to each other*. The ethics of OOO, then, aim to recuperate what David Abram would call the "more-than-human world" from human neglect and abuse.

Significantly, it is not just that withdrawn objects enter into relationships that function like (or as) metaphors: Actual metaphors themselves function *like OOO's idea of withdrawn objects*. As Kurz points out, "We can explicate a metaphor by, for example, generating circumlocutions [and] comparisons [*Vergleiche*], which, however, never reach the point where all has been said" (22). Thus, unsayability (here, the unsayability of "all"), a version of the topos we explored in a different variation in Rilke's *Broglie* cycle, once again moves to the forefront of our consideration of metaphor.

As I argued earlier in this chapter, metaphor is the language of empathy, and empathy is structured like a metaphor. As philosopher Ted Cohen maintains, "The construction and comprehension of metaphors, however those things are done, requires an ability that is the same as the human capacity for understanding one another" (1); further, "I am persuaded that understanding one another involves thinking of oneself as another, and thus the talent for doing this must be related to the talent for thinking of one thing as another; and it may be the same talent, differently deployed" (9).[29] Metaphor *makes us each other*, scrambles other and self, keeps both

---

29. Lee argues that a bodily basis for empathy lies at the root of our use and understanding of metaphorical language; see Benjamin Morgan 38–42. For a reading of the dependence of the ostensibly bodily or physiological understanding of *Einfühlung* on the use of metaphor, see Wilke 343–44.

in play at once: "Metaphor does not articulate a similarity; rather, it says 'this is that.' At the same time we are aware: 'this is not that'" (Kurz 23).

What, then, of *bad metaphor*, that which I have positioned under the broadly applied label "catachresis" and which so spectacularly performs the inadequacy of its saying—and therefore dwells as a neighbor to the topos of unsayability? From one perspective, such catachresis might be thought of as the paradigmatic case of *metaphor as such*, the marker of the relations of "withdrawn objects," and thus a preserver of our awareness of the ineffable and of Otherness. This is because catachresis (including, capaciously, the operations identified by OOO as "distortion" and "caricature") so immediately points to the "dark subterranean reality" (Harman, *Tool-Being* 1) of its tenor: Its vehicle will always remain inadequate to its subject or context, hinting at "inexhaustible," "unsayable"—or at least unexhausted, unsaid—depths. Catachresis is therefore perhaps, ironically, the most "adequate" metaphor for the withdrawnness of things. As such, it forms a bulwark against belief in the complete graspability of the Other: a tropic language of nonempathy or of a "gap" in "perfect" empathy many critics have seen as necessary for a genuine interpersonal ethics, if not, paradoxically, for interpersonal empathy itself.[30] If, to paraphrase Nietzsche, empathy is a metaphor that has forgotten it is a metaphor (that is, one that fails to acknowledge the infinity of the Other qua "withdrawn object"), catachresis reminds us of this gap: It defends us, as Morton writes in another context, against "the reduction of one entity to another's *fantasy* about it" (119).[31]

Thus we might find in Madeleine Broglie's unsayability, or "bad" sayability, an indication of her *inexhaustibility* in Harman's sense. And, returning to one of the images with which this chapter began,

---

30. See, for example, Coplan: "Empathy is a complex imaginative process in which an observer simulates another person's situated psychological states *while maintaining clear self-other differentiation*" ("Understanding Empathy" 5, my emphasis).

31. Cf. Nietzsche on "truths" as "illusions of which we have forgotten that they are illusions" ("On Truth and Lying" 878).

we might discover a different, diametrically reversed dimension to a defining catachresis:

> See: these eyes lay there: raiment,
> a face, a shine went into them
> as if they were – – well, what? – –:
>   the Grand Canal
> in its glory days before the burning –
> ‐
> and all at once Venice ceases to be.
> (*Gedichtkreis* 196) .

Here, it is perhaps not, as I suggested earlier, that the aggressive ridiculousness of the image (the eyes as "Canal Grande") destroys or erases Venice but that "bad" metaphor, indexing the limits of its own ability to grasp an "object," annihilates our *concept* of Venice: our failure to recognize withdrawnness, our thinking that we "know" the city (or eyes). As the row of dashes filling the space of an entire verse line intimates, what disappears is not Venice but our preconceived notions, our *thought*, of it. In this sense, catachresis is perhaps not coercion but our only access to the Other's "otherness," a reminder of it—and its protector.

Caution: Metaphors at Work!

In conclusion to this chapter, I offer a reading in the form of a parable (or, rather, a poem that functions *like* a parable, a simile or metaphor of a parable) that draws on both understandings of bad metaphor at once. The poem, written by Rilke in 1907 and published as one of the "thing-" or "animal-poems" in the second part of *Neue Gedichte*, describes a dog's experience of its relations with "the human." The text thus represents an imagined experience of one withdrawn object's experience of another withdrawn object: what Bogost calls *metametaphorism*, or "speculat[ing] . . . from the vantage point of the [object] itself" (80). I reproduce it here in its entirety:

Der Hund

> Da oben wird das Bild von einer Welt
> aus Blicken immerfort erneut und gilt.
> Nur manchmal, heimlich, kommt ein Ding und stellt
> sich neben ihn, wenn er durch dieses Bild
>
> sich drängt, ganz unten, anders, wie er ist;
> nicht ausgestoßen und nicht eingereiht,
> und wie im Zweifel seine Wirklichkeit
> weggebend an das Bild, das er vergißt,
>
> um dennoch immer wieder sein Gesicht
> hineinzuhalten, fast mit einem Flehen,
> beinah begreifend, nah am Einverstehen
> und doch verzichtend: denn er wäre nicht.

The Dog

> Up there the image [*Bild*] of a world
> of gazes is evermore renewed and counts.
> Only sometimes, secretly [*heimlich*], a Thing comes and places
> itself next to him when he thrusts himself through
>
> this image, wholly below, different than he is [*anders, wie er ist*];[32]
> not cast out and not set in his place [*nicht eingereiht*],
> and, as if in doubt, giving away
> his reality to this image, which he forgets,
>
> only to nonetheless hold his face into it
> again and again, almost supplicating,
> nearly comprehending, close to consenting [*Einverstehen*, "understanding
>   one's way into"]
> and nonetheless abstaining: for he would not be.

(641)

The poem so beguilingly imagines the dog's perspective that it is perhaps worth reminding ourselves that the text is a document of

---

32. On my translation of "anders, wie er ist," a polysemic formulation around which much of the poem's ambiguity turns, as "different than he is," see my discussion below.

human empathy—a projection of what a dog's experience of its own relation to the human Other might be like; the "feeling" of that experience. This speculation or "metametaphorism" is not without its hazards, both to humans and to dogs. The text thus also comes to be about not only the empathic seductions of metaphor but the resistance to it.[33]

The poem begins by emphasizing the importance, validity, and hazardousness of the *image*, the "Bild": "Up there the image [*Bild*] of a world / of gazes is evermore renewed and counts." Indeed, *Bild* is the most frequently repeated (in fact, the only repeated) noun in the text, occurring three times at key junctures: as what is "evermore renewed" and "counts"; as what must be or is "penetrated," "thrust through," perhaps giving rise to the arrival of the interposing (and possibly contrasting) "Thing" (*Ding*); and as that to which the dog nearly surrenders his "reality," even as he "forgets" the image itself.

Given the dog's (presumably) non- or barely linguistic world, it is reasonable to assume that the "Bild" in question is a visual one: as the poem puts it, evoking not just the exchange of looks that structures the dog's relation to humans but also the realm of visuality as such, the "image of a world / of gazes." But in the human world, "Bild" has clear additional connotations as *verbal* image, figurative language, trope, or metaphor: "Bilder" (images) and "bildliche Sprache" (figurative language, image language) are, after all, the bread and butter of poetry. The poem's world of images is thus our world, too—as well as, literally (or figuratively), *the poem's world*. It is, self-reflexively, the world of the "work" of the poem: The "image of a world" (*Bild von einer Welt*), or a world of images, is typically an essential part of what a poem "does." Either way, for the dog as for us (and the poem), it is the image that "counts" (*gilt*). For the dog, it is (in Bogost's terms) the animal's "metaphorism" of the human, the canine's limited and distorting experience of the human's withdrawn reality, the experience of the

---

33. For a different reading of "Der Hund," see Fick, who sees the poem as being about "the overcoming of the solipsistic way of seeing": "The intersection of two horizons, which are based on two different ways of being, is the theme of [the poem]"; "the Being of the observer seems to depend on whether and how the other being perceives him" (219–20).

interface through which the dog interacts with people. The same holds true for us. The fact that the text *sees the dog's seeing* as analogous to—figured by—the perception of "imagery" (*das Bild von einer Welt*) may be the first moment of metaphorism (in the service of metametaphorism, or, more simply, projective empathy) in the poem: We've (that is, Rilke's speaker has) understood the dog's *also* inexhaustible, also withdrawn or hidden reality in terms of our own actions—perceiving imagery, creating metaphors. Perhaps, to merge Lipps's "inside of imitation" and anthropomorphism, we "find" in the dog our own action of perceiving the world in terms of images because we have *first perceived the world in terms of images*. But, as Bogost warns, "once object relations become metaphorized, we must take care to avoid taking the constructed metaphor for the reality of the unit operation it traces" (72). From the (inaccessible) perspective of "reality," all metaphors are catachreses.[34]

The appearance of the "Thing" (*Ding*) in the middle of the first quatrain throws the opening verse of the second quatrain into syntactical confusion, leading to the most grammatically ambiguous formulation of the poem (to which I will return): "ganz unten, anders, wie er ist" ("wholly below, different than he is"—or, alternatively, "different, *as* he is"; "different, *like* him"). The Thing is already a profoundly cryptic entity, recalling the enigmatic nature of OOO's withdrawn objects. It seems to be positioned as the opposite of "the image": It only comes when the dog "penetrates" or "thrusts itself through" the image ("wenn er durch dieses Bild // sich drängt"), although even here it is unclear whether the dog's penetration of the image *causes* the Thing to appear or whether the two events merely happen concurrently, a correlation without causality.[35] Just as significantly, the meaning of the Thing

---

34. The word "image," while subtly suggesting a certain "framing of" or "remove from" what is seen, does not have to mean *metaphorical* image: It may denote the literal sense data of Vischerian "mere" seeing, particularly when this data is received in seemingly static "takes." That is, to assign the term "imagery" to the catalogue of figurative devices is already to use the term figuratively—to broaden its definitional scope and to play, as it were, on seeing.

35. The assertion that the Thing comes "only sometimes, ... when [the dog] thrusts himself through / this image" is similarly ambiguous. Does it mean that the Thing is generally absent but appears under certain narrowly defined circumstances ("sometimes"), namely "when[ever]" the dog "penetrates the image"? Or

remains obscure. Part feeling, part experience, part (perhaps) metaphorism of another, broader aspect of the dog's perception of the human, the Thing might also be thought of as a kind of *double* of the dog, a virtual dog, an emergent flicker of expanded awareness generated by some shift in the functioning of the "world of gazes." It is perhaps significant that the Thing arrives "heimlich" (secretly)—the word that forms the root of *unheimlich*, with its evocation of uncanny doubles, and that, as Freud famously demonstrated, ultimately means *the same thing* as "unheimlich" itself ("Uncanny" 929–34). Is this "Thing" and uncanny doubler a threat or helper, dog's best friend? Like the withdrawn object of OOO, it indexes a surplus or hidden reality: It disrupts and destabilizes the world of the image (the world *in the image of* the image), and thus, perhaps, certain parts of metaphorism.

Thus we arrive at the ambiguous line cited earlier, the formal hub around which much of the poem's mystery turns: "ganz unten, anders, wie er ist." Tellingly, the ambiguity hinges on the polysemy of the word *wie* (like, as)—the very marker of a metaphorical function (simile)—along with the syntax embedding it. I have translated the line as "wholly below, different than he is"—at first glance perhaps an odd choice, given that *wie* typically indicates similarity or equality ("like") in standard modern German, whereas *als*, in combination with *anders* ("anders als"), denotes inequality, difference, or comparison ("than"). However, historically, the usage of the two words was not always so strictly divided, and even today the employment of "wie" to express comparison is common in some forms of colloquial German (as in "anders wie du," "different than you").[36] The line might thus be read as "different than he is," as I have rendered it—not only in the sense of "different from the dog," "different than the way the dog is," but, in the light of the intervention of the Thing, *different from himself*: the *dog* as *other to himself*. It might also be understood as an affirmation of the flat fact or state of affairs of "being different" ("anders, wie er ist," "*different,*

---

does it mean that *even when* the dog penetrates the image, the Thing "only" appears "sometimes"?

36. For a typical older example, see Wirsel's 1854 dictionary for the deaf: "Das Wesen ... der Pflanzen ist ganz *anders, wie* das Wesen der Thiere" (the nature ... of plants is completely *different than* the nature of animals) (832, my emphasis).

as he [the dog] [simply] is"), or even as a paratactic and seemingly paradoxical, analogical juxtaposition of opposite truths: "anders, wie er ist," "different :: as he is."

This last possibility is particularly intriguing. For it is impossible to determine exactly *who* or *what* is "anders, wie er ist." Above, I read this as the dog, now split, doubled, or "Othered" from himself by his encounter with the Thing. However, the poem's formal ambiguity—its syntax, with its disorienting proliferation of commas at the end of the first and the beginning of the second quatrain—equally allows us to read the "who or what" as the Thing itself, positioned "next to" (*neben*) the dog. The formulation "anders, wie er ist" would then suggest that it is the *Thing* that is "different than the dog"; *or* "different, *[just] as* 'he' [the dog] [*also*] is [different]"; *or* "different *in the same way* that the dog is ('different, *like* him')"; *or* all three at once. Put otherwise, "anders, wie er ist" becomes a formal declaration (that is, a declaration articulated through *form*) of solidarity with the Otherness (or similarity) of the Thing. Ultimately, the divergent readings ("different from himself," "different than the Thing," "different, like the Thing") may not be so divergent after all: In each case, we find the same struggle and merger of sameness and otherness, like and unlike—the crux of both metaphor and empathy. Similarly, like catachresis in its function as the marker of relations between withdrawn objects, the Thing may not (only) be the image's (*Bild*'s) opposite, but (also) its "truer" double. That is, "Bild" becomes (or, more precisely, indexes) "Thing" when it is consciously understood as catachresis.

As the quatrain continues, the dog, "as if in doubt," begins to "give away his reality" to the image, which he "forgets" ("wie im Zweifel seine Wirklichkeit / weggebend an das Bild, das er vergißt")—a dangerous thing to do, if this forgetting means forgetting that the "Bild" is a "Bild," the metaphor a metaphor. But the Thing offers a potential escape path. In splitting and doubling the dog, it has perhaps made the dog not only Other to but also *more than* itself—or, more accurately, has unlocked *more of the dog*, a dimension usually "withdrawn" even from its own self-relation: a hidden reality into which the dog may momentarily break. Thus we may also understand the Thing as that which prevents the dog from dangerously giving away his "reality" to the overwhelming, because misunderstood, "Bild"—"for [then] he would not be."[37]

From one perspective, "Der Hund" depicts a rescue from the potential power of the colonizing image or "Bild"—one understanding of "bad metaphor"—to obliterate self or other. This "Bild" is now not just a spectacularly coerced and coercive catachresis like the Grand Canal but any metaphorizing of our relations with others in which we "forget" that the relation is metaphorical. Here, if the poem overtly treats the risks of the dog's metaphorizing of the human, it is clear that the text, both in its content and in its status *as* a poem that imagines the experience of an animal, is equally about *our* metaphorizing of the "withdrawn objects" we encounter. Even seemingly innocuous descriptions of the dog's "(almost) supplicating," "(nearly) comprehending," and "(close to) consenting" are manifestations of our own metaphorism of the dog, a point underscored by the text's use of the common simile marker "wie" (like) to "make sense" of the dog's actions: "*wie* im Zweifel," "*as if* in doubt" (my emphasis). The poem is thus a warning about the potential dangers of an empathy that loses awareness of its own projective qualities. In this warning, there is another understanding of bad metaphor to be lost, or found: the understanding of catachresis as an index of the object's withdrawal. From this perspective, the poem points to the safeguarding potential precisely *of* (this second understanding of) bad metaphor. If, as OOO suggests, all relations are, with respect to a withdrawn object's totality, not only metaphorical but also incompletely or "inadequately" metaphorical—by definition, "bad metaphor"—then bad metaphor becomes, paradoxically, *good*: a figure or form that, by making us "see" its "flawed" metaphoricity, reminds us of the limitations or dangers of a "colonizing" empathy, fosters greater awareness of the other (and Other), and defends against the self's possession *of*, or *by*, this Other.[38] As Steven Shaviro writes, "I very much doubt that the world

---

37. Cf. the last line of Stephen Cohn's translation of the poem, Cohn 275.
38. Bogost, following Jane Bennett, reaches a similar conclusion in the context of OOO's analysis of metaphorism: To have a genuine ethics, we must let

can be 'justified' as an 'aesthetic phenomenon,' as Nietzsche so stridently claimed.... But justified or not, the world is indeed, at its base, aesthetic. And through aesthetics, we can act in the world and relate to other things in the world without reducing it and them to mere correlates of our own thought" (*Universe* 156).

To summarize, empathy works like a metaphor, all relationships are catachrestically metaphorical, and the key is not to lose sight of the catachrestically metaphorical nature of these relationships. We might even say, from the standpoint of OOO, that the logical form of all metaphor is catachresis. We would seem, then, to have arrived at the groundwork for an ethics based in aesthetics.[39] However, there remains the vexing question, lurking at the margins since Vischer's original formulation of *Einfühlung*, of the origin, trajectory, and locus of feeling, form, and empathy. Even in OOO's object-world, so different from the materialist "dead nature" object-world with which we began, we might still ask: Where do feeling, form, and empathy or *Einfühlung* begin, with a "subject" or with an "object"? And how do we approach these matters if, as Lipps at least intermittently acknowledged, there is no "separation of myself and [the object]," only a "complete unity" (*vollkommene Einheit*) or "total state of affairs" (*Gesamtsachverhalt*) (*Grundlegung* 192, 182)? Although no less requiring of an answer, the question of empathy and ethics, intimately bound up with aesthetics, thrusts us "through the image" onto new terrain when we recognize that, strictly speaking, neither subjects nor objects, at least when conceived of in their traditional sense, in fact "exist."

---

awareness of our unavoidable anthropomorphism help guard us against anthropocentrism (65).

39. For a very different paradigmatic case of an ethics based in aesthetics, see Nietzsche's *Genealogy of Morals*.

Coda

The Afterlives of Einfühlung

As with metaphors and the withdrawn objects of OOO, we can "explicate" *Einfühlung*'s implicate order, but "never reach the point where all has been said" (Kurz 22). Nevertheless, let us recall some of the things we *have* said regarding *Einfühlung*'s implicit pre- and para-history. As Crary argues regarding technology, it is not the case that "an independent dynamic of mechanical invention, modification, and perfection imposes itself onto a social field, transforming it from the outside"; rather, technologies are "concomitant or subordinate part[s] of other forces" (8), expressing the logic of a historical moment or structure of consciousness. If we think of *Einfühlung* as formulated by Vischer as a conceptual or affective technology, then one of the "other forces" of which it is a part is the force of nineteenth-century disenchanted materialism, with its vision of a dead object-world. As Maskarinec writes in the context of modernism, "Empathy aesthetics provides one response to ... worries about our alienation from a world of things" (60). Inversely mirroring Vischer's claim that it is "natural love for [his] species"—a feeling that might reasonably be seen as encompassing interpersonal empathy as well—that makes *Einfühlung* possible (103), Lipps goes on to conceptualize interpersonal empathy on the basis of models of *aesthetic* empathy or *Einfühlung*. It seems understandable that in the midst of the twentieth century's shift from thinking of empathy in terms of the self-projection of human feelings into inanimate forms to foregrounding the term's now-dominant associations with interpersonal fellow-feeling (some of them themselves inaugurated by Lipps), the subterranean model of *Einfühlung* would continue to shape the transforming concept of empathy: It makes "internal sense" that an aesthetic idea, developed to think the relation of humans to things and ultimately to reanimate objects declared dead, should, from its conceptual foundations in this thing-world, go on to inform theories of intersubjective relations with other humans who are now also increasingly thought of as objects.

From one perspective, one might say that *Einfühlung*, growing from the roots of the vitalist-materialist conflict as a response to the "death of nature" and articulating the anxieties surrounding this death, had itself become the "form" of these anxious feelings by the time it took rhetorical shape in and as Vischer's "formulation": thus the pervasive subtext of the macabre, violent, uncanny, and demonic between the lines of his prose ("empathy, the revenant"; "empathy, a ghost story"). As Morton writes, "Form is memory" (91). But the path of the pre- or para-history of *Einfühlung* is not monolithic or univalent. Büchner and Stifter anticipate problems and perils, but also *possibilities* that lie latent in the developing conditions of an increasingly objectifying world; they thus prefigure both problematic and promising elements that will surface in later theorists of empathy, forms and feelings, and objects such as Vischer, Lipps, and Lee. Stifter, for example, as much ruminates on the problems of empathy with a human "Other" conceived of as "object" or "pure form" as he recognizes the potential of the body, both human and textual, as a site of resistance—including resistance, articulated through a Lee-like *Einfühlung* into the affective charges of the body "embodied" in textual form, to his own patriarchal investments and his century's increasing privileging of sight at the expense of other, viscerally felt senses. Stifter's *Innigkeit* (intensity) perhaps itself offers a clue for how *Einfühlung*'s dimensions could expand beyond Vischer's conceptualization and pave the way not only for a growing concern with intersubjective empathy but also for an empathy that paradoxically transcends the notion of the subject itself. As a "proto-(Massumian) affect theory," Stifter's poetics of intensity allows for empathic resonances both with *particular* bodies (Clarissa's, the text's) and with the energies that, though mediated in this case by specific forms (again, Clarissa's corporeal-emotional aggregate and the text's), exceed these individual channels. Lipps takes the "mentalizing" of *Einfühlung* furthest, even as he ties this mentalizing to the motions of the bodies of others. As Lanzoni describes it, it is the "abstracted projection of the ego's striving into the object of contemplation" ("Introduction" 289). As we have seen, it is also the conversion of the "real" other into a series of metaphors for the self. Rilke in turn transforms the implicit and explicit metaphoricity of Lipps's project ("everything is metaphor"; "everyone is a metaphor of me") into a version of empathy as (bad) metaphor that makes a virtue of this lack of perfect contact, thereby potentially "repairing" some of the problems introduced by the proliferating and uncanny "second selves," "transplantations," and "exchanges" of Vischer's idea of *Einfühlung*. If, in Vischer, self and other or subject and object can perhaps too easily become isomorphic near equivalents or (almost) "perfect metaphors" of each other, in Rilke's catachresis, as in OOO's radicalization of Kant, it is our *inability* to fully grasp the Other that "saves" us. It is in these ways that empathy, which begins its modern life as an aesthetic concept, remains an aesthetic problem, and one both implicitly and intimately linked to ethics. Looking at all of these developments, we might say that *Einfühlungstheorie*, and its relations to the intersubjective empathy with which it has from the beginning been both different and interwoven, have changed throughout the course of their history (and pre- and para-history), but also that these apparent changes brought to the surface or "explicated" implications that were already present, both in Vischer's initial formulation and in the developments leading up to it.

Afterlife One

Berlin, 1925. The age of *Einfühlung* was over, killed, supposedly, as art critic Franz Roh announced that year in his book *Nach-Expressionismus, Magischer Realismus* (*Post-Expressionism, Magical Realism*), by Worringer's abstraction (40)—or by Brecht's alienation, World War I, and the diminishing returns of psychological-aesthetic research into *Einfühlung* itself. But if we consider a typical citizen of the fledgling Weimar Republic making her way down an electrically illuminated, advertisement-glutted street on her way to the cinema, rumors of the death of *Einfühlung* seem to be greatly exaggerated. For *Einfühlung* left behind a conspicuously combined—and problematic—aesthetic, economic, and political legacy.

As Janet Ward writes in *Weimar Surfaces: Urban Visual Culture in 1920s Germany*, the German turn of the century "witnessed the gradual implosion of advertising into art, and art into advertising" (93). Electrical advertisements represented one of the most widespread and influential forms of this fusion of commerce and aesthetics: "Before the stock market crash of 1929 . . . , Germany's capital city had three thousand electric advertisements on display" (Ward 102). This "fusion of commerce and aesthetics" is likewise a paradigmatic locus for corresponding intersections of *Einfühlung* and empathy, feeling and form. As Ward explains, "The primary location for the phantasmagorical investiture provoked by 1920s advertising was in the public sphere of the metropolis, specifically *on the street*" (93). Here, the advertisements' flashing lines, rotating figures, and appearing and disappearing forms recall the diverse forms and shapes, including "simple," "abstract," and "spatial" ones (Maskarinec 13), that observers "feel themselves into" in the writings of Vischer and Lipps. Advertising's solicitation of feeling into form, however, has ideological effects on the total person. Through the "mysterious transplantation[s] and magical transformation[s]" (Vischer 104) of desire and identification evoked by the ads and their marketed commodities, ideology and capital reach into and affect the empathic observer's mind-body continuum.

Ward identifies multiple Weimar-era observers who describe the period's advertising culture in ways that evoke the uncannier aspects of Vischer's *Einfühlung*. Siegfried Kracauer, for example, in a suggestive illustration of self-other exchange, writes that when one views electrical ads, "one's spirit—which is no longer one's own—roams ceaselessly out of the night and into the night.... Some sort of magic spurs the spirit relentlessly amid the thousand electric bulbs, out of which it constitutes and reconstitutes itself into glittering sentences" (qtd. in Ward, 128–29). Perhaps even more strikingly, Ward describes Rudolf Seyffert's 1929 *Allgemeine Werbelehre* (*General Tenets of Advertising*) as arguing that advertising's purpose is "to provide a totally seamless combination of a will imposed from without and individual decision-making from within" (98)—a portrayal that might also apply equally well to a sinister account of German *Bildung*, the workings of ideological hegemony, or *Einfühlung* figured as the sort of "demonic possession" implied by Vischer's image of the seduced nobleman and devil-controlled hanged girl (that is, not possession of the other by the self but of the self by the other). As Lipps argues in "Einfühlung und ästhetischer Genuss," we experience *pleasure* when we surrender to the "demands" of an aesthetic object (105).

As Ward writes, Weimar advertising culture unfolded according to the principles of applied psychology, or *Psychotechnik*, introduced to Germany by Harvard professor (and Wilhelm Wundt student) Hugo Münsterberg. Münsterberg's popular 1912 book *Psychologie und Wirtschaftsleben* (*Psychology and Economic Life*), published near the height of the influence of *Einfühlungstheorie*, inspired 170 German companies to develop departments reliant on applied psychology in the following decade (Ward 96). Not surprisingly, Münsterberg himself was an empathy theorist, the director of a Harvard University laboratory that sought to wed the experimental insights of psychological aesthetics with *psychotechnische* techniques (Bruno 162; Brain, "Self-Projection" 329–37). And when our hypothetical Weimar citizen leaves the Münsterberg-influenced advertising nimbus of her electrified street to enter the cinema, she does not escape *Einfühlung* but plunges deeper into it. Indeed, Münsterberg, also a perceptive film theorist, understood cinema in terms of Vischerian and Lippsian *Einfühlung*, especially empathic projection. As he writes in his 1916 book *Das Lichtspiel: Eine psy-*

chologische Studie (*The Photoplay: A Psychological Study*), our minds "project" motion and depth onto the *literally* projected film—the static, rapidly changing, two-dimensional images or forms appearing on the screen. Similarly, in a combination of *Einfühlung* and a projective form of intersubjective empathy, we project our own emotions onto the film's characters and landscapes (64–78).

Münsterberg reminds us that "cinematography had been largely invented in laboratories of physiology and psychology, before going its own way as a medium of popular entertainment" (Brain, "Self-Projection" 334). More ominously, *Das Lichtspiel*'s surface-level panegyric to film art vividly (if perhaps unintentionally) exposes cinematic technique as realizing those fears of colonization, substitution, and possession (possession *of* and possession *by*) that haunted early *Einfühlungstheorie*. On the one hand, movies "*[tell] us the human story by* overcoming the forms *of the outer world, namely, space, time, and causality, and by* adjusting the events *to the forms of the inner world, namely, attention, memory, imagination, and emotion*" (129, my nonitalicized emphasis): "*The massive outer world has lost its weight, it has been . . . clothed in the forms of our own consciousness. The mind has* triumphed over *matter*" (153–54, my nonitalicized emphasis). On the other hand, when Münsterberg, in a seeming reference to his own *Psychotechnik*, argues that an observer watching events in a state of "involuntary" or externally controlled attention—a state he associates with the situation of the film spectator—has no *choice* how to respond but simply "*must* read the glaring electric signs [advertisements] which flash up" (*Photoplay* 80, my emphasis), we have reached the point where cinema and advertising merge to reveal their common roots in "automatic" and uncanny aesthetic empathy, and where this cinematic-commercial *Einfühlung* announces *its* connection to (ideological) mind control "from without" (Ward 98)—that is, to "demonic" possession.

Indeed, it is just such a merger that "transforms and transplants" the titular character of Robert Wiene's seminal Weimar-era horror film *Das Cabinet des Dr. Caligari* (*The Cabinet of Dr. Caligari*), released four years after Münsterberg's cinema book. The film's sinister asylum director is obsessed with Caligari, an eighteenth-century mystic who hypnotized a somnambulist, Cesare, into committing brutal murders. In an explanatory flashback toward the end of the film, the asylum director reels into the nighttime street; his thoughts—commands that reveal the controlling imperative at stake in the empathic—appear to him "from without" in the form of optically superimposed glowing words that repeatedly flash by, letter by letter, like time-phased electrical advertisements, all over the walls of the town: "You must become Caligari!" (1:02:11–1:03:12).[1] Thus the asylum director, "possessed" at the site of the formal union of film technique and advertising aesthetics, *does* "become Caligari," simultaneously mind-controlled and mind-controlling: He "feels his way into" the eighteenth-century Caligari, assumes the earlier figure's name, hypnotizes his "own" murderous Cesare, and so on. Resonating with Vischer's fears of the potentially "pathological" effects of *Einfühlung* and Lipps's theories of the "immediate" "inner imitation" of the perceived motions of others, Münsterberg writes of sensory hallucinations caused by film viewing, of the dangers of cinema-induced "psychical infection" or emotional contagion, and of the concern that seeing fictional crimes on-screen could lead to real "motor responses" in spectators and the, as it were, "empathic" commission of actual crimes by movie audiences (*Photoplay* 154).

Put otherwise: *Einfühlung* does not disappear in the 1920s but *disappears into* advertising and film—its "natural" refuge.[2] It is perhaps unsurprising that Walter Benjamin, in the second version of his essay on the work of art in the age of mechanical reproduction, writes in resonance with Vischer's terminology that the early twentieth-century cinematic public "*only empathizes [sich einfühlt] with the actor insofar as it empathizes with the camera [Apparat]*" (488).[3] At the furthest and darkest end of this spectrum of adver-

---

1. For Weimar-era descriptions of Germany's electrical advertisements appearing "letter by letter" and disappearing again, see Janet Ward 116.
2. The Weimar-era critical discourse on cinema seems to have "hidden" its "refugee" *Einfühlung* well. Despite the extraordinary popularity of *Einfühlung* as a theoretical category until at least the mid-1920s, an anthology of nearly 300 contemporary documents about film contains only four occurrences of the word "empathy," eight of Hugo Münsterberg's name, and no mention of either Vischer or, more surprisingly, Lipps (Kaes et al.).
3. Today a prime locus or "natural refuge" for the afterlife of *Einfühlung* is the role-playing video game. In miHoYo's open-world fantasy adventure game *Genshin*

tising and film, or advertising *as* film, we find filmic "advertisements" like Riefenstahl's *Triumph des Willens* (*Triumph of the Will*, 1935), a spectacle of dangerous *Einfühlung* into whose cheering masses, mobile or "animated" geometrical forms (marching crowds), gleefully cavorting fascist bodies, space-expanding (and dominating) long shots, intimacy-provoking close-ups, and rhythmic alternations of serenity and frenzy the spectator projects himself—and in whose introjected forms he simultaneously *forms himself*, as in a perverse Lacanian mirror stage. As Ward points out, "So many of the very same psychotechnicians of Weimar commerce went on . . . to become the . . . psychotechnicians of the Nazi regime. . . . It was all too easy for Nazism to adopt the psychotechnically dominated tendencies of the Weimar advertising industry for its own noncommercial aims of mass cultural rebirth" (100). Indeed, in a telling fusion of "abstraction" and "empathy," the mesmerizing marching formations, gleaming bodies, and laughing faces of fascism are precisely the commodities this film-cum-advertisement wants to sell.

The Empathy Zone

To conclude this fugitive reflection on the afterlives of *Einfühlung* on a less somber note, let us return briefly to the question of metaphor and aesthetics, including their intersection in object-oriented ontology. For the discourse of OOO not only gives pride of place to aesthetics and metaphor, as Graham Harman has stated (*Object-Oriented Ontology* 59–102): It also, as the previous chapter's discussion of Rilke suggests, forms an unacknowledged "refuge" for *Einfühlung* and its relation to intersubjective empathy. Indeed, OOO gives refuge to *Einfühlung* and empathy through reliance on a figural rhetoric of metaphor itself.

Impact, for example, the player's production of the movements of a third-person avatar and her maneuvering of the avatar through a represented geography that visually pivots, swivels, and otherwise responds to the player's haptic manipulation of keyboard controls provides a rich stage for Vischer's "kinesthetic imagination," Lipps's "inner imitation," and the overall self-projection into perceived form.

As we have noted, OOO posits a universe of innumerable, mutually "withdrawn" objects, each one inaccessible in its totality and unable to be "exhausted" by its relations with any other object. As the complete reality of any object remains hidden, all objects interact "aesthetically," by means of "metaphors" of themselves—metaphors *for* others. As Harman writes, "Two real objects in the world make contact not through direct impact, but only by way of the fictional images they present to each other" (*Object-Oriented Ontology* 163). These "fictional images," both of the other (object) and of myself (as object), are always partial; in their outward projection and corresponding reception, they meet in a liminal zone that might itself be figured as metaphorical. It is a zone, that is, of what the object is *like* (for me) and what I am *like* (for it). Additionally, if I interact, say, with a glass on a table, something (the glass) that is "like" something for the table is "like" something (else) for me—and in both cases, the "likeness" is only a partial *likeness* of the object's inaccessible totality.

The likenesses or "images," whether visual, tactile, chemical, atomic, or otherwise, presented by objects are *forms*. I project "myself"—the parts of me—into the parts of the object that can experience (the partial) "me" in its own terms, just as the object projects "itself" (the parts of itself) into the "me" that can experience it according to my own capacities: the parts of me to which it can become legible. Put otherwise, the object and I reciprocally project and receive the parts of ourselves that *correspond to our respective forms*. But because it acknowledges its own insufficiency, incompleteness, or lack of totality—its catachrestic nature or "badness"—this is a more ethically sophisticated version of Vischer's quasi-Kantian projection of the (form of the) self into the (form of the) Other, a process that simultaneously depends on and establishes (always imperfect) isomorphism and congruence. We might therefore restate Harman's argument in terms of Vischerian *Einfühlung*: All interactions between objects are *empathy*.

This empathy can of course lay no claim to complete "interobjectivity" (let alone "intersubjectivity"): It is always a mutually partial projection and reception, not a communion with what experience *is* (or is "like") for "them." It might perhaps be more accurately described as what it's like to be *part of them for me*. Yet this imperfect empathy might nonetheless open a space for (incompletely) shared, negotiated, or "parallel" experience—and thus for the troubling of conventional boundaries of subject and object (or "object and object").

An essay by Rilke's contemporary José Ortega y Gasset helps bring additional dimensions of this post- or para-historical legacy of *Einfühlung* to light. As Harman has noted on numerous occasions, Ortega's little-known 1914 essay on metaphor, "An Essay in Esthetics by Way of a Preface," served as the inspiration for Harman's development of object-oriented ontology (*Guerilla Metaphysics* 98; *Object-Oriented Ontology* 66–85). In a section of Ortega's piece that Harman does not discuss at length, we find aesthetic-empathic processes at work that evoke *Einfühlung*'s familiar dangers of possession and fears of being possessed; however, Ortega's analysis refuses to lock down the trajectory of these operations. I cite the passage in its entirety:

> Every image has, in a sense, two faces. From one side it is an image of something; from the other it is, albeit an image, something of mine. I see [a] cypress, I have the image, I imagine the cypress. So that, with respect to the cypress, it is *only* an image; but for me it is a real state of mine, it is a moment of my "I," of my being. Naturally, while my act—seeing the cypress—is taking place, the cypress is the object that exists for me; what "I" may be at that instant is for me an unknown. On the one hand, then, "cypress" is the name of a thing; on the other hand, it is a verb—my seeing the cypress; if, instead, this state or activity of mine is to become an object of my perception, I will have to place myself with my back to the "real" cypress, and from there, in the opposite direction, look inward and see the cypress gradually becoming unreal, transforming itself into my activity, into my "I." In other words, I will have to find a way to force the word "cypress," with its nominal value, to become active and erupt, assuming that of a verb. (144)

At first glance, Ortega's language seems to echo Vischer and Lipps at the height of their "possessing" mode: "I have the image," "it is something of mine," "it is a real state of mine, ... a moment of my 'I,' of my being." Indeed, when Ortega insists that he needs to "place himself with his back to the 'real' cypress, and from there, in the opposite direction, look inward and see the cypress gradually becoming unreal, transforming itself into his activity, into his 'I,'" he appears to anticipate Rilke's later, similarly Other-erasing call, in the *Ninth Duino Elegy*, for the "world" to "arise in us, invisible": "Earth, isn't this what you want: to arise within us, / *invisible*? Isn't it your dream / to be wholly invisible someday?—O Earth: invisible!" (203).

Conversely, Ortega's rhetoric also recalls the other—the "self-erasing"—side of Lipps's *Einfühlung*. As Ortega writes, "Naturally, while my act—seeing the cypress—is taking place, the cypress is the object that exists for me; what 'I' may be at that instant is for me an unknown." As Lipps had put it a decade earlier in his "Einfühlung, innere Nachahmung, und Organempfindungen" ("Empathy, Inner Imitation, and the Sensations of Organs"), "If I have fully given myself over to ... observation ..., then I am ... fully removed from what I am doing, e.g., the movements that I actually carry out. ... I am now wholly in the [other] moving form. ... I am transported into it. I am, as far as my consciousness is concerned, wholly and completely identical with it. ... This is aesthetic imitation. And it is at the same time aesthetic empathy" (190–91). Most importantly, however, when Ortega's cypress "gradually becomes unreal" and "transforms itself into his activity, into his 'I,'" it is impossible to limit the directional arrow of the transaction. On the one hand, the process seems to eliminate the tree—to assimilate it fully to the actions of the apprehending subject. On the other hand, the process might be read as the *tree's* transformation of the "I's" activity into *it*, such that "I" do not remain as I was.

It is the ambiguity of this "empathy zone" that opens the door to multidirectional communication, indeed potentially to mutual transformation. If this understanding of *Einfühlung* does indeed live on between the lines of the aesthetic concerns of contemporary philosophy, it may also open the door to communicative, transformative ways for the diverse forms of the world to *feel each other*.

Works Cited

Abram, David. *The Spell of the Sensuous: Perception and Language in a More-Than-Human World*. Vintage, 1997.

Adorno, Theodor W. *Ästhetische Theorie*. Edited by Gretel Adorno and Rolf Tiedemann. Suhrkamp, 1990.

Agosta, Lou. *A Rumor of Empathy: Rewriting Empathy in the Context of Philosophy*. Palgrave Macmillan, 2014.

Agutter, Paul S., and Denys N. Wheatley. *Thinking about Life: The History and Philosophy of Biology and Other Sciences*. Springer, 2008. https://doi.org/10.1007/978-1-4020-8866-7.

Alphen, Ernst van, and Tomáš Jirsa, eds. *How to Do Things with Affects: Affective Triggers in Aesthetic Forms and Cultural Practices*. Brill, 2019. ProQuest Ebook Central.

Altieri, Charles. *The Particulars of Rapture: An Aesthetics of the Affects*. Cornell University Press, 2003.

Anz, Heinrich. "'Leiden sey all mein Gewinst': Zur Aufnahme und Kritik christlicher Leidenstheologie bei Georg Büchner." *Georg Büchner Jahrbuch* 1 (1981): 160–68.

Arcade Fire. "Reflektor." *Reflektor*. EMI Music Publishing / Sonovox / Merge, 2013.

Arens, Katherine. *Austria and Other Margins: Reading Culture.* Camden House, 1996.
Aristotle. *Poetics.* Translated by Kenneth A. Telford. Henry Regnery Company, 1961.
Auerbach, Erich. *Mimesis: The Representation of Reality in Western Literature.* Translated by Willard R. Trask. Princeton University Press, 1953.
Bachelard, Gaston. *The Poetics of Space.* Translated by Maria Jolas. Beacon Press, 1969.
Barasch, Moshe. *Modern Theories of Art 2: From Impressionism to Kandinsky.* New York University Press, 1998. ProQuest Ebook Central.
Barthes, Roland. "The Reality Effect." In *The Rustle of Language*, translated by Richard Howard. University of California Press, 1989.
Baudelaire, Charles. "The Salon of 1859: Letters to the Editor of the *Revue Française*." In *Selected Writings on Art and Artists*, translated by P. E. Charvet. Cambridge University Press, 1972.
Baumgarten, Alexander Gottlieb. *Aesthetica.* G. Olms, 1961.
Baumgarten, Alexander Gottlieb. *Reflections on Poetry: Alexander Gottlieb Baumgarten's* Meditationes philosophicae de nonullis ad poema pertinentibus. Translated by Karl Aschenbrenner and William B. Holther. University of California Press, 1954.
Bayertz, Kurt. "Die Deszendenz des Schönen: Darwinisierende Ästhetik im Ausgang des 19. Jahrhunderts." In *Fin de Siècle: Zu Naturwissenschaft und Literatur der Jahrhundertwende im deutsch-skandinavischen Kontext*, edited by Klaus Bohnen, Uffe Hansen, and Friedrich Schmöe. Wilhelm Fink, 1984.
Begemann, Christian. "Gespenster des Realismus: Poetologie—Epistemologie—Psychologie in Fontanes *Unterm Birnbaum*." In *Realism and Romanticism in German Literature*, edited by Dirk Göttsche and Nicholas Saul. Aisthesis, 2013.
Begemann, Christian. *Die Welt der Zeichen: Stifter-Lektüren.* Metzler, 1995.
Behdad, Ali. *Belated Travelers: Orientalism in the Age of Colonial Dissolution.* Duke University Press, 1994.
Benjamin, Walter. *The Arcades Project.* Translated by Howard Eiland and Kevin McLaughlin. Belknap Press of Harvard University Press, 1999.
Benjamin, Walter. "Das Kunstwerk im Zeitalter seiner technischen Reproduzierbarkeit," In *Gesammelte Schriften*, volume 1.2, edited by Rolf Tiedemann and Hermann Schweppenhäuser. Suhrkamp, 1974.
Benjamin, Walter. "Kleine Geschichte der Photographie." In *Walter Benjamin: Ein Lesebuch*, edited by Michael Opitz. Suhrkamp, 1996.
Benjamin, Walter. "The Work of Art in the Age of Mechanical Reproduction." In *Illuminations*, edited by Hannah Arendt, translated by Harry Zohn. Schocken, 1968.
Bernstein, J. M. *Against Voluptuous Bodies: Late Modernism and the Meaning of Painting.* Stanford University Press, 2006.
Best, Stephen, and Sharon Marcus. "Surface Reading: An Introduction." In Leitch, *Norton Anthology of Theory and Criticism*, 3rd ed. Norton, 2018.

Bogost, Ian. *Alien Phenomenology, or What It's Like to Be a Thing*. University of Minnesota Press, 2012.
Bohm, David. *Wholeness and the Implicate Order*. Routledge and Keegan Paul, 1980.
Bollmer, Grant. "Empathy Machines." *Media International Australia* 165, no. 1 (2017): 63–76. PDF. https://doi.org/10.1177/1329878X17726794.
Bowie, Andrew. *Aesthetics and Subjectivity: From Kant to Nietzsche*. Manchester University Press, 2003.
Brain, Robert Michael. *The Pulse of Modernism: Physiological Aesthetics in Fin-de-Siècle Europe*. University of Washington Press, 2015. ProQuest Ebook Central.
Brain, Robert Michael. "Self-Projection: Hugo Münsterberg on Empathy and Oscillation in Cinema Spectatorship." *Science in Context* 25, no. 3 (2012): 329–53. PDF. http://doi.org/ 10.1017/S0269889712000166.
Braungart, Georg. *Leibhafter Sinn: Der andere Diskurs der Moderne*. Niemeyer, 1995.
Brazier, Mary A. B. *A History of Neurophysiology in the 19th Century*. Raven, 1988.
Brazier, Mary A. B. "Rise of Neurophysiology in the 19th Century." *Journal of Neurophysiology* 20, no. 2 (1957): 212–26. https://doi.org/10.1152/jn.1957.20.2.212.
Brecht, Bertolt. "Short Description of a New Technique of Acting Which Produces an Alienation Effect." In *Brecht on Theatre: The Development of an Aesthetic*, edited and translated by John Willett. Hill and Wang, 1964.
Breithaupt, Fritz. *The Dark Sides of Empathy*. Translated by Andrew B. B. Hamilton. Cornell University Press, 2019.
Breithaupt, Fritz. "Empathy and Aesthetics." *Zeitschrift für Ästhetik und allgemeine Kunstwissenschaft* 63, no. 1 (2018): 45–60.
Breithaupt, Fritz. *Kulturen der Empathie*. Suhrkamp, 2009.
Brinkema, Eugenie. *The Forms of the Affects*. Duke University Press, 2014. Project MUSE.
Brodersen, Silke. "Physiologische Körperfigurationen bei Adalbert Stifter." In *Organismus und Gesellschaft: Der Körper in der deutschsprachigen Literatur des Realismus (1830–1930)*, edited by Christiane Arndt and Silke Brodersen. Transcript, 2011.
Bruno, Giuliana. "Das Laboratorium der Affekte: Film, Ästhetik, Wissenschaft." In Curtis and Koch, *Einfühlung*.
Büchner, Georg. "An die Eltern." In *Gesammelte Werke*.
Büchner, Georg. *Gesammelte Werke*. Edited by Gerhard P. Knapp and Herbert Wender. Goldmann, 2002.
Büchner, Georg. "An Karl Gutzkow." In *Gesammelte Werke*.
Büchner, Georg. *Lenz*. Deutscher Klassiker Verlag, 1999. Rpt. in Sieburth, *Lenz*.
Büchner, Georg. *Lenz*. Translated by Richard Sieburth. In Sieburth, *Lenz*, English and German facing.

Büchner, Georg. *Mémoire sur le Système nerveux du Barbeau*. Translated by Otto Döhner. *Georg Büchner Jahrbuch* 8 (1995): 305–70.
Büchner, Georg. "Über Schädelnerven: Probevorlesung." In *Gesammelte Werke*.
Büchner, Georg. *Woyzeck*. Lesefassung, edited by Werner R. Lehmann. In *Werke und Briefe*, Münchner Ausgabe, edited by Karl Pörnbacher, Gerhard Schaub, Hans-Joachim Simm, and Edda Ziegler. DTV/Carl Hanser, 1988.
Burke, Edmund. *A Philosophical Enquiry into the Origin of Our Ideas of the Sublime and Beautiful*. Edited by Adam Phillips. Oxford University Press, 1990.
The Cabinet of Dr. Caligari. Directed by Robert Wiene. Decla Film-Gesellschaft Berlin. 1920. ZDF / ARTE, 1994. Transit Films / Friedrich Wilhelm Murnau-Stiftung / Kino International, 2002.
Campbell, Karen J. "Toward a Truer Mimesis: Stifter's *Turmalin*." *German Quarterly* 57, no. 4 (1984): 576–89. PDF. http://www.jstor.org/stable/404699.
Cassedy, Steven. *Flight from Eden: The Origins of Modern Literary Criticism and Theory*. University of California Press, 1990. http://ark.cdlib.org/ark:/13030/ft8h4nb55x/.
Cassirer, Ernst. *The Philosophy of Symbolic Forms*. Vol. 3, *The Phenomenology of Knowledge*, translated by Ralph Mannheim. Yale University Press, 1957.
Cazeaux, Clive, ed. *The Continental Aesthetics Reader*. 2nd ed. Routledge, 2011.
Chalmers, David J. "Facing Up to the Problem of Consciousness." *Journal of Consciousness Studies* 2, no. 3 (1995): 200–219.
Coen, Deborah R. *Climate in Motion: Science, Empire, and the Problem of Scale*. University of Chicago Press, 2018.
Cohen, Ted. *Thinking of Others: On the Talent for Metaphor*. Princeton University Press, 2008.
Cohn, Dorrit. "The 'Second Author' of *Death in Venice*." In *The Distinction of Fiction*. Johns Hopkins University Press, 1999.
Cohn, Dorrit. *Transparent Minds: Narrative Modes for Presenting Consciousness in Fiction*. Princeton University Press, 1978.
Cohn, Stephen, trans. "The Dog." By Rainer Maria Rilke. In *New Poems: A Bilingual Edition*. Northwestern University Press, 1992.
Coplan, Amy. "Understanding Empathy: Its Features and Effects." In *Empathy: Philosophical and Psychological Perspectives*, edited by Amy Coplan and Peter Goldie. Oxford University Press, 2014.
Coplan, Amy, and Peter Goldie. Introduction to *Empathy: Philosophical and Psychological Perspectives*, edited by Amy Coplan and Peter Goldie. Oxford University Press, 2014.
Corbett, Rachel. *You Must Change Your Life: The Story of Rainer Maria Rilke and Auguste Rodin*. Norton, 2016.
Crary, Jonathan. *Techniques of the Observer: On Vision and Modernity in the Nineteenth Century*. MIT Press, 1990.

Curtis, Robin. "Einführung in die Einfühlung." In Curtis and Koch, *Einfühlung*.
Curtis, Robin, and Gertrud Koch, eds. *Einfühlung: Zu Geschichte und Gegenwart eines ästhetischen Konzepts*. Wilhelm Fink, 2009.
Curtis, Robin, and Gertrud Koch, eds. Vorwort to Curtis and Koch, *Einfühlung*.
Curtius, Ernst Robert. *European Literature and the Latin Middle Ages*. Translated by Willard R. Trask. Pantheon/Bollingen Foundation, 1953.
Debes, Remy. "From *Einfühlung* to Empathy: Sympathy in Early Phenomenology and Psychology." In *Sympathy: A History*, edited by Eric Schliesser. Oxford University Press, 2015.
Deleuze, Gilles. *Difference and Repetition*. Translated by Paul Patton. Continuum, 1997.
De Man, Paul. *Allegories of Reading: Figural Language in Rousseau, Nietzsche, Rilke, and Proust*. Yale University Press, 1979.
De Man, Paul. "The Epistemology of Metaphor." *Critical Inquiry* 5, no. 1 (Autumn 1978): 13–30. https://www.jstor.org/stable/1342975.
Dennett, Daniel C. "Facing Up to the Hard Question of Consciousness." *Philosophical Transactions of the Royal Society B: Biological Sciences* 373, no. 1755 (July 30, 2018). https://doi.org/10.1098/rstb.2017.0342.
Diderot, Denis. *The Paradox of Acting*. Translated by Walter Herries Pollock. Chatto and Windus, Piccadilly, 1883. https://archive.org/details/cu31924027175961/page/n11/mode/2up.
Döhner, Otto. "Neuere Erkenntnisse zu Georg Büchners Naturaffassung und Naturforschung." *Georg Büchner Jahrbuch* 2 (1982): 126–32.
Donahue, Neil H., ed. *Invisible Cathedrals: The Expressionist Art History of Wilhelm Worringer*. Pennsylvania State University Press, 1995.
Donahue, William Collins. "The Aesthetic 'Theology' of Büchner's *Lenz*." In Fortmann and Helfer, *Commitment and Compassion*.
Downing, Eric. *Double Exposures: Repetition and Realism in Nineteenth-Century German Fiction*. Stanford University Press, 2000.
Etymonline: Online Etymological Dictionary. https://www.etymonline.com.
Feagin, Susan L. "Empathizing as Simulating." In Coplan and Goldie, *Empathy*.
Fick, Monika. *Sinnenwelt und Weltseele: Der psychophysische Monismus in der Literatur der Jahrhundertwende*. Niemeyer, 1993.
Fischer, Luke. *The Poet as Phenomenologist: Rilke and the* New Poems. Bloomsbury, 2015–2016.
Fortmann, Patrick. "Introduction: Georg Büchner's Perpetual Contemporaneity." In Fortmann and Helfer, *Commitment and Compassion*.
Fortmann, Patrick, and Martha B. Helfer, eds. *Commitment and Compassion: Essays on Georg Büchner: Festschrift for Gerhard P. Knapp*. Brill/Rodopi, 2012. ProQuest Ebook Central.
Foucault, Michel. "Different Spaces." In *Aesthetics, Method, and Epistemology*, edited by James D. Faubion, translated by Robert Hurley et al. Vol. 2 of

Essential Works of Foucault 1954–1984, series editor Paul Rabinow. New Press, 1998.

Freeman, Barbara Claire. *The Feminine Sublime: Gender and Excess in Women's Fiction*. University of California Press, 1995.

Freud, Sigmund. *Totem und Tabu: Einige Übereinstimmungen im Seelenleben der Wilden und der Neurotiker.* Vol. 9, *Gesammelte Werke, chronologisch geordnet.* Vischer/Imago, 1940.

Freud, Sigmund. "The 'Uncanny.'" Translated by Alix Strachey. In Leitch, *Norton Anthology of Theory and Criticism*. Norton, 2001.

Gallagher, Shaun, and Julia Gallagher. "Acting Oneself as Another: An Actor's Empathy for Her Character." *Topoi* 39, no. 4 (2020): 779–90. https://doi.org/10.1007/s11245-018-9624-7.

Gallese, Vittorio. "'Being Like Me': Self-Other Identity, Mirror Neurons, and Empathy." In *Mechanisms of Imitation and Imitation in Animals*, Vol. 1, *Perspectives on Imitation: From Neuroscience to Social Science*, edited by Susan Hurley and Nick Chater. MIT Press, 2005. ProQuest Ebook Central.

Gallese, Vittorio. "Mirror Neurons, Embodied Simulation, and the Neural Basis of Social Identification." *Psychoanalytic Dialogues* 19, no. 5 (2009): 519–36. https://doi.org/10.1080/10481880903231910.

Geulen, Eva. *Worthörig wider Willen: Darstellungsproblematik und Sprachreflexion in der Prosa Adalbert Stifters*. Iudicium, 1992.

Goethe, Johann Wolfgang von. "Erotica Romana VII" [Roman Elegy V]. Translated by J. Worthy. Accessed January 7, 2017. http://lettersfromthedustbowl.com/elegies.html.

Goethe, Johann Wolfgang von. *Faust: Der Tragödie erster und zweiter Teil*. Edited by Jörn Göres. Insel, 1998.

Goethe, Johann Wolfgang von. "Römische Elegien V." In *Deutsche Gedichte*, vol. 1, edited by Karl Krolow. Insel, 1991.

Goldman, Alvin I. *Simulating Minds: The Philosophy, Psychology, and Neuroscience of Mindreading*. Oxford University Press, 2006.

Greiner, Rae. "1909: The Introduction of the Word 'Empathy' into English." In *BRANCH: Britain, Representation, and Nineteenth-Century History*, edited by Dino Franco Felluga. https://branchcollective.org/?ps_articles=rae-greiner-1909-the-introduction-of-the-word-empathy-into-english.

Grillparzer, Franz. *Der arme Spielmann: Erzählung*. Reclam, 2021.

Groos, Karl. "Das ästhetische Miterleben und die Empfindungen aus dem Körperinnern." *Zeitschrift für Ästhetik und allgemeine Kunstwissenschaft* 4 (1909): 161–82.

Groos, Karl. *Einleitung in die Ästhetik*. J. Ricker'sche Buchhandlung, 1892. ECHO: Cultural Heritage Online.

Guillemin, Anna. "Mimesis of Everyday Life in the *Kunstgespräch* of Büchner's *Lenz*: Realist Aesthetics Between Anti-Ideal and Social Art." In Fortmann and Helfer, *Commitment and Compassion*.

Guyer, Paul. *A History of Modern Aesthetics*. Vol. 2, *The Nineteenth Century*. Cambridge University Press, 2018.

Häge, Elisabeth. *Dimensionen des Erhabenen bei Adalbert Stifter*. De Gruyter, 2018. ProQuest Ebook Central.
Halberstam, Jack. *Wild Things: The Disorder of Desire*. Duke University Press, 2020. muse.jhu.edu/book/78007.
Hamburger, Käte. "Die phenomenologische Struktur der Dichtung Rilkes." In *Rilke in neuer Sicht*, edited by Käte Hamburger. Kohlhammer, 1971. Internet Archive.
Hammermeister, Kai. *The German Aesthetic Tradition*. Cambridge University Press, 2002.
Hammond, Meghan Marie. *Empathy and the Psychology of Literary Modernism*. Edinburgh University Press, 2014. Cambridge Core.
Harman, Graham. *Guerrilla Metaphysics: Phenomenology and the Carpentry of Things*. Open Court, 2005.
Harman, Graham. *Object-Oriented Ontology: A New Theory of Everything*. Pelican, 2018.
Harman, Graham. *Tool-Being: Heidegger and the Metaphysics of Objects*. Open Court, 2002.
Harman, Graham. "The Well-Wrought Broken Hammer: Object-Oriented Literary Criticism." *New Literary History* 43, no. 2 (Spring 2012): 183–203. https://www.jstor.org/stable/23259371.
Heath, Malcolm. Introduction to *Poetics*, by Aristotle, translated by Malcolm Heath. Penguin, 1996.
Heidegger, Martin. *Being and Time*. Translated by John Macquarrie and Edward Robinson. Blackwell, 1962.
Heidegger, Martin. "Wozu Dichter?" In *Holzwege*. 9th ed. Klostermann RoteReihe, 2015.
Heidelberger, Michael. *Nature from Within: Gustav Theodor Fechner and His Psychophysical Worldview*. Translated by Cynthia Klohr. University of Pittsburgh Press, 2004.
Heller, Erich. *The Disinherited Mind: Essays in Modern German Literature and Thought*. Bowes and Bowes, 1975. Internet Archive.
Herder, Johann Gottfried. "Plastik." In *Herder und die Anthropologie der Aufklärung*, Vol. 2, *Werke*, edited by Wolfgang Pross. Carl Hanser Verlag, 1987.
Herder, Johann Gottfried. "Vom Erkennen und Empfinden der menschlichen Seele." In *Herder und die Anthropologie der Aufklärung*, Vol. 2, *Werke*, edited by Wolfgang Pross. Carl Hanser Verlag, 1987.
Hölderlin, Friedrich. "Bread and Wine." In *Poems and Fragments*, 4th ed., translated by Michael Hamburger. Anvil Press Poetry, 2004.
Höller, Hans. "Die sozialgeschichtliche Bedeutung der ästhetischen Wahrnehmung bei Adalbert Stifter." *Wirkendes Wort* 32, no. 4 (1982): 255–67.
Holub, Robert. *Reflections of Realism: Paradox, Norm, and Ideology in Nineteenth-Century German Prose*. Wayne State University Press, 1991.
Horton, David. "Modes of Consciousness Representation in Büchner's *Lenz*." *German Life and Letters New Series* 43, no. 1 (1989): 34–48. https://doi.org/10.1111/j.1468-0483.1989.tb00635.x.

Horton, Scott. "Mörike's To a Lamp." *Harper's*, August 3, 2008, https://harpers.org/2008/08/morikes-to-a-lamp/.
Hutchinson, Ben. *Rilke's Poetics of Becoming*. Legenda/Modern Humanities Research Association and Manley Publishing, 2006.
Imorde, Joseph. "'Einfühlung' in der Kunstgeschichte." In Curtis and Koch, *Einfühlung*.
Irigaray, Luce. *This Sex Which Is Not One*. Translated by Catherine Porter and Carolyn Burke. Cornell University Press, 1985.
Irle, Gerhard. *Der psychiatrische Roman*. Hippokrates, 1965.
Irmscher, Hans Dietrich. *Adalbert Stifter: Wirklichkeitserfahrung und gegenständliche Darstellung*. Fink, 1971.
Jakobson, Roman. "Two Aspects of Language and Two Types of Aphasic Disturbances." In Leitch, *Norton Anthology of Theory and Criticism*, 3rd ed. Norton, 2018.
Jameson, Fredric. *The Antinomies of Realism*. Verso, 2015.
Jennings, Michael W. "Against Expressionism: Materialism and Social Theory in Worringer's *Abstraction and Empathy*." In Neil H. Donahue, *Invisible Cathedrals*.
Kaes, Anton, Nicholas Baer, and Michael Cowan, eds. *The Promise of Cinema: German Film Theory 1907–1933*. University of California Press, 2016. ProQuest Ebook Central.
Kafka, Franz. "In the Penal Colony." In *"The Judgement" and "In the Penal Colony,"* translated by Malcolm Pasley. Penguin, 1995. Internet Archive.
Kant, Immanuel. *Immanuel Kant's Critique of Pure Reason*. Translated by Norman Kemp Smith. Macmillan and Co., 1929. Internet Archive.
Kant, Immanuel. *Kritik der Urteilskraft*. Edited by Wilhelm Weischedel. Suhrkamp, 1974.
Keen, Suzanne. *Empathy and the Novel*. Oxford University Press, 2007. ProQuest Ebook Central.
Keen, Suzanne. "Empathy Studies." In *A Companion to Literary Theory*, edited by David H. Richter. Wiley, 2008. https://doi.org/10.1002/9781118958933.ch10.
Kidd, David Comer, and Emanuele Castano. "Reading Literary Fiction Improves Theory of Mind." *Science* 342, no. 6156 (October 2013): 377–80. https://doi.org/10.1126/science.1239918.
Knapp, Gerhard P., and Herbert Wender. Nachwort to *Gesammelte Werke*.
Kofman, Sarah. "The Melancholy of Art." In *Selected Writings*.
Kofman, Sarah. "The Resemblance of Portraits: Imitation According to Diderot." In *Selected Writings*.
Kofman, Sarah. *Selected Writings*. Edited by Thomas Albrecht, Georgia Albert, and Elizabeth Rottenberg, translated by Jennifer Bajorek. Stanford University Press, 2007.
Korab-Karpowicz, W. J. "Martin Heidegger (1889–1976)." Internet Encyclopedia of Philosophy. https://www.iep.utm.edu.
Koss, Juliet. "Über die Grenzen der Einfühlung." In Curtis and Koch, *Einfühlung*.

Kotler, Steven. *Last Tango in Cyberspace*. St. Martin's Press, 2019.
Kotsko, Adam. "Tool-Being-Toward-Death: OOO's Misreading of Heidegger." *An und für sich* (blog). November 14, 2013. https://itself.blog/2013/11/14/tool-being-toward-death-ooos-misreading-of-heidegger.
Krell, David Farrell. Notes to *The Death of Empedocles: A Mourning-Play*, by Friedrich Hölderlin, translated by David Farrell Krell. State University of New York Press, 2008. ProQuest Ebook Central.
Kristeva, Julia. *Powers of Horror: An Essay on Abjection*. Translated by Leon S. Roudiez. Columbia University Press, 1982.
Kristeva, Julia. *Revolution in Poetic Language*. Translated by Margaret Waller. Columbia University Press, 1984.
Kurz, Gerhard. *Metapher, Allegorie, Symbol*. Vandenhoeck and Ruprecht, 2004.
Lacan, Jacques. *The Four Fundamental Concepts of Psycho-Analysis*. Edited by Jacques-Alain Miller, translated by Alan Sheridan. Norton, 1978.
Langer, Susanne K. *Feeling and Form: A Theory of Art*. Charles Scribner's Sons, 1953.
Lanzoni, Susan. *Empathy: A History*. Yale University Press, 2018.
Lanzoni, Susan. "Introduction: Emotion and the Sciences: Varieties of Empathy in Science, Art, and History." Special issue, *Science in Context* 25, no. 3 (2012): 287–300. https://doi.org/10.1017/S0269889712000105.
Lanzoni, Susan. "Practicing Psychology in the Art Gallery: Vernon Lee's Aesthetics of Empathy." *Journal of the History of the Behavioral Sciences* 45, no. 4 (Fall 2009): 330–54. https://doi.org/10.1002/jhbs.20395.
Lee, Vernon. "Aesthetic Empathy and Its Organic Accompaniments." Translated by R. L. Shields. In Lee and Anstruther-Thomson, *Beauty and Ugliness and Other Studies in Psychological Aesthetics*.
Lee, Vernon. *The Beautiful: An Introduction to Psychological Aesthetics*. Cambridge University Press, 1913. Internet Archive.
Lee, Vernon. "The Central Problem of Aesthetics." 1910. In Lee and Anstruther-Thomson, *Beauty and Ugliness and Other Studies in Psychological Aesthetics*.
Lee, Vernon. *The Handling of Words and Other Studies in Literary Psychology*. University of Nebraska Press, 1968.
Lee, Vernon, and C. Anstruther-Thomson. *Beauty and Ugliness*. In Lee and Anstruther-Thomson, *Beauty and Ugliness and Other Studies in Psychological Aesthetics*.
Lee, Vernon, and C. Anstruther-Thomson. *Beauty and Ugliness and Other Studies in Psychological Aesthetics*. Bodley Head, 1912.
Leighton, Angela. *On Form: Poetry, Aestheticism, and the Legacy of a Word*. Oxford University Press, 2007. ProQuest Ebook Central.
Leitch, Vincent B., William E. Cain, Laurie A. Finke, Barbara E. Johnson, John McGowan, and Jeffrey J. Williams, eds. *The Norton Anthology of Theory and Criticism*. Norton, 2001.
Leitch, Vincent B., William E. Cain, Laurie A. Finke, John McGowan, T. Denean Sharpley-Whiting, and Jeffrey J. Williams, eds. *The Norton Anthology of Theory and Criticism*. 3rd ed. Norton, 2018.

Levine, Caroline. *Forms: Whole, Rhythm, Hierarchy, Network*. Princeton University Press, 2015.
Lipps, Theodor. "Einfühlung, innere Nachahmung, und Organempfindungen." In *Archiv für die gesamte Psychologie*, vol. 1, edited by E. Meumann. Engelmann, 1903.
Lipps, Theodor. "Einfühlung und ästhetischer Genuss." *Die Zukunft*, no. 54 (January 1906): 100–14.
Lipps, Theodor. *Grundlegung der Ästhetik*. Vol. 1, *Ästhetik: Psychologie des Schönen und der Kunst*. Leopold Voss, 1903. Center for Research Libraries, https://utah-primoprod.hosted.exlibrisgroup.com/permalink/f/dtufc4/UUU_ALMA51554106880002001.
Lipps, Theodor. *Raumästhetik und geometrisch-optische Täuschungen*. E. J. Bonset, 1966.
The Lord of the Rings: The Fellowship of the Ring. Directed by Peter Jackson. New Line Cinema/WingNut Films, 2001.
Lovecraft, H. P. "Herbert West—Reanimator." In *More Annotated H. P. Lovecraft*, edited by S. T. Joshi and Peter Cannon. Dell, 1999.
Luke, David. Introduction to *Limestone and Other Stories*, by Adalbert Stifter, translated by David Luke. Harcourt, Brace, and World, 1968.
Lyotard, Jean-François. "The Sublime and the Avant-Garde." In Cazeaux, *Continental Aesthetics Reader*.
Mallgrave, Harry Francis, and Eleftherios Ikonomou. Introduction to *Empathy, Form, and Space: Problems in German Aesthetics, 1873–1893*, edited by Harry Francis Mallgrave and Eleftherios Ikonomou. Getty Center for the History of Art and the Humanities, 1994.
Margaroni, Maria. "'The Lost Foundation': Kristeva's Semiotic *Chora* and Its Ambiguous Legacy." *Hypatia* 20, no. 1 (2005): 78–98. https://www.jstor.org/stable/3810844.
Maskarinec, Malika. *The Forces of Form in German Modernism*. 1st ed. Northwestern University Press, 2018. muse.jhu.edu/book/60376.
Massumi, Brian. "The Autonomy of Affect." *Cultural Critique*, no. 31 (Autumn 1995): 83–109. https://www.jstor.org/stable/1354446.
Massumi, Brian. Notes on the translation and acknowledgments to *A Thousand Plateaus: Capitalism and Schizophrenia Vol. 2*, by Gilles Deleuze and Félix Guattari, translated by Massumi. University of Minnesota Press, 1987. Internet Archive.
Matravers, Derek. *Empathy*. Polity, 2017.
Maurer, Kathrin. "Close-Ups of History: Photographic Description in the Works of Jacob Burkhardt and Adalbert Stifter." *Monatshefte* 97, no. 1 (Spring 2005): 63–77. http://www.jstor.com/stable/30154207.
Mayer, Mathias. *Adalbert Stifter: Erzählen als Erkennen*. Reclam, 2001.
Mayer-Gross, Wilhelm [Wilhelm Mayer]. "Zum Problem des Dichters Lenz." *Archiv für Psychiatrie und Nervenkrankheiten* 62 (1921): 889–90. https://doi.org/10.1007/BF02029963.

McArthur, Tom, Jacqueline Lam-McArthur, and Lise Fontaine, eds. *The Oxford Companion to the English Language*. 2nd ed. Oxford University Press, 2018.
Merchant, Carolyn. *The Death of Nature: Women, Ecology, and the Scientific Revolution*. Harper and Row, 1980.
Merker, Emil. Nachwort to *Der Hochwald*, by Adalbert Stifter. Reclam, 1995.
Metz, Joseph. "'Eine eigentliche Durchdringung': Literary and National Identity, Gender, and Body in Rilke's 'Stifter Letter' to August Sauer." *German Quarterly* 76, no. 3 (Summer 2003): 314–28.
Metz, Joseph. "The Jew as Sign in Stifter's *Abdias*." *Germanic Review* 77, no. 3 (2002): 219–32.
Meyer, Richard M. *Berliner Tageblatt*, October 12, 1913. https://www.xlibris.de/Autoren/Zitate/Buechner.
Morgan, Benjamin. "Critical Empathy: Vernon Lee's Aesthetics and the Origins of Close Reading." *Victorian Studies* 55, no. 1 (2012): 31–56. https:/doi.org/10.2979/victorianstudies.55.1.31.
Morgan, David. "The Enchantment of Art: Abstraction and Empathy from German Romanticism to Expressionism." *Journal of the History of Ideas* 57, no. 2 (1996): 317–41. https://www.jstor.org/stable/3654101.
Morgan, Dermot. "The Problem of Empathy: Lipps, Scheler, Husserl and Stein." In *Amor Amicitiae: On the Love That Is Friendship: Essays in Medieval Thought and Beyond in Honor of the Rev. Professor James McEvoy*, edited by Thomas A. F. Kelly and Philipp W. Rosemann. Peeters, 2004.
Mörike, Eduard. "Auf eine Lampe." In *Stimmen im Kanon: Deutsche Gedichte*, edited by Ulla Hahn. Reclam, 2003.
Morton, Timothy. *Hyperobjects: Philosophy and Ecology after the End of the World*. University of Minnesota Press, 2013.
Müller, Johannes. *Handbuch der Physiologie des Menschen für Vorlesungen*. Vol. 2. Koblenz: Hölscher, 1840. https://gallica.bnf.fr/ark:/12148/bpt6k9738355t.
Müller, Johannes. *Elements of Physiology*. Vol. 2. Translated by William Baly. Taylor and Walton, 1842.
Müller Nielaba, Daniel. *Die Nerven Lesen: Zur Leit-Funktion von Georg Büchners Schreiben*. Königshausen und Neumann, 2001.
Müller-Sievers, Helmut. *Desorientierung: Anatomie und Dichtung bei Georg Büchner*. Wallstein, 2003.
Müller-Sievers, Helmut. *The Science of Literature: Essays on an Incalculable Difference*. Translated by Chadwick Truscott Smith, Paul Babinski, and Helmut Müller-Sievers. De Gruyter, 2015.
Müller-Tamm, Jutta. *Abstraktion als Einfühlung: Zur Denkfigur der Projektion in Psychophysiologie, Kulturtheorie, Ästhetik und Literatur der frühen Moderne*. Rombach, 2005.
Münsterberg, Hugo. *Hugo Münsterberg on Film: The Photoplay: A Psychological Study*. Edited by Allan Langdale. Routledge, 2002. EBSCOhost.

Nagel, Barbara N. *Ambiguous Aggression in German Realism and Beyond: Flirtation, Passive Aggression, Domestic Violence*. Bloomsbury Academic, 2019.
Nagel, Thomas. "What Is It Like to Be a Bat?" *The Philosophical Review* 83, no. 4 (1974): 435–50. https://www.jstor.org/stable/2183914.
Neuhuber, Christian. *Lenz-Bilder: Bildlichkeit in Büchners Erzählung und ihre Rezeption in der bildenden Kunst*. Böhlau, 2009.
Nietzsche, Friedrich. *The Gay Science, with a Prelude in Rhymes and an Appendix of Songs*. Translated by Walter Kaufmann. Vintage, 1974.
Nietzsche, Friedrich. *On the Genealogy of Morals: A Polemic*. In *Basic Writings of Nietzsche*, translated and edited by Walter Kaufmann. Modern Library, 2000.
Nietzsche, Friedrich. "On Truth and Lying in a Non-Moral Sense." Translated by Ronald Speirs. In Leitch, *Norton Anthology of Theory and Criticism*. Norton, 2001.
Noddings, Nel. *Caring: A Relational Approach to Ethics and Moral Education*. 2nd ed. University of California Press, 2013. ProQuest Ebook Central.
Noë, Alva. *Action in Perception*. MIT Press, 2004.
Novalis. "Die Lehrlinge zu Sais." In *Monolog, Die Lehrlinge zu Sais, Die Christenheit oder Europa, Hymnen an die Nacht, Geistliche Lieder, Heinrich von Ofterdingen*, edited by Ernesto Grassi and Walter Hess. Rowohlt, 1963.
Oberlin, Johann Friedrich. "Mr. L . . ." In Sieburth, *Lenz*.
Ortega y Gasset, José. "An Essay in Esthetics by Way of a Preface." In *Phenomenology and Art*, translated by Philip W. Silver. Norton, 1975.
Panero, Maria Eugenia, Deena Skolnick Weisberg, Jessica Black, Thalia R. Goldstein, Jennifer L. Barnes, Hiram Brownell, and Ellen Winner. "No Support for the Claim That Literary Fiction Uniquely and Immediately Improves Theory of Mind: A Reply to Kidd and Castano's Commentary on Panero et al. (2016)." *Journal of Personal and Social Psychology* 112, no. 3 (March 2017): e5–e8. https://doi.org/10.1037/pspa0000079.
Pearce, J. M. S. "The Law of Specific Nerve Energies and Sensory Spots." *European Neurology* 54, no. 2 (2005): 115–17. https://doi.org/10.1159/000088647.
Petraschka, Thomas. *Einfühlung: Theorie und Kulturgeschichte einer ästhetischen Denkfigur 1770–1933*. Brill mentis, 2023.
Petraschka, Thomas. "'Theirs Is the Future Way of Studying Aesthetics': Vernon Lee and the German Aesthetics of Empathy." In Petraschka and Werner, *Empathy's Role*.
Petraschka, Thomas, and Christiana Werner, eds. *Empathy's Role in Understanding Persons, Literature, and Art*. Routledge, 2023. https://doi.org/10.4324/9781003333739.
Pijarski, Krzysztof. "'Realism,' Embodied Subjects, Projection of Empathy." *Visual Literacy*. Special issue, *Teksty Drugie*, edited by Katarzyna Bojarska, no. 2 (2015): 147–67. https://doi.org/10.18318/td.2015.en.2.10.
Pörnbacher, Karl, Gerhard Schaub, Hans-Joachim Simm, and Edda Ziegler, eds. Kommentar to *Werke und Briefe*, by Georg Büchner, Münchner Ausgabe. DTV/Carl Hanser, 1988.

Prater, Donald. *A Ringing Glass: The Life of Rainer Maria Rilke*. Oxford University Press/Clarendon Press, 1986.
Preisendanz, Wolfgang. "Die Erzählfunktion der Naturdarstellung bei Stifter." *Wirkendes Wort* no. 16 (1966): 407–18.
Prinz, Jesse. "Vernon Lee's Aesthetics: Empathy, Emotion, and Embodiment." In Petraschka and Werner, *Empathy's Role*.
Ragg-Kirkby, Helena. *Adalbert Stifter's Late Prose: The Mania for Moderation*. Camden House, 2000.
Rancière, Jacques. *Aisthesis: Scenes from the Aesthetic Regime of Art*. Translated by Zakir Paul. Verso, 2013.
Reddick, John. *Georg Büchner: The Shattered Whole*. Clarendon Press, 1994.
Reddick, John. "Mystification, Perspectivism and Symbolism in *Der Hochwald*." In *Adalbert Stifter Heute: Londoner Symposium 1983*, edited by Johann Lachinger, Alexander Stillmark, and Martin Swales. Adalbert Stifter-Institut des Landes Oberösterreich, 1985.
Reuchlein, Georg. "'... als jage der Wahnsinn auf Rossen hinter ihm': Zur Geschichtlichkeit von Georg Büchners Modernität: Eine Archäologie der Darstellung seelischen Leidens im *Lenz*." *Jahrbuch für internationale Germanistik* 28, no. 1 (1996): 59–111.
Rich, Adrienne. "Compulsory Heterosexuality and Lesbian Existence." In Leitch, *Norton Anthology of Theory and Criticism*, 3rd ed. Norton, 2018.
Richards, Page. *Distancing English: A Chapter in the History of the Inexpressible*. Ohio State University Press, 2009.
Rilke, Rainer Maria. "Der Ball." In *Sämtliche Werke* [Complete Works], vol. 1.
Rilke, Rainer Maria. "Erlebnis." In *Sämtliche Werke*, vol. 6.
Rilke, Rainer Maria. *Fünfte Duineser Elegie*. In *Sämtliche Werke*, vol. 1.
Rilke, Rainer Maria. "Die Gazelle." In *Sämtliche Werke*, vol. 1.
Rilke, Rainer Maria. *Gedichtkreis für Madeleine Broglie*. In *Sämtliche Werke*, vol. 2.
Rilke, Rainer Maria. "Hetären-Gräber." In *Sämtliche Werke*, vol. 1.
Rilke, Rainer Maria. "Der Hund." In *Sämtliche Werke*, vol. 1.
Rilke, Rainer Maria. *Neunte Duineser Elegie*. In *Sämtliche Werke*, vol. 1.
Rilke, Rainer Maria. *The Ninth Elegy*. Translated by Stephen Mitchell. In *The Selected Poetry of Rainer Maria Rilke*, edited and translated by Stephen Mitchell. Vintage, 1989.
Rilke, Rainer Maria. *The Notebooks of Malte Laurids Brigge*. Translated by Burton Pike. Dalkey Archive, 2008.
Rilke, Rainer Maria. "Offener Brief an Maximilian Harden." In *Sämtliche Werke*, vol. 5.
Rilke, Rainer Maria. "Der Panther." In *Sämtliche Werke*, vol. 1.
Rilke, Rainer Maria. "Rose, oh reiner Widerspruch, Lust." In *Sämtliche Werke*, vol. 2.
Rilke, Rainer Maria. *Sämtliche Werke*. 6 vols. Edited by Ernst Zinn. Insel, 1955–1966.
Rilke, Rainer Maria. "Über den Dichter." In *Sämtliche Werke*, vol. 6.

Rilke, Rainer Maria. "Über Kunst I—<III>." In *Sämtliche Werke*, vol. 5.
Roh, Franz. *Nach-Expressionismus, Magischer Realismus: Probleme der neuesten europäischen Malerei*. Klinkhardt und Biermann, 1925. HathiTrust.
Roth, Udo. *Georg Büchners naturwissenschaftliche Schriften: Ein Beitrag zur Geschichte der Wissenschaften vom Lebendigen in der ersten Hälfte des 19. Jahrhunderts*. Niemeyer, 2004.
Ryan, Judith. "Dead Poets' Voices: Rilke's 'Lost from the Outset' and the Originality Effect." *Modern Language Quarterly* 53, no. 2 (1992): 227–45.
Ryan, Judith. "Rilke's Early Narratives." In *A Companion to the Works of Rainer Maria Rilke*, edited by Erika A. Metzger and Michael M. Metzger. Camden House, 2001.
Ryan, Judith. *Rilke, Modernism and Poetic Tradition*. Cambridge University Press, 1999.
Saussure, Ferdinand de. *Course in General Linguistics*. In Leitch, *Norton Anthology of Theory and Criticism*, 3rd ed. Norton, 2018.
Savoyen, Carel van. *Supper at Emmaus* [*Christ and the Disciples at Emmaus*]. 1640–1665. Wikimedia Commons. https://commons.wikimedia.org/wiki/File:Carel_van_Savoyen_-_Supper_at_Emmaus.jpg.
Schaub, Gerhard. Anmerkungen for *Lenz*, by Georg Büchner. In Georg Büchner, *Werke und Briefe*, Münchner Ausgabe, edited by Karl Pörnbacher, Gerhard Schaub, Hans-Joachim Simm, and Edda Ziegler. DTV/Carl Hanser, 1988.
Schiffermüller, Isolde. "Kunst und Wahnsinn in Adalbert Stifters 'Turmalin': Zur figurativen Praxis der Erzählung." *Quaderni di Lingue e Letterature* 19 (1994): 217–29.
Schiller, Friedrich. "On the Sublime (Toward the Further Development of Some Kantian Ideas)." Translated by Daniel Dahlstrom. In *The Sublime Reader*, edited by Robert R. Clewis. Bloomsbury Academic, 2019.
Schings, Hans-Jürgen. *Der mitleidigste Mensch ist der beste Mensch: Poetik des Mitleids von Lessing bis Büchner*. C. H. Beck, 1980.
Schnädelbach, Herbert. *Philosophy in Germany 1831–1933*. Translated by Eric Matthews. Cambridge University Press, 1984.
Schor, Naomi. "Reading in Detail: Hegel's *Aesthetics* and the Feminine." In *Feminist Interpretations of G. W. F. Hegel*, edited by Patricia Jagentowicz Mills. Pennsylvania State University Press, 1996.
Sebald. W. G. *Die Beschreibung des Unglücks: Zur österreichischen Literatur von Stifter bis Handke*. Residenz Verlag, 1985. Internet Archive.
Seigworth, Gregory J., and Melissa Gregg. "An Inventory of Shimmers." In *The Affect Theory Reader*, edited by Melissa Gregg and Gregory J. Seigworth. Duke University Press, 2010. https://doi.org/10.1215/9780822393047.
Selge, Martin. *Adalbert Stifter: Poesie aus dem Geist der Naturwissenschaft*. Kohlhammer, 1976.
Shaftesbury [Anthony Ashley Cooper]. "Soliloquy: or, Advice to an Author." 1711. In *Characteristics of Men, Manners, Opinions, Times*. edited by Lawrence E. Klein. Cambridge University Press, 1999.
Shaviro, Steven. *Post-Cinematic Affect*. O-Books, 2010.

Shaviro, Steven. *The Universe of Things: On Speculative Realism*. University of Minnesota Press, 2014.
Shell, Marc. *Money, Language, and Thought: Literary and Philosophic Economies from the Medieval to the Modern Era*. University of California Press, 1982.
Siderits, Mark, and Shōryū Katsura. *Nāgārjuna's Middle Way: Mūlamadhyamakakārikā*. Wisdom, 2013.
Sieburth, Richard, trans. *Lenz*. By Georg Büchner. Archipelago, 2004.
Sieburth, Richard. Notes to Sieburth, *Lenz*.
Sieburth, Richard. Translator's afterword to Sieburth, *Lenz*.
Sloterdijk, Peter. *You Must Change Your Life: On Anthropotechnics*. Translated by Wieland Hoban. Polity, 2013.
Smith, Matthew Wilson. "Georg Büchner, J. M. W. Turner, and the Materiality of Perception." In *Georg Büchner: Contemporary Perspectives*, edited by Robert Gillett, Ernest Schonfield, and Daniel Steuer. Brill/Rodopi, 2017. ProQuest Ebook Central.
Spinoza, Benedict de. *The* Ethics. In *A Spinoza Reader: The* Ethics *and Other Works*, edited and translated by Edwin Curley. Princeton University Press, 1994.
Staiger, Emil, Martin Heidegger, and Leo Spitzer. "A 1951 Dialogue on Interpretation: Emil Staiger, Martin Heidegger, Leo Spitzer." Translated by Berel Lang and Christine Ebel. *PMLA* 105, no. 3 (1990): 409–35. ProQuest.
Stephens, Anthony. "Cutting Poets to Size: Heidegger, Hölderlin, Rilke." *Jacket*, no. 32 (April 2007): http://jacketmagazine.com/32/stephens-heidegger.shtml.
Stifter, Adalbert. *Abdias*. In *Studien*. Artemis and Winkler, 1950.
Stifter, Adalbert. *Der Hochwald*. Reclam, 1995.
Stifter, Adalbert. *Tourmaline or The Doorkeeper*. In *Limestone and Other Stories*, translated by David Luke. Harcourt, Brace, and World, 1968.
Stifter, Adalbert. *Turmalin*. In *Bunte Steine: Journalfassungen*, edited by Helmut Bergner. Vol. 2.1 of *Adalbert Stifter Werke und Briefe: Historisch-kritische Gesamtausgabe*, edited by Alfred Doppler and Wolfgang Frühwald. Kohlhammer, 1982.
Stifter, Adalbert. *Turmalin*. In *Bunte Steine: Erzählungen*, edited by Helmut Bachmaier. Reclam, 1994.
Stifter, Adalbert. Vorrede to *Bunte Steine: Erzählungen*, edited by Helmut Bachmaier. Reclam, 1994.
Strowick, Elisabeth. "Poetological-Technical Operations: Representation of Motion in Adalbert Stifter." Translated by Amy Klement. *Configurations* 18, no. 3 (2010): 273–89. PDF. https://dx.doi.org/10.1353/con.2010.0019.
Stueber, Karsten. "Empathy." In *The Stanford Encyclopedia of Philosophy*, edited by Edward N. Zalta. Fall 2019. https://plato.stanford.edu/archives/fall2019/entries/empathy/.
Swales, Martin, and Erika Swales. *Adalbert Stifter: A Critical Study*. Cambridge University Press, 1984.
Tatarkiewicz, Władysław. *A History of Six Ideas: An Essay in Aesthetics*. Translated in part by Christopher Kasparek. Martinus Nijhoff/Polish Scientific Publishers, 1980.

Tieck, Ludwig. *Der Blonde Eckbert—Der Runenberg—Die Elfen: Märchen*. Reclam, 1952.
Titanic. Directed by James Cameron. Paramount Pictures / Twentieth Century Fox / Lightstorm Entertainment, 1997.
Titchener, Edward Bradford. *Lectures on the Experimental Psychology of the Thought-Processes*. MacMillan, 1909.
Tobias, Rochelle. "Rilke, Phenomenology, and the Sensuality of Thought." *Konturen* 8 (2015): 40–61, https://doi.org/10.5399/uo/konturen.8.0.3700.
Torgersen, Eric. *Dear Friend: Rainer Maria Rilke and Paula Modersohn-Becker*. Northwestern University Press, 1998.
Turing, A. M. "Computing Machinery and Intelligence." *Mind: New Series* 59, no. 236 (1950): 433–60. http://www.jstor.org/stable/2251299.
Varela, Francisco J., Evan Thompson, and Eleanor Rosch. *The Embodied Mind: Cognitive Science and Human Experience*. Revised edition. MIT Press, 2016.
Viëtor, Karl. *Georg Büchner: Politik, Dichtung, Wissenschaft*. Francke, 1949.
Vischer, Robert. *On the Optical Sense of Form: A Contribution to Aesthetics*. Translated by Harry Francis Mallgrave and Eleftherios Ikonomou. In *Empathy, Form, and Space: Problems in German Aesthetics, 1873–1893*, edited by Harry Francis Mallgrave and Eleftherios Ikonomou, Getty Center for the History of Art and the Humanities, 1994.
Vischer, Robert. *Ueber das optische Formgefühl: Ein Beitrag zur Aesthetik*. Hermann Credner, 1873.
Voltaire [François-Marie Arouet]. "An Essay on Taste." In *An Essay on Taste by Alexander Gerard, M.A., with Three Dissertations on the Same Subject. . . .*, edited by Alexander Gerard. A. Millar, 1759. Internet Archive.
Voss, Christiane. "Einfühlung als epistemische und ästhetische Kategorie bei Hume und Lipps." In Curtis and Koch, *Einfühlung*.
"WAHNSINN, m." *Deutsches Wörterbuch*. By Jacob Grimm and Wilhelm Grimm. Digital edition, version 01/23, Wörterbuchnetz of the Trier Center for Digital Humanities, https://www.woerterbuchnetz.de/DWB?lemid=W02565.
Waite, Geoffrey C. W. "Worringer's *Abstraction and Empathy*: Remarks on Its Reception and on the Rhetoric of Its Criticism." In Neil H. Donahue, *Invisible Cathedrals*.
Walker, John. "'Ach die Kunst! . . . Ach, die erbärmliche Wirklichkeit!': Suffering, Empathy, and the Relevance of Realism in Büchner's *Lenz*." *Forum for Modern Language Studies* 33, no. 2 (1997): 156–70.
Walker, John. "Two Realisms: German Literature and Philosophy 1830–1890." In *Philosophy and German Literature 1700–1990*, edited by Nicholas Saul. Cambridge University Press, 2002.
Ward, Janet. *Weimar Surfaces: Urban Visual Culture in 1920s Germany*. University of California Press, 2001.
Ward, Mark G. "Self-reflexive Discourse: An Aspect of German Realist Writing." In *Perspectives on German Realist Writing: Eight Essays*, edited by Mark G. Ward. Edwin Mellen Press, 1995.

Weber, Heinz-Dieter. Materialien for *Lenz und Oberlins Aufzeichnungen in Gegenüberstellung, mit Materialien*, by Georg Büchner and Johann Friedrich Oberlin, edited by Heinz-Dieter Weber. Klett Schulbuch, 1980.
Weber, Max. "Science as a Vocation." In *From Max Weber: Essays in Sociology*, edited and translated by H. H. Gerth and C. Wright Mills. Oxford University Press, 1946.
Weitzman, Erica. "Despite Language: Adalbert Stifter's Revenge Fantasies." *Monatshefte* 111, no. 3 (2019): 362–79. https://muse.jhu.edu/article/735555.
Wilke, Tobias. "Einfühlung als Metapher." *Deutsche Vierteljahrsschrift für Literaturwissenschaft und Geistesgeschichte* 88, no. 3 (2014): 321–44.
Wirsel, S. W. *Wörterbuch zur Fortbildung in der Sprache für diejenigen Taubstummen, welche bereits ihre Ausbildung erlangt haben*. H. Lange, 1854. https://books.google.com/books?id.
Wittgenstein, Ludwig. *Philosophical Investigations*. Translated by G. E. M. Anscombe. Blackwell, 2001.
Worringer, Wilhelm. *Abstraction and Empathy: A Contribution to the Psychology of Style*. Translated by Michael Bullock. Martino Publishing, 2014.
Wübben, Yvonne. *Büchners "Lenz": Geschichte eines Falls*. Konstanz University Press, 2016.
Yeats, William Butler. "Byzantium." Poetry Foundation, https://www.poetryfoundation.org/poems/43296/byzantium.
Young, Robert J. C. *Colonial Desire: Hybridity in Theory, Culture and Race*. Routledge, 1995.
Zinn, Ernst. Anmerkungen des Herausgebers for *Sämtliche Werke*, by Rainer Maria Rilke, vol. 6. Insel, 1955.

Index

Abram, David, 276
abstraction, 22–23, 224
Abstraktion als Einfühlung (*Abstraction as Empathy*) (Müller-Tamm), 48–50
Abstraktion und Einfühlung (Worringer), 22–23, 224, 268
acrobat, 255–56, 265
Adorno, Theodor W., 172
advertising, 289–90, 292–93
aesthetic empathy: decline of, 21–24; *Einfühlung* and pathways and possibilities for, 36, 37–38; as feeling of form, 29–30; as ghost story, 75–84; importance of bodily motion to, 186–87; and interpersonal empathy in *Lenz*, 101–2, 106; intersubjective empathy and, 136, 141; Lee on, 182–83; Lipps on, 17n14, 97–98, 287; Maskarinec on, 10; phases in history of theory, 79; Rilke's proximity to Lipps's understanding of, 223; Stifter as anticipating problems and implications of, 215–16; and theory of mind, 150; and uncanny, 80, 92, 96; Vischer on, 53–54, 55, 66–68, 74–75. See also *Einfühlung*; *Einfühlungstheorie*
aesthetic imitation, 97–98, 296
aesthetics: Breithaupt on interpersonal empathy and, 47; as coming together of feeling and form, 29; defined, 2–3; and empathy in Kotler's *Last Tango in Cyberspace*, 4; in German experimental science, 20; marriage of science and, 18–19; and object-oriented ontology (OOO), 293–94; physiological / psychological, 15–16, 70–75, 81; potential proximity of

aesthetics (*continued*)
pathological to, 80–81; trajectory of, 65; in *Über das optische Formgefühl*, 65; Vischer's "physiologization" of, 67. *See also* aesthetic empathy; aesthetic imitation; *Einfühlungstheorie*
affect: as form of relation, 192; intersection of intensity and, in *Der Hochwald*, 167–74; Massumi on emotion and, 214; and paradoxes of *Einfühlung*, 6; and problem of feeling, 30–31; relocation of human, in things, 60; Wundt on, 30
affect engine, 175–82
affective sounds, 254, 256, 258
affectus, 93, 204, 266
affordances, 28, 29, 171
Agosta, Lou, 21n22
ahnungsvoll, 77
aísthesis, 2, 24, 258, 265
alienation, in "Erlebnis," 265, 268
Altieri, Charles, 30, 93
altruism, 43
analogy, 222
Anstruther-Thomson, Clementina, 5, 26, 187, 189, 191, 201
applied psychology, 290
Aristotle, 176, 222
Arneth, Antonie von, 132n4
art: advertising as, 289; Benjamin on epochs and new forms of, 185–86; death of nature and rise of, 82–83; and Lee's studies on sensory physiology, 187–90; Lenz's theory of, in *Lenz*, 90–91; realist, 158; relation of *Lenz*'s uncanny rhetoric of resurrection to, 108–15; scanning and, 67; Vischer on life and, 65–66. *See also Kunstgespräch*
artificial intelligence, 11, 35, 38, 44–45, 126, 136, 147, 162, 215
Auerbach, Eric, 128
"Auf eine Lampe" ("To a Lamp") (Mörike), 121–23
Augenblick, 245

Babbage, Charles, 148
bad metaphor(s): in Broglie cycle, 236–51; in "Erlebnis," 265; as good, 284; in Harden letter, 228–36; and "Der Hund," 278–84; of Lipps, 253–54; and object-oriented ontology (OOO), 270–76; of Rilke, 218–19, 221–22, 225–27, 288. *See also* catachresis
Barthes, Roland, 152
Baudelaire, Charles, 158
Baumgarten, Alexander, 2–3, 4, 20, 65, 150
Baumgartner, Andreas von, 193
Bayertz, Kurt, 55n1
beautiful, the, 196–97
Beauty and Ugliness (Lee and Anstruther-Thomson), 5, 26, 189–90, 191, 201
Begemann, Christian, 200n40
Benjamin, Walter, 11, 141, 159, 160, 185–86, 292
Bennett, Jane, 284n38
Bernstein, J. M., 82
body: aesthetic empathy and movement of, 186–87; alternating stases and flows, 174; Groos on discernment of form and, 188–89; Lee on bodily basis for empathy, 276n29; and Lee's studies on sensory physiology, 187–92; maternal, 206–7, 213; Stifter on, as site of resistance, 287–88
body-object isomorphism, 59–60
Bogost, Ian, 269, 275, 278, 281, 284n38
Bohm, David, 9. *See also* implicate order (Bohm)
Bollmer, Grant, 78, 145, 150, 153–54
Bowie, Andrew, 25
Brain, Robert Michael, 15–16, 23, 44
Bratranek, F. T., 127–28, 168
Braungart, Georg, 17n15, 47n34, 136–37
Brazier, Mary A. B., 70, 72n13, 73
Brecht, Bertolt, 23, 143, 289

Breithaupt, Fritz: on empathic sadism, 170–71, 175–76, 177, 178; on empathy and media, 141; empathy triggers, 179; on interpersonal empathy, 12–13; on necromantic empathy, 53; scholarship in literary empathy studies, 45–47; on theater and empathy, 136; on vampiric empathy, 140
Brinkema, Eugenie, 32–33, 192
Brodersen, Silke, 127–28
Brücke, Ernst, 73
Büchner, Georg: cites Müller's *Handbuch*, 72; connections between Vischer and, 8–9, 56–57; and dialectical image, 11; as empathizing interpersonally with Lenz, 42; as exemplar of intersubjective empathy, 100–101; failed resurrection in *Lenz*, 54; historical positioning of, 87; *Mémoire sur le Système nerveux du Barbeau*, 104–6; and pre- or para-history of *Einfühlung*, 287; similarities between Stifter and, 126–27; and transition from vitalism and *Naturphilosophie* to scientific materialism, 55; "Über Schädelnerven" ("On Cranial Nerves"), 87–88, 96. See also *Lenz* (Büchner)
Büchner, Ludwig, 87
Bunte Steine (Many-Colored Stones) (Stifter), 128
Burke, Edmund, 17, 176, 196–97

Das Cabinet des Dr. Caligari (The Cabinet of Dr. Caligari) (Wiene), 291–92
Campbell, Karen J., 131, 143
cannibalism metaphor, in Harden letter, 231–33, 234–35
Carritt, E. F., 15
Cassirer, Ernst, 83n20
Castano, Emanuele, 43
catachresis: destruction of, in Broglie cycle, 248; as forced empathy, 227; and "Der Hund," 284; linked with imposed empathy in Broglie cycle, 241; logical form of metaphor as, 285; metaphors as, 281; as revenant of unsayable in Broglie cycle, 238; Rilke and linking of empathy with, 216; and two senses of Rilke's bad metaphors, 225, 277–78. See also bad metaphor(s)
celebrity hall, in *Turmalin*, 140–41, 158–59
Cézanne, Paul, 39, 252
Chalmers, David, 27
chora, 205–7, 210, 211, 214–15
Christ and the Disciples at Emmaus (Savoy), 90, 109–12
cinema, 290–92
circulation, image of, in Broglie cycle, 248–50
citations, unattributed, in *Lenz*, 102–3
Coen, Deborah R., 127
coerced-coercive metaphor, 226–27
coercion: nexus of metaphor and, 226; in Rilke's poetic project, 225–26; and Rilke's reliance on the metaphoric field of cannibalism, 234–35
Cohen, Ted, 226–27, 276
coins, as metaphors, 238, 249–51
colliding forms (Levine), 29, 33, 163–67
colonial desire, 259
Condillac, Étienne Bonnot de, 21n20
convention, 251
Copernican Revolution, 19
correlationism, 270–71, 272, 275
Crary, Jonathan: Dubois-Reymond's pursuit of cross-connecting nerves, 99–100; on Goethe's *Farbenlehre*, 18; on law of differential sensitivity, 169; on Müller's *Handbuch*, 72, 73–74; on "new sign" of nineteenth-century industrialization, 157; and nineteenth-century ambiguity surrounding sight, 201; on photography, 157, 159–60; on Schopenhauer, 20; on senses as subject to manipulation and derangement, 96–97; on subjectivizing of vision, 19; on technology, 286

cruelty, of *Der Hochwald*'s narrative, 175–82

Dark Sides of Empathy, The (Breithaupt), 46–47
death: and *Einfühlung* as projection, transfusion, and transplantation, 69; Otherness of, 78; uncanny links among *Einfühlung*, reanimation, and, in *Über das optische Formgefühl*, 56; and Vischer's artistic models, 66–67. See also resurrection
Debes, Remy, 13, 15
Deleuze, Gilles, 31
de Man, Paul, 225–26, 244
demonic: Lenz's excesses of proto-*Einfühlung* as inseparable from images of, 96–97. See also possession; Satan
Descartes, René, 72
dialectical image, 11–12
Diderot, Denis, 142
difference, empathy and erasure of, in *Turmalin*, 152–57
differential sensitivity, law of, 169
divided loyalties, in *Der Hochwald*, 163–67
Döhner, Otto, 89
doppelgänger, 53, 76, 211
Downing, Eric, 167, 194
Du Bois-Reymond, Emil Heinrich, 73, 99–100

Einfühlung: afterlife of, 289–96; ambiguity in term, 5; coining of term, 2; defined, 58; and distinguishing between borders of self and other, 5–6; versus empathy, 3; exploration of untreated stakes of, 9–10; as feeling of form, 60; form in, 5; in historical context, 49; history of, 12–24; implicate order existing before, during, and after appearance of term, 9; as inseparable from artistic or aesthetic perception, 62; and nearness to pathology, 80–81; neurophysiology and understanding of, 4–5; pre- or para-history of, 286–88; as product and catalyst of and reaction against neurophysiological-materialist modernity, 55–56; as projection, transfusion, and transplantation, 68–69; and psychological aesthetics, 4–5, 15–16, 20, 23, 30, 55–56, 70, 80–81, 94; as resistance to modernity, 160; as resurrection or reanimation, 52–54; retranslation of term, 14; rise of, 16–17; scholarship on German literature and, 45–49; uncanniness of, 56, 57, 58–59, 67–69, 75–84, 121–24. See also aesthetic empathy; *Einfühlungstheorie*; empathy
Einfühlung (Empathy) (Petraschka), 47n34
Einfühlungsästhetik, 223
Einfühlungstheorie: anxieties beneath birth of, 10; compensation provided by Vischer's, 10; decline of, 23–24; interpretation of Stifter through lens of, 11; in Kotler's *Last Tango in Cyberspace*, 4; and linkages of feeling and form, 7–8; Müller-Tamm on, 15; and necromantic empathy, 55; Rilke's writing as seeming apotheosis of, 223–24; role of nervous system in physiologization of aesthetics, 70. See also aesthetic empathy
electrical ads, 289–90, 292
Eliot, George, 129
emotion, 168, 214
empathic sadism (Breithaupt), 170–71, 175–78
empathy: abstraction and, 22–23; and ambiguity in term *Einfühlung*, 5; as carrying ethical stakes, 12–13; defining, 13–14; and distinguishing between borders of self and other, 5–6; early theory and meanings of, 2–3; versus *Einfühlung*, 3; literary-critical empathy studies, 43, 45–49; and metaphor, 276–77, 285; phases

in history of theory, 79; vampiric, 140. *See also* aesthetic empathy; interpersonal empathy; intersubjective empathy; narrative empathy; necromantic empathy
Empathy and the Psychology of Literary Modernism (Hammond), 45
empathy effects, 151
empathy engine, 180
empathy machine, 144–52, 154, 157–61
enactivism, 26–27
entoptic phenomena, 80–81
Epic theatre, 143
"Erlebnis" ("Experience") (Rilke), 262–69
Esquirol, Jean-Étienne, 95
"Essay in Esthetics by Way of a Preface, An" (Ortega y Gasset), 295
eye imagery / eye motif: in Broglie cycle, 221–22, 225, 226, 239–41, 245–48; in *Der Hochwald*, 182–83. *See also* sight; vision

Farbenlehre (*Theory of Colors*) (Goethe), 18, 259
fascism, 293
Feagin, Susan L., 201
Fechner, Gustav, 20, 48, 81, 169
feeling: linkages of form and, 6, 7–8, 29–33; problem of, 30–31; use of term, 31
feminine: the beautiful as linked to, 196–97; and *Innigkeit* in *Der Hochwald*, 208–9, 210; narrator of *Der Hochwald* as exchanging bodies with, 211–15. *See also* gender
Fick, Monika, 47–48, 56, 72–73, 262, 264, 266n21
Fifth Roman Elegy (Goethe), 62
Fischer, Luke, 223–24, 262
Flaubert, Gustave, 129
Florence, and woman-as-city metaphor in Broglie cycle, 241–42, 243, 244
Forces of Form in German Modernism, The (Maskarinec), 45
"Formgefühl," 29–30

form(s): colliding (Levine), 29, 33, 163–67; in *Einfühlung*, 5; empathy-inspiring, 7; linkages of feeling and, 6, 7–8, 29–33; as pivotal to foundational empathy theory, 5; and political power, 28–29; problem of, 24–28; understandings / definition of, 24–25, 28; Vischer on emotional content and, 143–44; Vischer on feeling, 60–61
forms of resistance, 130, 294
Fortmann, Patrick, 100
Freud, Sigmund, 21n22, 77, 99

Gallese, Vittorio, 16, 21n22
Gedichtkreis für Madeleine Broglie (*Poem Cycle for Madeleine Broglie*) (Rilke), 221–22, 223, 226, 236–51, 278
gender: and empathy and erasure of difference in *Turmalin*, 154–55; and *Der Hochwald*, 172–74; and *Innigkeit* in *Der Hochwald*, 208–9, 210; scrambling of, in Broglie cycle, 250–51; and semiotic chora, 206–7; and vast and minute and sublime and beautiful in *Der Hochwald*, 193–200. *See also* feminine; masculine
gender essentialism, 173, 207
Genshin Impact, 186, 292n3
German Expressionism, 23
German literature, scholarship on *Einfühlung* and, 45–49
German realism, 107, 128–29
German Romanticism, 18
Geulen, Eva, 134–35, 137, 141
ghost story: *Einfühlung* as, 10, 56, 75–84; "Erlebnis" as, 267, 268; *Lenz* as, 37, 56; *Turmalin* as, 146
Goethe, Johann Wolfgang von, 18, 19, 62, 67, 77, 84, 85n24
Grand Canal, and eye imagery in Broglie cycle, 221–22, 225, 226, 239–41, 245–48
Gregg, Melissa, 6, 168, 192
Grillparzer, Franz, 156

Groos, Karl, 26, 27, 31–32, 98, 177, 188–89, 192
Grundlegung der Ästhetik (*Foundations of Aesthetics*) (Lipps), 252–53, 254, 256
Guattari, Félix, 31
Guillemin, Anna, 109, 110
Gutzkow, Karl, 89, 128
Guyer, Paul, 14–15, 42, 60, 64, 95, 190

Haller, Albrecht von, 21n20
hallucinations, 95
Hammermeister, Kai, 2
Hammond, Meghan Marie, 13, 45, 150, 218
Handbuch der Physiologie des Menschen (*Elements of Physiology*) (Müller), 71–72, 73–74
Harden, Maximilian, Rilke's letter to, 220, 221, 226, 228–36
Harman, Graham, 269, 270, 271, 272, 274, 293, 294, 295
Heath, Malcolm, 178
Hebbel, Friedrich, 198
Hegel, Georg Wilhelm Friedrich, 82, 83, 109, 157
Heidegger, Martin, 271
Helmholtz, Hermann von, 20, 73
Herbart, Johann Friedrich, 21n20, 143, 162
Herder, Johann Gottfried, 17
Der Hochwald (*The Mountain Forest*) (Stifter): affective excess and cruelty of narrative of, 175–82; and affect theory, 167–69, 172; as anticipating problems and implications of aesthetic empathy, 215–16; constraint versus escape in, 171–72, 174, 209–11; divided loyalties and colliding forms in, 163–67; eye imagery in, 182–83; forms of resistance in, 130–31; gendered economies of word and gaze in, 193–200; *Innigkeit* in, 169–70, 174, 207–11; intersection of intensity and affect and empathy and *Einfühlung* in, 167–74; and Lee's studies on sensory physiology, 190–92; link of human and textual body in, 191, 204–5; link of rhythm, punctuation, and syntax to intensity, affect, and body, 167, 172, 174, 201, 216; metamorphosis of Ronald in, 212–15; motion effects in, 184–87; narrator of, as exchanging bodies with feminine, 211–15; as patriarchal text, 193–94, 198–99; and semiotic chora, 200–211; sublime and beautiful and gendering in, 193–97
Höller, Hans, 129
Holub, Robert, 111
Horton, David, 102
Hume, David, 17
"Der Hund" ("The Dog"), 278–84
Husserl, Edmund, 261n17

Ikonomou, Eleftherios: on abstraction and empathy, 23; defines Vischer's "Formgefühl," 29; on Herbart's influence on experimental science, 21n20; on Kant and form, 26; on movements of wood in *Über das optische Formgefühl*, 118n47; on parallel development of Vischer's and Lotze's theories, 16; on scanning, 59, 62; and translation of *Einfühlung*, 14; on Vischer's neologisms for microsubtleties of affective response, 30
image: in "Der Hund," 280–84; and object-oriented ontology (OOO), 294
imitatio Christi, 90–91, 111, 112
imitation: inner / inside of, 177, 188–89, 192, 255–56, 260; Lipps on aesthetic, 97–98, 296; proposed, in *Lenz*, 109; Turing on mindedness and, 148. *See also* photography
immediate metaphoricity, 254–56
immensity, and sublime in *Der Hochwald*, 194–95
Imorde, Joseph, 259–60
implicate order (Bohm), 9, 10–11, 35, 41, 50, 125, 215, 286

imposed empathy, in Broglie cycle, 241, 248
industrialization, 157
inner / inside of imitation, 177, 188–89, 192, 255–56, 260
Innigkeit (intensity), 169–70, 174, 207–11, 287–88. *See also* intensity
intensity: in "Erlebnis," 266; intersection of affect and, in *Der Hochwald*, 167–74. See also *Innigkeit* (intensity)
interpersonal empathy: and aesthetic empathy in *Lenz*, 101–2, 106; Lipps's combination of *Einfühlung* and, 252–53, 287; Lipps's conceptualization of, 287; in literary-critical empathy studies, 43, 47
intersubjective empathy: aesthetic empathy and, 136, 141; Büchner as exemplar of, 100–101; and *Einfühlung*, 41–42, 43–44, 218; and theory of mind, 150
Irigaray, Luce, 214
Irmscher, Hans Dietrich, 144

James-Lange hypothesis, 189
Jameson, Fredric, 129
Jentsch, Ernst, 59, 77, 78
Jesus Christ, Lenz's identification with, 90–91
Jirsa, Tomáš, 31

Kafka, Franz, 142
Kant, Immanuel: on the beautiful, 197n36; correlationism, 270–71, 272, 275; and Müller's formulation of law of specific nerve energies, 71; and object-oriented ontology (OOO), 270, 275–76; and physiological idealism, 20; and problem of form, 25–26; and rise of *Einfühlung*, 17–18, 19; sublime, 193, 194–96
Keen, Suzanne, 17n14, 43
Kidd, David Comer, 43
Kofman, Sarah, 78, 109, 116, 157, 161, 162
Kotler, Steven, 1–2, 3–5, 6

Kracauer, Siegfried, 290
Krell, David Farrell, 170, 209
Kristeva, Julia, 172, 174, 205–7
Kulturen der Empathie (Cultures of Empathy) (Breithaupt), 45–46
Kunstgespräch, in *Lenz*, 86–87, 108–15
Kurz, Gerhard, 274, 276, 277

Lacan, Jacques, 76
Lange, Joseph, 132n4, 158
Langer, Susanne K., 30
language: Lee and form body of, 188; Lee on movement of, 191n30, 203; relevance of metaphor to considerations of, 274–75
Lanzoni, Susan, 4, 13, 15, 50–51, 136, 186–87, 288
Last Tango in Cyberspace (Kotler), 1–2, 3–5, 6
law of differential sensitivity, 169
law of specific nerve energies, 49, 71, 80, 88, 96, 200–201
Lee, Vernon: on affect and form, 31–32; on bodily basis for empathy, 276n29; and bodily processes in form, 26, 201; empathy theory of, 171; *Der Hochwald* and theory of *Einfühlung* of, 183–84; Lipps and, 189–90; on movement of language and body, 203; reading Stifter's style in light of, 11; and rhythm and pattern of form in *Der Hochwald*, 212; studies on sensory physiology, 187–92; on subjective pattern of feelings and objective pattern of form, 5; on *Things*, 272–73; Vischer and, 9
"Die Lehrlinge zu Sais" (Novalis), 18
Leibhafter Sinn (Incarnate Sense) (Braungart), 47n34
Leighton, Angela, 24–25, 79
Lenz (Büchner): Büchner as empathizing interpersonally with, 42; and connections between Vischer and Büchner, 56–57; narrative voice and compositional strategy in, 100–108;

Lenz (Büchner) *(continued)*
  paradox of successful and unsuccessful resurrections in, 115–16; pathologies of empathy in, 90–100; as philosophical forerunner for uncanny resurrection scene in *Über das optische Formgefühl*, 116–21; rebirth, reanimation, and resurrection in, 54, 83–90, 108–15; relation of resurrection and *Kunstgespräch* in, 108–15
Lenz, J. M. R., 84–85, 100
Lessing, Gotthold Ephraim, 136–37
Levine, Caroline, 25, 28, 29, 167, 174
Lichtenberg, Georg Christoph, 21n20
Das Lichtspiel: Eine psychologische Studie (*The Photoplay: A Psychological Study*) (Münsterberg), 290–91
life: and relation of resurrection and *Kunstgespräch* in *Lenz*, 108–15; rise of art and fall of, 82–83; Vischer on art and, 65–66. *See also* nature
Lipps, Theodor: on aesthetic enjoyment of representations of others' misfortunes, 177; on aesthetic imitation, 296; on art's effects, 188; characterization of empathy as the inside of imitation, 255–56, 260; coerced and coercing metaphors in empathy theory of, 227; conceptualization of *Einfühlung* as complicating concept of metaphor, 254; conceptualization of interpersonal empathy, 287; on creating visual line, 182; and decline of aesthetic empathy, 21–22; on *Einfühlung*, 224; on empathy and theory of mind, 150; on form, 26; *Grundlegung der Ästhetik* (*Foundations of Aesthetics*), 252–53, 254, 256; as influence on growth of phenomenological thought, 22n23; Lee and, 189–90; and "mentalizing" of *Einfühlung*, 288; and merger of *Einfühlung* and intersubjective empathy, 218; and metaphoricity versus immediacy, 254–56; on motor mimicry, 97–98; on object of empathic experience, 32–33; on possession of empathized objects, 28; possible influence on Rilke, 252–62; Rilke as student of, 223, 252; on separation of self and object, 285; and simulation theory, 138; on surrendering to demands of aesthetic object, 290
literary-critical empathy studies, 43, 45–49
Lotze, Hermann, 16, 183n27, 192
Lovelace, Ada, 147–48
loyalties, divided, in *Der Hochwald*, 163–67
Luke, David, 170
Lyotard, Jean-François, 196

Madhyamaka, 123n51
madness, of Lenz, 84–86
Mallgrave, Harry Francis: on abstraction and empathy, 23; defines Vischer's "Formgefühl," 29; on Herbart's influence on experimental science, 21n20; on Kant and form, 26; on movements of wood in *Über das optische Formgefühl*, 118n47; on parallel development of Vischer's and Lotze's theories, 16; on scanning, 59, 62; and translation of *Einfühlung*, 14; on Vischer's neologisms for microsubtleties of affective response, 30
Malte Laurids Brigge (Rilke), 224–25
Margaroni, Maria, 207, 211
masculine: sublime as linked to, 193–96. *See also* gender
Maskarinec, Malika, 10, 23, 32–33, 45, 286
massiveness, and sublime in *Der Hochwald*, 194–95
Massumi, Brian, 6, 31, 33, 168–69, 172, 174, 212, 214
materialism, 72n13, 73, 79–80, 87
materialist unconscious, 57, 115–21
maternal body, 206–7, 213

Matravers, Derek, 13–14
Maurer, Kathrin, 157–58
Mayer, Mathias, 127
Mayer-Gross, Wilhelm, 56–57, 99, 106–7
Meillassoux, Quentin, 270
Mémoire sur le Système nerveux du Barbeau (Büchner), 104–6
Merchant, Carolyn, 10, 87
metametaphorism (Bogost), 278–80
metaphoricity, 238, 254–56, 284, 288
metaphorism (Bogost), 275, 280–84
metaphor(s): cannibalism, in Harden letter, 231–33, 234–35; as catachreses, 281; coerced-coercive, 226–27; coins as, 238, 249–51; and empathy, 276–77, 285; in "Erlebnis," 265, 267; Lipps's conceptualization of *Einfühlung* as complicating, 254; and object-oriented ontology (OOO), 274–76, 293–94; relevance to considerations of language and linguistic turn, 274–75; river scene in "Über den Dichter" as, 258–59; use of term, 222. *See also* bad metaphor(s)
Method acting, 138
miHoYo, 186, 292n3
mind, theory of, 150
mindedness, 148–50
minute, form of descriptions in *Der Hochwald* as, 197–200
mirror neurons, 13n10, 21n22
modernity: celebrity hall as space of, in *Turmalin*, 141; and photography, 157–58; rise of *Einfühlung* as resistance to, 160; Stifter's relationship to, 128
monism, 47–48
Morgan, Benjamin, 188
Morgan, David, 78, 79, 80
Mörike, Eduard, 121–23
Morton, Timothy, 270–71, 277, 287
motion / movement: Groos on discernment of form and, 188–89; in *Der Hochwald*, 184–87; importance of, to early *Einfühlungstheorie*, 4; and Lee's studies on sensory physiology, 187–92
motor mimicry, 97–98
Müller, Johannes, 19–20, 49, 71–74, 80, 81, 88, 95, 96, 200–201
Müller Nielaba, Daniel, 89
Müller-Sievers, Helmut, 88, 102–3, 104–6, 107, 112–13
Müller-Tamm, Jutta: on abstraction and empathy, 23; *Abstraktion als Einfühlung* (*Abstraction as Empathy*), 48–50; on aesthetics in German experimental science, 20; on conditions for appearance of *Einfühlung*, 16–17; on *Einfühlung*, 15; on Kant and contributors to prehistory of *Einfühlung*, 26; on Lipps, 190; on marriage of science and aesthetics, 18–19, 20; metaphor in understanding of projection, 227n4; on Müller's formulation of law of specific nerve energies, 71; on nature in Vischer's theory of aesthetic empathy, 74; on Nietzsche and Helmholtz, 21n21; on Nietzsche's "Über Wahrheit und Lüge im außermoralischen Sinne," 234n6; on physiological idealism, 20; on precursors to "physiological idealism" and projective *Einfühlung*, 21n20; on problem of form, 27; "thought-figure" of projection, 5
Munich Circle, 22n23
Münsterberg, Hugo, 290–91
muscular motion, 205, 258

Der Nachsommer (*Indian Summer*) (Stifter), 128
Nāgārjuna, 123n51
Nagel, Barbara N., 176n22, 198n39
Nagel, Thomas, 275
narrative empathy: in *Der Hochwald*, 175, 178, 182; in *Lenz*, 42, 101–2; in literary-critical empathy studies, 43; merger of actor and part as, 137

narrative voice: in *Der Hochwald*, 164, 165–66, 167, 211; in *Lenz*, 91–92, 100, 102; in *Turmalin*, 154–55
nature: described in macro- and micro-details in *Der Hochwald*, 194–95, 197–200; need for "real" in *Lenz*, 114; organic and inorganic, and resurrection scene in *Über das optische Formgefühl*, 117–19; rise of art and death of, 82–83; struggle between vitalist / *naturphilosophische* and materialist conceptions of, 87; in Vischer's theory of aesthetic empathy, 74. *See also* life
Naturphilosophie, 10, 55, 72, 73–74, 87, 88–89
Nazism, 293
necromantic empathy: in Büchner's *Lenz*, 54, 80; in Vischer's *Über das optische Formgefühl*, 52–54
nerves / nerve sensations: as emblem of vitalist-materialist conflict in German thought, 73; and rise of physiological or psychological aesthetics, 70–75; Vischer on, 61–62, 70. *See also* law of specific nerve energies
Neue Gedichte (Rilke), 223–24, 239, 278–84
Neuhuber, Christian, 95
neurophysiology, 4–5, 18–19, 37, 70, 72, 200–201
Nietzsche, Friedrich, 21, 119, 233–34, 238n11, 277
Ninth Duino Elegy (Rilke), 273
Noddings, Nel, 153, 154
Noë, Alva, 27
Novalis, 18, 89

Oberlin, Johann Friedrich, 85–86
object-oriented ontology (OOO), 270–76, 284, 285, 293–95; and *Einfühlung*, 272–73
object-sphere, speaking, 274
"Offener Brief an Maximilian Harden" (Rilke), 219–21, 223, 228–36
Oken, Lorenz, 88

order, implicate (Bohm), 9, 10–11, 35, 41, 50, 125, 215, 286
origin, locus, and vector of experience or self, problem of, 27–28, 63–65, 68, 93, 112, 121–24, 137, 182, 253, 261
Ortega y Gasset, José, 274, 295–96
Other: absorption by self, 68–69, 77–78; absorption of self by, 68–69, 75, 77–78; and bad metaphor, 277–78; death as, 78; replacement or possession of self by, 69, 75, 78–79; as self in "Erlebnis," 262–65; Stifter on problems of empathy with human, conceived of as object, 287
other minds, 148–51
Ott, Joseph, 219–21, 228–36
Ott, Pepi, 219–21, 228–36
Ott, Poldi, 232

Paget, Violet. *See* Lee, Vernon
pantheistic monism, 79, 80
"Der Panther" ("The Panther") (Rilke), 4n3, 219, 239
pathetically sublime, 176
pathological: pathologies of empathy in *Lenz*, 90–100; potential proximity of aesthetics to, 80–81
patriarchal sadism, 211
performance of mindedness, 148–50
Petraschka, Thomas, 47n34
phenomenology, 22n23, 261
photography, 66–67, 157–60
physiological idealism, 20
physiological perception and projection, 49
physiological / psychological aesthetics, 15–16, 70–75, 81
"physiologization" of aesthetics, 67
Pijarski, Krzysztof, 157, 158, 201
Plato, 214
pleasure: in surrendering to demands of aesthetic object, 290; in tragedy, 176–78
political power, form and, 28–29
possession: in *Lenz*, 96–97, 107–8; and Ortega's aesthetic-empathic

processes, 295–96; in resurrection scene in *Über das optische Formgefühl*, 119–21; in *Turmalin*, 140
Prinz, Jesse, 26
problematic of empathy, Harden letter as case of, 228–31
projection: Guyer on, 64; Lipps on, 218; metaphor in Müller-Tamm's understanding of, 227n4; Müller on, 49–50; and object-oriented ontology (OOO), 294; Vischer on, 64–65
Psychologie und Wirtschaftsleben (Psychology and Economic Life) (Münsterberg), 290
psychology, 15–16; applied, 290
psychonarration, 264–65
Psychotechnik, 290–91, 293
Purkinje, Jan Evangelista, 18, 19

quotation, as tropic strategy in Büchner, 105

Ragg-Kirby, Helena, 127, 129, 130
Rancière, Jacques, 255
realism, German, 128–29
realist art, 158
reality, and object-oriented ontology (OOO), 270, 271
reanimation. *See* resurrection
rebirth, 82–90. *See also* resurrection
receptivity, 262
Reddick, John, 88, 211n45, 212
resistance, forms of, 130
resurrection: *Einfühlung* / empathy as demonic, in *Über das optische Formgefühl* and *Lenz*, 52–54, 55, 57, 96, 98, 108, 116–17, 119–21; in *Lenz*, 83–90, 99, 103, 108–15; *Lenz* as philosophical forerunner for uncanny, in *Über das optische Formgefühl*, 116–21; paradox of successful and unsuccessful, in *Lenz*, 115–16; return of Romanticism as, 79–80; uncanny links among death, *Einfühlung*, and, in *Über das optische Formgefühl*, 56

return, thematic and generic staging of, in Broglie cycle, 248–50
Rich, Adrienne, 210
Richards, Page, 238n10
Riefenstahl, Leni, 293
Rilke, Rainer Maria: bad metaphors in, 218–19, 221–22, 225–27, 288; bad metaphors in Broglie cycle, 236–51; bad metaphors in Harden letter, 228–36; and dialectical image, 11–12; in *Einfühlungstheorie* timeline, 223–24; "Erlebnis" ("Experience"), 262–69; "Der Hund" ("The Dog"), 278–84; influence on Kotler's *Last Tango in Cyberspace*, 3; interest in Ott murder case, 219–21; Lipps's possible influence on, 252–62; as Lipps's student, 223, 252; *Malte Laurids Brigge*, 224–25; *Neue Gedichte*, 223–24, 239, 278–84; *Ninth Duino Elegy*, 273; and object-oriented ontology (OOO), 272–74; on problem of form, 218–19; "Über den Dichter" ("Concerning the Poet"), 256–60; "Ur-Geräusch" ("Primal Sound"), 266n21; versus Vischer, 288; Vischer and, 9
Rodin, Auguste, 39, 219, 252
Roh, Franz, 289
role-playing video game, 186, 292n3
Romanticism, 75, 79–80, 89–90
Roth, Udo, 72n13, 88, 89
Rousseau, Jean-Jacques, 178
Ryan, Judith, 228n5

sadism: empathic, 170–71, 175–78; patriarchal, 211
Satan: Lenz's identification with, 96–97, 115. *See also* demonic
Savoy, Carel van, 90, 109–12
scanning, 59–63, 67
Scheler, Max, 22n23
Schelling, Friedrich Wilhelm Joseph, 72, 73, 87
Scherner, Karl Albert, 16

Schiller, Friedrich, 176, 177, 230
schizophrenia, 84–85
Schmidt, Julian, 107
Schopenhauer, Arthur, 20, 21n21, 126
Schor, Naomi, 198
Sebald, W. G., 127
Seigworth, Gregory J., 6, 168, 192
self: absorption by Other, 68–69, 77–78; absorption of Other by, 68–69, 75, 77–78; doubling of, 69, 75, 76, 78–79; as Other in "Erlebnis," 262–65; replacement or possession of, by Other, 69, 75, 78–79
semiotic chora, 205–7, 210, 211
sensory physiology, 20
Seyffert, Rudolf, 290
Shaviro, Steven, 169, 284–85
Sieburth, Richard, 85n24, 86
sight: nineteenth-century ambiguity surrounding, 200–201; Vischer on, 204. *See also* eye imagery / eye motif; vision
simile, 222
simulation theory, 138–39, 253
Sinnenwelt und Weltseele (*Sense-World and World Soul*) (Fick), 47–48
Sloterdijk, Peter, 273–74
small, form of descriptions in *Der Hochwald* as, 197–200
Smith, Adam, 17
sounds, affective, 254, 258
speaking object-sphere, 274
specific nerve energies, law of, 49, 71, 80, 88, 96, 200–201
Spinoza, Benedict de, 31, 32, 93, 204, 266
stage effects, in *Der Hochwald*, 179–80
Stein, Edith, 22n23
Stifter, Adalbert, 125–31; as anticipating problems and implications of aesthetic empathy, 215–16; *Bunte Steine* (*Many-Colored Stones*), 128; and dialectical image, 11–12; as inviting interpretation through lens of *Einfühlungstheorie*, 11; *Der Nachsommer* (*Indian Summer*), 128; and pre- or para-history of *Einfühlung*, 287–88; relationship to "the modern," 128; similarities between Büchner and, 126–27; *Studien* (*Studies*), 128; stylistic experimentalism of, 129–30; and Vischer and Lee, 9. *See also Der Hochwald* (*The Mountain Forest*) (Stifter); *Turmalin* (*Tourmaline*) (Stifter)
Strowick, Elisabeth, 184n28
Studien (*Studies*) (Stifter), 128
subjectivity, 63–64
subject-object dualism, collapse of, 27–28, 41, 121–24, 261, 273–74
subjunctive, 222
sublime, 193, 194–96
suffering, taking pleasure in others,' 176–78
Swales, Erika, 126, 130, 166, 211n46
Swales, Martin, 126, 130, 166, 211n46
sympathy, 13, 17

Tatarkiewicz, Władysław, 24
technology, 286
theater: and empathy and erasure of difference in *Turmalin*, 152–57; as framework for experiment on empathy in *Turmalin*, 132–35, 161–62; *Turmalin* characters as united by trope of, 136–44
Theocritus, 117–18, 119
theory of mind, 150
Thurn und Taxis, Marie von, 263
Titchener, Edward, 98, 186–87; translates *Einfühlung* as "empathy," 2
touch, scanning as inseparable from, 61–62
tragedy, taking pleasure in, 176–78
Triumph des Willens (*Triumph of the Will*, 1935), 293
Turing, Alan, 136, 148
Turmalin (*Tourmaline*) (Stifter), 131–36, 161–63; and artificial intelligence, 126, 136, 147–48, 150, 162, 215; characters of, as united by

trope of theater, 136–44; empathy and erasure of difference in, 152–57; empathy machine in, 144–52, 157–61; forms of resistance in, 130; and Rentherr's daughter as figure for pure formalism, 134–36, 143, 147–52, 162; and virtual reality, 126, 144, 145, 148–49, 150–52

Über das optische Formgefühl (Vischer): aesthetics in, 65; close analysis of, 44; concern with inanimate objects and uncanniness of *Einfühlung* in, 58–59; *Einfühlung* as projection, transfusion, and transplantation in, 68–69; feeling of form in, 60–61; genesis of, 143–44; *Lenz* as philosophical forerunner for uncanny resurrection scene in, 116–21; necromantic empathy in, 52–54; nerve sensations in, 70; phases of empathy theory history in, 79; problem of origin, locus, and vector of experience or self in, 63–65, 68, 121–24; projection in, 64–65; scanning in, 59–62; summaries of, 58; uncanny anxieties aroused by concept of *Einfühlung* in, 54–55, 75–84; uncanny links among *Einfühlung*, death, and reanimation in, 56
"Über den Dichter" ("Concerning the Poet") (Rilke), 256–60
"Über Schädelnerven" ("On Cranial Nerves") (Büchner), 87–88, 96
"Über Wahrheit und Lüge im außermoralischen Sinne" ("On Truth and Lying in a Non-Moral Sense") (Nietzsche), 233–34
unattributed citations, in *Lenz*, 102–3
uncanny: and aesthetic empathy, 80, 92, 96; *Einfühlung* as, 56, 58–59, 67–69, 75, 79, 121–24; Lenz's excesses of proto-*Einfühlung* as inseparable from images of, 96, 99; in *Über das optische Formgefühl*, 54–55, 56, 58–59, 75–84, 116–21

uncanny double, 69, 80, 89, 115, 134, 194, 282
unsayable / unsayability (*Unsäglichkeit*): in Broglie cycle, 238, 240, 242, 244, 245–46; and *Innigkeit* in *Der Hochwald*, 209
"Ur-Gerausch" ("Primal Sound") (Rilke), 266n21

vampiric empathy (Breithaupt), 140
van Alphen, Ernst, 31
Varela, Francisco J., 123n51
Venice, and woman-as-city metaphor in Broglie cycle, 244, 246–47, 278
video game, role-playing, 292n3
virtual reality (VR), 11, 35, 38, 44–45, 50, 126, 144, 145, 186, 260
Vischer, Friedrich Theodor, 16, 74, 143
Vischer, Robert: aesthetic / artistic models of, 66–67; on art and life, 65–66; coins term *Einfühlung*, 2; compensation provided by *Einfühlungstheorie* of, 10; connections between Büchner and, 56–57; defines *Einfühlung*, 14–15, 213; and dialectical image, 11; familiarity with Müller and Wundt, 74; on feeling form, 60–61; on feeling oneself into objects, 42; on form, 5; on form and content, 143–44; on form and physical boundaries, 93–94; "Formgefühl," 29–30; and Herbart, 21n20; on life, 113; on love and empathy, 3; on nerve sensations, 61–62, 70; and rise of *Einfühlung*, 16–17; on scanning, 59, 61, 63, 67; Stifter as anticipating, 125; on subjectivity, 63–64; and transition from vitalism and *Naturphilosophie* to scientific materialism, 55; understanding of *Einfühlung* in terms of metaphors of self-other identification and exchange, 216; and vector of empathy, 28; versus Rilke, 288. See also *Über das optische Formgefühl* (Vischer)

vision: subjectivizing of, 19; Vischer on, 204. *See also* eye imagery / eye motif; sight
vitalism, transition to scientific realism from, 10, 55, 73–74. See also *Naturphilosophie*
vitality, 109, 113, 168–69, 172
Voltaire [Francois-Marie Arouet], 231
Voznesensky, Andrei, 275

Walker, John, 72n13, 129
Ward, Janet, 289, 290, 293
Ward, Mark G., 129
Weber, Aloisia, 132n4
West, Herbert, 62–63

Wiene, Robert, 291–92
Wilke, Tobias, 65–66
withdrawn object, 269–72, 275–77, 278, 281, 283–84
Wittgenstein, Ludwig, 251
woman-as-city metaphor, in Broglie cycle, 241–42, 243, 244, 246–47, 278
Worringer, Wilhelm, 22–23, 224, 268
Wübben, Yvonne, 56–57, 87, 104, 106, 107–8
Wundt, Wilhelm, 16, 20–21, 30, 62, 74

Yeats, William Butler, 76
Young, Robert J. C., 259

www.ingramcontent.com/pod-product-compliance
Lightning Source LLC
Chambersburg PA
CBHW030116240426
43673CB00041B/1299